THE NEW YORK TIMES

MANAGEMENT READER

THE NEW YORK TIMES

MANAGEMENT

READER

*Hot Ideas and Best Practices
from the New World of Business*

Correspondents of *The New York Times*
with chapter introductions by David Leonhardt

EDITED BY
Brent Bowers and Deidre Leipziger

FOREWORD BY
Harold J. Leavitt, Ph.D.

Times Books

HENRY HOLT AND COMPANY | NEW YORK

Times Books
Henry Holt and Company, LLC
Publishers since 1866
115 West 18th Street
New York, New York 10011

Henry Holt® is a registered trademark
of Henry Holt and Company, LLC.

Library of Congress Cataloging-in-Publication Data
The New York times management reader : hot ideas and best practices
from the new world of business : correspondents of the New York times
with chapter introductions / by David Leonhardt ; edited by Brent Bowers
and Deidre Leipziger ; foreword by Harold J. Leavitt.—1st ed.
    p. cm.
Includes index.
ISBN 0-8050-6742-6 (hb)
    1. Leadership. 2. Employee motivation. 3. Employees—Training of.
4. Technological innovations—Management. 5. International business
enterprises—Technological innovations—Management. 6. Industrial
management. I. Leonhardt, David, 1973– II. Bowers, Brent.
III. Leipziger, Deidre. IV. New York times.

HD57.7 .N49 2001
658—dc21

                                            2001017159

First Edition 2001

Printed in the United States of America
1 3 5 7 9 10 8 6 4 2

History is philosophy learned from examples.

—Thucydides

Contents

Foreword xi

1. The Real World: *When Theory Meets Practice* 1

2. Revolutionary Thinking: *Entrepreneurial Management* 26

3. Moving with the Times: *Old Economy Meets New* 57

4. Redrawing the Borders: *Managing Globally* 99

5. Getting Hitched: *The Next Generation of Mergers
and Acquisitions* 123

6. The Talent Squeeze: *Recruiting and Retaining Employees* 152

7. When Managing Becomes Leading:
Getting the Most Out of Your Team 177

8. Running the Show: *Handling Transitions at the Top* 212

9. 9-1-1: *When Things Go Wrong* 246

10. Visiting Olympus: *The Corporate Legends* 275

Afterword: *Wheeling and Dealing, Old School* 314

Acknowledgments 319

Index 321

Foreword

Whether you're just getting started in the profession of management—as a beginning M.B.A. student, for example—or even if you're a newly minted, degree-in-hand M.B.A., or a veteran executive, or just a thoughtful citizen in search of a big, clear picture of the business world 2000, this is the book you should read. For that's what this volume does. It gives you a wide-angled panoramic view of the here, now and real organizational world; a picture that helps answer some of the tough questions I've been asked repeatedly over many years of teaching and consulting: Are organizations (this year) truly in the midst of a major revolution or is that just hype? What's really new, but also what's *not* new on the managerial scene? Are organizations becoming better places for human beings to work in? Or, was a wise old executive right when he told one of my classes, "All organizations are prisons. It's just that the food is better in some than it is in others"? This book will not provide clean, simple answers to questions like those. What it will do, though, is help you get a fix on which managerial "trends" and "revolutionary" changes are for real, and which ones are nothing more than transient old fads, repackaged and recycled.

There are at least three good reasons that this book will help you separate managerial wheat from chaff and truth from rhetoric:

Reason #1: These verbal snapshots, taken together, provide a panoramic view of the *actual* organizational world circa 2000. No ribbons and bows here, no airbrushed warts and scars, just sharp, clear pictures of the new, whirling managerial world, a world that will surely be whirling even faster by the time new M.B.A.s are ready to jump aboard a year or two from now. These reporters' sharp lenses catch how things *do* play out, rather than how they *should,* with everything from pettiness and chicanery to overweening ambitions and insatiable greed. But they also catch instances of great humanity, creativity, compassion and wisdom.

This volume documents many of the major business and near-business events of the last two years: Ford's rather successful handling of its takeover of Mazda; the Mannesmann/Vodafone war inside Germany; GE's Jack Welch and the mantra of Six Sigma; even the Harvard Business School's move into Silicon Valley—where the real action used to be. The book also covers smaller, more human events. It tells the tale of a neighborhood coffeehouse's struggle to survive the arrival of a huge new neighbor, Starbucks. And it describes, empathically, the culture shock experienced by executives *returning* from overseas assignments. This book, that is to say, does what I always wanted my high school history books to do: it reports what's going on in different locales and on different social levels at the same instant in time.

Reason #2: In this era of volatility and impermanence, of mergers and takeovers and of wild markets, these readings remind us of a reality too easily forgotten: that much of organizational management has *not* changed. The frustrations and rewards of the workplace, the conflicts, the power struggles, the bureaucratic foul-ups, the occasional wise, insightful leaders, the pain-in-the-derrière bosses, the personal search for meaning through work—all those were around yesterday and the day before, and they will be around tomorrow. They are the background rhythms—good, bad and ugly—that have always been the subtext to the natural lives of organizations. The image that comes to mind is the sea, calm and unchanging a few fathoms down, even as blustery gales and crushing waves ravage the surface.

For example, the snapshots of modern movers and shakers in this volume—Sandy Weill, Warren Buffett, Bill Gates—might well have been written one hundred or fifty or twenty years ago. Only the names have changed. As it was with the Fords, Stanfords, Morgans, Geneens, Packards, Sculleys, some of today's well-knowns are clearly good guys, while others wear, if not black, at least dark gray hats. Sagacity, integrity, imagination and idealism intermix, as they always have, with overblown egos and insatiable lustings after wealth and power.

One old managerial area, however, does seem finally to be changing: the internal managing process itself. Issues that researchers and consultants have sermonized about for over half a century—participation, motivation, teamwork and such—are now making a real dent, though they are still found more in preachings than in practice.

Still, consultants and gurus need not rush to take credit for this managerial enlightenment. It is the roiling winds of change, not our weak urgings, that are pushing organizations toward greater openness and more humanistic managerial styles. Organizations finally recognize they need their people's ingenuity and creativity, the same ingenuity and creativity they used to bottle up, fearful lest it disrupt their prized stability and orderliness. Often tentatively and reluctantly, a little bit at a time, they have begun to let the genie of human imagination out of the bottle.

Reason #3 is, perhaps, the most important reason that these brief, candid essays are worth reading: they spotlight something far more than this year's managerial beasts and beauties, and more than the unchanging, deep heartbeats of organizations. They catch the new, new thing: the speed, turbulence and instability that have sharply and permanently differentiated the new organizational surround from all its predecessors. Indeed, several of these reporters updated their stories, probably because leaving their readers with stale news violates their journalistic standards, but also because, in the racing new organizational world, this morning's news may well be stale this afternoon.

Consider how quickly and definitively things have changed: In the late 1980s and even the early '90s, America lagged and Japanese successes preoccupied us. We fought back. Two words, "quality" and "productivity," became the American industrial mantra. To achieve them, we imported quality circles, reengineered the corporation, built teams, downsized, TQMed and Just-in-Timed. And we returned to preeminence. Remember?

That was yesterday. Today quality and productivity no longer take center stage. They're alive and well, but they've left the headlines, relegated to an inside page. The new keywords are "speed" and "flexibility." Those are much harder concepts to get one's arms around. Quality and productivity are readily operationalized. Speed and flexibility aren't, especially when speed keeps increasing. As for flexibility, it remains a loosey-goosey notion.

Some managers think the way to cope is by flattening and federalizing. Others want their organizations to grow larger while acting smaller. Neither of those is likely to be sufficient. No clear formulae have yet emerged—and none may—as organizations try to make their way through their unpredictable, unfamiliar, ever-changing new environments. There are no postponements on today's global gridiron, no time-outs or rest periods, no final whistles and darn few rules.

We used to believe that large organizations were permanent establishments, indestructible, all steel and stone. No longer! Any organization—corporate, not-for-profit, educational, or governmental—that is here today may well be gone tomorrow. Hostile takeovers (Qwest, U S West, Frontier and Global Crossing), "friendly" mergers of "equals" (Daimler-Benz and Chrysler) and just plain deaths of venerable institutions (Montgomery-Ward) are occurring faster than ever before. Even some nonbusiness organizations, beset by high costs and tough competition, are forced to risk novel routes to survive. This book contains a report, for example, on the effort of Stanford University's medical establishment to merge with UC Berkeley's medical facilities. It looks easy. The physical distance between the two is only a few miles. Of course, it didn't turn out to be easy.

The stresses on organizations are necessarily also visited upon their individual members. For if the mother organization cannot feel secure, how can her children feel career-safe? This volume documents rapid rises and falls of some of the mighty and the not-so-mighty members of contemporary management. For example, CEOs of massive corporations are dropping at an unprecedented rate, unable to keep their wriggling, amoebalike behemoths on course. And at every hierarchical level, stable old career patterns are disappearing even though new ones have not taken shape.

Yet, fear not! Not all modern managers are doomed to fail. Some have managed their enterprises very well, despite extremely rough seas. Witness, for example, the tales herein of Jack Welch of General Electric and Warren Buffett of Berkshire Hathaway.

Down the hierarchy, among, as they used to say, "the rank and file"—though organizational ranks and files aren't what they used to be—a paradox appears. The downsizing butchery of the early '90s left survivors who no longer trust the organizations to which they had long been loyal. Now, however (or perhaps last week—depending on when this book goes to press), we are shown some highly imaginative efforts those same organizations are using to attract new employees and hold on to their old ones. Thus *people*—treated as intolerable corporate costs just a year or two ago—have quickly transmuted into "our most valuable assets." Was it willful, vacillating managers who were responsible? Or the willful, shifting winds of change? Will those winds soon shift again?

Those, then, are some downsides of this book's candid photos of managing 2000, but there are plenty of upsides. I had never, for example, until I read this book, thought of modern managers as very much like *explorers*. In today's—and even more in tomorrow's—uncharted organizational waters and ever-changing environs, managing is coming to be near synonymous with exploring. More and more of managing now involves going where no one has gone before, venturing into deep, dark, dangerous caverns, confronting fire-snorting competitive dragons and learning to interact with strange, semisavage cultures of geeks and nerds.

No longer must managers confine themselves to the stultifying routines of planning and organizing and the other stuff of quaint old management textbooks. The new managing, driven by the racing new world, may even liberate the managerial soul, providing opportunities for challenge, novelty and a rewarding sense of having done something worthwhile. Isn't that the kind of forward-moving life pattern that managers—and the rest of us—deserve?

I don't want to conclude this introduction without fulminating a bit about the *why* question. Even though much remains the same, today's organizational world certainly isn't the one I grew up with. The two couldn't be more different. *Why? Why* have speed and flexibility supplanted order and stability as top organizational priorities? *Why* is today's environment so much more fast-moving, volatile and uncertain than yesterday's? *Why* is the managerial environment likely to be even more turbulent tomorrow?

If a collection of readings such as this one had been prepared in 1970 or 1980, it would also have shown that organizations were not standing still. Of course things were changing then, too. Yet, in those decades, managers seemed able to maintain reasonable control over their institutions. Organizations changed mostly when and because their leaders chose to change them. Now organizational leaders seem to be "the driven" at least as often as they are "the drivers." Again, why? Why globalization now? Why a continuing orgy of takeovers, alliances and acquisitions? Why a crazy, roller-coaster stock market?

A large part of the answer seems clear: technology. Many other forces certainly play their part, but, far more than any of the others, it is burgeoning technology that bubbles and spits at the core of the great volcano of organizational change. It is technology, especially the long, wide reach of information technology, that has *forced* globalization, *forced* the flattening of hierarchies, *forced* organizations to grow larger, *forced* alliances and mergers, and *forced* organizations to remain constantly on the qui vive lest they be gobbled up by passing predators. It is technology, too, that has changed the whole notion of what constitutes a lifelong career.

Yet, despite all that technology-driven organizational change, the people in organizations—executives and file clerks alike—seem hardly to have changed at all. The people in today's organizations are neither more nor less bright, selfish, ambitious, curious, lazy or competitive than those of a half century ago. What has changed is the technology-driven environment in which they labor. That sharply altered environment has also changed the managerial relevance of each of those human qualities, raising the value of some and shrinking the value of others. Fortunately, that recalibration of the human attributes organizations most need looks like it will take us in the right direction—toward severing some of the bonds that have traditionally prevented managers and others from, as they say, fulfilling their human potential.

That wasn't true of older technologies that supplanted and extended human arms, legs and eyes but did almost nothing to free the human spirit.

Another point worth noting: although organizations seem to have taken charge of information technology, it has also taken charge of them. Organizations exploit new technology for profit. They buy technologists. They take at least partial control over university-based science and technology, and they gobble up little hi-tech start-ups. All that makes it appear that they're running the show. But organizations also depend on technology. They simply can't, in today's world, live without it. Since technology is expanding faster and faster, organizations are caught in a continuing race to keep up with the multidirectional swarm of innovations those technologies are continuously spawning.

Regardless of other economic trends, technology itself has neither brakes nor an OFF button, so the new world is unlikely either to slow down or to level off. Information technology has a long way to go before it comes into full flower, and other world-changing technologies are ripening close behind. Genetic-tech is about to burst open and nano-tech is in bud, with consequences beyond imagining.

Technology shrinks time as well as space and that makes me want to see the 2010 edition of this book—if books still exist in 2010. Measured the old way, that would be at least a century from now. By 2010 more than the technology will have changed. One can bet that the secondary and tertiary social fallout from all this technology will be looming very large. What new technological goodies await us out there? And what not-so-goodies? What tensions will have developed between the *have* and *have-not* sectors of our world? And what great moral dilemmas will have been posed by emerging applications of genetic technologies?

On all these fronts, this worthy book made my mental and emotional juices flow, as these ramblings must attest. No preachings in these reports, no editorials, no talking heads, no guruistic nostrums, just many competent reporters' dispassionate observations of this year's real managerial world.

—Harold J. Leavitt, Ph.D.

THE NEW YORK TIMES

MANAGEMENT READER

· 1 ·

THE REAL WORLD

When Theory Meets Practice

I think the biggest lesson from the success of *Harry Potter* is that you need to try not to follow a trend. You have to follow your heart.

—Arthur Levine, editorial director,
Arthur A. Levine books, October 13, 1999

My income was the tips I got from delivering [groceries] to Mrs. Davis and Mrs. Griffith, and I realized the faster I got there and the better I treated them, the bigger the tip I got. That's a basic, fundamental lesson of any business.

—Gerard R. Roche, chairman,
Heidrick & Struggles International, February 2, 2000

Michael Sheldrake, meet Joseph Schumpeter.

For twenty years, Sheldrake was living the kind of life that some people dream of retiring to. He ran a coffee shop on the California coast, and his days were defined by the aroma of coffee beans and by the banter of customers he called friends. Soggy mornings, long commutes, office cubicles were all strangers to Sheldrake.

Then, one day in 1994, a grinch arrived—in the form of a siren standing inside of a green circle. When the ubiquitous logo of Starbucks Coffee, a chain with more than thirty-five hundred outlets around the world, went up in the neighborhood of his Polly's Gourmet Coffee, Sheldrake knew he faced an agonizing choice—a choice you will read about in the coming pages.

The battle between Polly's and Starbucks may have played out on a single street in a resort city south of Los Angeles, but it holds much larger significance. Over the last decade, the combination of an increasingly global economy and rapidly evolving new technologies have posed new threats, and created new opportunities, for businesses on an almost weekly basis.

Perhaps the most popular way to describe this process is "creative destruction," a term invented by Joseph Schumpeter, an early-twentieth-century economist from Austria. All profit derives from innovation, Schumpeter argued. As soon as companies are selling the same thing in the same way, be they steam engines or nonfat cappuccinos, none will make a profit—until one finds a new angle.

For much of the last century, Schumpeter's academic vision has remained just that, thanks to inefficient flows of information and regulatory boundaries, among other things. Lately, however, governments have begun dismantling many of their tariffs and regulations, while technology has allowed for rapid imitation and market entry.

The result is a new stage of instability, one in which seemingly ascendant companies can quickly lose their way. Today, companies have to compete with all kinds of new rivals, be they foreign companies, small start-ups or firms that once seemed to operate in an entirely separate industry. Just as important are the technological shifts that have forced companies to make enormous bets that can turn sour within months.

"People are dealing with more variables at one time than they ever did in the past, and a lot of the changes are of a fundamental nature," says William Esrey, the chief executive of Sprint, who was elected in 2000 as chairman of the Business Council, a group of more than one hundred chieftains. "The pace of change is clearly at an unprecedented level."

No wonder that popular management tomes bear titles like *Blur* and *Blown to Bits*. And that chief executives have started leaving their jobs—voluntarily or otherwise—in record numbers. And that stocks routinely lose, or gain, billions of dollars of market capitalization after a single piece of news emerges.

Across corporate America, executives have confronted larger versions of Sheldrake's conundrum of how to deal with a new threat. Merrill Lynch, for example, drastically cut its fees to head off competition from Internet brokerages like Ameritrade. AT&T responded to deregulation by attempting to remake itself into a new kind of company, only to backtrack dramatically and split itself in pieces.

This chapter offers a glimpse into the lives of managers who are dealing with the vexing issues of a new era. By the time you are done reading, you will even find out what happened to Sheldrake in his Davidlike battle over roasted coffee beans.

The Brand or the Product

Karl-Heinz Kalbfell carefully held a cast-iron sculpture of the Rolls-Royce hood ornament, the "flying lady" who reaches into the wind and whose feet seem to lift off the ground.

As director of Project Rolls-Royce at the German automaker Bayerische Motoren Werke AG, Kalbfell is planning to introduce an entirely new line of Britain's most prestigious name in cars. But thanks to a stalemate between BMW and Volkswagen AG, which both wanted to buy Rolls-Royce in 1998, he has to wait until 2003, when Volkswagen will relinquish control over the celebrated name.

"It is a little strange," he admitted. "We came into a situation which was indeed unique. But we have to cope with that."

Unique does not begin to describe the challenge. Until BMW acquires the name, Kalbfell is not supposed to even pose in front of current Rolls-Royce models, much less promote them in any way. And even when it gets the name, BMW will not be inheriting any factories and will not be manufacturing current models like Silver Seraph or Corniche. Instead, it has designed an entirely new car, which has not been shown in public. The only things certain to remain the same will be the flying lady, the distinctive Rolls front grille, and price tags that begin at about $210,000.

All this stems from a Solomon-like deal in which Volkswagen and BMW essentially split the British company in two. Beginning in 2003, BMW will get rights to the Rolls-Royce name and its icons. But Volkswagen acquired the factories and the entire operations of Bentley Motor Cars, the sportier but equally expensive line of cars that accounts for about two-thirds of Rolls-Royce sales.

It is not yet clear which company was more clever: was it BMW, which paid $65 million for the name, or Volkswagen, which paid $780 million for the company?

It is clear that BMW plans to start Rolls-Royce as an entirely new operation. It will not produce current models, though it may well use the names. Nor will it use the same engines or chassis.

"We will be starting from scratch," Kalbfell said in an interview at BMW headquarters here. "We want to make sure that the way we market is in the good tradition of Rolls-Royce. But at the same time, and this is very important, too, it has to be in a direction that is right for the future."

To smooth the transition, Volkswagen has agreed to produce the Silver

Seraph after 2003 if there is demand. But Volkswagen is more interested in competing with Rolls-Royce than supporting it, and BMW does not want to pay Volkswagen for making its cars.

Neither BMW nor Volkswagen wanted to split up Rolls-Royce. Both wanted to buy the entire company when its former parent, Vickers PLC, put it up for auction in 1998.

But the two essentially trapped each other. Volkswagen trumped BMW's bid by offering $780 million for the company, which produces fewer than two thousand cars a year at prices of $210,000 to $360,000 apiece.

BMW struck back by capturing claims on the name itself. It did so by striking a deal with Rolls-Royce PLC, the aircraft engine manufacturer that had split off from the car company years earlier.

Rolls-Royce PLC had the right to block a transfer of the coveted name to non-British owners, and agreed to sell the right to BMW for $65 million. After weeks of furtive negotiations, Volkswagen agreed to surrender the name to BMW and focus on the Bentley as its lead luxury car.

Kalbfell is not the kind of person who would normally drive a Rolls-Royce. He created BMW's motor sport division, which makes racing versions of its road cars and other specialized sport vehicles. He also orchestrated BMW's reentry into Formula One racing several years ago.

Despite Rolls-Royce's association with history and tradition, BMW executives decided they had no choice but to build a new company from the ground up. They say it would be impractical to adopt what is essentially a built-by-hand production of the existing models to a new line of cars. And they argue that Rolls-Royce cars were due for a makeover anyway.

Though Vickers had rescued Rolls-Royce from bankruptcy, it kept the company on a tight budget for developing new models. To keep costs down, the company began buying engines and many other components made by BMW.

But BMW's engines were designed for speed and acceleration, not for the silent smooth ride of a car created for people with chauffeurs.

"The idea to adapt BMW engines was something of a mistake, and it was one that I think was recognized by executives in the company," said Philip Hall, chief executive of the Sir Henry Royce Memorial Foundation, a nonprofit organization that keeps extensive archives on Rolls-Royce.

Indeed, sales of Rolls-Royce cars dropped 26 percent in 1999, from 600 cars to just 444. Part of the reason stemmed from the high value of the British pound, which made the cars extremely expensive on the European continent. But given that Bentley sales declined only 1.8 percent, the fall also reflected unhappiness among consumers and lack of interest by VW.

One of Kalbfell's first decisions was to stop using BMW engines, and come up with something similar to the big V-8 engines that powered Rolls-Royces for nearly forty years.

"What we intend to do is integrate all the available competence of the BMW group, but that doesn't mean that it will be made from BMW parts," Kalbfell said.

Engines are comparatively simple to select. Far more delicate, however, is the task of creating a design that still evokes Rolls-Royce's history while avoiding the cars' increasingly fusty image.

Upon taking over Project Rolls-Royce, Kalbfell assembled a group of designers from California, Britain and Germany under the leadership of a Scottish engineer, Ian Cameron.

The group was divided into competing teams and leased offices in a bank building near Hyde Park. Kalbfell picked the location because it has one of the highest rates of Rolls-Royce ownership in England.

"We wanted them to become immersed in the culture," Kalbfell said. "We needed to get away from the influence of the R & D Center here in Munich."

BMW designers pored over archives at the Rolls-Royce foundation. They also courted Rolls-Royce dealers and owners' clubs, especially in England and the United States.

BMW says it has selected a design and built a prototype car, but it has not shown it yet to people outside the company.

Kalbfell has also laid plans for a new factory in Goodwood, in the south of England far away from Rolls-Royce's old home in Derby, in central England. The company will employ about 350 people and be able to produce about one thousand cars a year.

By comparison with Volkswagen, BMW's plans are cautious. Volkswagen is spending several billion dollars on expansion and plans to introduce a new series of "midpriced" Bentleys. Volkswagen's goal is to increase Bentley sales tenfold, to about ten thousand cars a year.

But BMW is still reeling from its last catastrophe in Britain, the disastrous acquisition of Rover Cars. After losing $6 billion over six years, BMW essentially gave away most of Rover in the spring of 2000 and ignited widespread wrath in England for what was viewed as reneging on its commitments.

Rolls-Royce is a much smaller challenge. Despite its reputation as a producer of cars for royalty, rock stars and the simply rich, Rolls-Royce is an infinitesimally small company that produces fewer than six hundred cars a year.

And there will be competition. DaimlerChrysler will be introducing the Maybach limousine, bigger and more expensive than even the biggest Mercedes, in 2003. And Volkswagen, in addition to expanding Bentley, is also pushing high-end sport cars from Lamborghini and Bugatti.

Rolls-Royce enthusiasts are waiting to see what emerges. But many Rolls-Royce car dealers have to decide whether to side with Bentley or Rolls-Royce.

Though Bentley and Rolls-Royce had already drifted apart in distribution, as many as a quarter of Rolls-Royce dealers in Britain still handle the Bentley as well.

In England, the two biggest dealers in Rolls-Royce and Bentley—H.R. Owen and Jack Barclay—decided to merge in the fall of 2000. The combined company will market both lines of luxury automobiles, but it will separate them into two dealership operations.

"We do not see them being sold alongside one another," said Nicholas Lancaster, the president of H.R. Owen.

Other dealers will have to decide which way to go. But given that Volkswagen's goal is to sell ten thousand Bentleys a year, compared with BMW's goal of one thousand Rolls-Royces, more are likely to stay with Volkswagen.

Lancaster is ready for both rivals. "We are in an age when more people are becoming rich than ever before," he remarked. "The choices are so small at the very top range of these vehicles that there is definitely room for more."

Edmund L. Andrews
September 23, 2000

CASE 2

Social Responsibility, For Profit

They all played their classic roles once word got out in November 1998 that a Dow Chemical Company contractor had repeatedly spilled toxic dust intended for Dow's incinerator in Michigan.

Denunciations poured forth from outraged environmentalists like Diane K. Hebert, chairwoman of a local group called Environmental Health Watch. "We are shocked by the carelessness and indifference that allowed these dangerous spills to occur," Hebert told the *Detroit Free Press*. "Dow's negligence has endangered our community's health."

And Dow was a predictable corporate heavyweight, announcing that it was cooperating with an investigation by state regulators and barred from saying much. Local coverage, trotting out old descriptions of the wastes at the plant site, made it appear that Jeffrey Feerer, the environment, health and safety manager for the manufacturing operations in Midland, was minimizing the presence of dangerous dioxin by characterizing the spills as little more than "sand and dead microbes."

But even as the adversaries squared off in public, they quietly continued collaborating on a novel two-year drive to slash toxic chemical emissions from Dow's vast chemical complex on the eastern edge of town. The two sides were out to discover whether environmentalists armed with detailed information about a company's business needs and processes could help it find and carry out profitable ways to cut waste.

It was an uncomfortable alliance from the start, fraught with risks for both sides. Some people at Dow feared that giving some of their harshest critics such an intimate look at operations would blow up into a public relations nightmare or lead to leaks of confidential information to competitors. Hebert and the other environmentalists involved agonized over whether Dow might exploit the exercise to make itself look environmentally responsible without producing meaningful changes.

And, as the November 1998 clash and previous public battles over a new waste-water treatment project here proved, even the most successful collaboration could not paper over all of the adversaries' long-standing differences.

Still, everyone stayed the course. By the time the project was completed, in April 1999, Dow was on track to cut production of a list of toxic chemicals selected by the environmentalists by 37 percent and to reduce the release of the chemicals to the air or water by 43 percent. To the surprise of both sides, the project had beaten a goal of 35 percent reductions on both measures, which had seemed a stretch in the beginning.

Moreover, Dow's investment of $3.1 million to make the changes was expected to save it nearly $5.4 million a year and, for some businesses, improve product quality or add to production capacity.

Companies and environmental groups have worked together in the past on pollution prevention. But the depth and length of Dow's relationship with the environmental activists is prompting talk of a new era of cooperation.

"This partnership will almost certainly become a model nationally among companies looking to improve the environment and improve their bottom line," said Carol M. Browner, administrator of the Environmental Protection Agency.

Edwin Mongan, manager of environmental stewardship for DuPont, the nation's largest chemical company, said he was impressed by what he heard at a Dow briefing for the industry in Washington. "It looks promising," Mongan said.

The groundwork for the project was laid in 1996 by Dow and the Natural Resources Defense Council, the environmental policy group based in New York. They recruited five longtime local critics of Dow, a step that both agreed was crucial to the project's credibility and impact on local managers.

The challenge was to find big reductions that would actually save Dow money—a search for so-called low-hanging fruit. In addition to Hebert, the critics were Mary Sinclair, who led protests that squelched Dow's efforts to have a nuclear power plant built here in the 1970s; Terry Miller of the Lone Tree Council in Bay City, Michigan; Anne Hunt of Citizens for Alternatives to Chemical Contamination in Lake Michigan; and Tracey Easthope, director of environmental health at the Ecology Center in Ann Arbor.

Dow believed there were few opportunities for reductions, because the site had been working on pollution controls for two decades. The environmentalists, assuming that businesses were adept at spotting profit-enhancing environmental projects, also had their doubts.

But Dow managers and their new environmentalist advisers quickly found a startling array of prospects that had been routinely overlooked.

Dow, for example, discovered that introducing new chemical catalysts and making other innovations in the manufacture of resins, combined with modifications in the processing equipment, eliminated a nasty by-product, formaldehyde-laced tars. The onetime cost of the project was $330,000, while the savings at Dow's waste-treatment plant totaled $3.3 million annually.

Dow managers became especially intrigued by the money-saving moves turned up by Bill Bilkovich, a tireless environmental engineering expert based in Tallahassee, Florida, who spent more than two years at the site. In one embarrassingly simple case, Bilkovich pointed out that Dow could save thirty-four thousand dollars annually and cut thirty-four thousand pounds of emissions of a toxic chlorine compound used in making Saran plastic products by transferring it to storage tanks twice a day instead of all at once. By filling only half the tank the first time, vapors no longer had to be vented to the incinerator.

"Many of these projects were too small to be seen as real business opportunities," said Linda E. Greer, an environmental toxicologist with the Natural Resources Defense Council, who worked with Dow to recruit the local environmentalists and organize the project.

As surprising as the savings were, the most provocative aspect of the project was the crucial role the environmentalists played and Dow's willingness to lower its guard.

"It was a heroic decision to bring in their most vocal critics," Greer said.

Dow let the environmentalists choose which toxic chemicals to go after. It accepted their list of twenty-six without argument, even though many were selected mainly because they can produce dioxin when burned. That required stifling any impulse to defend the company's long-standing position that critics exaggerate dioxin's health risks and industry's role in creating dioxin.

The company also accepted the aggressive, 35 percent reduction target and, with many qualms, the environmentalists' refusal to sign any confidentiality agreements.

The environmentalists reviewed and signed off on Dow's desire to use Bilkovich as an independent expert in hunting for pollution-prevention opportunities. Both sides agreed on retaining John Ehrman, a mediator with the Meridian Institute, a nonprofit group in Dillon, Colorado, to keep them focused on the narrow goal of reducing toxic wastes. To ensure that the environmentalists felt confident about the data they were receiving, Dow agreed that they could hire Steven Anderson, an environmental consultant based in Bordentown, New Jersey, to review Dow records and advise on technical matters.

Perhaps most unusual, Dow told the production managers and technicians who actually produced the plastic packaging, pesticides, drugs and myriad other products at the complex's forty plants that they would have to present their pollution prevention projects directly to the environmentalists for approval and, once the projects were started, show them their progress reports. Normally, employees in the operating trenches are shielded from the scrutiny of outside critics by health and safety intermediaries like Feerer.

As the months went by, the apprehensive Dow managers were surprised by the cordiality of the environmentalists and their interest in the intricacies of the businesses. The environmentalists were not always equally relieved, especially when listening to managers who they said seemed uninterested in the impact of toxic chemicals as long as their operations were complying with all environmental regulations.

"I was ready to bite my tongue in half listening to some of the presentations," said Hebert of Environmental Health Watch. "They really didn't understand why we were concerned."

For all the tension, though, the exercise bore fruit.

Dow clearly wanted the Michigan Source Reduction Initiative, as the project was formally known, to succeed. It took pains to get that message across to the midlevel managers involved. Senior executives like Vince Smith, the site manager, and Jerry Martin, the corporate vice president in charge of environmental affairs, attended every quarterly meeting with the environmentalists to underscore the company's commitment.

"Face time with senior management and the chance to impress them is a great incentive for many young managers," Feerer said.

One manager, Michel Piche, the head of a latex-manufacturing unit, said he was struck by the thoroughness of Bilkovich's research into Dow's problems with butadiene, a chemical used to make rubber and resins. To gather data proving that Dow could cut the amount of butadiene it loses to incineration if a supplier would refrigerate it before shipment, Bilkovich studied one thousand railcar loads of the highly reactive chemical to show how concentrations of an unreactive form of butadiene called dimer build up with time and heat.

Dow now knows that refrigeration will slow the buildup of dimer, enough to improve the efficiency of a recycling system in the latex operations that has to be flushed when dimer levels threaten to clog it.

"Very often you collect ideas but lack the resources to pursue them," Piche said.

In some cases, the gains from the project came not from new ideas but from making sure that old ones were executed. For example, Dow had installed a $750,000 steam-based system in 1995 to recover toluene and chloroethane, two toxic chemicals needed to make Ethocel, a stabilizing and binding agent used in products as varied as construction materials and time-release drugs. But the Ethocel production group had put off figuring out how to adjust the size of the Ethocel granules to make the recycling system efficient, and the system had often been bypassed for weeks at a time.

Now, said Dave A. Midkiff, manager of the unit, the production adjustments have been made, and if the recovery unit goes down for a shift, technicians are called in even if it means paying overtime. Midkiff said he had tied a portion of his engineers' pay to the performance of environmental equipment.

The fragile trust established by so much effort hung in the balance for several weeks after news of the waste spills in November 1998. In the end, thanks largely to the counseling of Ehrman, the mediator—who had been hired in anticipation of just such a crisis—no one walked away.

The project can point to achievements beyond its stated goals and deadlines. There have been major reductions in emissions of chemicals not specifically selected for the project. Also, the gains reported for the selected chemicals did not include those expected from proposed improvements that did not have budget approval by April 30. And other projected gains—like a plan to reduce wastes by shipping toxic chemicals to Dow recycling plants in other states—were excluded from the official results because the environmentalists oppose putting hazardous materials on the roads.

Dow is planning to duplicate the Midland experiment at its even larger petrochemical complex in Freeport, Texas.

One hope is that next time around, Dow and the environmentalists can achieve a goal they call "institutionalization." Basically, that means measurably changing the corporate culture so that low-level managers routinely look for the kinds of improvements made here—something that everyone involved agrees eluded the Midland project.

Such mental readjustments are tougher to track than waste reductions. The Midland project conducted a survey in early 1999 on the attitudes of business managers toward pollution, but the project failed to figure out how to link the data to institutionalization.

The company and its environmental critics agree that pollution prevention is likely to stall if business managers do not embrace it. Businesses have many reasons to forgo waste-reduction opportunities. For instance, other undertakings may offer greater returns on investment.

In addition, testing to prove the value of a pollution prevention plan may take too much engineering time, or the changes could interrupt production.

At any rate, environmentalists say, the financial payoff from being environmentally friendly is too small to make much of an impression on the corporate mind-set. They say that the projected annual savings of $5.4 million from the three-year waste-reduction program in Midland represents just five-tenths of a percent of the $1.31 billion Dow earned the previous year on sales of $18.44 billion.

"It's spit in the ocean," said Easthope of the Ecology Center.

Dow executives say such comments underestimate how much environmental savings add up. They also say that their commitment to pollution prevention goes far beyond today's bottom line, citing, for instance, corporate goals for cutting worldwide emissions of hundreds of toxic chemicals by 50 to 90 percent in the ten years ending in 2005.

"No one knows exactly what a sustainable company looks like, but pollution prevention has to be a first step," Feerer said.

Dow's environmental partners here worry that reports of the project will "greenwash" Dow, making it look more environmentally responsible than they think it is. They also fear that critics of regulation, if not Dow itself, will trumpet the success as an argument for depending on voluntary measures to improve the environment. Cooperation like this project, they say, should not hide the need for stricter government oversight.

"I expect we'll get criticism from environmentalists over this," Easthope said. "I'll probably agree with a lot of it."

Barnaby J. Feder
July 18, 1999

Two of Dow's seventeen projects were tougher to implement than expected, and through the end of 2000 only $2.2 million of the $3.1 million budgeted for projects had been spent. Annual savings from the implemented projects was $4.7 million, compared to the projected $5.4 million. The completed projects cut waste production by 29 percent instead of the 37 percent expected overall, and cut emissions by 31 percent instead of the 43 percent expected total, falling short of Dow's 35 percent total reduction goal.

Dow has continued to apply the group's criteria in looking for cost-saving and waste-reduction opportunities, and has identified additional projects that will reduce waste creation by 2.2 million pounds on top of the 6.1 million-pound reduction already achieved.

CASE 3

The Cost Cutters

"I could take off my shoe and show you I don't have a cloven hoof," said David Hunter, putting a self-mocking spin on his contentious line of work.

Famous as a slash-and-burn cost cutter who can do the dirty work that floundering hospitals cannot bring themselves to tackle on their own, Hunter is often greeted as the Devil incarnate. No one's job is safe when his seventy-member consulting firm, Hunter Group, wields the ax: Along with thousands of clerks, technicians, nurses, doctors and other workers, Hunter has displaced chief executives at major university-affiliated teaching hospitals in Chicago, Detroit and San Francisco. The company also produced an emergency rescue plan in 1999 for the premier medical center in Philadelphia.

No question, these institutions and others like them are staring at daunting problems. Battered by big cuts in Medicare payments, rising drug costs and managed care plans that force them into below-cost deals, teaching hospitals around the country face mounting financial stresses. The hardest-pressed among them, generally large hospitals in inner cities, find themselves with no choice but to cut costs drastically to keep their doors open.

That is when Hunter, a no-nonsense management expert with more than a decade of experience operating on wounded hospitals, is called in by hospital trustees. "If they are using guys like us," he said, "the problems have to be enormous." He calls the hostile reception he often gets "a shoot-the-messenger issue," adding that "the problems were there before we got involved."

But critics say Hunter Group's shock therapy endangers the triple mission of the medical centers: educating doctors, treating patients of all income levels and conducting the breakthrough medical research that has little or no place at for-profit hospitals. Officials of medical faculty associations and nursing unions, for example, say the job cuts tend to be of the meat-ax, across-the-board variety, hitting vital services as hard as ancillary areas.

"What is happening today is the invisible destruction of the great academic medical centers," said Dr. William N. Kelley, chief executive of the financially troubled University of Pennsylvania Health System. "We will be more efficient and able to deliver care at a lower price, but we will not be able to do the things that made us great," like experimenting with new surgical procedures.

"Our ability to develop the medicine of tomorrow is going away," Kelley said.

Academic medical centers play a vital role in American health care that is important even to people who never set foot in them. They treat the toughest cases and train the best new doctors, who often hone their skills serving the poor before beginning practice elsewhere. Teaching hospitals develop and test new medicines and surgical procedures on the frontiers of medical knowledge. In many cities, academic medical centers are also the largest employers of both skilled and entry-level workers.

But as inflation in health care revs up after a four-year lull, the great hospitals are under growing pressure from government and private payers to take yet another tuck in their world-class expenses.

Hunter Group's forte is emergency work, and it loses no time once an engagement begins. Teams of operations and finance experts move from the home base of St. Petersburg, Florida, into nearby hotels and motels and shuttle to the troubled hospital in hired limousines and rental cars paid for by the client.

Referring frequently to a portfolio of "benchmarks" like the ratio of nurses to beds or floor polishers per square foot, drawn from consulting stints at one hundred hospitals across the country, they analyze the hospital's operations from the wards and surgical suites to the billing department to the executive suite. "We take a real hard look at the expense side," Hunter said.

Within fourteen weeks in most cases, the consultants present a plan to a steering committee of hospital board members and senior management:

- Cut jobs 20 percent, they said in Philadelphia, where the prestigious University of Pennsylvania Medical Center had an operating loss of $198 million in the 1998–99 fiscal year. The hospital said that it would eliminate twenty-eight hundred health services jobs out of fourteen thousand over the next fourteen months.
- Close a money-losing satellite hospital that serves the poor, they said in San Francisco, where a merger of two nationally acclaimed hospital systems was bleeding $2 million a month in operating losses. Though the two medical centers, those of Stanford University and the University of California at San Francisco, said that they would dissolve the merger, UCSF said it would go ahead with the closing of in-patient and emergency room services at Mount Zion Hospital. A similar recommendation in Detroit led to the closing of Mount Sinai Hospital there.
- Find a new chief executive, they said in Detroit, Chicago and San Francisco. Someone from Hunter will mind the store in the meantime. David Hunter himself became interim chief executive of California-Stanford. A longtime aide of Hunter ran the Detroit Medical Center and later the University of Illinois at Chicago Medical Center.
- Flatten management, reduce the numbers of laboratory tests and electrocardiograms, get rid of hundreds of salaried physicians, reduce support money flowing to medical education from patient fees and pare teaching budgets, they say nearly everywhere.
- When the financial problems seem intractable, simply sell the hospital. An 80 percent stake in the George Washington University Medical Center in Washington, for example, was sold in 1997 to a for-profit chain, Universal Health Services.

The discussions between the Hunter team and the client hospital can be tense, said a top hospital executive who has participated in such meetings.

Not every recommendation is accepted: in Boston, the New England Medical Center spurned a Hunter Group proposal that it should sell out to a for-profit company, later arranging its own merger with a nonprofit health care system in Providence. But it is hard for hospital boards to say no when management is temporarily ceded to the consultants.

Rank-and-file doctors, nurses and technicians at the hospitals say they get little or no chance to contribute suggestions or influence the consultants' decisions on cuts. "We knew we were on the chopping block," said a nurse at the San Francisco hospital. "We heard about it on the whisper circuit."

Hunter Group gets the lion's share of assignments to turn around troubled academic medical centers, said Larry Lewin, director of hospital strategy for Lewin Group, a Washington-based consulting firm. But a growing number of health care turnaround firms are competing for the business, and Ernst & Young, the giant accounting and consulting firm, also jumped in recently.

Candidates for the consultants' ministrations have been exploding in number since cuts in Medicare payments to hospitals in 1998. In 1999, the nation's 120 academic medical centers operated two hundred hospitals, but some hospital executives doubted that they could all survive without severe cutbacks and closings. A 1999 survey of its members by the University Health System Consortium of eighty big teaching hospitals found that two in five had losses in operations in their most recent quarterly results.

In New York City, the five big academic medical centers were headed for a drop of $100 million in their combined annual operating income in 1999, and shortfalls at the three teaching hospitals of the State University of New York were straining the university system's statewide budget.

"Academic medical centers are the crown jewels of our health system," said Dr. Bernard Ferrari, a consultant at McKinsey & Company, the management consulting firm. "They often deliver the most expensive care to the people who are least able to pay. They are an endangered species." A handful have large endowments or other sources of investment income that have tided them over while the stock market has been booming, but even they are now struggling with declining revenue.

Medical schools are attracting fewer applicants than they were a few years ago, but health care economists debate whether the centers are still training too many specialists, too many general practice doctors, or both. Though union officials and politicians stress the importance of the centers in providing tens of thousands of jobs and vital health services for low-income people in cities, deteriorating finances are robbing many of them of the ability to play these roles and still be self-sustaining.

"It is questionable whether Boston, Philadelphia, Washington and New York can support multiple big medical school organizations," Hunter said.

The hospitals that recently sought help from Hunter Group all have especially steep losses.

The Detroit Medical Center posted operating losses of $160 million in 1998 and $93 million in the first seven months of 1999. The University of Pennsylvania Health System in Philadelphia lost $288 million on operations in two years.

University of California-Stanford Health Care projected a $65 million surplus for the first two years after it was created by merging the hospitals of Stanford and the University of California in November 1997. The projection was overly optimistic by $111 million; the center lost $46 million. The two top executives at California-Stanford resigned in 1999.

Still, in some cases, critics say, Hunter-inspired economizing made it harder, not easier, to stanch the losses. Senior physicians at the New England Medical Center said it took much longer for the hospital to collect outstanding bills after it made deep cuts in its billing department. At the same hospital, a profit-generating liver transplant unit was out of action for a week until replacements could be found for blood bank technicians whose jobs were cut.

But Hunter's fans point to a return to profitability at beleaguered hospitals in several cities as evidence that broadly, his methods work.

Hunter, a former hospital executive at Duke University and in Mount Holly, New Jersey, started Hunter Group with two partners in 1988. He and his partners sold the firm to sixteen of its executives in 1998 for an undisclosed price. Hunter stayed on as chief executive on contract and retains a financial interest in the company.

"We can do things that existing management can't do," he said in a conversation on the front porch of his century-old stone house in Newtown, Pennsylvania, outside Philadelphia. For one thing, most academic medical centers operate by consensus among turf-guarding medical superstars not known for small egos. Decision-making in such an environment can be excruciatingly slow, and resistance to outside criticism can run high.

"Ninety-five percent of our members are trying to keep David Hunter out of their institutions," said Robert Baker, president of the University Health System Consortium.

When the Hunter Group is brought in, it is typically for a few months of drastic cutting. "We're not there long-term," Hunter said, and clients rarely sign up for a return engagement. "They never want to go through it again."

Many of the problems that lead a medical center to call the Hunter Group were all too evident in the short, unhappy merger in the San Francisco area.

Stanford Health Services and the University of California San Francisco Medical Center both ranked among the nation's top ten hospitals in independent surveys before their merger, which was motivated by a desire to overcome the challenges of operating in the vortex of one of the nation's most intense markets for health care plans.

The merger, however, just made the financial problems worse, at least for the short run. Instead of cutting staffs and eliminating duplication, the merged entity wound up adding one thousand employees, including new managers to coordinate hospitals forty miles apart at Palo Alto and San Francisco. Unforeseen millions were spent on computers and consultants, including $100 million for Year 2000 upgrades.

Desperate to reverse the trend, the hospital's board called in Hunter Group, at a cost of $414,000 a month plus expenses.

The consultants found that the merged medical centers were spending fifteen thousand dollars more for each patient than other large hospitals did, reflecting teaching, research and treating the indigent. The number of emergency patients increased sharply, adding to unreimbursed costs, after the medical center expanded emergency room capacity at its main hospital in San Francisco.

To attack the cost problems, Hunter consultants negotiated staff reductions with the medical school faculty and the managers of hospital departments and examined ways to get better prices on supplies. Taking care of poor people is both a duty and a financial drag. The merged medical center loses $80 million annually on uncovered services to Medicaid patients, said Peter Van Etten, who was chief executive until August 1999.

Susan Cieutat, a pediatric intensive care nurse who is active in the California Nurses Association, said cuts in staffing levels are causing problems. "There used to be one nurse for three or four patients," she said. "Now it's five or six patients. Nurses are exhausted, stressed, demoralized. Many are looking for work elsewhere."

Hunter acknowledges that cutting the nursing staff can be a delicate matter because good nursing is crucial to quality of care. And in some places there is a shortage of nurses ready to do stressful jobs. "It's more 'Can we get them?' than 'Can we cut them?'" he said.

As for revenues, Hunter proposed trying to renegotiate contracts with managed care companies that were based on capitation—a flat monthly fee for each health plan member—or on fixed day rates for hospital care; both are money-losers for the hospital, he said, and it would be better off with a fee schedule that varies with the patient's diagnosis. That will not be easy in California, a bastion of managed care.

The cost of care for poor people poses an even more difficult revenue problem. Costs that hospitals have to swallow have been rising as health plans raise their premiums, causing a growing number of working people who are not eligible for Medicaid to drop their coverage. Hospitals are stuck with much of the cost of caring for such patients.

Dr. Warren Gold, chairman of the UCSF medical school faculty association, noted that Hunter Group had recommended "a major cutback in physician practice support payments"—subsidies given by the medical center to faculty members who provide primary care to patients. According to Dr. Lee Goldman, the acting dean of the medical school, the main concern was to retain money in the hospital to buy state-of-the-art equipment like $3 million gamma knives for delicate brain surgery.

"What is really at risk here is clinical innovation, the interface between a faculty that does research and tries to make advances, and the clinical care," Goldman said.

"The U.S. is indisputably the leader in this," he added. "In the 1860s it was Germany. Now everybody comes here. It's a great American triumph. But we could screw it up."

The real choice facing the most troubled medical centers, Hunter argued, is not one of preserving research financing or cutting it back; it is a choice of ruthlessly cutting expenses or closing the doors. Like it or not, the money to operate the old way simply will not be there in the future, he said.

Hunter predicted that revenues at academic medical centers would fall by at least 10 percent a year for the foreseeable future, though he acknowledged his estimate might be colored by his close-up knowledge of hospitals in deep trouble. "We're not," he said, "looking at the Miss Americas."

Milt Freudenheim
October 31, 1999

Dr. William N. Kelley has stepped down as chief executive of the University of Pennsylvania Health System. Some Medicare cuts were restored in 2000. All four hospitals that sought help from Hunter in the late 1990s experienced improvements in their financial results, though those in Chicago and

San Francisco were slowest to do so. The medical center in Philadelphia made the most progress, showing an operational profit in late 2000.

The Category Killers

For two decades, Michael Sheldrake was the coffee king of Second Street in Long Beach, California. With virtually no competition within twenty miles, his Polly's Gourmet Coffee dominated the market in the affluent Belmont Shores section of the city.

But Sheldrake's idyll, like those of many other small-business owners, was disrupted by the coming of the "category killer" chains. In his case, he found himself up against arguably the most formidable mass retailer of this decade, Starbucks. Polly's sales fell 10 to 15 percent when a Starbucks store appeared a few blocks away in Long Beach in 1994. And in 1998, another Starbucks opened just seventy-eight yards from Polly's.

"We were getting despondent," Sheldrake said. "We were just trying to hang on. We had a chain problem and didn't know what to do."

Perhaps no phenomenon has more profoundly transformed American main streets in the 1990s than the "chain problem." From tony Annapolis, Maryland, to the Melrose district of Hollywood to bohemian Harvard Square in Cambridge, Massachusetts, retail streetscapes have been steadily homogenized as heavily marketed national chains have outgunned and displaced locally owned rivals, whose resources and organization generally pale in comparison with the likes of Starbucks.

But the way Polly's responded to the chain problem demonstrates that resistance is not futile. In a turn of events that suggests some hope for small-scale retailers, Polly's fought back, and has managed to grow and thrive even with two Starbucks in its neighborhood. Sales rose 40 percent in 1998 and were expected to climb 30 percent in 1999.

With help from a retail consultant, Bob Phibbs, who specializes in helping independent businesses cope with chain-store competitors, Polly's decided to take aim at Starbucks in two ways: beating the chain at its own game by operating even more efficiently, and exploiting the inherent vulnerability of many chains. "The problem with a chain is that it's like a mall: It's all mechanical, and there's no relationship with the customers," said Phibbs, whose other clients have included independent hotels and pet stores. "I think people are getting sick of the megastores. People are disaffected."

In the case of Polly's, Phibbs advised the company to stress the fact that the store roasts its own coffee on site, which is impractical for a sprawling chain like Starbucks, and to emphasize the wider variety of coffees Polly's offers. Starbucks, considered trendy by many of its customers, was derided in Polly's local advertising as a mere purveyor of "ordinary" coffee.

But Polly's resurgence was built on more than positioning. Phibbs urged the store's management to adopt the chains' best organizational and management ideas, like putting an end to a plethora of special arrangements between employees and longtime customers for free or cut-rate services and tightening cash management procedures. Employees attended mandatory classes to improve their sales skills.

"The advantages of the chains are their procedures and administration," Phibbs said. "If an independent doesn't learn how to be just as efficient, they're going to be dead, fast."

Many retail experts say the chains' organizational advantages and economies of scale will eventually overwhelm most independent businesses, even if a few, like Polly's, swim against the tide for a time. Yves Sistron, a principal at Global Retail Partners, a venture capital company based in Los Angeles that invests in aspiring chains, observed that mass retailers are continually invading once secure small-business preserves, even in areas like cosmetics, educational toys, watches, fruit juices and Chinese food.

To Sistron, who has invested in successful chains like Jamba Juice and P. F. Chang's China Bistros, it is only a matter of time before well-financed and -managed chains gobble up just about everything on Main Street. "Who gets beat up?" he said. "The smaller independent stores, the mom-and-pops. I'm not saying it's not dreary. But it's true." In the future, he said, if shoppers want to find anything like a traditional Main Street, "it's going to be Main Street, Disneyland."

Certainly, the continuing success of Starbucks lends credence to Sistron's view. The company's sales at stores open at least a year were 8 percent higher in September 1999 than they were in September 1998, and Starbucks has bought out one smaller competitor after another. In October 1999 it had twenty-five hundred stores, up from just eleven a decade earlier. Starbucks's chairman, Howard Schultz, has spoken of growing to twenty thousand outlets, rivaling McDonald's twenty-five thousand stores for sheer ubiquity.

Yet it is Starbucks's concentration on growth, Phibbs said, that gives companies like Polly's their opportunity. The bigger Starbucks gets, he said, and the further afield it goes, the more trouble it will have maintaining consistent high quality in its products and in customer service.

The chain's expansion into other kinds of drinks, including sweetened iced coffees, and Schultz's Internet ambitions to turn the Starbucks Web site into a dominant "premier lifestyle portal" have not yet excited much enthusiasm on Wall Street, where analysts are concerned about a perceived lack of focus. Translated into Main Street terms, Phibbs said, Starbucks risks squandering its cachet as an upscale coffeehouse. "Starbucks is not a coffee business any more," Phibbs said. "It's a drinks business—a McDonald's of the 1990s."

Starbucks doesn't see itself as Goliath to the independents' David. It says it doesn't look at competition on a neighborhood-by-neighborhood basis. "We couldn't be happier that this guy is doing great business," Arthur Rubinfeld, Starbucks's senior vice president for store development, said of Sheldrake and Polly's, because it enlarges the market for everyone: "More people are on the street looking for a coffee experience, and the higher-end coffee ends up doing better." But he took issue with the claim that in-store roasting gives Polly's a quality advantage over Starbucks. "It's not relevant in this day and age. We source and roast the best quality beans," he said.

Still, for entrepreneurs like Sheldrake, any weakness that might appear in the strategic focus of a powerful chain represents a chance to survive and thrive. But given the chains' marketing muscle, Sheldrake said, he knows that independents like Polly's can never afford to backslide or become lazy.

"A small business can stand up to a chain," Sheldrake said. "But you can only do it if you have procedures as good as theirs—and better coffee, too."

Joel Kotkin
October 24, 1999

CASE 5

A New Business Model

In the mid-1990s, a success story at the John G. Shedd Aquarium in Chicago came perilously close to morphing into a public relations disaster.

Built in 1930, Shedd could handle up to nine thousand visitors a day. Then, in 1991, it opened an oceanarium that featured dolphin shows, drawing new visitors. But the oceanarium could accommodate only seventy-five hundred people, and on busy days guards had to turn away hundreds of visitors, some of whom were angry after having driven for hours with their children to see the shows.

The overcrowding threatened to get worse if nothing was done before Shedd finished two exhibitions to reproduce the environments of the

Amazon River and the Philippine coral reefs. Those additions will also have limited space.

For a solution, Shedd turned to one of the country's preeminent strategic consulting firms, Bain & Company, which charges corporate clients multi-million-dollar fees but like its competitors also does work free for nonprofits. Sure enough, by teasing out patterns in a sea of details the aquarium had compiled on visitors, from their ZIP codes to their ages and number of children, Bain came up with a plan to persuade local groups to visit on slow days.

Not so long ago, that achievement would have been soon forgotten, just another good deed by a consulting firm with corporate clients around the world who pay Bain an estimated $700 million annually for advice.

But now, because of a project that was nine years in the making and that was officially started in 2000, such sophisticated advice forms the backbone of a new initiative by Bain. The initiative, the Bridge Group, has close ties to Bain but is a legally separate nonprofit organization. It has a staff of twelve of the best and brightest consultants from Bain's ranks who have committed themselves to stints at Bridge of six months to a year, even though they have to take pay cuts ranging from 80 percent for million-dollar-a-year Bain executives to 20 percent for junior consultants.

The Bridge Group is something entirely new in the world of big-league business consulting—a general-purpose strategic consulting firm that will help other nonprofit organizations for a fee.

Its aim is to complement the piecemeal, pro bono approach that Bain and others have long taken toward helping nonprofits solve management and logistical woes. The group will offer the consistent, sustained advice that has helped big business wring more profit out of each invested dollar. It will also enhance the quality of help now provided by a plethora of non-profit consultants, ranging from one-person shops to niche agencies, mostly focused on fund-raising or management.

It is, Bain consultants believe, a long overdue step. After all, the United States has about 770,000 nonprofits, not counting religious organizations, which took in an estimated $750 billion in fees, grants, donations and investment earnings in 1999. But despite accounting for 8 percent of the economy, nonprofits get little attention in the business pages or from big consulting firms precisely because they are not in business to make investors rich.

Many nonprofit experts expect a wave of consolidation among non-profits, just like the mergers that have swept through corporations over the last decade, as organizations seek the scale necessary for success in the twenty-first century. The creation of a strategic consulting firm for non-profits is likely to encourage such a trend. For all its growth, however, the nonprofit sector is highly fragmented, with many organizations too small to accomplish much and many duplicating the works of other organizations.

"There simply is no force to push consolidations and to move organizations to an appropriate scale to fulfill their mission," said Thomas J. Tierney, Bain's worldwide managing director and father of the idea for the Bridge Group.

Moreover, about half the growth in nonprofit revenue in the last two decades came from fees charged for services that range from counseling troubled families to renting out space in churches to daycare providers. Donations accounted for only 8 percent of the growth.

Tierney's vision is not just to help individual nonprofits, but to build a storehouse of knowledge that can be applied to common problems among nonprofits in the same way that Bain can help a ketchup maker improve profits by reviewing work it did for mustard and pickle makers.

"Pro bono consulting for nonprofits often doesn't produce results because it is in and out," Tierney said. "They often have no follow-up because the ugly fact is that, ultimately, you get what you pay for."

Each project will include follow-up consultations so the insights that Bridge Group consultants develop do not gather dust on a shelf but are adopted and refined through practical experience.

The Bridge Group's consultants all have full access to the wealth of knowledge that Bain has stored in its Bain Virtual University, a database in which every corporate client's project is reduced to a case study, called a "knowledge module," so that the wheel does not get invented over and over again. This gathering and storing of information is a critical element in the efficiency and profitability of big consulting firms.

The Bridge Group, which has small offices in Boston and San Francisco, will charge fees that will generally be only about one-fifth what Bain charges for-profit corporate clients and in many cases will be paid by foundations, said Jeffrey L. Bradach, a former Harvard business professor who is the managing director of the Bridge Group.

Bridge expected to handle perhaps ten clients in 2000, one of them a major foundation that Bradach declined to identify. "The presenting problem was that they give away tens of millions of dollars a year but don't know what they really produce for that money," Bradach said.

The Bridge Group will analyze the donations, trying to show the foundation how to get results that further its agenda. That kind of insight into how grant-making can produce tangible results has been the Holy Grail of non-profit evaluators. Bradach says his staff has the expertise to apply strategic consulting, over time, to improve the effect of grants.

The Bridge Group began with an idea sketched on the back of napkins at a Mexican restaurant in Silicon Valley. Tierney and Paul L. Carttar, another Bain consultant, were reviewing what they had learned from work for various charities in the San Francisco Bay Area, including the San Francisco United Way, and were bemoaning the lack of a vehicle to apply what they had learned to other nonprofits.

"Because these were pro bono projects, there was no knowledge capture," Tierney said, using consultant jargon to explain that valuable insights were not reduced to case studies and stored for use by other consultants on future projects.

As the two men looked at the stack of napkins covered with notes, Tierney recalled, he told Carttar: "Gosh, there has got to be a way to do this in a sustainable manner." Seven years later, when Tierney first sketched his idea for a reporter, it did not have a name. But soon two teams from Bain began working on the idea and, after eighteen drafts of a business plan, they came up with a low-cost model built around highly motivated consultants working at low pay for fixed periods.

Bain made a $1.3 million grant for the project and then Tierney, Carttar and Bradach, the cofounders, went looking for outside financing, securing a total of $5.5 million from the Edna McConnell Clark, Rockefeller Brothers and Surdna foundations, all in New York, and the Irvine Foundation in San Francisco.

Edward Skloot, executive director of the Surdna Foundation, which has a $650 million endowment, said the Bridge Group was a critical step in improving nonprofit governance and management. "We see value in developing knowledge that can be shared" with other nonprofits, he said.

For Tierney, starting the Bridge Group is a chance to create a legacy in the world of big-league consulting, an idea that could transform nonprofit management.

"If we can prove this model works, then someone else is going to do it and we want that," he said. "If one of the other big consulting firms doesn't do this in the next few years, it would be a mark against our idea."

The project has become his consuming passion. As he spoke, he took a sheet from a legal pad and, without pausing in his remarks, sketched a matrix comparing the Bridge Group model with the existing system under which firms and nonprofit consulting agencies both do cut-rate or free work for charities.

Soon, Tierney's jotting had grown into twenty-eight boxes, an illustration of how consultants take reams of information that can easily overwhelm both corporate and nonprofit managers and reduce it to its basic components, then devise ways to deal with those components efficiently.

One question that Tierney and his cofounders say they repeatedly encountered as they sought financing was: What does Bain get out of this?

For one thing, it gets a relief valve for star consultants who might otherwise leave to become chief executives at corporations but now have the option of spending six months or more on socially redeeming work instead of helping condiment makers squeeze more profits out of their factories. Indeed, more than one-third of Bain's twenty-four hundred full-time professionals have volunteered to work at the Bridge Group.

Only the best will get the chance, Tierney said, and they will "have to be very, very, very good." So will the host of potential clients who have begun sending proposals to the Bridge Group, which when fully staffed will be able to handle about forty a year. "We must be very careful about who our clients are," he said, "because as consultants you can't be any better than your client base."

David Cay Johnston
February 2, 2000

The Bridge Group changed its name to The Bridgespan Group. Thomas J. Tierney stepped down as worldwide managing director of Bain to become chairman; he continues to be a Bain director.

REVOLUTIONARY THINKING

Entrepreneurial Management

My life as Lycos chief executive—and sole employee—began in a cubicle. It was exciting. I felt I was building something, though I wasn't sure exactly what, with an awful lot of opportunity. First, I put a computer on my desktop. Then I learned to use a PC. Meantime, I was trying to start a business. What should a logo look like? Who should the employees be, and what should they do?
—Robert J. Davis, chief executive officer,
Lycos Inc., May 17, 2000

I started my first business, a Web design company called I/O 360, at age thirty-six. . . . I had this romantic notion of what it would be like to be my own boss. I didn't know it meant all this work and no pay.
—Bob Clyatt, chief executive officer,
HorizonLive.com, March 29, 2000

We hear it again and again: This is the age of entrepreneurship. Technology has freed workers from the drudgery that is corporate America and allowed them to step forth on their own. A new business on the Internet is just one good idea, and a few clicks, away. Lacking even that, other people can become "e-lancers," selling their graphic-design or computer-programming skills over the digital transom.

The reality, of course, is a whole lot more difficult. In fact, in recent years, the number of people who are their own boss has actually dropped slightly. This decline has come at a time when the United States created millions of jobs, making self-employment a noticeably smaller part of the economy than it was a decade ago. Rather than hanging out their own shingle, more people are deciding that big offices, along with the camaraderie, computer training and health insurance that they offer, trump self-employment.

But what if you can't shake the bug? What if you know that owning a business is what you want? How, then, can you overcome the early obstacles—long days, no benefits, little initial pay—and succeed?

You can start by knowing that it will not be easy. The end of the dot-com euphoria that had gripped the stock market means that ideas have a much harder time finding money than they did in the 1990s. You want to sell candles on the Internet? Go ahead. Just don't expect a venture capital company to give you any money to hire a staff or set up a warehouse.

If you want support, and a reasonable chance at success, you need to tend toward the radical. At a time when information moves more quickly than it ever has, incrementally new ideas do not retain an advantage for long.

This chapter profiles some of the entrepreneurs who have come up with daring ideas. Michael R. Bloomberg, for instance, saw obscure financial data as the gateway to a multibillion-dollar information network. Geraldine Laybourne thought like a child, and was able to build an entirely new television network as a result. She then had the guts to leave a sure thing to start a high-risk venture.

Often, radical ideas aren't enough. One of the biggest leaps entrepreneurs have to make is from launching a start-up to running an organization. Many fall short.

Among the keys to success seems to be aggressiveness. Sometimes that zeal can border on the offensive. In this chapter, you'll also meet one man who is no stranger to displays of vulgarity and another who keeps a metal skull on his desk.

Even if your style is more subdued, and even if you never expect to leave company life, there are lessons here. Around the world today, corporations are trying to figure out how to act more entrepreneurially, precisely because of the rapid flow of information. To raise profits year after year requires original ideas in ways that it never before has.

"We've reached the end of incrementalism," Gary Hamel, the management guru, writes in *Leading the Revolution*, his newest book, "and only those companies that are capable of creating industry revolutions will prosper in the new economy." Continue reading, and start fomenting.

CASE 1

Eponymous Leadership

Seth Ruskin, a global equities trader in Florida who was about to change jobs, made it a point to insist on one thing from his new employer, Wanger Asset Management of Chicago. The firm had only a few computer terminals providing the Bloomberg financial data service, and he wanted to be sure he had one.

"Everybody's using it," he explained. Through the Bloomberg service, he said, "I'm in contact with everyone, and it's so easy to use."

Just as Federal Express created a new paradigm in the 1980s, revolutionizing the shipping of documents and small items, Bloomberg LP in the 1990s created one for the dissemination and use of business and financial information. In the process, the company changed the landscape of the $7 billion financial data industry, marginalizing once-proud competitors like Dow Jones's Telerate system.

As much as any founder could, Michael R. Bloomberg shaped his company in his own image. Beginning in the early 1980s with a business that provided arcane financial data to bond traders, he built a unique information powerhouse whose news reports are published in newspapers worldwide, whose television programming in 102 countries and whose data flow to about 111,000 trading desks, executive suites and newsrooms—anywhere that instantaneous financial information is in demand. In the process, the dapper Bloomberg became a billionaire.

But what it takes to forge a revolution is not the same as what it takes to govern. Bloomberg's challenge now is to guide his company through its transformation into a corporate giant stable enough to manage a huge, competitive business and nimble enough to outsmart other entrepreneurs—the men who would be Bloomberg.

These days, the privately held Bloomberg LP is now coping with the problems of a mature company. Cost controls have a new, high priority. A lavish bonus system has been reined in. The sales force has been beefed up as the company sets its sights on foreign markets, where every gain will be hard won. All this as the eponymous Bloomberg box through which the data flow is being phased out in favor of a personal computer–based system.

Yet for all the changes, the company is still an unmistakable reflection of its founder.

Like the system he built, Michael Bloomberg is enormously complex. He is generous: The company pays well, and he is an active philanthropist. He is also an obsessive worker, and numerous employees complain of a punishing work schedule. He has been aggressive in hiring women, but is not shy about using brusque sexual language in the office. Though he can be tough in pushing longtime associates aside, he is slow to dismiss anyone.

As the company has grown to nearly five thousand employees and has expanded around the globe, Bloomberg has withdrawn slightly, devoting more time to philanthropy and nurturing gossip about possible political ambitions. At the same time, his company must grow—in many different directions at once—if it is to maintain its momentum.

Of Growth and Culture

In a 1999 interview at his Manhattan headquarters, Bloomberg, dressed impeccably in his trademark dark suit, white shirt and dark tie, said Bloomberg LP's future would depend on its ability to reinvent itself.

"The world is such that you have to constantly provide the public— whether the public is an institutional public or a retail public—with new things," he said. "Partly because they get bored. But also because the competitors out there, whether it's better kinds of cereal or widgets or information or whatever it is, they're doing it better."

That leaves Bloomberg watchers with two fundamental questions. First, where will new growth come from, when the company must confront the London-based Reuters Group PLC on its home turf overseas and watch out at home for Internet-based services that offer much less but come far cheaper? Reuters had worldwide 1998 revenue of $5 billion—from financial data systems and news, photo and video services—compared with an estimated $1.5 billion for Bloomberg.

In 1998, Bloomberg had net installations of 19,800 systems, just five hundred more than the previous year, according to company figures. The growth of its installed base was 22 percent—hardly a poor showing, but lagging behind the 1997 rate of 28 percent and the 1996 rate of 25 percent.

"With Bloomberg in the United States, I think they've reached a peak," said Angela Wilbraham, an editor with Waters Information Services of New York, a leading research organization in the financial information and services field.

The second question concerns the company's corporate culture, which was forged in a period marked by hyperenergetic work schedules, hypergrowth in data-processing capacity and a sometimes hypercritical management. Can Bloomberg LP outgrow its adolescence and achieve steady, if less spectacular, growth, while managing its expanding work force in a more measured way?

Bloomberg is betting that the increasing complexity of the financial world will inexorably bolster demand for a system like his—a system intended to make opaque financial data transparent.

"If securities prices were all that mattered—if everything was open, high, low, close on the New York Stock Exchange—Yahoo.com could do it fine, and we'd be out of business," he said.

As for the bruising corporate culture, Bloomberg said: "Look, I hope the company is better tomorrow than it is today. The world changes. You become bigger. When you are a small company, you don't have policies. As you get bigger, you get to be more, codified, if that's the word."

From Humble Beginnings

The pressure to keep delivering new information—data, equations to analyze the data and real-time news—is evident at the company's Manhattan headquarters at Park Avenue and Fifty-ninth Street. Starting before 7 A.M., reporters, programmers and sales representatives reach across one another for bowls of fruit and cups of coffee at the food nook, the operation's main intersection.

All around them, Bloomberg LP's computers are silently compiling financial data and other information, and spitting them out for those who need them. Any news headline about an Asian insurrection, any stock transaction on an obscure Latin American market, any change in a local water authority's bond price—information from eight hundred separate sources—can be sent through the company's servers at the rate of twelve thousand discrete items of information a second.

Bloomberg began building this empire in 1981, after he was unceremoniously ousted from Salomon Brothers when it merged with the Phibro Corporation. He had been a successful bond trader and head of equities before becoming the brokerage firm's chief of information systems. In that capacity, he developed a system for providing Salomon's traders with data and numerical analysis. Still, his personality did not meld with those of the other partners.

Bloomberg used his partnership proceeds from Salomon to begin building his own company, designing a data system for bond traders with the same needs he once had. No off-the-shelf computer of the period could accommodate the system's needs, so he built his own dedicated computer terminals, eventually naming them for himself. By 1990 he was leasing ten thousand boxes a year for about twelve hundred dollars each. The Bloomberg, as the box is known, provided streams of data in newly accessible formats, including a reservoir of historical information that lent depth and perspective to every market decision. With the push of a button, complex calculations about prices and trends could be retrieved.

"We let investment professionals focus on their business rather than the mathematics of it," Bloomberg said.

That service was augmented in the early 1990s with a news service that began by providing financial bulletins and has grown into a broad-based service with a worldwide staff of seven hundred reporters covering financial and political news for Bloomberg customers, America Online subscribers and others.

The popularity of the system brought rich rewards to the company's founder. And Bloomberg, who is worth an estimated $2 billion, came to cut a wide swath in the world of philanthropy. He joined the board of the Metropolitan Museum of Art and donated $100 million to Johns Hopkins University, where he is chairman of the board.

Bloomberg's profile rose as rumors began circulating that he might enter politics—perhaps with a run for mayor of New York. He neither encouraged nor discouraged that notion. When the subject came up in a 1999 interview, Bloomberg paused, sweeping his hands outward, as if to embrace eighteen years of accomplishment certified by the dozens of framed newspaper clippings that cover his office walls.

"I think we can agree that we've done this successfully," he said. "Number one, you don't want to do something for the rest of your life if you have the option. Number two, I've always been—envious isn't quite the word—but people who do public service deserve our admiration."

After the Revolution

Bloomberg has shared his success with his employees, winning the loyalty of many. Given the rapid growth of the company, its bonus system—based on the number of new customers—proved lush. For example, journalists a few years out of school could make ninety thousand dollars a year.

So when the bonus system was recently revamped, it received considerable notice internally. The changes reduced the sales base on which bonuses were calculated and made the bonuses more sensitive to annual sales fluctuations. Though employees can, theoretically, receive windfalls as big as ever, some are anxious about the overhaul.

"People here are used to the market appreciating a certain rate, and they are starting to feel like their wealth has gone down," said one longtime senior employee, speaking on the condition of anonymity.

The company's managers, including Bloomberg, see the change as a necessary adjustment, one of many reflecting tighter controls as the company tries to shave costs and rein in what have been rather loosely run operations.

For example, the company's investigation of purchasing practices at its offices in Princeton, New Jersey, led to Bloomberg's filing a lawsuit in 1999 against two former employees, accusing them of embezzling more than $1.5 million.

Meanwhile, journalists' expenses are coming under closer scrutiny, and Bloomberg employees have been given electronic passes to monitor their comings and goings.

The new strictures may test morale at a company that thrives on the intensity of its work ethic. A further test may come from challenges to a culture that, some employees say, has transported Wall Street's locker-room language uptown at a time when more women are willing to challenge such behavior, in court if necessary.

While the atmosphere has improved in recent years, employees say, the change did not happen fast enough to avert three lawsuits accusing the company of sexual harassment. All make reference to a work environment in Bloomberg LP's sales organization in which explicit sexual comments were commonplace.

One plaintiff, a former saleswoman named Sekiko Sekai Garrison, contends in her suit that women in the sales department were encouraged to wear provocative clothing and were subjected to vulgar descriptions of their figures. Men, she says, spoke openly of female colleagues as potential sexual conquests.

According to her suit, which was pending in Federal District Court in Manhattan, Bloomberg himself joined in the banter. "Bloomberg regularly made sexual comments about women to company employees and clients," the suit says. None of the suits, however, accuses Bloomberg of making sexual overtures toward female employees.

Bloomberg does not deny that he occasionally uses bawdy language, but he says that neither he nor the company misbehaved. Bloomberg instituted awareness sessions about sexual harassment in 1994 and, he noted, a news bureau chief was dismissed after the company concluded that he had harassed a female colleague.

Bloomberg is dismissive of the lawsuits.

"All three of their lawyers called up and said, 'If you give us cash, we'll go away,'" he said. "As far as I am concerned, that is out-and-out extortion, and I think companies caving in to that sort of thing are making a terrible mistake. And we will go and fight all three of these. And I, in my heart of hearts, believe that we have done nothing wrong."

Ronald Shechtman, the lawyer who filed the suit for Garrison, said he had had extensive, but ultimately fruitless, settlement talks with the company's lawyer. "There was a serious and sustained effort to resolve the case," Shechtman said.

"The Bloomberg Way"

Like Bloomberg's sales representatives, its journalists built their organization from scratch, beginning in 1990. Besides having to win respect for a fledging news operation, they were working for a management that pushed its vision of journalistic excellence relentlessly.

Matthew Winkler, the former *Wall Street Journal* reporter who is editor in chief of *Bloomberg News,* is credited both inside and outside the company with establishing a high quality of basic financial reporting. And these days, Bloomberg is supplementing its wire service staples with columns and in-depth articles, like an exposé in December 1998 about companies' selective disclosure of information to analysts at high-priced retreats.

(That is a far cry from the early days, when Bloomberg journalists were being rejected for press credentials that would enable them to cover Federal agencies. Then, Winkler offered Bloomberg boxes free to newspapers, including the *New York Times,* if they would run Bloomberg articles. That arrangement is ending, though news organizations may be eligible for discounted rates.)

The service, about one-third the size of the news operation at Reuters, was built on Winkler's rigid rules, presented in a booklet called "The Bloomberg Way." Among its injunctions are prohibitions on words like "flat." ("People would never say that a market's curved or round, so don't write that it's flat.")

Its clientele's voracious appetite for information leads to a punishing work schedule, even given the company's high pay scale. Present and former reporters say eleven-hour days are routine.

Winkler, who routinely arrives at work at 6 A.M. and stays until after 7 P.M., said, "I would never ask anyone to do what I haven't done myself or what I'm doing." He added, "You put in the time that's necessary as the story is unfolding."

Certainly, long hours are a staple in many news organizations, as are arguments among strong-minded journalists. Still, Bloomberg alumni with experience in other organizations describe a management culture pock-marked by debilitating confrontations, a workplace in which stories about personal humiliations have become the stuff of corporate legend.

In a 1993 incident, Winkler criticized two Washington-based reporters who, while working fifteen-hour days, neglected to return a call from another reporter in Princeton. In his weekly employee newsletter, Winkler headlined his observations "Proud to Be Stupid" and characterized the behavior as "shocking" and "the antithesis of what this news organization stands for."

Winkler did not defend his handling of the situation, but asked that his reviews of reporters' work be assessed as a whole. Indeed, the tone of his write-ups became less acerbic, with praise more forthcoming. "You get older and wiser," he said.

Bloomberg is quick to defend Winkler. The editor, he said, "is a perfectionist, and I don't see anything wrong with that."

Sharing the Wealth

Employees who stayed with the company benefited handsomely as it grew. Figures provided by one investor indicate that Bloomberg LP, which does not release financial numbers, made about $270 million in 1998 on sales of $1.5 billion, giving it a pretax profit margin of about 18 percent. These people think that Bloomberg had debt of about $315 million.

Bloomberg said the numbers were generally correct.

As a limited partnership, Bloomberg LP's profits—and tax bills—pass to its shareholders, though under the arrangement, equity owners receive 60 percent of profits, with 40 percent plowed back into the company.

Merrill Lynch owns about 20 percent of Bloomberg LP. Bloomberg owns about 72 percent, and six longtime employees have a total of about 8 percent. Their stake, along with Bloomberg's, is in a holding company called Bloomberg Inc.

In 1996, when Merrill chose to reduce its stake from 30 percent, the holding company borrowed to pay Merrill $200 million for 10 percent of the operating company, thus valuing all of Bloomberg LP at $2 billion.

At the time of the Merrill deal, Bloomberg also agreed to buy out two of the eight smaller shareholders to whom he had given stock in the company's early days, when he was looking for ways to recruit and retain key employees.

One of those shareholders, a computer programmer named James Jong who left in 1995, said recently, "I was bought out for forty cents on the dollar, and the payment took a year." Bloomberg, he said, told him that he lacked the cash to pay a higher price and that, in any case, a minority shareholder like Jong would have no other potential buyers.

Asked about that account, Bloomberg said: "I would never do that. And Jong's numbers were inaccurate." Bloomberg omitted any mention of Jong from his autobiography, *Bloomberg by Bloomberg* (Wiley, 1997), although he cited all the company's other minority shareholders, including another investor who sold his stake but who remained with the company.

For the moment, Bloomberg wants no more shareholders. If Bloomberg LP were public, stockholders might raise their eyebrows at continuing losses in its television operations.

Bloomberg Television is carried in the mornings over the USA cable network and local stations like KDFW-TV, Channel 4, the Fox affiliate in Dallas. For the most part, Bloomberg LP's TV revenues come from selling ads during this programming, but sales have yet to come close to covering expenses, a spokeswoman said.

With a private company, Bloomberg need not defend his money-losing investment in what the company calls "audio-visual" journalists. In any event, he says that Bloomberg's TV and radio reports help extend the brand name.

"Most guys I know who run public companies claim they wish they were me," he said.

Tinkering with the Formula

Bloomberg's future rests not on television, however, but on sales of its data systems. Its growing sales force of a thousand is the largest staff in the company.

The product that those representatives are selling is no longer a stand-alone machine but a system that runs on personal computers. That change reduces the company's overhead somewhat, since Bloomberg LP will no longer have to manufacture or service the terminals itself. (Existing terminals will be phased out and replaced by the PC system.)

Reuters, the longtime market leader, sends data to 445,000 screens, according to Robert Crooke, a company spokesman. Unlike Bloomberg LP, which has been selling a one-size-fits-all product for an average of $1,200 a month, Reuters offers a range of products priced from $100 to $1,200. Its high-end Reuters 3000 PC-based service is designed to challenge the depth and versatility of Bloomberg. Bridge Information Systems is offering Telerate Plus, a bond analytics product that sells for $825 a month. Bridge bought Telerate from Dow Jones in 1998 in a fire sale, after Dow Jones lost more than $1 billion on its investment. Bridge's purchase of that and another service, ADP, brought its installed base of terminals to about 300,000, or nearly triple the number of Bloomberg terminals.

Bloomberg LP, Reuters and Bridge operate systems designed in an era when the Internet was not a factor in the market data universe. Now, though Bloomberg maintains that his company and Reuters are actually the world's biggest Internet companies, he is well aware that there are many advertiser-supported sites—from Yahoo.com to CNNfn.com to Marketwatch.com—that offer basic data on United States equities. And users get much of the information free.

Bloomberg, in internal memos, has said he sees a threat from "small, nimble entrepreneurial companies" that might cut into his market.

But in the short run, some analysts say, he needs to challenge Reuters's domination overseas and in the currency markets generally. According to one Bloomberg executive, speaking on the condition of anonymity, in 1999 Bloomberg LP had eight hundred institutions providing it with currency data. Reuters had five thousand. Bloomberg LP also introduced a system for completing trades in certain limited markets, as a competitor to Reuters's Instinet system. And it has developed a product called Data License, which provides end-of-the-day data to financial professionals who do not need minute-by-minute price information.

Yet according to some financial analysts and executives of other data companies, the biggest threat to companies like Bloomberg LP is most likely to come from their own large customers: Banks and brokerage houses may develop their own internal systems that render Bloomberg's higher analytic functions superfluous.

Bloomberg is acutely aware that there may be other, younger Michael Bloombergs out there. But at the moment, his name still has a magical resonance. Traders check "the Bloomberg"; some Merrill Lynch executives, who transmit messages over their machines, use the verb "to Bloomberg" as a synonym for sending e-mail.

Still, Bloomberg is hyperconscious of the speed at which a company can spiral into oblivion. "I started Bloomberg in 1981," he said in March 1999. "I've gone back and looked at the then-Fortune 500 companies. How many do you think are still in the Fortune 500?" His answer: "One hundred sixty, as of a few months ago."

"There are very few companies that survive through multiple market cycles and technological evolution," he added.

Will his? "Well," Bloomberg said, "I can guarantee you that if we don't keep changing, innovating, giving our customers more for their money, we will not survive."

Felicity Barringer and Geraldine Fabrikant
March 21, 1999

CASE 2

Building a Vision

Sam LeFrak was pounding his palms on a conference table so hard the telephone was bouncing. He was yelling. He was cursing. Someone tried to get a word in, but it was no use.

LeFrak was happy. And he was on a roll.

"This," he said, with a bang on the table, "will be one of the stops on the Gray Line bus tour." (Bang.) "This will be shown by every boat." (Bang.) "There's Newport! There's Newport!" (Bang.) "And when you see what we started with, you'll know why it will be the proudest moment of my life."

He brought his ruddy face up close to a visitor's: "Now, I'm not trying to influence you."

Newport is the $10 billion apartment and office complex that LeFrak, the billionaire developer, and his son, Richard, are building on what not long ago was a rotting stretch of Jersey City, New Jersey, waterfront. Never mind that boat captains will probably miss it while pointing out Manhattan across the way or the big green statue nearby.

It is what LeFrak, who has built more apartments in the New York area than any other private developer, calls his "baby," his "Mona Lisa" and, more tellingly in his eighties, his "swan song."

And when the giant gated city is finished sometime in the early part of the third millennium, it promises to be perhaps the only one of LeFrak's vast creations that will measure up to his gargantuan ego.

With twelve thousand apartments, it will dwarf Lefrak City, the largest apartment complex in Queens and once the largest privately developed complex in the country, which LeFrak built in the 1960s. (He only later capitalized the F in his family's name, saying he wanted to stress a French heritage.)

Newport will have about two Empire State Buildings' worth of office space. The property, all of which the LeFraks own, is about the size of Rikers Island, and includes the land above and below the New Jersey end of the Holland Tunnel.

LeFrak said, and it was hard to tell if he was joking, "We are going to let them keep the tunnel there."

For a generation raised on the flashy self-aggrandizement of Donald J. Trump, it may be hard to imagine that he had a kind of spiritual forefather in Samuel J. LeFrak. In the late 1950s, when LeFrak took over the successful construction company that his father, Harry, founded, he set out to transform the name itself into a synonym for middle-class urbanity outside Manhattan.

He emblazoned his name in huge orange letters on Lefrak City, alongside the Horace Harding Expressway, next to signs that needled weary drivers: "If We Lived Here Daddy, You'd Be Home By Now." He courted governors and mayors, but most of all reporters, for whom he played a role unlike any real estate developer before him: outrageous, always available, willing to make almost any claim and answer any question, if not always accurately.

He frequently claimed that one out of every sixteen New Yorkers lived in a Lefrak apartment (a plausible calculation, though he never explained his math). When articles about his finances upset him, he called up reporters offering to open up his books. When he was singled out by the federal government in the early 1970s in a housing discrimination case, he angrily pronounced it the worst disaster since Pearl Harbor, and, after a dispute with the city over federal housing funds, he briefly but loudly threatened to stop building in New York and move his headquarters to Los Angeles.

During the last two decades, his prominence has dimmed because he eventually did all but stop building in New York City. This was largely because of disagreements over Battery Park City—he wanted it to be more middle-class than luxury—that led him to walk away as a primary developer of that complex in the early 1980s.

He constantly complains that city officials have long made it too difficult and expensive to build in New York City. But while other real estate families have stumbled in economic downturns, LeFrak and his son have continued, slowly, methodically, and largely with their own money, to build and fill more apartments and offices.

"Inflation, deflation, stagflation, even rent control," LeFrak likes to say, his voice jumping an octave, "this family has survived it."

If anything, his hyperbole has grown with age. He has called Newport "probably the largest job that has ever been built since the pyramids." He also increasingly seeks the kind of recognition—as a statesman, an educator, a patron and an architectural visionary—that has eluded him as a creator of mostly plain-vanilla complexes.

But it remains to be seen whether history will judge him as more than an extraordinarily resourceful, prolific builder. "I really don't think he has influenced the course of architecture any more than he has influenced foreign policy or education or art or any of the other issues to which he would like to have you believe he has made a major contribution," said Paul Goldberger, the architecture critic for the *New Yorker*.

"He produced a lot of housing economically, which is an admirable accomplishment," Goldberger added. "I like to think that one could have done it better than he did, but the city did need a lot of housing and he filled that need."

It is an assessment that at one time LeFrak proudly made himself. "They were basic," he wrote in a 1974 article that appeared in the *New York Times* about the standard six-story Lefrak apartment buildings that dot nearly every Brooklyn and Queens neighborhood. "The windows opened and closed. You opened them in the summer and closed them in the winter. Middle-class New Yorkers could afford to live in them and raise families."

But now LeFrak would like to be remembered for more than concrete and profit figures. He sometimes compares Newport to Frank Gehry's Guggenheim Museum in Bilbao, Spain. At a lavish eightieth birthday party at the Solomon R. Guggenheim Museum in Manhattan in 1998, he draped himself with a red sash and Finnish knighthood medal, one of several he has sought and received over the last two decades.

"Look at this guy—he's got his fruit salad on," said the actor Eli Wallach, a longtime friend and the narrator of a documentary that the Lefrak Organization commissioned for the birthday celebration. "There's just no one like Sam." His oversized business cards say Sir Samuel J. LeFrak and copies of his speeches that his company distributes announce him as Dr. LeFrak. (He has received several honorary doctorates.)

Now in his eighties, with a fortune estimated at more than $1.5 billion and an estimated ninety thousand apartments in the city (the LeFraks will not disclose their exact holdings), LeFrak remains an almost unbelievable mix of sophistication and street grit. He is a major benefactor and trustee of the Guggenheim Museum in Manhattan, and his vast art collection ranges from van Goghs to Warhols. Yet walking through the polished marble lobby of a Newport apartment tower recently, he asked a reporter if it wasn't "beauty-full."

"This is what we give the people," he said. "I get all the X Generation coming out here now."

Many real estate experts say his business instincts remain as sharp as ever. "Newport is not going to be a creative masterpiece," Goldberger said. "But the real creative thinking was just in going over there."

LeFrak, who had looked longingly on the crumbling railheads and warehouses along the Jersey waterfront for years from the deck of his ninety-four-foot yacht, told his son in the early 1980s that building there would fulfill a dream of his, to create a kind of rival skyline across from lower Manhattan.

"It would have been most people's nightmare," his son, Richard LeFrak, said. "The spot where all this is now was the worst kind of urban decay you could possibly look at." But the land sat atop a PATH train line, was surrounded by highways, had sweeping views of lower Manhattan and stretched along more than a mile of the Hudson.

A dozen years after construction began—with $1 billion invested, including their own money to install sewers and roads—Newport is more than a quarter completed, with eleven million square feet of offices and apartments. A Tokyo computer services company has taken nearly half a million square feet of office space, which the LeFraks say is the largest lease ever undertaken in the United States by a Japanese corporation. The first six high-rise rental buildings, with twenty-three hundred apartments and rents ranging from $750 for a studio to $2,800 for a large two-bedroom, have been completely rented.

LeFrak, wearing his trademark Panama hat and bright red tie, can be seen most days cruising around the complex in his Mercedes, like a brand-new potentate.

One day recently, he led a reporter out to a grassy spit of land that seemed within touching distance of lower Manhattan. He turned and surveyed the mini-city rising behind him. Was it a fitting retort, he was asked, to those who he says pushed him away from New York City to New Jersey?

He smiled wickedly. "You know what this is an international symbol for?" he said, making an impolite gesture with a gloved finger.

"Well, that's what Newport is going to be for those guys when they look across the river."

Randy Kennedy
December 31, 1998

CASE 3

The Personal and the Profitable

Robert L. Johnson remembers well a scene from his early days in cable television. In a bar with a number of cable executives, he was, as usual, the only black person in the group. An executive, a man Johnson had known for years, told a tasteless joke about the Ku Klux Klan and the miniseries *Roots*.

Reminiscing in his office at his Washington, D.C.–based company, BET Holdings Inc., Johnson's point in retelling the story was not its questionable humor. It was how as an African-American in the upper echelons of corporate America he often found himself confronted with a choice. Should he express his hurt or anger at racial slights? Or should he bury them for the sake of getting ahead?

"Being in business you swallow things that you don't like just because I'm trying to get this deal," he said. "So, OK, fine. I'll laugh at your jokes.

"So sure, you swallow those kinds of things," he continued. "Sometimes it does go overboard and you've got to decide at what point do you draw the line, and say this is beyond deal making; this is beyond trying to sell your product."

At the bar that day, Johnson said, he chuckled at the colleague's joke and told one of his own. If the joke bothered him he wasn't about to show it.

"I don't internalize a lot of the kind of stuff that comes at me from the standpoint of white society," he said. "I've adopted a saying, 'Welcome to the NFL,'" the National Football League. "In the NFL if you run into the line, you're going to get hit. That's why you put on a helmet and shoulder pads. If you're a black American, expect to get hit, and don't start crying when somebody comes up and hits you."

That philosophy—keep emotions in check, don't let issues of race get in the way of the deal—has helped Johnson become one of the country's most successful black entrepreneurs, indeed one of the most successful business executives of any race. In the last twenty years he has used his business savvy and his ability to attract white investors with deep pockets to build Black Entertainment Television—and later BET Holdings—into an entertainment giant worth, he says, more than $2.5 billion.

He also used his corporate connections to place himself in the position to become one of the few African-Americans ever to own a commercial airline. As part of the proposed merger between United Airlines and US Airways, Johnson will acquire a spinoff of US Airways' operations—including routes, planes and personnel—at Reagan National Airport in Washington.

But if Johnson has put his ties with corporate chieftains to good use, they too may have looked to see what they can glean from their friendship with him. It was Steven Wolfe, the chairman of US Airways, who proposed that Johnson acquire the airline's operations in Washington, which is called DC Air. Several analysts hinted that such a move might make the

Justice Department reluctant to block US Airways' merger with United since that would also mean blocking an African-American from acquiring an airline.

Johnson has also come in for criticism from some black intellectuals and civil rights advocates who see him as an African-American business executive who subordinates racial pride and solidarity to making a dollar.

Intellectuals sometimes grumble that BET, perhaps the most recognizable African-American brand name since the days of Motown, is filled with mindless and salacious music videos rather than meaningful black programming. Johnson is mercilessly skewered in the black syndicated comic strip *Boondocks*, one of whose characters has described the cable network as not particularly black and certainly not entertaining.

To Johnson, this is all mere carping. He is filling the market's demands. If the videos he broadcasts did not bring in an audience, he would put on what people did want to watch.

"See that video right there," Johnson said, pointing to the wall of his office where a television screen showed a BET video of women in skimpy bikinis writhing suggestively. "I didn't make that video. I had nothing to do with it. I didn't know that video was being made. They sent it to us because we have a mutually beneficial relationship. That artist wants to be seen. I want to put on programs. Somebody's watching that video right now. And because somebody's watching, the advertiser's going to put some money in it."

He added: "Believe me, if they send me videos with no nude women, if that's all they made, that's all I'd play. I don't pick up the phone and say, 'Hey, give me some more bump and grind.'"

That he can easily shrug off the criticism of black people and the slights of whites is a testament to what Johnson believes is his complete comfort and confidence in himself. His background of growing up in Freeport, Illinois, a town that was about 90 percent white, and attending the University of Illinois and Princeton University has made him comfortable dealing with whites.

Moving between worlds, while at times painful and daunting, is something he counsels young black people to experience.

"Obviously I think in a world that's shrinking every day, the smartest thing to do is get as much exposure as you can," he said. "If you can interact with other people and other cultures, then do so. Get to know them; get to know how they think; get to know their value system, their sense of humor; get to know what motivates them and what intimidates them. The more you know about people, the more comfortable you can be with them and the more you can communicate with them."

Steven A. Holmes
May 29, 2000

In November 2000, Viacom Inc. said it would buy BET Holdings for an estimated $2.3 billion in stock. Under the deal, Robert L. Johnson would become a major Viacom shareholder and would remain in control of Black Entertainment Television.

CASE 4

Inventing the Shelf

Peter Kindersley bicycles from his London home across the River Thames every morning, slicing through traffic to his office in Covent Garden, his suit pants bound with steel clips to avoid catching in the sprockets. Kindersley, chairman and former chief executive of the British publisher Dorling Kindersley, then marches up four flights of stairs, dismissing the lift as simply a modern excuse for laziness.

Kindersley admits up front that he is not exactly in the mainstream of a business now dominated by global conglomerates. "I was trained as a painter and not a business person at all," he said in 1999, sitting in the office that he shares with James Middlehurst, who took over as chief executive in August 1998 to supply the financial skills that Kindersley admittedly lacks. "I run the company as much more a workshop session rather than as a hierarchical business."

Kindersley is a publishing throwback—one whose old-fashioned independence of mind is such that he and his partner in the company's 1974 founding have largely ceased speaking to each other over Kindersley's resistance to selling out.

Kindersley has changed little since he toiled away on the company's first book, illustrating photography techniques for tradesmen.

But the company has.

Though modest by the standards of the industry's giants, Dorling Kindersley now publishes more than three hundred titles a year. In 1999, capitalizing on its reputation for distinctive illustration, the company reached deals to publish licensed books—tied to brands or products—for

Mattel's Barbie line, for the National Football League and for the Star Wars series (an exclusive, seven-year deal initiated by George Lucas).

Yet in a consolidating industry, the company has remained stubbornly independent. Kindersley, whose gentle demeanor belies a determination to chart his own course, would not have it any other way. Walt Disney, W.H. Smith of Britain and Microsoft are among the suitors who have approached him, but he has rebuffed every offer.

Kindersley began Dorling Kindersley with no grand ambitions. "I set up the company because I had a wife and two children to feed, and I had fallen out with my previous company in a fairly serious way," he said. The issue was what Kindersley calls the failure of that company, also a publisher, to make good on the promise of a 5 percent stake for becoming art director.

His old experience and his new predicament inspired him to start a new kind of publisher. "I was so horrified by how boring it was because it was so word-based—there was no interest in what a book looked like," he said. "It was just this sort of university mentality where every shred of aesthetic had been pressed out of them. I thought I must do something about this or I'll never survive."

After that first photography book, he moved into children's and reference books. Since 1991, the company has also sold more than forty million of its Eyewitness Guides travel series.

All these books have made Kindersley rich. He holds a 7.8 percent stake in a company worth $348 million.

Yet he still feels poor. "It was strictly survival then and it is still survival today," he said. "I begin to feel poor if the company doesn't do well."

Dorling Kindersley has always been a family affair. His wife, Juliet, an artist, has been a board member since the company's founding. His son, Barnabas, took the photographs for Dorling Kindersley's 1995 children's best-seller, *Children Just Like Me*. His daughter, Rosie, is the company's food editor.

Though Kindersley treats most of the staff like family, his refusal to sell out has alienated his original partner, Christopher Dorling, who retired in 1987 but remains a board member.

With trademark elements like the DK logo on every cover and spine, "You can spot a Dorling book a mile off," said Lorna Tilbian, an analyst at West LB Panmure in London. But Kindersley's business acumen does not match his flair for design, Tilbian added, saying, "There is nobody in this industry who can combine creative skills with financial skills."

It was wobbly financial performance that helped prompt Kindersley to hand day-to-day operations over to Middlehurst, a former entertainment executive. The company lost 77 percent of its stock market value from 1996 to 1998 as it struggled to introduce a line of CD-ROMs and manage its investments in emerging markets.

But Kindersley would much rather talk about books than finance.

After much prodding, he finally explains why Kindersley remains second in the company name. It is for aesthetic, not business reasons. "KD doesn't work so well, does it?" he said. "DK sounds better."

Andrew Ross Sorkin
October 31, 1999

In May 2000, Dorling Kindersley was sold to Pearson PLC, the British media conglomerate whose holdings include Penguin Books and the Financial Times, *for $466 million. Kindersley, who received about $150 million from the deal, sold the company after disastrously poor sales of its* Star Wars *book series. Pearson said it would fold the company into Penguin.*

CASE 5

The Anti–Silicon Valley High Tech Exec

"We are not an amorphous sea of communists," Henry T. Nicholas III, cofounder of the Broadcom Corporation, said, rolling his eyes in disgust.

He had just arrived at his southern California office—forehead damp from a morning workout, three-piece suit snug against his six-foot-six frame—and already he was ripping into one of his pet peeves of the new economy: open cubicle space.

Sure, Andrew S. Grove, the Intel chairman, had a cubicle, "but it was ceremonial," Nicholas said. "If an employee wants to shut his door, he should be able to do it." That is what his colleagues used to do when he worked as a young engineer in the once-vibrant aerospace industry here in the Los Angeles region, far from precious northern California.

In fact, a lot of things bug Nicholas about the way Silicon Valley technology companies are run these days—like executives who allow employees to bring dogs to work, turning offices into playgrounds. Or the way venture capitalists have become all but gods in the new technological order.

But Broadcom, whose engineers design silicon chips that quickly send voice, data and video over cable lines, has risen to the top of its game as the photographic negative of a Silicon Valley company. And its leader is the antithesis of the new age, new economy Zen master. At Broadcom, as Nicholas makes clear, "I run the show."

In practice that means rousing subordinates from their beds past midnight when he wants to talk about a project, or dictating the company's dress code: suits for engineers and managers when customers visit, and no khakis or jeans. "We like to think of ourselves as the anti–Silicon Valley company," said Nicholas, who is known as Nick. "You are not going to be worshiped here, but you will spend time getting to build a product that only you can do."

It is no wonder he is called Darth Vader by fans and competitors alike. For like Darth Vader, Nicholas wants to rule a universe—in this case the wired universe.

It was in 1991 that the former silicon chip designer, who has a Ph.D. in electrical engineering, teamed up with Henry Samueli, his friend and former professor, to start Broadcom. Their timing was impeccable. The Internet was just taking off and networking equipment makers needed chips to convert slow-moving analog signals into faster digital ones.

Broadcom's chips are in 90 percent of all digital television set-top boxes and cable modems and 65 percent of local area computer networks, analysts estimate. So far, only Lucent Technologies and Intel's Level One subsidiary have challenged Broadcom's networking products, and Texas Instruments is its only rival in cable modems. And Broadcom has taken the lead in making chips for the burgeoning market for broadband home networking.

Market share like that is hard to come by. So it is no surprise that Broadcom was one of the brightest initial public offerings of 1998—up 500 percent from its offering price by the end of that year and up 1,095 percent from its offering through the first half of 2000—making Nicholas and Samueli, who each own 16 percent of the company, worth more than $5 billion each.

That competitive advantage could well continue, said Joseph Osha, senior semiconductor analyst for Merrill Lynch. He predicts earnings at Broadcom, which has a market capitalization of $35 billion, will grow 125 percent in fiscal 2000 as consumers and businesses crave more interactive capabilities over the Internet.

Osha attributes a slump in early 2000 in Broadcom's stock price (down 35 percent in three months) to overall technology malaise. "It's fairly difficult to counterinvade their space," Osha said. Add to that the notion that Internet shopping and entertainment are fast becoming one, and Broadcom's technology looks even more valuable.

But Nicholas keeps pressing Broadcom to maintain its edge. "The joke is he gets by on liquid protein and two hours of sleep a night," Osha said, which may not be far from the truth. Broadcom's corporate culture reflects Nicholas's own tendency to work eighteen-hour days until a project is done.

"You have to take yourself to the absolute limits of human behavior," he said, his arms slicing the air. "The whole concept is you leave nothing in reserve."

As if to prove his point, he pulled out a random page from his running schedule from the summer of 1997 and recounted in gory detail a day in June when he was so sick he threw up in a patch of grass and logged that season's worst workout. But twenty days later, he said with pride, he tied his personal best. "It was complete focus on getting a task done," he said. "That is the culture we are trying to create here."

And how do the citizens of that culture respond?

Engineers are attracted to Broadcom for the same reasons they flock to Silicon Valley: stock options that are worth millions. But while Nicholas and his currency may attract talent, it is Samueli, now the company's chief technology officer, who patches up hurt feelings after Nicholas's frequent expletive-laced tirades.

"They view me as more their mentor and father," Samueli said. "I'm there for them to complain to."

Mehdi Hatamian, an engineer and project director who has worked at Broadcom for four years, recalled an incident in late 1996 when one of the chips his team was designing had a flaw that needed fixing. Nicholas was displeased with the time it was taking and called a meeting to tell the team so. For several minutes he raged, demanding to know who was responsible for the flaw. He finally turned to Hatamian, who said Nicholas angrily growled, "You are responsible for this."

"Nick, did you come here to blame me or get a problem solved?" Hatamian shot back, challenging Nicholas to fire him. Hatamian then outlined his plan for fixing the chip design, and after a two-hour grilling, returned to his office and, for several days, worked until 3:30 A.M. until the problem was fixed.

Even board members have asked him to ratchet down, Nicholas acknowledged. At one directors meeting, he said, some questioned whether it was wise for their highly visible chief executive to continue sky diving. He scoffed at the suggestion that he stop, citing statistics that showed his hobby—which he practices several times yearly—was safe. Besides, Nicholas said drolly, "They know if I died it would be the ultimate failure, and I hate to lose."

Still his antics, at times, are nothing short of a public relations nightmare. He has the same sort of toys as his Silicon Valley peers—the Lamborghini Diablo Roadster, the fifteen-thousand-square-foot estate, the jet leasing company. And in 1999 he and Samueli flirted with buying the Anaheim Angels baseball team and the Mighty Ducks hockey team.

But unlike the rich men up north, he is more outlandish in his boyish tastes. He loves the rock band Metallica, keeps a metal skull on his desk and a personal trainer on call twenty-four hours and brags about all-night drinking binges in Las Vegas.

Once, Nicholas recalled, he tried to strip an investment banker at a winter conference in Utah and roll him in the snow because he thought the banker was too uptight. "I love to torture those guys," he said. And New Year's Eve 1999, he sponsored a battle of the bands at a party at his house in Laguna Hills, offering the best group a two-thousand-dollar grand prize. Why? He wanted to teach the bands a lesson. "I made it a competition because the world is competitive," he said.

But he caused the biggest stir on his fortieth birthday in October 1999 when he invited MTV's band of the year, Orgy, to play at his home. Nicholas laughed when asked about the porn star who showed up at the party and the police officers who told him to turn the music down. Yes, they were there, he said. "We had a lot of beautiful women show up unattached." But it was not so funny when the party was reported in the *Los Angeles Times* and he got a call from his mother. "I mean, my mom read that stuff," he said recently, his sheepish grin fading.

Nicholas's wife of thirteen years, Stacey, a former electrical engineer with whom he has three children, said she had come to terms with his bad boy reputation.

"I trust his judgment," she said. Recently, they had spent three days with her college friends, river rafting, and Nicholas left the cell phone and attitude behind.

"People at Broadcom see the game face all the time," she said. "His favorite line is, 'Don't tell anyone. Don't let them know.' "

And how do his hijinks play in the investment community? "As far as I'm concerned, if they put up the numbers, who cares what he does?" said Osha, the analyst.

Nicholas was born in Cincinnati in 1959. After his parents divorced in 1965, he moved with his mother to Malibu, California. He graduated from Santa Monica High School in 1977 and attended the United States Air Force Academy, in part to rebel against his liberal upbringing and the southern California surf culture that shaped his teenage years. He quickly learned that Malibu's hang-ten aesthetic was the exception in society, not the norm.

"Imagine my surprise when I realized that by rebelling I began to conform like everybody else," he said.

But when he learned he was too tall to fly fighter jets, he left the academy and enrolled at the University of California at Los Angeles, where he graduated with a degree in electrical engineering in 1981. That same year, he met Samueli at the military contractor TRW Inc., where they both worked. Later, Samueli went to teach in the engineering department at UCLA, and Nicholas followed, becoming his first Ph.D. candidate and completing the degree in 1997.

The two men's lives are intertwined. While studying for his doctorate, Nicholas left TRW and, in 1988, became a founding consultant at PairGain Technologies, a maker of communications equipment, which Samueli cofounded with two other partners. But he wanted to run his own company, he said, so he started Broadcom in his bedroom in 1991. Samueli joined the company full-time four years later.

With business success has come celebrity—if not notoriety. Nicholas is aware of the names he is called, some too profane to repeat. "People ask engineers all the time here, 'How could you work for that jerk?'" he said. But Nicholas says his behavior is often misunderstood, and his wildest antics are intended more to shock than to offend.

"I'm kind of a sarcastic guy," he said. "I love to engage people in conversations, like saying, 'Maybe ritual human sacrifices are OK.'"

Of course, he is joking. But "people will take me seriously," he said, "or they'll agree with me."

This he chalks up to his fabulous wealth; people are accepting of his outrageous behavior. "Wealth doesn't change people," he said. "It changes the way people treat you."

While he spends plenty on toys, Nicholas is also generous with charities. He likes theater and has donated millions to the South Coast Repertory and the Orange County Performing Arts Center. He also gave ten thousand Broadcom shares to the University of California at Irvine's intercollegiate athletic department, which was earmarked for the crew team, of which he was a member at UCLA.

And having fun is as much a response to his grueling work schedule as it is making up for lost time. "I end up doing more extreme things because I have less of a life," he said. "I figure I pull an all-nighter for work. Why not do it for fun?" And if there is any doubt, consider his cross-country adventure in January 2000. Nicholas had planned to fly a helicopter from Miami to California with the goal of gaining enough hours to earn his solo helicopter pilot license.

He had two distractions. First, he was fatigued. He had slept on the plane from Irvine to Miami the morning after his all-night New Year's Eve party. When he arrived in Miami that afternoon, he found himself "loading up on five cups of coffee" to stay alert.

He also had an investor meeting scheduled back in California for January 3, which meant he had a little more than two days to complete the helicopter flight. The first day he left Miami late and spent the night in a small hotel in Tampa, Florida, mosquitoes buzzing in his ears. Still tired on the second day, he did not get as far as he had expected he would. So he ended the flight in Louisiana, calling for a jet to take him home, while the instructor flew the helicopter back to its hangar.

Looking back, he said his expectations were unrealistic and he should have allocated a week for the trip. Even simply recounting the incident still makes him visibly angry. "I really wanted to power through it," he said.

Laura M. Holson
June 26, 2000

CASE 6

New Medium, New Market

From the day in 1950 when the first bulky television set was installed in her childhood home, Geraldine Laybourne, three years old, fantasized that she was part of the new medium.

Her mother, a former radio soap opera actress and producer, greeted the addition to the living room with the welcoming yelp, "Hello TV!" And the television answered with, "Hello out there in TV land!"

And so it went. Young Geraldine got all dressed up when it was time for Hopalong Cassidy because she assumed the cowboy could see her. She begged her mother to let her climb inside the back of the set and join the fun. Her mother, in turn, turned off programs in the middle and encouraged the girl to make up the end. "I've been trying to do interactive TV since I was born," Laybourne said.

These are stories that have been told and retold by Laybourne, perhaps the most prominent female executive in television. She made her mark as president of Nickelodeon, took a brief turn as head of cable networks for Disney/ABC and finally launched Oxygen Media, a high-risk venture that combines original cable programming and Web sites for today's cheeky, irreverent woman.

The legend of Laybourne also includes lessons from her father, a stock-broker, who decided that his middle daughter had a head for business. He took her to the office each Saturday and tested her instincts by describing a company and asking her investment advice. He didn't always listen, she said, but if he had, he would have died a rich man.

Still, she was at sea when she graduated from Vassar College in 1969, on the cusp of a revolution. She dabbled in architecture but found her calling through the man she would marry, Kit Laybourne, five years her senior, who was teaching media studies at a Philadelphia high school. She followed him into teaching and then into independent television production, where one of their first clients was Nickelodeon, the nascent children's cable net-work that she would later turn into a powerhouse.

The Laybournes are together again in Oxygen's duplex loft above the Chelsea market. She is in the executive office, huddled with groups of men in suits, negotiating contracts with cable operators. He is in the animation studio, directing a crew of twentysomethings with pierced noses and spiky hair, who are creating cartoons for women as rowdy as Nickelodeon's *Ren & Stimpy*.

Kit Laybourne has no envy of his wife's fame. "He gets his juice from other things," she said. "He's one hundred percent creative." He is also a natural teacher, of their own two grown children (one a comedian working on a television pilot called *Running with Scissors*, produced by Marcy Carsey, an Oxygen partner, and the other a teacher of English and dance) and of the more than five hundred young Oxygen employees.

Kit Laybourne is buoyed by spending his time as an animator—and the Pied Piper for his overcaffeinated team. "They want to ignite, burn, work for twelve hours, drink for another five and then see who gets here first in the morning with the worst hangover," he said.

His wife has the more conventional task of selling cable operators on her new venture, when the field is crowded and the newest entrants are expected to pay for subscribers rather than be paid for their programming, a business model Laybourne rejects. She has yet to crack the New York market, or most of Los Angeles, though she has contracts for twenty-seven million viewers elsewhere.

But she is confident that New York is within reach, a development con-sidered more likely as a result of the proposed merger, between Time Warner and America Online, one of Oxygen's investors. "You have to earn everything," she said, disputing that her relationship with AOL means a done deal.

Oxygen began with the Laybournes' picking the brains of the Internet generation, who knew more than they did about convergence. First, they hired five friends of their children, put them in a conference room and asked them to surf the Web, evaluate what was out there for women and look for unmet needs.

Then it was time to create interactive programs and Web sites. Everyone's ideas were welcome, pitched to a committee of elders that included Carsey, Tom Werner and Caryn Mandabach, the creators of *The Cosby Show* and *Roseanne*, and Oprah Winfrey, an Oxygen partner, with two shows of her own.

This "green light process," as Laybourne called it, produced *We Sweat*, a sports program; *Women's Hands,* an e-commerce site for artisans; and *Be Fearless,* currently in production, about political advocacy. All the programming is created jointly for television and the Web. *Trackers,* for instance, a late-afternoon package of shows for adolescents, is the handiwork of a former producer from Viacom and another from Teen People On-Line.

One of the hallmarks of Laybourne's management style is that she considers mistakes opportunities. On her office door at Nickelodeon there was a sign that said, "If It Ain't Broke, Fix It Anyway," hardly the conventional wisdom.

At Oxygen, that impulse makes sense because viewers and Web surfers weigh in instantaneously on message boards, with praise and blame, which can alter programming overnight. "That to me is what's so exciting about this," Laybourne said. "You have to fix it every day."

Jane Gross
April 21, 2000

In December 2000, Oxygen announced a new investment of $100 million from Vulcan Ventures, one of its original backers. The company also said it would lay off about sixty-five employees, a little less than 10 percent of its workforce, and was scaling back its Internet business. The cable channel, which now has some presence in New York and has made additional inroads in the Los Angeles area, had cut back production and laid off eighteen employees in the summer of 2000.

CASE 7

The Brand Is the Man

For an entrepreneur who was down on his luck it was almost too good a deal to pass up.

Wally Amos had long ago lost control of Famous Amos, the cookie company he founded in 1975, and had even lost the right to use his name or the famous likeness of himself with his salt-and-pepper beard, Panama hat and embroidered Indian shirt. At one point, he lost his house. He was reduced to calling his own cookie line Uncle Noname, and the business was struggling.

Then in March 1999 the Keebler Company, the new owner of Famous Amos, offered Amos a two-year contract to promote his old brand. And Keebler was willing to let him use his name for his own business.

Amos was hardly in a position to play the tough negotiator. Yet, after sampling the cookies that Keebler was selling, he couldn't help himself.

"Somehow or another caramel coloring had been added and I don't know why that was," Amos said, the lines in his forehead becoming more pronounced. "And they were using a real low-grade vanilla flavoring, and I always used vanilla extract. One of the first things I shared with Keebler when we met was that I couldn't promote the product they were currently selling, that if I were going to be a part of it we had to make some adjustments so that it could be closer to a Wally Amos product."

Keebler, a unit of Flowers Industries, which had inherited the reformulated cookies, agreed to meet Amos's conditions. "Certainly Wally Amos carries the namesake, so it was an obvious place to look" for a spokesman, said Bruce Grieve, Keebler's vice president for new-business development. "People really know the name and so many people still recognize the face."

So a decade after losing his company, Amos is back bragging about Famous Amos, like a proud father showing off his now-grown firstborn.

He has pitched the cookies at a food-marketing trade show in Chicago, and has been appearing at supermarkets, shaking the hands of shoppers who still recognize him.

"It's a full-circle kind of thing," said Amos, who still flashes the toothy grin shown on cookie packages and television talk shows two decades ago, though his chocolate-colored face is creased with more lines these days.

But he has been chastened by failure, acknowledging that in some respects he walked into a trap awaiting many entrepreneurs. While he created a thriving business, he did not have all the skills he needed to run it as it grew.

"An entrepreneur has an enormously high energy level and has a very low attention span typically," said Paul Karofsky, executive director of the Center for Family Business at Northeastern University. "They can conceptualize brilliantly but then struggle to implement."

Amos started the original Famous Amos Cookie Company with $25,000 from the singers Marvin Gaye and Helen Reddy, celebrity friends he knew from his days as a talent agent. The company sold $300,000 in cookies that year, and by 1982, revenue reached $12 million.

Amos was a rising star. His hat and shirt were added to the Smithsonian Institution's advertising collection. In 1986, President Reagan presented him with one of the first Awards of Entrepreneurial Excellence.

But the heady times would soon end. A high school dropout who eventually earned a general equivalency diploma, Amos knew little about business basics and failed to hire managers who did. By 1985, the year before America's free-market president was hailing him as a hero, his company lost $300,000 as revenue slipped to $10 million.

And though few people knew it, Amos's personal affairs were in such disarray that during the worst of it, he was fifteen months behind on the mortgage for his house in Hawaii. "I was in Salt Lake City doing some promotion and I discovered that day that my house had been auctioned off," he recalled.

With the help of a friend, Amos eventually got the house back. Ever the optimist, he views the experience as yet another reminder of the power of faith and positive thinking.

"If you sit around starting to feel sorry for yourself, and blaming everyone else for your position in life, it is like being in quicksand," he said. "In quicksand, if you start flailing all about and panicking with each movement you go in deeper, but if you just stay calm and look about, chances are you'll see a twig or something you can reach to pull yourself out. Or, if you stay there long enough someone will come and rescue you."

Hindsight being what it is, Amos is now able to reflect philosophically on the low points. But "it was a shocker at first." He sought help to save the company, and ultimately himself.

Several investors stepped in, but Amos said they took more of his equity stake each time and never stayed long enough to turn the company around. In 1988 the company lost $2.5 million, and the Shansby Group purchased it for $3 million. Amos became a paid spokesman but left in frustration the next year.

"I'd lost the company really because I didn't use to listen to people a lot because I was Famous Amos," the founder now acknowledges. "The first couple of years after I left Famous Amos, I didn't even make cookies anymore, and I used to always make cookies at home. I didn't even want to talk about chocolate-chip cookies, really. I shaved my beard and stopped wearing hats."

But even without Amos on board, the Shansby Group began to turn the business around, cutting costs and pushing sales through vending machines. With the company propped up, it sold Famous Amos to President Baking for $61 million in 1992. Keebler acquired the brand in 1998, becoming its fifth owner.

Amos's cookie craving had returned in the meantime. In 1992, he started producing high-priced hazelnut cookies under the name Wally Amos Presents. But Famous Amos sued, contending trademark infringement, so he changed the name to Uncle Noname.

By then, competition in the high-priced cookie business had intensified, and Uncle Noname could not keep up. "It was just an uphill battle, looking to establish a new cookie company without having the resources and still in the minds of everybody being Famous Amos," he said.

Amos again found himself in a money-losing venture on the verge of collapse. Debt mounted to $1.3 million and Uncle Noname filed for Chapter 11 bankruptcy protection in 1997, emerging finally in the spring of 1999.

His entrepreneurial spirit intact, Amos switched to a line of low-fat and fat-free muffins. Now, under terms of his deal with Keebler, he has regained the right to use his name and he sells the muffins as Uncle Wally's.

"I can even use my picture on here," he said, seemingly astonished.

He now leaves the day-to-day operations of his Long Island, New York, company, which is based in Hauppauge, to a partner, Lou Avignone, who is a former owner of a larger food distributor.

Despite the company's poor financial history, and the fact that Uncle Wally's muffins have not become the huge hit with consumers that Famous Amos cookies once were, the business had modest revenues of about $3 million in the last year and the product is winning fans, Avignone said. The muffins, for instance, are a leading brand in Pathmark supermarkets in the New York area and are available nationally in stores like Costco warehouse clubs and Edwards supermarkets.

Letting an industry insider run the business has freed Amos to pursue a wide range of other interests. He frequently travels, giving motivational speeches or working on behalf of charities like Literacy Volunteers of America, of which he is spokesman. He has cowritten several books of inspiration, including one capitalizing on his failures at Famous Amos. It is entitled *Man with No Name: How the Founder of the Censored Cookie Company Lost Everything, Including His Name—and Turned Adversity into Opportunity*. And he has become somewhat of an e-mail fanatic, sending a network of cherished friends and associates regular morale-boosting messages. And with his Keebler deal, Amos is back on the promotional circuit.

Neither he nor Keebler would disclose how much the company was paying him to bite into Famous Amos cookies in public and urge people who spot him in airports to buy them.

"It is like Dave from Wendy's," said Clive Chajet, president of Chajet Consultancy, which advises companies on brand-building strategies. "If Dave left Wendy's and came back after ten years because things had not gone well the message is signaling change that 'We're going back to the way we used to be.' That's not a bad pitch."

Of course, it will take more than Amos's paid seal of approval to revive the brand. In addition to getting closer to the original recipe, Keebler also plans to introduce new flavors, like toffee chocolate chip and chocolate chip and walnuts, and to use its vast resources to get the brand before more consumers.

"We can dramatically increase distribution of the brand and that is everything from building its presence in convenience stores, mass merchandisers, obviously grocery stores and drugstores," Grieve of Keebler said.

Amos is happy to do his part. And even though he has no ownership in Famous Amos and is making Uncle Wally's his priority, he acknowledges that his first company is still in his blood. Whatever his former ties to it, he said, "I will always be Famous Amos."

Dana Canedy
July 3, 1999

·3·

MOVING WITH THE TIMES

Old Economy Meets New

[Army Airborne] Ranger school prepared me more than anything else for what I do now—managing in the controlled chaos of the Internet. If you can execute a mission under stress and motivate people who are worn down, then getting a group of people—who did eat today and did sleep last night—aligned around a common vision is not that difficult.

—Sunny Vanderbeck, chief executive officer,
Data Return, May 10, 2000

Keep the Internet in perspective. Yes, it's revolutionizing some things, but I know basic business rules just aren't changing, and above all that means you have to run a company with smart, talented people.

—Gerald Kearby, chief executive officer,
Liquid Audio Inc., October 20, 1999

It was 1995, the early days of the Internet as a mass medium, and the executives at Bertelsmann wanted to put down some roots in cyberspace. To many at the German media company, the choice seemed clear: start a new online service in Europe with the help of Microsoft. Bill Gates and his minions in Redmond, Washington, were ready to do the deal.

Thomas Middelhoff had another idea, though. A rising manager at Bertelsmann, Middelhoff saw potential in a different American company, one that had nowhere near as successful a track record as Microsoft.

Bertelsmann's board of directors was skeptical, forcing Middelhoff to strike a less ambitious deal than he had wanted. Even after the agreement had been struck, some of Middelhoff's colleagues referred to their new corporate partner as "Thomas's little toy."

In hindsight, that toy came to look like a piggy bank with the ability to mint its own money. The company was America Online, and the 5 percent stake that Bertelsmann bought in it grew to be worth billions. The deal helped catapult Middelhoff above more senior executives to become the chief executive of a media conglomerate that includes Random House, Doubleday and BMG Entertainment. He won the job in large part because the board saw him as the person most capable of transforming Bertelsmann from an old-economy publisher to a multimedia new-economy juggernaut.

In a striking example of the inventiveness with which traditional companies are embracing Internet upstarts, Bertelsmann startled the music industry in late 2000 by announcing that it would invest in Napster, the music-sharing Web site that several record companies, including BMG, had accused of abetting copyright infringement. It made the move to help finance Napster's conversion into a paid membership service instead of one that let users copy music from one another free over the Internet.

At the core of Middelhoff's foresight has been a willingness to look beyond immediately intuitive solutions. That is a theme you will find throughout this chapter, in stories both of success and of failure. Sometimes both happen at the same company. A few years back, the nation's major television networks assumed that their enormous audiences would simply gravitate to Web sites like Snap.com—run by NBC, a unit of General Electric—after seeing broadcast advertisements for them. Instead, Web surfers chose better-designed sites with less impressive pedigrees, and network executives were sent back to the drawing board to design a more sophisticated strategy.

Meanwhile, another GE division—the appliances unit—found some success in cyberspace because its executives were willing to dig deep from the outset. They forgot about some of their most basic assumptions and instead used a tried-and-true quality control method known as Six Sigma to analyze every aspect of a new Internet site. The surprising result: They put smaller, lower-quality photographs on the site than they had planned to, and they took their time in delivering new dishwashers to customers. Huh, you ask? For an explanation, read on.

As you do so, you may want to keep in mind an idea from some of the most recent thinking on Internet strategy. In *How Digital Is Your Business?*, Adrian J. Slywotzky and David J. Morrison of Mercer Management Consulting argue that good ole business issues—what customers want, how much something costs—must come first. Then executives can start worrying about how to digitize the solutions.

A Race to the Future

Oh, the might-have-beens. Picture Thomas Middelhoff, chief executive of Bertelsmann, on a global stage, sharing a photogenic—if stilted—group hug and high-fives to celebrate the stunning union of his German media conglomerate with America Online.

Instead, the beginning of 2000 found a solitary Middelhoff marooned by a snowstorm in his stark office on the twenty-fourth floor of the Bertelsmann tower overlooking Times Square in Manhattan. In a hastily arranged conference call, he resigned from America Online's board, prompted by the company's announced merger with Bertelsmann's media archrival, Time Warner.

The parting was friendly, even sentimental, by corporate standards. Stephen M. Case, the chief executive of America Online, said he would never forget how Middelhoff, as a rising Bertelsmann official, had nurtured a struggling AOL with timely investments in the mid-1990s.

But Middelhoff—a Düsseldorf altar boy turned Concorde-commuting media titan—had little time for wistfulness. Though he still believes that Bertelsmann, the world's fourth-largest media conglomerate, would have been the "best partner" for AOL, Middelhoff professes no disappointment that key members of the foundation that owns Bertelsmann refused to surrender the 164-year-old company's independence.

Besides, who has time for hypotheticals when your job is achieving nothing less than cultural transformation—on the Internet's frantic schedule—in a rigidly traditional corporation with its heartbeat and headquarters in a small German city and with seventy-eight thousand employees around the world?

"We have to reach every brain to explain that we have nothing less than an industrial revolution," Middelhoff said in an interview. "That makes it necessary to change how we see and run our business. That means speed is king. That means we have to be decentralized on the one hand and also more corporate. We have without any question a generational change at Bertelsmann."

Middelhoff's manner is so relentlessly cheerful that some company executives joke that it must mask something sinister. But his task is daunting. To compete in a landscape of exotic new media hybrids like CBS-Viacom or AOL Time Warner—the latter further engorged by its deal that same month to absorb the EMI Group's music business—he must reinvent the structure and customs of a global empire made up of six hundred separate businesses.

In the fourteen months after Middelhoff assumed leadership of Bertelsmann in December 1998, he proved a fervid evangelist, promoting the necessity of increasing the pace—and the risk-taking—in Bertelsmann's efforts to integrate its core music, magazine, book publishing and printing businesses into the digital economy.

Bertelsmann, he says, must move like "a fleet of fast, maneuverable frigates"—instead of a huge ocean liner—toward his goal of digitizing every element of the company's sprawling holdings, from the written word to distribution.

"We want to be number one in media e-commerce business," Middelhoff said with a strong German accent. "And from Bertelsmann's perspective, it's more important for us than to own a share in AOL."

With Time Warner's deal making, Middelhoff's preaching has taken on a more urgent tone. Bertelsmann, he said, intends to increase sharply its budget for acquisitions—in part by spinning off more of its Internet properties, giving the company some of the cyberstock that is today's media-deal currency.

The goal of the shopping spree, he said, will be to strengthen Bertelsmann's position in magazine publishing, where it ranks second in the world, and in music, where the Time Warner–EMI deal leaves it a badly trailing fourth.

Some analysts say media executives like Middelhoff should be focusing on deals that preserve access to online services—deals, say, like Time Warner's with America Online. "They need to ensure that they have access to distribution in the new economy, as well as access to talent and capital in sufficient amounts, and the ability to make decisions very quickly," said David Brodwin, an associate partner at Andersen Consulting. "Few have been able to do this without partnering or acquiring."

Middelhoff said that he, too, was prepared to make deals with Internet companies, but that for now his focus was to gain dominance in media sectors, like music.

There had been reports in London that Bertelsmann would make a counteroffer for EMI's music business, but Middelhoff denied such plans. Bertelsmann, he said, discussed a deal with EMI executives in 1998, only to break off conversations because the price they were demanding was too high—and that price, he noted, was a figure less than half of what Time Warner paid to fold EMI's music holdings into a fifty-fifty joint venture.

"So now the question is: Do we have the financial power to develop our positions—or, let me say, to protect them?" Middelhoff said.

Answering his own question, he said Bertelsmann was prepared to take what for it would be a dramatic step to maintain its competitiveness.

Historically, the decisive measure of success or failure for Bertelsmann's companies has been a formula that some of its American executives call the Holy Grail but in German is rendered *gesamtkapitalrendite*—the return on assets, or on total capital employed.

For almost two decades, the rate has been set at 15 percent, a value established by Reinhard Mohn, a fourth-generation descendant of the company's founder. Mohn created the contemporary Bertelsmann, building the company from a publisher of Protestant hymnals into a book-club power-house and now a multimedia giant.

But after the Bertelsmann Foundation rejected a deal with America Online in November 1999, Middelhoff said Mohn—who still serves on the foundation's board—decided in principle to reduce the return he expects.

The new figure hasn't been established, but relaxing the standard will free yet more money for acquisitions, Middelhoff said, "depending on what dog comes along." Already, Bertelsmann has budgeted at least 20 billion marks—a little more than $10 billion—for deal making in 2000 and 2001.

The company wants to deepen its pockets, too, by taking some units public.

"We have a clear strategy. The entire Bertelsmann organization got the wake-up call much earlier than any other media company," he said. "We don't see any reason to face any disadvantage in our style of organization—as long as we are not sleepy and are aggressive."

Working at "Thomas Speed"

As chief executive since November 1998, Middelhoff if nothing else lives at the pace he is convinced Bertelsmann must adopt if it is to thrive.

From offices at the company's headquarters in Gutersloh—a city of one hundred thousand on the edge of the Teutoburg Forest, about two hours from Düsseldorf—and his suite in Times Square, he presides over the unwieldy conglomerate through travel so constant that he sometimes wakes up wondering where he is. His international e-mail messages number about 120 a day; the father of five, he also uses the keyboard to keep in touch with his older children.

When a hit-and-run skier smashed into him in the Italian Alps recently, Middelhoff continued his Paris–to–New York flights with a broken collarbone. Some Bertelsmann executives say he roams the globe at "Thomas speed," his own personal time warp, but others worry that he's charging ahead too quickly, leaving stunned underlings trailing behind.

He was chief executive–designate when Bertelsmann acquired Random House early in 1998, solidifying its position as the largest English-language publisher in the world. Later that year, Middelhoff struck a deal to become partners in an online bookselling venture in the United States with Barnes & Noble, after briefly flirting with Amazon.com when his negotiations with Leonard Riggio, Barnes & Noble's chief executive, grew testy.

In 2000, he established a joint venture combining the titans of the book club business, Time Warner's Book-of-the-Month Club and Bertelsmann's Doubleday Direct.

Underlying the spate of deal making has been Middelhoff's calculated strategy to drive Bertelsmann deeper into digital territory.

The Barnesandnoble.com partnership, for example, enabled Bertelsmann to scrap expensive plans to start its own online bookstore in the United States; the company was also able to cash in when part of the electronic bookseller was spun off in a public stock offering. But the alliance has not been a perfect match. The stock has drifted, and top officials, including the chief executive, have swiftly shuffled in and out.

Along with its investments in AOL Europe and Lycos Europe, Bertelsmann has created a string of electronic bookstores called BOL.com, with Web sites individually tailored for various European countries. In April 1999, the company joined with Seagram to create Getmusic.com, a Web site that promotes artists from the two companies' labels and sells CDs online. And in Germany, Bertelsmann created an electronic auction house called Andsold in just three months.

"I would have said Bertelsmann was clearly ahead of the pack with respect to the Internet," said Peter A. Kreisky, a consultant for Mercer Management Consulting, which advises media and entertainment companies. "Bertelsmann got it very early on, because of Thomas Middelhoff and only because of Thomas Middelhoff. He integrated the Internet as an intrinsic part of every single business."

But with Middelhoff's departure from the America Online board and the transformation of AOL into a media rival, Bertelsmann may have lost something indefinable, but crucial, Kreisky said.

"What AOL did was give them a seat at the front of the train, able to really view the track ahead without any filtering," he said. "They were standing next to the driver, and they could see very clearly."

Between Old and New

On a cool autumn night in Berlin, Middelhoff reveled in the new media order. His driver and Mercedes awaited him outside a painfully hip party at Dresdner Bahnhof, a train station transformed for the evening with dangling chandeliers, shag rugs and hooded male and female dancers in ice-blue leotards.

He was almost giddy that night as he mingled among twelve hundred guests celebrating Bertelsmann's public stock offering for Pixelpark, a Web site designer it had acquired. "This is my world!" he exulted as he left the party. "And do you understand that I like this world?"

Middelhoff had reached this universe on a career track as swift as the pace he prizes in business.

In 1997, the Bertelsmann board skipped over a generation of older executives and anointed him the company's next chief executive. Eleven years earlier, he had signed on as a managing assistant at the Mohndruck Graphische printing plant in Gutersloh. He quickly rose to become the head of the Elsnerdruck printing plant, where, in an act that has become company legend, he fired his predecessor, who was planning to help him in the transition.

Middelhoff's roots are in Westphalia, in northern Germany, a rural area once known for its thriving textile factories. Battered by competition with Asian plants, many of those factories closed in the 1980s, including his father's business; his mother is a physician-turned-homemaker.

Early in his career, he drew the attention of top executives; by the late 1980s, some German followers of the company said, his name appeared on a list of ten potential successors to Mark Wossner, the chief executive since 1983.

By all accounts, he assured his rise in the leadership through a risky bet in 1995, early in the digital epoch.

Instead of investing with Microsoft to start an online service in Europe, Middelhoff negotiated a deal to acquire a 14.9 percent stake in America Online. The Bertelsmann board balked at that deal—some in the company derisively referred to it as "Thomas's little toy," giving Middelhoff a taste of what it was like to lead a company in new directions. Eventually, Bertelsmann bought a 5 percent stake, an investment that rocketed in value and gave Middelhoff a shiny Internet glow. The fifty-fifty joint venture in Europe followed.

Two years later, in designating him for the top job, the board passed over a more seasoned executive, Michael Dornemann, now chairman of BMG Entertainment, the company's music business. Like Wossner before him, Middelhoff was relatively young and could lead Bertelsmann for up to fifteen years before reaching sixty, the company's mandatory retirement age.

But it was also Middelhoff's more open and engaging manner that the leadership found appealing. The board was looking for someone who could cultivate contacts with international business leaders.

Middelhoff "came across as the great communicator and visionary," recalled Rudi Gassner, the chief executive of Bertelsmann's BMG Entertainment International, who retired in January 2000. "People talk about his American spirit, because without fear or reservation he approaches people."

As chief executive, Middelhoff has consciously set out to make contacts with influential people and celebrities in the United States. He has flown to Kennebunkport, Maine, for lunch with former President George Bush, a Random House author. He regularly sends gifts of CDs, current books and hand-signed notes to prominent business leaders.

His free spirit has not always been well received, Gassner said. "Most of the traditional employees are kind of stunned and don't really know how to deal with it, especially if they are older," he said. "One of the things that I've been saying to Thomas is that when you charge ahead the way he is, don't forget to look behind, because you may not have your troops behind."

But some analysts wonder if Middelhoff is himself too sluggish—especially in Europe—despite his mantra that speed equals survival.

"Bertelsmann is rather weak," said Carsten Schmidt, an analyst for Forrester Research in Amsterdam. "They've done too much in too many directions, and they're always late." Though Andsold was created quickly, he noted that it nonetheless was the fourth player in its market; likewise, Bertelsmann's electronic bookstore trailed—and copied—Amazon.com in Britain.

Bertelsmann, Schmidt said, remains secure in its partnership with America Online in Europe, because "Time Warner's content doesn't match Bertelsmann's European offerings." At the same time, he and other analysts still expect that Bertelsmann may have to find a partner in the United States to secure its access to digital consumers.

The deals are sure to keep coming. In January 2000, Mannesmann, Germany's biggest cellular company, confirmed talks with Bertelsmann and American Online to join in their European venture—a link that would give Bertelsmann another channel to media consumers. And in October 2000,

Bertelsmann announced an arrangement with Napster to distribute music over the Web for a fee.

Changing the Culture

As he faces these challenges, Middelhoff continues to try to tweak the Bertelsmann culture—always with the ultimate aim of moving faster. He has eliminated the cherished academic titles that people used in addressing one another around the German headquarters, replacing "Dr." with a simple "Herr" or "Frau." The formality created walls and probably stifled challenges from lower-level employees, he said.

Inevitably, there have been tensions between the old and new generations that have tested even the close relationship between Middelhoff and Wossner, chairman of the Bertelsmann Foundation, with offices across a swan lake from Middelhoff's in Gutersloh.

Wossner sent shudders through the company with his candid remarks in an article in the summer of 1999 in *Der Spiegel*. In particular, he was irritated with Middelhoff's comments at a news conference in which he used a German term for gnat waste to describe a television station that the company sold.

The tensions were smoothed over by the fall, but even then the two men could not agree on a description of their complicated relationship. Middelhoff had a habit of saying that Wossner, sixty and silver-haired, was akin to his father. In an interview, Wossner was quick to describe himself as Middelhoff's "elder brother."

Whatever Wossner's qualms, he publicly supports Middelhoff. "You have to be the right man in your time," he said. "And Thomas is without a doubt the man that is exactly right for the company that we have become."

Doreen Carvajal
January 30, 2000

Throughout 2000, Thomas Middelhoff continued to move with all deliberate speed. Among the moves: Bertelsmann was in talks with the EMI Group to combine music operations, to create the music industry's largest company. Bertelsmann also announced plans to invest in Napster, a freewheeling Internet phenomenon with thirty-eight million users who share music files, to help it develop a fee-based service. In November 2000, just days after the Napster deal, Michael Dornemann, head of Bertelsmann's music business, announced that he would be leaving in mid-2001.

CASE 2

From Military Contractor
to Service Company

When Hughes Electronics was first developing a service to beam television programs from satellites to home antennas, skeptics joked that DBS, the industry shorthand for direct broadcast satellite, actually stood for "Don't Be Stupid."

But no one is laughing now—except, perhaps, for Hughes executives and investors. DirecTV, the service Hughes started in 1994 that transmits as many as two hundred channels of digital television to pizza-sized rooftop dishes, has become a major threat to cable television.

At 8.1 million subscribers and growing rapidly, Hughes, based in Los Angeles, has become the third-largest provider of pay television in the United States, behind the leading cable operators, AT&T and Time Warner. As the nation's largest distributor of pay-per-view movies, it is a force to be reckoned with in Hollywood. And because it offers multiple channels of Home Box Office, Cinemax and all the Turner Broadcasting services, it distributes more programming created by Time Warner than does Time Warner Cable.

With its agreement in January 2000 to sell its satellite manufacturing operations to Boeing for $3.75 billion, Hughes has finished a transformation that no other company has made so completely—from military contractor to consumer and business service company. It took the first big step in that transition late in 1997, by selling its military business to Raytheon.

"We've got a new company again for the second time in two years," said Michael T. Smith, the bookish chairman and chief executive of Hughes, a subsidiary of General Motors. Smith said the company expects revenue growth of 20 percent to 40 percent a year for the next five years and earnings growth—excluding interest, taxes, depreciation and amortization—of 50 percent a year.

No defense company performs anything like that, and Wall Street certainly likes what it has seen. Shares of General Motors Class H, the tracking stock for Hughes, doubled in the last six months of 1999, while shares of cable companies have performed sluggishly as investors anticipate more inroads by satellite TV.

But Hughes will not be able to just sit back and let the money roll in. DirecTV now has positive cash flow but was still not profitable—and would not be until 2001, Smith said. It is also purely a distributor of entertainment at a time when many distributors are vertically integrated with program providers.

So Hughes is beginning to move into the "content" business, taking stakes in programming ventures and, with its war chest from the Boeing sale, continuing to look for acquisitions. Further evolution is expected, meanwhile, in Hughes's relationship with GM, perhaps ultimately leading to the spinoff that many investors are craving.

The biggest challenge, however, involves DirecTV, which now contributes about two-thirds of the company's revenue. Cable operators are investing heavily to upgrade their systems from analog to digital, allowing them to multiply the number of channels they offer and to close the gap with DirecTV. Cable systems are also adding two-way transmission capacity, so they can sell high-speed Internet access and telephone service, potentially leapfrogging what satellite television can offer.

Indeed, America Online, which agreed in August 1999 to invest $1.5 billion in Hughes to deliver Internet service over satellites, agreed to spend one hundred times that much in January 2000 to buy Time Warner, in part to gain access to its cable systems. Even Smith's old boss, the former Hughes chairman C. Michael Armstrong, has switched sides. Now chairman of AT&T, he has made it the nation's largest cable operator through purchases of Tele-Communications Inc. and MediaOne.

So for Hughes, the moment is now. It must try to quickly lock in new subscribers before all these new cable systems are in place. And it also must scramble to provide Internet service from space; indeed, the company is promising to begin offering two-way data communications as early as the end of 2000.

"Cable's spending all kinds of money to catch up, and when they catch up, we want to be ten steps ahead of them," Smith said.

The company's steps into content are being taken gingerly, executives acknowledge, though the logic is clear: Having exclusive content would help DirecTV differentiate itself from cable as cable begins to erode DirecTV's advantage in the number of channels offered, and it could also be a new source of profits.

"Good content is something we are going to want to carry no matter what," said Eddy W. Hartenstein, president of DirecTV since its inception. "If that's the case, why not get in on the front end?"

But with its aerospace heritage, it is not clear that Hughes has the mindset for entertainment. Smith, who friends say can remember numbers from presentations he has seen months before, spent much of his career in finance at General Motors and ran Hughes's defense business. Hartenstein, an aerospace engineer by training, began his career working on projects like a spacecraft to Venus.

Of course, the company's founder, Howard Hughes, wooed starlets and produced movies even as he built and flew planes. But he ended up a billionaire recluse, spending his days sitting naked in a Las Vegas hotel room—and Hughes's leaders today are not out looking for the next Jean Harlow or Jane Russell.

"We're not going to buy a studio or anything like that," Hartenstein said in an interview in his office overlooking Los Angeles International Airport, a reminder of the company's roots.

Rather, because DirecTV is in a strong position to nurture new programming services by giving them distribution, it will take equity stakes in some of the most promising. Hartenstein cited a deal with the Action Adventure Network, which produced some shows that had premieres on DirecTV's pay-per-view service. Now the shows are being sold into syndication, and DirecTV gets part of the proceeds.

Hughes is also expected to announce an investment in NeTune Communications, a company that will use satellites to transmit images shot by movie makers in remote locations back to studios.

The big question—the one that is most on investors' minds—is whether GM will eventually spin off Hughes, which it bought for about $5 billion in 1985 and is now worth about $50 billion.

In February 2000, GM announced transactions that would reduce its ownership of the tracking stock to about 35 percent, from 68 percent. But the automaker, which owns 100 percent of Hughes's assets, reiterated that it did not intend to give up the company; GM sees Hughes as integral to its plan to provide on-the-road communication services in cars.

The plan did little to relieve pressure from shareholders for a spin-off. Some GM holders want Hughes sold to break out its value from the automaker's limping stock; some Hughes shareholders think the company could grow faster if it were independent. Both stocks slid in that month—until Hughes jumped 17 percent and GM rose 6 percent, in part on an analyst's report that GM indeed was likely to complete a spin-off by 2002.

Even Hughes executives hint that more may be coming. "You can't get free in one fell swoop," said Smith, whose older brother, John F. Smith Jr., is chairman of GM. Possibly in preparation for a spin-off, Hughes has for the first time begun recruiting independent board members. Having sold its auto electronics and satellite manufacturing businesses, Hughes is now selling its research laboratory in Malibu. So there is less technology it can offer GM.

What remains is a company that has three main businesses, and all seem well positioned.

Besides DirecTV, there is Hughes Network Systems, the largest provider of satellite systems used for such purposes as connecting gasoline stations to headquarters for credit card authorizations, or auto dealers to their head-quarters to order parts. The third business is Hughes's 81 percent owner-ship of PanAmSat, the largest owner and operator of commercial satellites used by paging and telephone companies and by cable programming serv-ices like Home Box Office.

Still, it is DirecTV that has fueled Wall Street's enthusiasm. Indeed, as well as Hughes's stock has performed lately, the stock of its pesky satellite TV rival, EchoStar Communications, has done far better, rising eightfold in 1999. That is because EchoStar is a pure play in satellite television.

A desire to come closer to that profile was one reason that Hughes sold its satellite manufacturing business—which had also been suffering from manufacturing problems and is being investigated for possible violations of national security laws for its dealings with China. The other reason for the sale was the need for money to finance DirecTV's growth. But Smith said there are no plans to spin off DirecTV to shareholders as a truly pure play, because developing Internet services will require coordination between DirecTV and Hughes Network Systems.

Satellite television has attracted not only rural dwellers who do not have access to cable but also urban consumers who want more channels than cable can provide or are disenchanted by their local cable monopoly's service. Some 70 percent of DirecTV's new subscribers live in areas where cable tele-vision is available. DirecTV subscribers pay an average of fifty-eight dollars a month, compared with about forty-one dollars for cable subscribers.

The Carmel Group, a market research firm, forecast that satellite televi-sion companies would add 4 million new subscribers in 2000 to the 11.4 million they had at the end of 1999, while cable providers would lose five hundred thousand. "It's not a huge loss, but it's a wake-up call," said Jimmy Schaeffler, a Carmel analyst. Cable was estimated to have sixty-seven million subscribers.

Having between them acquired all their competitors, DirecTV and EchoStar enjoy a duopoly. DirecTV had 8 million subscribers at the end of 1999, compared with 3.4 million for EchoStar, which began what it calls its Dish Network in 1996. (Some 1.4 million of DirecTV's customers are subscribers of Primestar, which DirecTV acquired in 1999.) The two companies are running neck and neck in the race for new subscribers, with DirecTV adding 1.6 million and EchoStar 1.5 million in 1999.

DirecTV has more movies and sports and stronger retail distribution, and several big electronics retailers carry only DirecTV equipment. So EchoStar has fought back with low pricing and promotions.

In 1996, when satellite dishes were still selling for $500 or more, EchoStar dropped its price to $199, catching Hughes off guard. In response, Hughes decided to defer profits in a race for market share, much as Internet companies now do. DirecTV is now spending about $500 in advertising and incentives to attract each customer—an amount it says it recoups in seventeen months.

In January 2000, EchoStar—whose scrappy chief executive, Charles Ergen, delights in his role as industry renegade—filed a federal antitrust suit accusing Hughes of paying or pressuring retailers not to carry EchoStar equipment. The suit, filed in Denver, also accused Hughes of unfairly locking up rights to National Football League games.

The suit noted that DirecTV stopped doing business in 1999 with Sears, Roebuck, EchoStar's biggest retailer. "They never directly said it was because of EchoStar," said Chuck Cebuhar, Sears vice president for home electronics and home-office products. But, he added, "If you look at their activity, it says they would obviously prefer not to be on the floor with anybody else."

Hughes said the suit was without merit. Hartenstein said that DirecTV had "no stated policy" of demanding exclusive distribution and that retailers are dropped for not performing well. Sports leagues, he added, often make exclusive deals with broadcasters.

Both DirecTV and EchoStar should get a big boost from a new law that will allow them for the first time to offer local television channels. Until now, satellite subscribers had to get their local channels over the air or by cable—a situation that has been one of the biggest drawbacks of satellite television.

For now, the satellite services generally are offering the four major network channels. DirecTV says that as many as 60 percent of subscribers in some cities have opted for the added service at six dollars a month, and Hughes is expecting that it will help DirecTV attract two million new subscribers in 2000.

Cable, meanwhile, has increased its capacity to carry more than the recent norm of forty to eighty television channels—albeit at a tremendous cost. At the end of 1999, digital cable service was available to one-third of all cable customers. But there were 3.75 million digital subscribers, just over 5 percent of all cable customers, following $30 billion in spending by the industry to upgrade its systems since 1996.

The expanding bandwidth of cable services is already allowing Time Warner to test a video-on-demand service in a suburb of Honolulu. Many cable companies are offering high-speed Internet access, and some sell local telephone service as well—the latter being a big part of AT&T's cable strategy, for example.

Hughes is playing catch-up on the Internet front, arguably the most important for its future growth. The company offers Internet access through its DirecPC service, which can transmit information from satellites to personal computers at four hundred kilobits a second—slower than cable modems but about eight times as fast as a conventional modem.

DirecPC has attracted only about one hundred thousand subscribers, in part because it requires a telephone line to send information from users' computers. But the investment by America Online will give Hughes the money for a DirecPC promotion intended to add a million customers in three years. It also plans to offer two-way communications without the need for a phone line.

Still, DirecPC is seen as an interim solution. Hughes is banking most on Spaceway, a $1.4 billion, three-satellite system that is scheduled to begin service in 2003 and will offer higher speeds and higher capacity.

Hughes is also starting to look beyond satellites to other forms of distribution. The company gave up making cell-phone equipment, but does make equipment for wireless broadband, which uses radio waves to distribute data or video in a city. Hughes might use that technology to offer local channels, Smith said, freeing up satellite capacity.

The company is also trying to bolster its management. Divisions have been run as independent fiefs, and it remains to be seen whether Smith can make the whole greater than the sum of its parts.

Charles H. Noski, Hughes's chief operating officer, left recently for AT&T. Hartenstein, seen as being better at growing companies than at managing a big one, was promoted to oversee all consumer operations for Hughes, including DirecTV and Internet operations.

At the beginning of 2000, the company was looking for an experienced manager to run DirecTV in the United States. Hartenstein, meanwhile, will devote more time to DirecTV's Latin American service, which has been going through a restructuring, and its operations in Japan, where DirecTV lags behind its rival, Sky PerfecTV. Hartenstein hinted that Hughes might seek to merge the Japanese operation with Sky PerfecTV, owned by the News Corporation, Sony, Softbank and others.

Still, in the United States, at least, satellite television still has some running room, even as cable strives to catch up. "We see the growth not slowing down till we get to thirty million," Smith said of satellite television in general. And he fully expects Hughes to garner the biggest part of that growth.

Coming Soon, Downloads from Up Above

The battle to offer high-speed Internet access is often seen as being between cable modems and digital subscriber telephone lines. Hughes Electronics and other satellite companies beg to differ. Hughes executives say Spaceway, their satellite-based data system, could be as big a business as DirecTV.

The $1.4 billion, three-satellite system, scheduled to begin service in 2003, will offer consumers download speeds of about 1 megabit a second, equivalent to what people get with cable in 2000, although businesses will be able to get speeds of up to 108 megabits a second.

Cable and high-speed phone lines have a head start. They are already available to some consumers—and they do not require subscribers to put dishes on their roofs. "Cable currently has the edge in the urban markets," said Tom Eagan, an analyst with PaineWebber.

Still, by 2004, one-quarter of all homes in the United States will still not have access either to cable modems or to digital subscriber lines, according to the Yankee Group, a market research firm.

Many other companies are also planning satellite-based Internet service, including DirecTV's big rival, EchoStar Communications; Rupert Murdoch's News Corporation, Teledesic, the satellite company backed by Craig McCaw, the cellular telephone magnate; and a start-up called iSky Inc. that is backed by, among others, Liberty Media, the AT&T unit led by John Malone.

Hughes executives are banking on Spaceway's sophisticated design to give it an edge—especially among corporate customers, which they expect to be the biggest users. Most satellites receive signals from earth and broadcast them down again in a wide swath. But Spaceway satellites will be like computerized telephone switches in the sky, so that two offices or homes with Spaceway dishes can communicate with each other.

But some experts say it does not make sense to put computer processing in space, where systems cannot be readily upgraded as technology improves. Moreover, some say, there might not be much demand for one-to-one communications, given the ease of using the Web.

"Now all we want to do is plug into the Internet," said Thomas E. Moore, president and chief executive of iSky. Because it uses a simpler satellite design, iSky says it will spend half as much as Spaceway and be in service two years earlier.

Andrew Pollack
February 27, 2000

By the end of 2000, DirecTV had more than nine million subscribers. General Motors, which previously said it had no interest in selling Hughes, acknowledged that it was exploring the sale or spin-off of the subsidiary or an alliance with another company. In April 2000, Hughes hired Odie Donald, a former senior executive at BellSouth, to run DirecTV in the United States.

CASE 3

Six Sigma on the Web

It seems intuitively obvious: Anyone who is buying a new refrigerator or washer wants it delivered as soon as possible. So, an appliance manufacturer setting up a Web-based order-and-delivery system would put next-day delivery high on the list of lures, right?

Right—if the Web designer was trusting to intuition. But one thing that the folks at General Electric have had drummed into them since the mid-1990s— or, ever since the company embraced the quality-control regimen known as Six Sigma—is that they act on gut instinct at their peril.

No matter that the Six Sigma sensibility evolved out of old economy rules; it is informing every aspect of GE's push into new economy mode.

Consider what happened when GE Appliances decided in 1999 to set up a Web-based system to arrange delivery of GE products to people who bought them at Home Depot. GE Appliances used focus groups, what-if scenarios and other Six Sigma methodologies to discern how much value customers placed on having new appliances show up in twenty-four hours.

Shock one: The answer was, not much value at all. "Six Sigma eliminated any perceived need for evening deliveries, next-day deliveries, Sunday deliveries, all sorts of costly things that we had wrongly thought would be important to customers," said Michael P. Delain, GE Appliances' quality manager for local delivery service.

Shock two: If the delivery people had a professional, soothing demeanor, customers would tolerate just about anything, even late deliveries or damaged products.

"Sure, customers cared that we accommodated their choice of a delivery date, and that we showed up in the window that we promised," said Steve LeClair, program manager for e-business at GE Appliances. "But Six Sigma studies showed that they cared most about the softer, less measurable skills."

The resulting system, which is operating in about six hundred of Home Depot's 980 stores, lets sales representatives enter a customer's order onto the Web, and arrange for delivery to the customer's home directly from a GE warehouse. GE Appliances, meanwhile, now trains installers and delivery personnel on people skills.

Six Sigma, of course, is the quality program that big companies including Motorola, Honeywell and GE have credited with squeezing billions of dollars in costs out of products and processes, without losing quality or service. It is a statistical method of breaking a customer's requirements into tasks or steps, and setting the optimum specification for each part of the process, based on how the parts interact.

It means taking nothing for granted, checking out even those things that seem intuitively obvious, and running countless what-if scenarios to see what kind of cascade effect changing even seemingly innocuous variables can have on the result. When GE Medical Systems designed its Lightspeed diagnostic scanner, for example, Six Sigma studies showed that widening a few tungsten wires could increase the machine's accuracy—something that the design team had thought would require a costly tube redesign.

And Six Sigma means having all GE departments, from accounting to production to customer service, analyze the impact that their ways of interacting with each other could have on a customer's total experience with GE.

At the dictum of GE's chairman, John F. Welch Jr., Six Sigma has been a way of life at GE. The company has applied it to pretty much every aspect of its business—designing products, interacting with customers, fine-tuning delivery.

So early in 1999, when Welch said he expected every GE business to have an e-commerce strategy up and running by that spring, it took just nanoseconds for most to realize that Six Sigma was a natural for guiding GE onto the Web, particularly if they thought of a Web page as a product and of e-business as a process. All the GE businesses met Welch's deadline.

"Six Sigma processes let us demystify the whole concept of e-business," said Piet C. van Abeelen, GE's vice president for Six Sigma Quality. "They let us get organized without handing off pieces of the process among fifty-five people."

Industry experts say that GE is way ahead of other old economy companies in embracing the Web. Indeed, it is turning its Web savvy into a business itself. In June 2000, GE announced a joint venture with Cisco Systems that would help manufacturers use Internet technology to tie their factory data systems in with their office systems. GE also introduced a host of new Web-related services for small businesses.

"They've figured out how to transfer their brand identity to the Internet," said Geri Spieler, an e-business analyst with the Gartner consulting firm. "They grab people with depth and breadth of services, and keep them with multiple opportunities to click for more."

Indeed, GE Lighting, GE Appliances and others have Web-based programs that let architects and builders design lighting systems and kitchens from a list of specifications. Most GE businesses have self-help sites that give users step-by-step guidance for fixing or maintaining products. And all of them give browsers a chance to buy things.

"Each of their businesses is transactional on the Web, and no other old-line company can say that," said Nicholas P. Heymann, an analyst at Prudential Securities. "Six Sigma was a real turbocharger for them."

Examples abound. Through Six Sigma analyses, many GE businesses concluded that customers, given a modicum of extra information, would willingly handle a lot of repair work themselves. Other studies showed that if information about optional features was easy to find, many customers—businesses as well as consumers—would configure their own products, without waiting for a sales representative to call.

For GE, that meant saving a fortune on service personnel and "selling" to customers who are either geographically remote or too small to warrant sales calls.

One problem, the Six Sigma studies showed, was that customers often could not find the model numbers on their appliances or machines. So, several GE businesses put "how to find your model number" sections on their Web pages.

And, several GE businesses have given their Web sites so-called configurators and wizards—electronic guides that enable customers to customize their own systems, be it a redone kitchen or a lighting system for a new plant, and even help customers fix them in the future.

Six Sigma analyses also showed that house builders—prime customers for GE Appliances—want to give their own customers a way to design their homes at one Web sitting. So, GE is designing Web sites for major builders that enable the builder's customers to configure what GE appliances they want in their homes, but that also help them explore what's available in cabinetry, carpeting and other essential home items that GE does not sell itself. One such site, called Selectioncenter.com, is being tested at the U.S. Home Corporation.

"It's going to be an important site for builders, and for distributors like us," said Joe Dumstorf, president of Trend Technologies, a distributor of building products that helped GE design the site.

Almost every GE business can point to ways that Six Sigma forged a path to the Web. When GE's CNBC unit first put up a Web site in 1999, for example, the home page seemed to take an awfully long time to load. Instead of blaming traffic or Internet glitches outside GE's control, analysts used Six Sigma methods to deconstruct the page; they discovered that one of the page's distinctive features, the trailing stock ticker at the bottom, was slowing up the loading time. The site designers gave viewers the option of loading without the ticker, which cut the upload time in half, to 4 seconds. They have since whittled it down to 2.46 seconds.

And when GE Appliances wanted to lure consumers to check out new products on its Web page, the company performed a Six Sigma analysis to determine what kind of information customers wanted, how many mouse clicks they would be willing to make to get it, and whether they would settle for schematics of appliances that could be loaded quickly rather than full-color digital photos that might take forever to load.

"Intuition told us the bigger and more detailed the picture, the better," recalled Joseph J. Deangelo, vice president for e-business at GE Appliances. "Six Sigma analysis showed that customers preferred speed to detail when they were first comparing models, and were only willing to wait for detailed pictures when they were close to a decision."

Six Sigma has also played a role as GE's consumer businesses have set up Web-based help desks. GE's telephone help centers had been through their own Six Sigma rigor, which had led to a computerized body of knowledge that operators could consult to answer any question. Now questions that come in by e-mail, by direct query on a Web site or by phone all receive answers from that same database within twenty-four hours.

"A tenet of Six Sigma is that you take variability out of results," Deangelo explained, "and this enabled us to get rid of an entire category of potential defects, which is wrong, incomplete or late answers."

There was another Six Sigma tenet at play with the help sites: running what-if scenarios on how to convert questioners to self-help mode enabled GE to fine-tune the information offered through self-help mechanisms on the Web.

For example, owners of GE's new Advantium Oven, which cooks with a combination of light and microwave energy, often write in with questions on how to translate recipes for use with the Advantium. GE Appliances refers such questions to home economists on its staff, e-mails answers to the questioners, and then includes the information on its self-help sites, where anyone hoping to try a similar recipe can find it.

All told, Six Sigma means approaching every problem with the assumption that it has a data-oriented, tangible solution in the end. The process does not yield perfection, but it provides a handle on how much variability from a standard, be it a product specification or a delivery time, customers will tolerate before they perceive it as a defect.

The collaboration between GE Appliances and Home Depot is a case study. Until 2000, GE shipped a small assortment of appliances to Home Depot, which kept them in inventory until they were sold and then delivered them to customers. Home Depot wanted to offer more items but to stock less inventory.

So GE Appliances and Home Depot worked out a Web-based model whereby Home Depot sales representatives could use a kiosk at the store to enter a customer's order for any GE appliance. The kiosk transmits the order to the nearest GE warehouse via the Internet, and the item can be shipped from the warehouse to the customer's home.

"This lets us offer quicker delivery of a wider assortment of products, without maintaining big warehouses full of products," said Donald E. Galloway, Home Depot's national product manager for appliances.

The concept was simple, but the economics were not. Home Depot wanted to offer the service to every customer; GE used Six Sigma analyses to discern how wide a geographic radius around each warehouse it could economically serve.

Both GE and Home Depot finally agreed that it made sense to forgo servicing a handful of customers in order to guarantee stellar service to the vast majority. For customers who do not fall within the delivery radius, Home Depot resorts to the old methods—it places an order with GE, which ships the appliance to the store, which arranges delivery to the customer's home.

The process of applying Six Sigma continues, as GE moves toward being ever more Web-centric. According to Gary Reiner, GE's chief information officer, GE has dedicated about one thousand employees to its e-commerce effort. And 80 percent of those e-business mavens are homegrown; most old-economy companies hire their Web expertise from the tech world.

"It was essential that our Web sites reflect our customers' needs, not our organizational structure," Reiner said. "That kind of customer focus is an underlying principle of Six Sigma."

Claudia H. Deutsch
June 12, 2000

CASE 4

The Fragmented World Wide Web

If there were any established companies ready-made for the Internet, they should have been the big television networks. Or at least that was how it seemed in 1998.

"We have what is needed to compete because of the great depth in our brands and the great consumer loyalty to them," Michael D. Eisner, chairman of Walt Disney, said on the eve of the debut of Disney's Go Network.

The broadcast networks, after all, are still the most powerful media forces in America, accounting for two-thirds of the seven hours of television the average household watches each day. And they have an arsenal of advantages: lots of money, libraries of programming and decades of experience in attracting and keeping big audiences. And most important, the networks have the ability to promote their Web sites with unlimited amounts of advertising on television, which is still the most persuasive medium.

But after great effort and hundreds of millions of dollars of promotion, the networks are still also-rans on the Web. Traffic to their various sites badly lags behind the big portals like Yahoo, America Online and Microsoft's MSN, which are the closest thing the Web has to major networks.

Certainly Wall Street has all but written off the broadcast companies as Internet players. The publicly traded shares of NBC Internet and ABC's online cousin, the Walt Disney Internet Group, were down more than two-thirds in the first seven months of 2000—a steeper decline than those suffered by the stocks of their larger competitors.

And in August 2000, NBC Internet, citing slowing ad sales, said it would lay off 20 percent of its workforce.

CBS, meanwhile, has delayed plans to spin off its Internet operations into a separate company. And CBS's new parent, Viacom, has postponed the offering of shares in its online music business, the MTVi Group.

"Right now investors are not rewarding the Internet activities of Disney, NBC and Viacom," said Tom Wolzien, an analyst with Sanford C. Bernstein. "They are small, and the market prefers the big players like Yahoo and America Online."

It has been a humbling comedown for the networks and their owners, who are more accustomed to being mighty media monoliths than niche players scrounging for audiences.

Eisner now says he was given bad advice about how much the Internet differed from Disney's other businesses. The company developed the first version of its portal, Go.com, in six months, he noted, to keep pace with the notion of hyperfast Internet time.

"People told me we had to be like Microsoft and put out version one and two and three, and eventually we would get it right," Eisner said. "We did that with Go, then people told us it wasn't as good as Yahoo or America Online. I've never been involved with anything where I didn't believe what we did wasn't the best. But here we were, experimenting in front of the public."

What went wrong?

To begin with, the networks overestimated their own strengths. Their vaunted promotional abilities, for example, were helpful in persuading people to try their Web sites. But lacking the depth and sophistication of features that the successful portals had, many of the network sites could not turn the merely curious into steady customers.

And for all their early confidence, the network companies have been uncertain whether to make their Internet operations independent, to emulate the fast-moving style of other Web companies, or to keep them part of their broadcast operations, to take best advantage of their popular media content and packaging skill.

"The mistake made over and over again by traditional media companies is that they dabble in new media rather than doing something strategic to integrate with their core assets," said Tom Rogers, chief executive of Primedia and former head of NBC's cable operation and much of its Internet activities.

As it turns out, the networks' biggest Web successes have been the efforts most closely aligned with broadcast programming—as when ABC and its cable cousin ESPN promote the sports content of ESPN.com, or when CBS newscasts cite the financial reports on CBS MarketWatch.com. But those successes in specialized areas of coverage stand in stark contrast to the typically more disappointing results whenever the network companies have tried to reach broader audiences.

And even one unqualified hit is giving little glory to an outfit that could use some. MSNBC.com, backed by the combined promotion of NBC's cable network and Microsoft's MSN Internet site, has grown rapidly to become the top news site on the Internet. MSNBC even was profitable for NBC in 1999, executives say. But according to the terms of the deal, MSNBC's audience counts toward MSN's ratings, and the site sends little traffic to NBCi.

The networks' experience is not simply a tale of hubris, of media moguls glibly assuming they would show those goateed and pierced Web kids a thing or two.

In large measure, it was Wall Street that pushed the networks into the game, by demanding in 1998 that the network companies mount a credible Internet strategy. So, all too gamely, the networks plunged ahead.

Disney, the owner of ABC, and NBC, with the blessing of its corporate parent, General Electric, each made a series of acquisitions, combined with internal operations, to build Internet portals that were meant to challenge Yahoo and America Online. For ABC-Disney it was the Go Network, built from the Infoseek search engine. For NBC, it was Snap, bought from Cnet.

But the best days of both Go and Snap seem to be behind them. It is true that Go was the Web's sixth-most-popular site in June 2000, according to the research firm Media Metrix. And Snap, counted along with the other sites run by the NBC Internet unit, ranked ninth. But on the Internet, both audience and revenue appear to be concentrating in a handful of leaders at the very top. Indeed, for the year ended in August 2000, Go and NBCi actually lost audience share, even as the leaders—America Online, Yahoo and MSN—all increased their shares by more than ten points.

CBS, meanwhile, has taken a different tack. Rather than trying to create a network-scale portal, the company backed a dozen independent, specialized Web services, like MarketWatch, Sportsline and Iwon.

Among CBS.com and sites in which Viacom-CBS have investments, none was among the top fifty—except Iwon.com, a site that gives cash prizes to users, which ranked twenty-first.

(CBS.com had been losing audience share in 2000, but bounced back somewhat on Web traffic related to the network's hit show, *Survivor*.)

"The networks looked at the Internet and had to do something, if for no other reason than defensively," said Dean Daniels, a former CBS executive who is now president of Theglobe.com, a youth-oriented online community site. "There are huge audiences online that are spending less time watching television. The problem is that none of the networks are getting it right."

Time Warner, which runs the CNN, Turner and WB networks along with myriad other media properties, felt so flummoxed by the rise of new media that it agreed in January 2000 to sell itself to America Online.

And the News Corporation, which owns the Fox network and endured an expensive Internet flop in 1997, has kept a lower profile since then. Fox now hopes to capitalize on the rollout of high-speed, or broadband, Internet connections that are much better suited to disseminating video signals than are conventional telephone lines. One example of this strategy, already available, is Toohotforfox.com, a site that offers video outtakes from the Fox network's so-called reality programming.

"The game is over, and the major media companies didn't win it," said Peter Chernin, the News Corporation's president. "We didn't win. Disney didn't win. AOL and Yahoo did. So we're going to the next game, which is broadband, and that's wide open."

Meanwhile, the three big broadcast networks are reassessing their strategies. NBCi, which in 2000 said ad sales would fall short of Wall Street's expectations, will scrap the heavily promoted Snap name and more than a dozen other brands and focus on a redesigned site under the name NBCi.com. And Disney, recognizing the futility of going portal-to-portal with either Yahoo or AOL and learning from the success of its own ESPN.com, will focus its Web effort on entertainment and leisure activities.

ESPN.com is the top sports site, followed by CBS Sportsline, both of which are incessantly promoted on their networks' sportscasts.

"We are focused on the marriage of the Internet and on-air," said Fred Reynolds, Viacom's chief financial officer, who held the same position at CBS, where he looked after the Internet activities.

Indeed, CBS's Web strategy may be the one that is likely to change the least. All along, the company tended to buy partial stakes in specialized Internet sites like Sportsline in return for broadcast advertising time rather than cash. And much of that advertising comes not from the network's inventory of thirty-second commercials, but within the programming itself. "Every time Dan Rather introduces the business news from MarketWatch, we get credit," Reynolds said.

There are also signs that the networks are figuring out how to create Web sites tied to their broadcast entertainment programming. Traffic was brisk at the sites for CBS's hit shows *Survivor* and *Big Brother*, the latter featuring video feeds of contestants twenty-four hours a day.

And ABC has developed Web programming meant for viewers to browse while watching certain programs. Some 150,000 people competed during each *Who Wants to Be a Millionaire* broadcast, for example, to see if they could answer the questions before the contestant did. Not only does that site earn a profit from the Internet ads it sells, but ABC believes it also helps build a loyal TV audience.

In essence, it appears that the networks are concluding that their bets for the Web may spring from individual programs, rather than their entire programming portfolio. Ah, the virtues of hindsight.

What has been much harder has been to figure out the digital incarnation of the networks themselves. CBS, NBC and ABC are some of the most powerful brands in the country, but what exactly do they stand for with ".com" affixed to the end?

A major television network is, after all, an aggregation of many types of programming—news, sports, comedy, drama and, these days, voyeurism. So it seemed natural that the corollary of the network in the digital age was the Internet portal—a one-stop shop full of entertainment and information, bundled with a search engine and lots of other useful features like news and e-mail. Portals were doubly appealing because, then as now, they get the lion's share of the traffic and advertising revenue on the Internet.

But once they waded in, the networks soon found themselves up to their knees in a swamp of tedious portal necessities like building business directories and creating retail transaction services that have little to do with the media companies' expertise.

"I learned I don't want to sell insurance or create a yellow pages," Eisner said. After a year of struggling to beat Yahoo at its own game, Eisner decided in 2000 to pull back from the portal business. "It's not us. Our company stands for travel and entertainment and having a good time," he said.

NBC, by contrast, is still focused on building a broad portal. But the emphasis will be on shopping.

"You can't be all things to all people, and that was NBCi's problem," said Marty Yudkovitz, president of NBC Interactive Media.

Notably, the only network-affiliated portal that is growing rapidly is Viacom-CBS's Iwon.com, which has no explicit links to the CBS network. In less than a year that site, which promises users the chance to win as much as $10 million, has grown to a monthly audience of 8.4 million people, according to Media Metrix.

Now CBS is considering buying or building a broader portal to present a unified view of its two hundred local stations and its affiliated Internet sites. But Reynolds said the company would not give up its strict financial discipline that kept it from entering the sort of deals its rivals did.

"We will not be a second citizen online," he said. "We are willing to invest a lot of money, but at the end of the day you have to have a business that produces more cash than you spend."

Saul Hansell
August 14, 2000

CASE 5

Old Economy Principles

In the relentless search to find something unprecedented in the new economy, many business gurus, and even some well-trained economists, now say that the theoretical principles underlying it are novel as well. Don't bet on it. Increasingly, it looks as if old-economy principles are saving the day.

The main claim is that we now live in a "network society," one in which profits and economic growth can reach heights that will make other industrial revolutions seem pallid. Lawrence H. Summers, the Treasury secretary, displayed just such new-age thinking in a speech in the spring of 2000. Citing an example used by many a new-economy guru, he noted that one fax machine is useless, but when we have two and more, we have a network. If there are one hundred thousand fax machines, we have ten billion possible relationships.

Because of such networks, the argument goes, profitability does not diminish as investment expands. (Diminishing returns are supposedly old-economy ideas.) Rather, there are now "positive feedback loops" because it costs so little, sometimes almost nothing, to reach a new customer or make a new connection. Thus, the bigger the network, the higher the returns on investment. The ultimate network is, of course, the World Wide Web and the countless private Internet-like systems run by large corporations and institutions.

But how new is all this? Has the Treasury secretary ever heard of telephones? Or television? Or A&P, for that matter, which was started in the late 1800s? Granted, television and A&P were not the sort of networks that could isolate twenty-five or twenty-five thousand people, as ideally may happen on the Internet. But the basic economic advantage was the same: positive feedback loops. One A&P was only a large mom-and-pop store. Two or more, and we had a network. With every additional outlet, the owners increasingly enjoyed the benefits of large-scale purchases of inventories, aggressive advertising and the mass distribution of their product. The more they invested, the lower their average costs.

Or consider steel. In 1880, steel rails cost about sixty-eight dollars a ton to produce. But largely because of economies of scale, the price fell to about eighteen dollars a ton by 1900. The fixed cost to put up a modern steel mill was high, but the cost of producing extra rails was small. Thus, the more rails that could be sold, the lower the average cost for each ton. Those who sold the most could underprice the competition, spend more on marketing and lower costs still more.

The same economies of scale that worked in the late 1800s and throughout most of the 1900s may also be creating rapid productivity gains in the new economy. New companies are selling standardized products to enormous mass markets, just as in the good old days. Industry after industry back then exploited the advantages of scale, from petroleum companies to cigarette manufacturers to rail lines to automakers to retail chains. Huge companies came to dominate their markets.

In the new economy, standardization and economies of scale are clearly back. It is too early to get precise data on this. Moreover, many of these new economies of scale are being earned in service industries, and as John Kwoka, a George Washington University economist, points out, the government does not gather data about them.

But has there ever been a more standardized product in America than MS-DOS, Microsoft's operating system, or Windows? Consider today's most successful companies—Microsoft, Cisco Systems, America Online, Oracle, Sun Microsystems, Dell Computers, eBay and so on. All have enormous shares of their particular markets, and all enjoy economies of scale based on standardized (if complex) products. The more these companies sell, the higher their productivity as they reduce labor costs per unit to a minimum. The national economic data shows that most of the outsize gains in productivity are being created in just such computer and software companies.

Technologists tell us it will be the next generation of software that will ultimately connect the niche markets. My guess is that true profitability will continue to come to those businesses that sell products with the broadest appeal. AOL wants more subscribers, eBay desires more participants and Amazon.com hopes to reach the huge critical mass needed to make it profitable at last. In fact, the Internet probably gives even more advantage to large companies than they had in the past because the non-marketing costs of reaching one additional customer are virtually nil. The real advantage will be to those companies that either have a piece of technology that cannot be duplicated or can afford to advertise aggressively enough to win brand-name recognition in the mass market.

For antitrust authorities, old questions, not new ones, are being raised. The new networks give rise to monopolies. But the economic benefits of such big business should not be underestimated. Through economies of scale, stable markets, uniform standards, investment in research and development, and permanent, well-trained labor forces, big business has long been a boon to America.

On the other hand, monopolies can go too far by suppressing innovation and keeping prices high. Especially now that size may have a renewed advantage, the antitrust authorities are correct to be vigilant. Moreover, there are other traditional concerns. In the pursuit of more scale, mergers among media companies threaten principles of free speech. The consolidation of financial services makes us more vulnerable to crisis. The concentration of wealth has skewed political power toward the rich.

The real niche economy was the one started by Japanese auto companies in the late 1970s. Consumers demanded a wide choice of products, and our sleepy big businesses did respond, albeit slowly, with innovative ways to meet these needs more productively. But they could not raise productivity as rapidly as they did in the more standardized century between the Civil War and the 1970s. In my view, this contributed to America's historically slow growth from the 1970s to the early 1990s.

In the mid-1990s, that changed radically. Business again made standardized products that corporations and consumers craved in mass volume. For good and ill, welcome back the old economy.

Jeff Madrick
July 6, 2000

CASE 6

Adding Silicon Valley
to the Syllabus

If there is an intellectual center of big business, it is the immaculately maintained faux-Georgian campus of Harvard Business School, for nearly a century the training ground for the people who run and advise the world's largest companies. From turning out future chief executives of IBM, Merck and Procter & Gamble to being the home of strategy gurus like Michael E. Porter, Harvard has practically stamped its crest on the large industrial companies that defined the twentieth-century economy.

But "the West Point of capitalism," as the school is known, has spent the last few years behaving like anything but an academy of big business. Instead, Harvard has undergone a transformation worthy of the case studies that are the hallmark of its MBA curriculum. This one goes something like this: Fearing new kinds of competition, an industry giant changes how it does business to remain relevant and retain its dominance under a new set of economic rules.

The crux of the changes is an effort to reorganize Harvard around the study of entrepreneurial ventures, be they dot-com start-ups or divisions of large companies trying to act like small companies. Those are the places that many Harvard students want to work today, and they are the businesses that occupy the thoughts of the nation's most sought-after academics. The shift has touched every Harvard student and has caused the business school—the world's richest, best-known and most influential—to start a series of initiatives in Silicon Valley, where Stanford, its most important rival, is preeminent.

The M.B.A.s who received their diplomas in the spring of 2000 here, across the Charles River from Harvard University's main campus in Cambridge, were the last who were required to take general management, once the school's signature course. Students now must enroll in a first-year class called "The Entrepreneurial Manager."

In the 1999–2000 school year, more than one-quarter of the electives chosen by second-year students were in the entrepreneurship department, which twenty years ago consisted of just two classes. In 2000–01, forty students will opt out of regular classes for two months to receive credit for working inside mostly small companies in Silicon Valley and Massachusetts. Officials have taken to boasting that Harvard sends more graduates to the valley than any other business school.

"We need to change, indeed get out in front of the parade, to continue to attract these bright twenty-five-year-olds," said Jay Light, a Harvard professor for thirty years and one of the school's senior associate deans overseeing the curriculum changes. "If we don't maintain our relevance for what they want to do with their lives, there's a problem."

The shift brings some significant risks. In essence, Harvard has allowed its current students' interest in working for small companies—an interest that cynics might brand a grasp for instant riches—to play a major role in shaping its curriculum for the next decade. And while the Internet may be here to stay, the stock market's volatility suggests that entrepreneurial fervor may be more fleeting. The consolidation spree of the last decade also indicates that large companies—indeed, ones larger than in the past—will continue to dominate the economy.

Yet Harvard, as it reinvents itself, could alienate the big-company recruiters who have faithfully trekked to Boston every autumn for decades. The school has made "quite a radical set of changes," said Adrian J. Slywotzky, a vice president at Mercer Management Consulting near Boston who has often written about large organizations' attempts to reinvent themselves and who received his M.B.A. from Harvard in 1980. "Companies could say, 'I'm not sure how Harvard is serving me,'" Slywotzky said.

Harvard professors, however, say that the economic changes of the last five years have forced them to act and that, in any event, they are not really leaving behind the study of big companies. Almost like a mantra, the professors repeat word-for-word a definition of entrepreneurship that they say applies to General Electric as well as it does to a dot-com operated out of a garage: the pursuit of opportunities beyond means that are currently available.

"We think of entrepreneurship not as a personality type or as a stage in the life cycle of a business but as a way of managing," said Kim B. Clark, the dean since 1995, whose overhaul of the business school has earned him mention as a candidate for Harvard University's presidency. "The concepts of leadership that are important now and are going to be important in the future spring out of an understanding of entrepreneurship."

Rosabeth M. Kanter, a professor of management, added, "Big companies are dying to behave more like start-ups."

In the broadest sense, Harvard is simply catching up to its alumni. The school teaches students to think like general managers—chief executives or presidents—but not all of the eight hundred–plus Harvard M.B.A. graduates each year can end up in such jobs at big companies. In fact, about one-third of graduates who have been out of Harvard for at least fifteen years own their own businesses, according to studies done by the school.

Now Harvard is arguing that it, more than any other institution and more than the hands-on experience of working at a start-up, can help today's students become entrepreneurs quickly. That argument is part realpolitik and part intellectual. The school gives students access to one of the economy's most powerful professional networks—a Harvard *keiretsu* that includes all those earlier entrepreneurs, as well as dozens of venture capitalists and the founders of dozens of recent dot-coms.

At the same time, the two years away from working life gives students time to think through a broad range of business problems, to take risks that they could not if actual dollars were at stake and, possibly, to even come up with their own business plans. "We run a simulator where people are taking live shots at them," said William A. Sahlman, a longtime professor of entrepreneurship. "This is the big time, but still low risk. You can't get that in the outside world."

Regardless of whether Harvard's transformation ultimately succeeds, it is already being felt far beyond Boston. Every year, Harvard sells some six million copies of the school's famous case studies to other business schools and organizations. So unlike, say, Berkeley's physics department or Yale's law school, Harvard Business School has a direct and immediate effect on the curriculum of hundreds of its peers.

In other words, it just isn't at Harvard that business students are now learning about companies that most of them had never heard of.

Playing Catch Up

Professor Paul Marshall was settling in to plan the last week of the semester when one of his teaching assistants offered a blunt assessment of the situation. "It's coming apart!" he said. One of the final case studies for Harvard's new core class in entrepreneurship would contain sensitive information that eStyle—the Internet retailer that was its subject—was unwilling to release on Harvard's timetable.

The professor would have none of it. "Then pick up the pieces and run across the finish line," Marshall recalled telling the assistant. Sure enough, Harvard got eStyle to release the case in time for it to be printed, though students had to rush through reading it in two days, rather than the usual few weeks. Call it business school on Internet time.

"The faculty is scrambling like hell" to keep up with developments in the business world, Marshall said.

Students say the class was uneven at times, but most agree that it was still much better than studying how Caterpillar might cut costs by a percentage point or how a Procter & Gamble manager should market a new brand of tissues—the sort of topics and companies on which Harvard's case studies had focused for decades.

This is just one way that the school is a very different place than it was in 1995, when Clark became dean. Netscape Communications had just gone public, and thousands of college students across the country were already addicted to e-mail. But Harvard Business School, one of the richest of any kind and one supposedly with a foot in the real world, had not given e-mail accounts to its students.

"We were so far behind; we were, like, way, way behind," Clark said.

He figured that the school could prosper by helping managers think about how to deal with the ways that technology was altering the corporate landscape—or that it could fall behind its peers quite rapidly. "My sense was that we were at an inflection point, and we needed to seize the moment and take action," Clark said.

Some of the changes were straightforward. By the first week of 1996, every student and professor had an e-mail account and could connect to it from all over campus. Harvard's case studies soon included spreadsheets tied to real-time data sets and videos.

Altering the curriculum was more complicated, and more profound. Until the mid-1980s, the school offered only one or two entrepreneurship courses; many faculty members saw the subject as unworthy of rigorous study. "It was pretty lonely," said Howard H. Stevenson, who has taught entrepreneurship at Harvard since the early '70s.

As the technological shifts of the last twenty years took hold, however, the market changed all that. Students clamored for such classes, and the faculty's interest grew, too. The entrepreneurship department now offers some eighteen courses taught by twenty-eight professors, who range from lifetime academics to a cofounder of the Staples office supply chain.

The most significant change is the switch of the required first-year class from general to entrepreneurial management. In 1990, the case subjects for the class included Bank One, Caterpillar, Colgate-Palmolive, General Electric, Honda, Nike and Pepsi-Cola. In 2000, the lineup included perhaps only two companies that a layman would recognize as major corporations—Charles Schwab and Intuit. Among the others were Bitstream, Chemdex.com (now part of the Ventro Corporation), Go Fish and Onset Ventures.

Marshall and his teaching assistants are not the only ones to find the transition bumpy. In 1999, Clark felt it necessary to send a memo to professors forbidding them to serve on the boards of companies started by current students. And students have been pushing the career services office to do more to help them wade through the dozens of dot-coms that would eagerly hire a Harvard M.B.A.

The more important question, however, may be what the changes will mean for corporate America. After all, generations of Harvard M.B.A.s have filled the ranks of the country's consulting firms, investment banks and corporate giants. Now many of the most talented students are starting their own businesses or joining smaller companies.

Harvard's decision to cater to that clientele, some people fear, could produce a group of budding executives with a much firmer understanding of how to raise venture capital than of how to steer a global enterprise. All the while, the world's corporations are becoming ever more complex as they swallow up rivals and stretch across international borders.

"There is a risk to our generation all working in ten- and fifty-person companies," said Kevin M. Lalande, a member of Harvard's class of 2001 who started two companies between his undergraduate work and business school. "Later on, it's going to be much more difficult to find people who have the kind of experience to run a multinational."

Rivals? What Rivals?

Harvard University is not given to paying much heed to its competition, and the business school generally fits the institutional mold. "We don't think of ourselves as competing with other schools," said Light, a senior associate dean, when asked to name Harvard's closest rival. "We think of ourselves as producing knowledge."

That is often a surprisingly insular process. Of the twenty-eight professors in the entrepreneurship department, thirteen hold a Harvard M.B.A.; an additional seven have other Harvard University degrees. Ask them where they studied and some pause briefly before replying, "Here." The answer is so obvious that the question seems almost to take them by surprise.

But "here" is not exactly the center of the new economy; that would be three thousand miles west of Boston, and Stanford Business School is in the midst of it.

Stanford admits only one of every thirteen applicants, making it almost twice as selective as Harvard by that measure. By reputation, Stanford has won a place alongside Harvard as one of the two best business schools in the country, most students agree, a notch above the University of Pennsylvania's Wharton School, the University of Chicago, Northwestern and Columbia. In the most recent ranking by *U.S. News & World Report,* Harvard and Stanford tied for first. "We are each other's biggest competition, by far," said Robert Joss, Stanford's dean. "In fact, our second-most-important competition is students who decide not to go to business school."

All of this presents a challenge to Harvard. It may have the advantage of better name recognition than Stanford, and more resources, but as the case studies often point out, such benefits do not guarantee success in the new economy. Indeed, if Harvard became the school of big business and the old economy while its cross-country rival was identified as a training ground for the new economy, it could look forward to the same kind of problems that business icons like General Motors have suffered in recent years.

The analogy is not lost on Clark. A graduate of both Harvard College and Harvard's doctoral program in economics, he spent much of his academic career studying innovation at automobile companies, among others. It was Clark who, during yet one more long trip to the Bay Area a few years ago, conceived the notion that Harvard should establish a beachhead in northern California.

After a typically frustrating search for Silicon Valley real estate—agents offered sites like the third floor of a decrepit Victorian house and an office without a single parking place—the California Research Center finally opened on Sand Hill Road in Menlo Park in 1997. And if the name on the door and the address are impressive—America's most prestigious university setting up shop on Silicon Valley's BMW-lined boulevard of venture capital and innovation—the research center is not much to look at. It is a typically charmless suite of small second-floor offices that Harvard shares with a technology development firm.

"We have visitors come in, especially from Asia, and say, 'This is it?'" acknowledged Christina Darwall, the office's director and a former software entrepreneur. "A lot of these people pull up in their big, long limousines. They're expecting marble."

There is no marble, but a steady parade of Harvard professors—more than a third of the faculty, so far—have tramped through the research center since it opened. Darwall and a small staff keep in closer touch with Silicon Valley companies than Harvard professors ever could from Boston, writing some case studies themselves and opening doors for the faculty to write others.

"People are busier here, and it doesn't mean as much to them to be in a case," Darwall said.

At the same time, Harvard wants its paying customers to feel that studying at the business school can include time in Silicon Valley. So the center helped organize a job-hunting trip that sent more than five hundred Harvard students to California during their winter vacation. Harvard has also begun conducting executive education programs in the valley, with about half of the students coming from the region.

Of course, all this has raised a few eyebrows at Stanford, which has not exactly welcomed its eastern counterpart with open arms. When Harvard officials were planning the research center, they approached Stanford about collaborating. Stanford never responded, Darwall said. Still, Joss,

Stanford's dean, says he is not worried about Harvard's presence. "We welcome the fact that they're interested in and engaged in the ideas out here," he said. "We have the real benefit of being right in the heart of the action."

Indeed, many people in Silicon Valley consider Stanford the more forward-thinking of the two. "They still think Harvard is an old school that teaches old tricks," said David Cowan, the managing general partner of Bessemer Venture Partners in Menlo Park, who received a Harvard M.B.A. in 1992. Yet based on his discussions with students and professors now at Harvard, Cowan believes the school has changed significantly.

"When I went, I felt at the time I had made a mistake and should have gone to Stanford," he said. Now, he said, "I sure wish I had gone to Harvard Business School more recently than when I did."

Harvard professors, true to their institutional instincts, tend to brush off the notion that they are increasingly competing with Stanford—noting, for example, that they often collaborate with Stanford professors.

But there may be a bit more rivalry than the professors acknowledge. One does not have to spend much time on the Boston campus to hear a few disparaging, if often lighthearted, comments about the Palo Alto campus. Sahlman, the entrepreneurship professor, even has a Stanford parking permit and a tattered Stanford pennant pinned up in his office.

The permit reminds him of one downside of crowded Silicon Valley. The pennant was a gift from a class of students, Sahlman said, "because I made fun of Stanford so much."

David Leonhardt
June 18, 2000

In November 2000, Harvard Business School announced that it and Stanford University were teaming up to design—and sell—executive education classes that will be taught over the Internet.

CASE 7

Culture Clash

The negotiation was one part corporate diplomacy and one part Dilbert.

The young executives of methodfive Inc., a Web design firm, were planning a Halloween party in their loftlike headquarters in Greenwich Village.

The partners of PricewaterhouseCoopers, the giant accounting and consulting firm that had recently bought a stake in methodfive, couldn't decide whether they should wear costumes.

Donning disguises would make them seem hip, the partners thought. But they worried that they also might end up looking silly in front of clients who would be at the party. So they vacillated. "One day, they would be wearing costumes; the next day they wouldn't be wearing costumes," said Alaina Yoakum, methodfive's marketing manager, who had frequent conversations with a public relations executive at Pricewaterhouse about the party.

Eventually, they decided that the most senior partner coming to the party would wear a costume so long as methodfive's chief executive did, too. Somehow, though, Andrew B. Zimmerman, the partner, got a garbled message and came in a suit, while Adeo Ressi, the executive, came as Obi-Wan Kenobi, light saber and all.

Zimmerman could do little but try to laugh off the mix-up and rescue himself by joking in a speech to his audience—including Austin Powers, a werewolf and a sack of potatoes—that he was really a consultant who had come dressed as an accountant.

The Halloween party was more than just an amusing turn in the cultural acclimation taking place since the button-down Pricewaterhouse bought a 12 percent stake in the cutting-edge methodfive in 1999. It was also a stark illustration of the communications gap that more and more workplaces are experiencing as bricks-and-mortar behemoths team up with Web companies. The plan by America Online to acquire Time Warner is only the grandest of such partnerships. These "clicks and bricks" alliances give established companies, many of which have failed to figure out the Internet, an immediate entry to the online world, and they give dot-com ventures a scale that might otherwise take decades to build.

The rationale for the methodfive-Pricewaterhouse deal was similar. Methodfive would quickly gain a foothold with hundreds of Pricewaterhouse clients around the world (as well as an infusion of cash). Pricewaterhouse would add sparkle to its enormous but staid information-technology consulting practice, contending that it, too, could tap the minds of creative twentysomethings who truly understood the Internet.

From the beginning, however, employees of both companies realized that the strategic vision was the easy part. Melding the two workplaces would be the problem.

Pricewaterhouse, the result of a multibillion-dollar merger, employs

150,000 people in 150 countries. Its consultants zip in and out of airports, offering executives advice about "adding value." The top consultant holds an M.B.A. from the Wharton School at the University of Pennsylvania.

Methodfive opened its doors in 1996, the result of an idea by Ressi, who was then a twenty-three-year-old dropout from the University of Pennsylvania's undergraduate program and had already sold one Internet start-up. Methodfive employs eighty people, most of them in a tenth-floor office lighted as much by the glow of computer screens as by dim bulbs overhead. Elsewhere in the building are a discount rug store and a nutrition newsletter. When boredom strikes, methodfive's employees try to throw a stuffed dog into a trash can from across the office.

It was Ressi who received a call from Zimmerman in the summer of 1999. The two had lunch and hit it off; before long, they had agreed on the broad outlines of a deal. Then came the first lesson in what it is like to work with an enormous company. Pricewaterhouse said it had to study the proposed agreement to make sure it did not violate Securities and Exchange Commission rules. Throughout the summer, methodfive added clients, hired new workers and waited for word from Zimmerman. "That is not Internet speed," Ressi said of the delay.

Not only that, but he found the decision-making machinery at Pricewaterhouse difficult to fathom. "You think: 'This dude is in charge. I speak to him. It gets done.' That's not really true at PWC," he said. "One guy has three or four different bosses."

To find their way, methodfive's workers set up an internal public-relations group to treat Pricewaterhouse as a potential client to which it must sell itself. Ressi said he had traveled to Pricewaterhouse offices around the world to "evangelize." Yoakum, the marketing manager, spends almost one day a week talking up methodfive to Pricewaterhouse.

Pricewaterhouse's consultants do not dispute the methodfive workers' description of the cultural divide. The differences in both style and substance, they say, are why Pricewaterhouse invested in methodfive. "We need to make sure we protect their brand and not pull it too close to us and turn it into oatmeal," said Michael G. Macesich, a Pricewaterhouse partner.

Keith J. Wymbs, one of three Pricewaterhouse consultants on a yearlong loan to methodfive, got a quick taste of culture shock shortly after arriving in December 1999. Sitting with two methodfive employees at an impromptu meeting, he began talking about "value chains" and "core competencies," he said. Their reaction? "Blank stares."

"Coming from a large organization, you get embodied with consultant-speak," Wymbs said. "Being here made me take a step back and say, 'I can eliminate this.'"

Not everything has worked out, to be sure. Several employees who didn't like the idea of linking up with a consulting giant have left, for example.

But the remaining employees said they saw the benefits of alliance. Working with Pricewaterhouse has taught them to attack problems more systematically and to be tougher negotiators with clients, they said. They have even begun showing up a little earlier in the morning, some as early as nine. "A year ago, no one was in the office at nine,'" Ressi said. "Not a soul."

David Leonhardt
January 26, 2000

CASE 8

A 1930s Guide to the New Economy

In 1932, a twenty-one-year-old professor by the name of Ronald Coase gave a lecture to students of the School of Economics and Commerce in Dundee, Scotland. He explained why businesses exist as they do—why, for, instance, they choose to produce some goods themselves and contract with outside companies to provide the rest.

Five years later, Coase turned the lecture into a paper, "The Nature of the Firm," which in 1991 was cited by the Royal Swedish Academy of Sciences as it awarded him the Nobel Prize for economics. Despite that fame, Coase's ideas on the nature of business were rarely mentioned inside corporate boardrooms and executive offices.

Then came the Internet economy.

Coase, now a professor emeritus at the University of Chicago's law school, has recently witnessed a revival of his ideas, particularly among dot-com executives and leaders of established companies as they forge Internet initiatives. And though his theories do not provide a road map for e-commerce success, they do provide a compass for executives whose strategic vision has been blurred by a sandstorm of alliance offers, shifting business models and new competition.

"What Coase—and everything that follows from him—helps us do is answer the question, 'What's the boundary of the firm, and how hard should that boundary be?'" said Charles Conn, chairman of Ticketmaster

Online/CitySearch. "It helps you think about things like whether to buy, build or partner."

At the core of Coase's theory is this notion: When a company tries to determine whether to farm out or instead produce goods or services on its own, market prices are not the sole factor. Rather, there are significant "transaction costs," in Coase's language, generated by the search for the right company to strike a supply agreement with, and the time and expense of cutting the deal. Those costs, he theorized, frequently determine whether or not a company will seek an outside supplier or service provider.

At the time Coase wrote his theory, transaction costs were prohibitively high. Because information flowed at a glacial pace, and supplies moved only slightly faster, companies strove to manage the entire chain of production within the walls of their own corporations. For instance, the Ford Motor Company, a paragon of the "vertically integrated" corporation of the early 1900s, once bought a rubber plantation rather than cede control of that part of tire manufacturing.

Sixty years later, transaction costs have plunged, thanks to the Internet. Within the so-called new economy, information itself is typically the product, and that information moves at the speed of a T1 line. As a result, companies can get complete information about potential suppliers and business partners within a few clicks, and can therefore set up supplier agreements or form alliances with other companies for a fraction of what it would have cost even a decade ago.

That, in turn, helps explain why Internet companies have cluttered the airwaves with alliance announcements since 1998. Of course, part of that owes to the fact that before the dot-com bubble burst, Internet companies frequently trotted out alliance partners as a way of building pre-IPO buzz. But analysts say that even with the window-dressing alliances, Coase's theory still holds: With diminished transaction costs, more alliances are inevitable.

"With lower transaction costs, companies are able to focus on narrow product slivers or business activities, and have other parties do the rest," said David Ernst, leader of the global alliances practice of McKinsey & Company, the consulting firm.

The implications are that "there are a lot more big winners—and big losers," Ernst said. "Because if you have a network of partners you can attract incremental business, and plug the revenues back into your core business," he added. "But if you don't, then you're the one whose market share is getting taken away."

David Jefferds, cofounder of CyberElves, a Web development company with about forty employees, said he understood the pressure to partner up. "Since we're a small- to medium-sized company, we don't have every skill set, like Web hosting," he said. "And we could probably target that by partnering with firms, getting expertise, and then making the buy-versus-build decision."

But an alliance "isn't always necessarily a perfect fit, because you're still referring your client to someone else," Jefferds said. "So you're taking a risk with a client that you're really not compensated for," he added.

Ernst said that managing alliances was critical, "because the outcome of your business depends increasingly on how you do that." Still, he said, most companies have "mixed results with their alliances and are struggling to be proactive, amidst a huge deal flow."

Rather than have a one- or two-person business development staff overseeing partnership programs, Ernst said companies should "invest more heavily in building the business development staff to track the performance of each alliance, and link those performance metrics to the corporation's overall performance metrics." But, he said, fewer than one in four are doing such things.

Of course, managing alliances is sometimes a strange science, particularly given the array of relationships that can result from an alliance network. Conn, of Ticketmaster Online, pointed out that among his company's alliances, two were with competitors, Yahoo and the *Denver Post*. "In the old economy, the question was, 'Compete or buy?'" he said. "Now, anything goes."

As for how to manage the boundaries of his own company and the dozen or so companies he has invested in, Conn said he applied Coase's theory about transaction costs to a few other truths of the modern economy. "Now that workers are the principal source of a company's cost, and they're all shareholders, there's a real advantage of having people see the value of their work on a daily basis," he said. "So where that's true, there's an advantage to having a smaller operation."

To maintain that spirit, he said, "it often makes sense to have alliances and partnerships, rather than buy and merge."

For his part, Coase predicts that understanding transaction costs in the new economy will bring people back to the ideas of the economist Adam Smith. "It enables you to have more specialization and greater production, because you're more efficient," he said in a telephone interview from his home in Chicago. "You'll get more small firms as a result, but large firms will also get larger, because they can concentrate on core activities and contract out what they can't do well."

For all the attention his theory is getting in the dot-com context, Coase said he was not paying much attention to e-commerce. "So much is wrong with economics that I'm trying to correct some other things now," he said. "And one doesn't need to study the actuarial tables to know there isn't a lot of time for that."

Bob Tedeschi
October 2, 2000

In November 2000, Ticketmaster Online/citySearch changed its boundaries, agreeing to buy the Ticketmaster Corporation, its former parent.

4

REDRAWING THE BORDERS

Managing Globally

I find the biggest gap has been between what I can actually
accomplish here versus what I was used to accomplishing in the
States with the same or fewer resources.
—Howard Holley, general manager,
Xerox (China) Ltd., September 20, 2000

Remember when going global was the latest fashion in corporate boardrooms, back before e-commerce and e-strategy and e-enabling and all those
other e's overwhelmed management discussions a half-decade ago or so?

Well, guess what: international vision seems to be just as much a key to
business success in the twenty-first century as the Internet. While the Net
may eventually fundamentally change the way consumers buy many of
their goods, it won't necessarily prod people into buying more goods. Few
families will buy a third car, for example, or double their milk consumption, just because it's easier to order those products on the Web.

For established companies looking for gaudy increases in revenue, new
markets are necessary, and as you will see in this chapter, an Internet presence doesn't automatically give you a global base. How, then, can a company sell its wares overseas?

There are no easy answers.

The Ford Motor Company, for instance, is often held up as a model of
how to establish an overseas partnership, particularly in an industry that
has often flubbed the task. Over the last two decades, Ford slowly increased
its investment in the Mazda Motor Corporation. Finally, in 1996, it took
over the Japanese company, and since then has earned high praise for the
way it handled the inevitable tensions of a cross-border merger.

But Ford fell short on the measurement that business people tend to like the most: the bottom line. The company barely turned a profit on Mazda and didn't appear to be on the verge of reaping a windfall either. Instead, it focused on the long haul, shunning cost-cutting moves that could create dissension in the ranks. While the approach might seem painfully cautious in an age enamored of Internet speed, it does have the advantage of being farsighted.

And it is farsightedness and the assiduous planning that goes with it that unlock the door to the global economy. The right foreign partners must be found; a new set of laws, accounting practices and ways of doing business must be mastered; and American managers must be uprooted and sent overseas to face unfamiliar challenges. There are sensible strategies to confront such challenges, as you will read in the coming pages.

The best advice, though, may come from Nigel Brackenbury, the head of Ford's operation in Moscow, a particularly hard market to crack: Plan ahead and then improvise. "When will the crisis end?" he asked in 1999, speaking of the unpredictability of doing business in a country that is still lurching clumsily from a centrally planned economy to an open market. "It won't," was his terse reply to his own question. "It's the challenge for all of us in Russia to put together strategies to promote growth in the conditions we have."

CASE 1

Slow Returns

A candid version of the advice that the Ford Motor Company might offer its competitor, Renault S.A., on making an investment in a Japanese car company would probably be something like this: Get ready for a long, hard trek, because the payoff won't come quickly.

Ford's twenty-year, $624 million odyssey with a Japanese car maker, the Mazda Motor Corporation, has so far produced a lot of headaches. But since Renault has already plunked down $5.4 billion to buy a 36.8 percent stake in the sputtering Nissan Motor Company, Japan's second-largest automaker, avoiding the potential potholes is no longer an option.

So what lessons has Ford learned that might be useful to Renault? Grasp authority and hang onto it for dear life. Expect nasty surprises. Hand responsibility for a turnaround to your partner and its employees. Respect the sacred cows, but don't kowtow to them.

And read the life story of Mother Teresa, for hers is the sort of tenacity and forbearance that you will need.

These principles have led to what industry executives regard as the beginning of a turnaround at Mazda's headquarters and sprawling factories in Hiroshima. The company has gained market share in Japan despite slipping sales and an extremely weak domestic car market; in the fiscal year ended March 31, 1999, it posted its first overall profit, including the performance of subsidiaries, in six years. Operating profits doubled, and, thanks to a more than $2 billion reduction in costs, the break-even point for Mazda alone, exclusive of subsidiaries, has plummeted almost 40 percent.

All of this has been accomplished without the cultural clashes that many people expected when Ford took control of Mazda in 1996 after seventeen years as a major stockholder. After all, international auto mergers have a history of ending badly, with the two best-known examples involving Renault: the managerial chaos at the American Motors Corporation, which Renault controlled through most of the 1980s and sold to Chrysler in 1987, and Renault's failed merger with Volvo of Sweden in 1993.

Not surprisingly, Renault and Nissan executives have been trying to understand why Ford and Mazda have gotten along so much better. "That relationship between Ford and Mazda is very good, and that is one example of two cultures working," Yoshikazu Hanawa, the chief executive of Nissan, said in an interview.

Indeed, it is clear that the French are trying to follow Ford's blueprint. Ford increased its stake in Mazda in 1996 by giving it cash for new shares, and Mazda spent the cash to reduce debt, bankroll vehicle-development programs and meet other urgent financial needs. Now Nissan has issued new shares to Renault and has plans for similar kinds of spending.

Also following Ford's lead, Renault is trying to combine its product line-ups with its Japanese partner's to eliminate duplication, but without sending lots of managers to Japan. "It is not about merging corporate structures; it is about working together to develop and sell cars, which is not quite the same thing," said Louis Schweitzer, chairman of Renault.

Still, the rapport between Ford and Mazda obscures an awkward fact that can only trouble Renault's shareholders: Ford has made little money on its Japanese investment and is unlikely to make much anytime soon. Rather, Ford has behaved to some extent as an indulgent sugar daddy, willing to bail out its Japanese partner and providing gentle nudges rather than risking blunt action that might upset managers at Mazda's headquarters.

Ford, eight times the size of Mazda, is the world's second-largest company in sales, after General Motors, so it can afford to make generously financed, long-term bets on the Japanese market. Renault does not have that luxury. It is slightly smaller than Nissan in sales and less than one-third the size of Ford. Nissan's problems are bigger than Mazda's ever were, mainly because Nissan has continued to bleed financially as the Japanese auto market has crumbled since 1996, while Ford has taken some steps to stanch Mazda's losses.

Nonetheless, Schweitzer, delighted at the scope of his deal, declared soon after the ink was dry in March 1999 that it would offer a "shortcut to the world growth status we were looking for." If Ford's experience is any guide, however, the road ahead of Renault may be more of a meandering detour.

Grab the Wheel

For a long time, Ford's investment in Mazda, starting in 1979 with the purchase of a 25 percent stake for $140 million, amounted to little more than an expensive visitor's pass for Detroit engineers and managers to tour Japanese factories. One of Ford's goals was to figure out why Japanese automakers seemed able to build more reliable and affordable cars than American automakers, and it did pick up valuable tips on quality and efficiency. But it had little success in influencing Mazda's overall strategy—failing, for example, to persuade Mazda not to produce cars that competed directly with Ford models.

Through the first seventeen years of the partnership, in fact, Mazda executives largely ignored their American partners. Indeed, in the early 1990s, Mazda went on a panicked spending spree, building a modern factory for the equivalent of several hundred million dollars and opening three new sales divisions while the Japanese economy tumbled into its worst recession since World War II.

Senior Mazda executives appointed by Ford, meanwhile, were not even invited to key meetings and did not always receive full information about Mazda's activities, said Henry D. G. Wallace, a career Ford executive who served as Mazda's executive vice president in the mid-1990s.

The situation changed in 1996, when Ford spent $484 million to raise its holdings to 33.4 percent after Mazda found itself losing money and struggling to meet its debt payments. By itself, such a stake usually does not confer control in Japan. But Ford imposed a crucial condition on its investment: that it have the right to appoint Mazda's president.

Wallace got the job, becoming the first foreigner to oversee a Japanese automaker. And he was no figurehead. At Mazda, as in most large Japanese companies, whoever is president is virtually an absolute monarch; his wishes rarely go unfulfilled, no matter how unreasonable, unprofitable or ill-conceived. No longer, Wallace said, was he outside the loop. He was the loop.

Ford also had a powerful ally in Sumitomo bank, Mazda's main lender.

Sumitomo and Ford had a close, long-standing relationship; it was Sumitomo officials, for example, not Mazda executives, who convinced Ford to make its initial investment in Mazda, and it was Sumitomo officials who put Ford on a white horse to rescue Mazda in 1996.

"What Ford wanted to see was that the relationship with Mazda would go smoothly, and when it was necessary, we did talk to Mazda to insure its cooperation," said Sotoo Tatsumi, the retired Sumitomo chairman who first approached Ford in the early 1970s, when he was a general manager. "Until a few years ago, not all the people at Mazda welcomed Ford."

The former Ford managers who are now Mazda executives consider the Sumitomo relationship crucial to their success. "It's not just Ford and Mazda at work here," James E. Miller, Wallace's successor as Mazda's president, often says. "It's Ford, Mazda and Sumitomo."

Though Renault's 36.8 percent stake in Nissan is slightly larger than Ford's holdings in Mazda, Renault does not appear likely to wield as much control. Renault installed Carlos Ghosn, one of its best executives, at Nissan in the summer of 1999, but as the chief operating officer, and while Nissan's executive vice presidents will report to him, he will report to Hanawa.

Confront the Unexpected

Ask top American or European auto executives about their Japanese rivals these days, and they are likely to repeat dark rumors about how much debt the Japanese companies have—and how much of it lurks in hidden business partnerships.

The extent of Nissan's liabilities off the balance sheet apparently had a lot to do with a decision by DaimlerChrysler AG not to invest in the company. But Renault says it has not been scared by what it has found in poring over Nissan's books.

There are many stories in the auto industry about how much debt Ford might have discovered at Mazda after taking control, mostly at dealerships that were owned by Mazda. Kaoru Kurata, an auto analyst at Goldman Sachs (Japan) Ltd., estimates that Mazda's dealership-related debts may be as high as $3.66 billion.

Ford executives say their full year of research before taking control adequately documented these debts. But Gary K. Hexter, a Ford manager who is now Mazda's chief financial officer, acknowledged that there had been some surprises elsewhere. "Yes, we've found some liabilities that hadn't been adequately identified, both at Mazda and at the subsidiary companies," he said. "It's inevitable."

William C. Ford Jr., chairman of Ford Motor, said there had not been any major shocks. "We have a very firm idea of where Mazda is," he added.

To prevent any future shocks, however, Hexter has the thankless task of trying to bring order to Mazda's books, pulling together figures on roughly 180 affiliates and subsidiaries. He has established borrowing limits; he also requires preapproval of major new spending and reviews new business proposals.

"We have made a lot of progress, but it has been slower in the domestic subsidiaries and dealerships," he said. "There's such a huge range of businesses, which makes it difficult to manage them centrally."

Set Goals That Stick

Ford executives have long believed that there is nothing like tangible success to help win friends and allies. So the Ford managers dispatched to Mazda have made a practice of setting all sorts of targets and then making it clear that they expect them to be met.

That is a big change for Mazda, said Kei Kado, a director in charge of product development planning and international business planning. "Most Japanese workers would feel that a target is a sort of challenge," Kado said. "But the people from Ford regard it as a commitment—and in Japan, if you don't meet your commitments, you put a knife in your stomach."

One of his tasks was to achieve a 40 percent reduction in the variable costs of car production—the expenses left after subtracting things like profit margins, fixed costs, advertising and the price of logistics from the price of a car. He accomplished that, and now Miller is asking him to save 30 percent to 40 percent more.

Mazda's dealers and directors were shocked when he began pushing a plan that consolidated back-office dealership operations regionally, eliminated unprofitable shops and pared the number of dealer chains from five to three. All of Mazda's Japanese directors opposed the plan, but Miller persisted. Then the results came in. "Our monthly expenses went down by nearly one hundred million yen," exclaimed Yoichi Suzuki, president of the consolidated dealership operation in Saitama prefecture, still somewhat in awe of the results.

"Their approach is brilliant in terms of business," Suzuki said of the Ford officials. "They are energetic, speedy and clear about what they want. The Japanese style is more ambiguous, dependent on mood and human relationships."

By now, though, Mazda's Japanese managers have become accustomed to once-startling changes. Among other things, Mazda has eliminated the time-honored Japanese practice of shuffling unneeded white-collar workers off to affiliates for two-year job stints, rather than laying them off. Instead, it now dispatches them to its own assembly line, where staffing is relatively lean.

Be Sensitive, but Show Spine

In the United States, Ford has been criticized for not moving faster at Mazda to reduce capacity, cut jobs and use other tools favored by American companies overhauling their operations. In Japan, however, it has been praised for the same cautious approach. "I did not give them any specific advice," Sumitomo's Tatsumi said, "but I knew Ford understood it would need a soft touch."

Although Mazda has eliminated about six thousand jobs, it has winnowed its ranks through attrition, early retirement and leaner hiring practices, softening the effects on the Hiroshima area, where the company is crucial to the economy.

But Ford's genius has been in differentiating the truly sacred cows from the merely privileged ones. Consider taxicabs. In 1995, Mazda was producing cars for sale to taxicab companies, a business dominated by Toyota and Nissan, and it wasn't making money on the operation. Wallace's suggestion that Mazda exit the cab business met with protest from Japanese executives. But the cries were quickly silenced when he asked whether they wanted to be riding in Mazda taxis after the company went bankrupt.

At the insistence of managers sent from Ford, Mazda also slowed research into rotary engines, a product for which the company was famous but which had limited usefulness. "That was painful, because a lot of people felt it was the heart and soul of the company," said Wallace, now group vice president for Asia-Pacific operations and affiliations at Ford's headquarters in Dearborn, Michigan.

To soften this sort of pain, Ford's executives have tried to adopt local customs whenever possible. Miller has stunned his Japanese colleagues with his whole-hearted embrace of the after-hours carousing that is an integral part of Japanese business. His stamina in keeping up with the parties that migrate from restaurant to bar to bar has astonished Mazda employees. And like Japanese executives, Miller often takes to the public-address system to rally the troops, reading haltingly in Japanese to make announcements, issue exhortations and pay compliments for jobs well done.

His cosmopolitan ways reflect one of Ford's biggest assets at Mazda—its unusually large corps of globe-trotting executives. Miller is an American, but his curriculum vitae reads like that of the most seasoned international executive: president of Ford New Zealand from 1989 to 1993; head of

Eastern Europe and exports at Ford Europe to 1994; president of Ford's South African subsidiary until 1997, when he joined Mazda.

Four of the six group vice presidents at Ford grew up outside the United States, including Wallace, a Scot. So did Jacques Nasser, the new chief executive and president, who was raised in Lebanon and Australia and speaks fluent Arabic, French, Spanish and Portuguese, in addition to English.

Ghosn, the top Renault executive going to Nissan, was born in Brazil, and the company has long had a large and successful business in South America. But Renault's leaders are clearly worried that they may be short of top managers with international experience. "Probably we would look outwards for a few new talents at Renault," said Schweitzer, the chairman.

Get Ready to Wait

While it appears that Ford has pulled off at least the beginnings of a turnaround at Mazda, the true benefits of its investment remain to be seen. "While we've climbed mountains," Miller said, "there are higher mountains in the range to climb."

The first synergies will not appear until after 2000, when the two companies are expected to begin producing sport utility vehicles with common suspensions, engines, transmissions and other components.

In the meantime, its Mazda stake gives Ford a foothold in the Japanese market, which can only prove valuable whenever car sales rebound there. Ford officials hope to sell Mazdas in other Asian markets, as well.

With these benefits hard to measure in dollars and cents, it is difficult to make a case for the wisdom of Ford's investment. The company got a bargain in 1979 by securing a quarter interest in Mazda for the equivalent of $318 million in today's dollars; that is a pittance compared with the $6.5 billion that Ford paid in March for Volvo's car-making operations, a smaller but more consistently profitable business than Mazda. And Ford has also collected $100 million in dividends from Mazda over the years.

Yet if Ford had invested the money it sank into Mazda in 1979 in its own stock instead, the shares would have been worth $8.4 billion in mid-1999, a 6,000 percent return. And for $8.4 billion, Ford could buy controlling stakes in several Mazda-sized companies today.

Still, many auto executives are betting that the industry will eventually consolidate into five or six big companies. Each of these leviathans will need sizable operations in Japan. And given the impossibility of starting from scratch there, American and European automakers are going to be in business with the Japanese one way or another.

By that reasoning, Ford's years of losses at Mazda might someday not seem like such a waste of money. And Renault, in taking an even bigger gamble than Ford, can only hope to have as much success.

Schweitzer, conscious of his company's failures in the past, said he is determined to form a close partnership with Nissan. His Japanese partner may not be a beauty now, but he nonetheless uses the language of love to describe his plans for the courtship.

"To build a good relationship," he said, "you should not look at each other but do things together and look in the same direction."

Stephanie Strom and Keith Bradsher
May 23, 1999

Nissan prospered in 2000, partly by cutting costs and partly by introducing attractive models that were designed before the deal with Renault. Sales at Mazda faltered, and the company was pursuing deeper cost cuts, following Nissan's example. James Miller was replaced as president of Mazda by Mark Fields, the youngest man ever appointed to head a major Japanese corporation.

CASE 2

New Ground Rules

The words came quietly, spoken without a hint of threats or gloating: "Klaus, you're going to lose."

According to people present, Klaus Esser, the chief executive of Mannesmann AG, stared coldly ahead of him, not looking at or even acknowledging hearing Chris Gent, the chief executive of Vodafone AirTouch PLC.

For three months, Esser had been fighting off Gent's $180 billion hostile takeover bid for Mannesmann—the biggest attempted corporate takeover in history. The outcome of the battle would determine which company would dominate Europe's market for wireless telephones.

Then, meeting on a Sunday morning in January 2000 at the Hyatt Regency Hotel at Charles de Gaulle Airport in Paris, Gent gently dropped a bombshell: Without discussing specifics, he hinted that he had wooed away Esser's longtime partner in France, Vivendi SA.

Until a day before, Esser had been furiously trying to negotiate his own full merger with Vivendi, hoping to stave off Vodafone. But he knew it was a long shot, and he got a call late the previous evening from Vivendi's chairman, Jean-Marie Messier, with the bad news: Vivendi's board had decided against the merger.

Esser suspected that Gent had outmaneuvered him, but it was not until Sunday afternoon, when Vodafone and Vivendi held a news conference in Paris, that he learned how. Gent offered to sell Vivendi part of Mannesmann's stake in Cegetel, the holding company that owns France's second-largest wireless network. If Vodafone conquered Mannesmann, Messier would then take control of Cegetel and form a venture with Vodafone offering Internet services across Europe.

For Esser, it was a devastating betrayal by his partner—and friend—Messier. At an emergency meeting that Mannesmann convened that evening, one of Esser's lieutenants said of Vivendi, "They stabbed us in the back and our backs are now against the wall," according to a participant in the meeting.

By the following Thursday, as it became clear that most Mannesmann shareholders intended to sell their stock to Vodafone, Esser capitulated and agreed to a peaceful deal.

It was the first time that Germany had seen a hostile takeover of a German company, inside or outside the country's borders. It is also a watershed for European history, a deal certain to prompt a new wave of cross-border mergers and freewheeling Anglo-American capitalism.

Interviews with executives on both sides tell the story of a takeover fight that reached a level of Machiavellian intrigue rivaling anything by American corporate raiders in the 1980s.

After Vodafone announced its takeover plan in November 1999, Mannesmann, based in Düsseldorf, set up a sprawling war room on the second floor of a U-shaped building that houses its Eurokom telecommunications subsidiary. Both companies employed armies of Wall Street investment banks: Vodafone hired Goldman Sachs and Warburg Dillion Read; Mannesmann used Morgan Stanley Dean Witter, Merrill Lynch, J. P. Morgan and Deutsche Bank.

Mannesmann bankers, summoned from London, lived for three months at the Steigenberger Park Hotel in Düsseldorf, trying to return home for weekends by taking the last British Airways plane out of town each Friday night—a flight they came to call the Advisers Express.

As a practical matter, the battle took place on two very different fronts. The first was what the public saw: a loud and boisterous publicity campaign by both sides to win the loyalty of Mannesmann shareholders. That battle entailed almost continual barnstorming campaigns to court institutional investors in Germany, London and New York. It also entailed a massive advertising and public relations effort by both sides.

But the more important battle was outside the public eye. That, according to people involved, was the struggle to win corporate allies—most crucially, Messier and Vivendi.

Esser and Messier phoned and faxed each other frequently in early January 2000. And their executives held lengthy "due diligence" meetings at Vivendi offices in Paris, examining the feasibility of a merger.

But Messier, in the best tradition of Europe's old balance-of-power politics, decided to play the two combatants against each other and hold out for the best possible deal.

Not long after Esser had begun intensive talks with Vivendi, Messier called Gent of Vodafone to see what kind of a deal he might want to consider. Throughout the month, people involved say, Messier continued to toy with both companies and give each the impression that a deal was possible.

The three-way struggle smacked of the old Europe, when industries were still divided along national boundaries and when cross-border deals were so politically sensitive that companies tended to limit themselves to delicate alliances rather than outright acquisitions.

Yet, those boundaries had largely crumbled by the time Vodafone began its hostile bid for Mannesmann. By then, it was clear one of them would become Europe's preeminent wireless company—an enviable position, given the skyrocketing use of mobile phones and Europe's rapid embrace of high-speed wireless data technologies.

Vodafone, which began in 1985 and owns Britain's biggest mobile telephone network, had minority stakes across Europe and in many other countries around the world. Mannesmann, by contrast, was focused entirely on Europe. But it had controlling stakes in its three biggest markets, Germany, Italy and Britain.

For both sides, Messier and Vivendi represented crucial missing pieces: that French wireless stake. Vivendi also had other attractive holdings in Canal Plus SA, Europe's biggest pay-television company; Havas SA, the media and publishing company; and B Sky B, the British satellite broadcaster.

By January 2000, Esser knew he needed something dramatic to repel Vodafone's bid. Mannesmann's stock had soared from 158 euros a share in October 1999 to nearly 300 euros, or roughly $295—a clear sign that many investors viewed the Vodafone deal as desirable.

Esser tended in public to come off as dull and humorless, in comparison with the garrulous Gent. Reaching for jokes as he presented Mannesmann's formal defense on January 14, Esser belittled Vodafone's holdings in places like Fiji and Uganda. The market was not amused: Mannesmann stock jumped 10 percent that day, a further sign that Vodafone's offer was favored.

Gent spent countless hours on the phone and in person with his team of advisers, which was led by Scott Mead, cohead of Goldman Sach's global communications, media and entertainment group—the banker who had previously negotiated Vodafone's acquisition of AirTouch Communications and its alliance with Bell Atlantic.

Esser's confidants included Kurt Kinzius, the Mannesmann board member responsible for European activities; Dietrich Becker, a top banker at Morgan Stanley who had worked closely with Esser for years; and Colin Roy and Daniel Dickinson of Merrill Lynch. But according to some members of the circle, Esser remained opaque—seeming not to recognize the rising tide in favor of Vodafone and unwilling to acknowledge that he might actually lose.

Behind the scenes, people on both sides say, Esser held more frequent meetings and maintained telephone contacts with Gent—conversations in which Esser spurned offers to negotiate a key job for himself in the combined company if Vodafone prevailed.

In the end, it was the Vivendi agreement that forced Klaus to acknowledge the unthinkable.

"Obviously, the Vivendi deal was insurance against Mannesmann doing a deal," a Vodafone executive said. "It wasn't the greatest deal in the world, but it wasn't bad."

Certainly as a tool in persuading shareholders, it was sensational. So, from Vodafone's standpoint, were Messier's remarks at the news conference in Paris announcing the deal, when he made clear he thought Vodafone would win control of Mannesmann.

The next day, advisers to both companies urged Esser and Gent to sit down and talk again, this time alone. A day later, the two men met in a secluded conference room in the Steigenberger. The meeting lasted a little more than an hour, and both exectives came away feeling more amenable to merging, though they still differed strongly on price and management issues.

Gent was set to do a German TV interview the next day, either from London or Düsseldorf. Mannesmann advisers convinced him to come to Düsseldorf for the interview and to meet with Esser.

At a meeting on the twenty-first floor of Mannesmann's headquarters that night, Gent met with Esser and Canning Fok—the managing director of Hutchison Whampoa, the Hong Kong company that holds a 10 percent stake in Mannesmann—who leaned on Esser to do a deal.

People involved in the meeting described it as grim, but by about 1:30 A.M., Esser and Gent had hammered out a basic deal. For months, Esser had insisted that Mannesmann shareholders would need a stake larger than 50 percent of the new company. But he now settled for 49.5 percent, giving Vodafone slim control.

As Gent flew back to London on his private jet before dawn, advisers continued drafting the terms of the deal that would be submitted to Mannesmann's supervisory board.

The Mannesmann board, whose members include Jurgen Schrempp, chairman of DaimlerChrysler AG, met that afternoon at Mannesmann headquarters, as advisers from both sides huddled nearby. Gent, who had flown back to Düsseldorf, was also on hand.

After three months of conflict and a night without sleep, both camps had short tempers and high suspicions. According to an investment banker close to Mannesmann, the supervisory board ended its meeting after a board member overheard a hallway conversation in which a Mannesmann banker said that a Vodafone adviser wanted the Mannesmann board to disband immediately.

People close to Vodafone insist they never made a formal demand like that. Whatever the case, the board meeting ended and was not reconvened that night.

The next few hours were chaos. Countless reporters and television teams camped outside Mannesmann offices, all of them understanding that a handshake deal had been reached the night before.

Without the supervisory board, Esser still managed to complete an agreement in principle that he planned to present to the board and was confident they would accept. On the twenty-first floor, clapping erupted as both executives signed and shook hands on the deal.

Around 10:15 P.M., the two executives then walked through an underground tunnel to an adjacent building to make the announcement, avoiding direct contact with about one hundred reporters who had camped out in Mannesmann's lobby.

After the news conference, Gent and Esser quickly left the building. Gent headed to the airport with his advisers to return to London on the company jet. Haggard yet victorious, they popped a bottle of champagne on the flight back. A car supplied by Vodafone dropped Esser at home.

Edmund L. Andrews and Andrew Ross Sorkin
February 7, 2000

By January 2001, the Vodafone takeover of Mannesmann was complete. Klaus Esser, the former chief executive of Mannesmann, resigned as expected and joined a venture capital firm. He received more than $30 million in severance payments—not unusual in the United States, but quite shocking to Germans. Despite enormous anxiety in telecom markets about the massive costs of building so-called third-generation wireless networks, Vodafone had weathered fairly well.

CASE 3

The Dauntingly Native Global Village

Falling stock prices are not the only numbers giving e-commerce executives heartburn these days. Equally unsettling to some Internet merchants is the flood of statistics suggesting that to keep their businesses growing, they have to look outside the United States.

A report released in May 2000 by IDC, an Internet research firm, predicts that two-thirds of all e-commerce spending will take place outside the country by 2003. In that year, IDC says, consumer spending on Web sites in the United States will reach $119 billion, but overseas sites will garner $209 billion of business.

And yet, with the investment community demanding that Web merchants find a speedier path to profitability, the merchants can hardly justify the expenses associated with rolling out sites aimed at other nations.

Those expenses can be substantial. According to Eric Schmitt, an analyst with the Forrester Research consulting firm, retailers can spend "a couple million dollars in the first year of international efforts."

"And this is a treadmill," he said. "You don't just build the Spanish version and walk away. It's a beast that needs to be fed."

In May 2000, Boo.com, a British fashion e-tailer, went out of business a mere six months after it started up its Web site. The company had quickly become insolvent—in large part because of the strain of trying to start up in eighteen different countries simultaneously.

Barry Parr, author of the IDC report, said that even when e-commerce companies have the money to devote to overseas expansion, "these markets can be very difficult to address." In addition to the obvious language hurdles, he said e-tailers faced regulatory challenges with import and export rules, taxation and technology issues, and wrinkles in each country's customer service and fulfillment approaches.

Industry executives said that any of these items could, if mishandled, torpedo a company's international efforts. But fulfillment issues are particularly problematic. When the e-commerce trend took off in 1998, some analysts predicted that Web merchants would overturn traditional retailing, which tended to be based on customers who shop within ten miles of their homes.

Indeed, that revolutionary sentiment partly fueled investors' enthusiasm for companies like Amazon and CDNow, which quickly found customers throughout the world who were willing to shop on their sites. But since 1999, consumers and businesses have acknowledged that many customers prefer to do business with retailers that can serve them both on the Web and in a local store if they want to return items.

At the very least, analysts said, consumers want to shop with an Internet retailer that can handle customer service problems and returns from the same continent.

For Web merchants with global aspirations, that frequently means building and staffing customer service centers on different continents—as Amazon did when it set up a phone center in the Netherlands in 2000—as well as working with local distributors or manufacturers.

Despite such a daunting list of investment and cultural challenges, Parr of IDC said globalization plans were imperative for Internet retailers.

"I tell companies that before they leap into wireless initiatives, they should figure out their international strategy. It has to be part of the plan."

In devising that strategy, analysts say one crucial decision is how a company manages its foreign Web sites. On one hand, if a company chooses to manage the global operations from the United States, its foreign sites are far more prone to make linguistic and merchandising mistakes—for instance, selling goods that might be offensive in certain cultures, or offering product instructions that are delivered with the wrong tone.

"In Japan, you wouldn't say 'Don't turn the left knob,' because that's too direct," said Charles Baxter, chief executive of eTranslate, a consulting company. "You'd say something like 'It would be much better to turn the right knob.'"

Such mistakes are less likely if companies hire a team in each foreign market to handle the Web site, analysts said. But that, too, can lead to problems for companies trying to convey a consistent brand message.

"Customers can spot inconsistencies," Forrester's Schmitt said. "If you have to deal in multiple countries, you don't want ten sites with a different look and feel at every one, and companies don't want to have ten different backend systems."

One of the earliest successes in e-commerce globalization was Dell Computer, which began selling on the Web in 1996 and now has sites aimed at eighty-five different countries and territories. According to Frank Muehleman, senior vice president of Dell's worldwide division, the company uses a decentralized approach with its international sites.

Dell created a common technology platform for each of its global sites, including a template for ordering and product information, which ensures a consistent user experience across the sites. In addition several hundred specialists give advice and training to the local managers. "Then we let the local team handle the rollout," Muehleman said.

Just as important, Muehleman said, Dell built manufacturing plants in each of the regions it serves, including Brazil, Ireland, China and Malaysia. And because the company employs local customer service staff, he said, "every time a customer picks up the phone, they're dealing with someone local."

The Internet companies that have been the most active on the global front are the so-called portals, like Yahoo, Altavista and Lycos. In May 2000, Lycos agreed to be acquired by Terra Networks, the Internet arm of the Spanish telecommunications company Telefónica de España. The portals' expansion into other nations, while not easy, has been a relative snap compared with the travails of companies that must actually move goods across borders.

And even e-commerce companies that do not sell goods on the Web, like financial firms, have encountered plenty of obstacles in other countries. When the online broker Schwab.com started a site for clients in Britain in 1998, for instance, many customers there balked at online trading because they were accustomed to exchanging paper stock certificates in each transaction. Chiefly because Schwab.com refused to give paper certificates to its online customers, the site generated just fifteen thousand new accounts between June 1998 and June 1999, according to Russ Shaw, senior vice president of marketing for Charles Schwab Europe.

The site then offered thirty days of commission-free trading to new customers in the summer of 1999, and generated nearly thirty thousand new customers in about two months. For both the customers and Schwab, Shaw said, "it's been an education process."

Analysts say that most e-commerce companies are reluctant to begin that process, given the already steep learning curve they have encountered in the domestic market. But some alternatives may emerge.

American e-tailers, for example, could form partnerships with retailers in other nations that want e-commerce sites of their own but lack the expertise to build them. Parr, the IDC analyst, said that under such an approach, an American e-tailer could lend its technology, and perhaps its name, to a foreign counterpart, which in turn would offer its local distribution and customer service systems and expertise. The companies would then share the revenues.

Martin McClanan, chief executive of Red Envelope, a gift site, said he had been approached several times with similar offers, but so far he had demurred. "Our plan is to bring this business to scale in the U.S. first," he said. "Then, when we can dedicate a twenty-person team to another country, we'll do that." The company might consider global expansion plans after the 2000 holiday season, he added.

"It's so easy to want to boil the ocean and do everything," he said. "But in retail it's all about execution. And getting this business to profitability is still first and foremost."

Bob Tedeschi
May 22, 2000

CASE 4

Emerging Capitalism

Caterpillar had just cleared away a patch of spindly trees in Tosno, Russia, a town outside St. Petersburg, and begun building a new $50 million factory when, one day in August 1998, the Russian financial system collapsed.

Overnight, the Russian government devalued its currency and simultaneously defaulted on $40 billion in domestic debt. Prices rose by two-thirds over the following seven months, and the spending power of ordinary Russians decreased 40 percent. The ruble, worth around fifteen cents before the crisis, fell to about four cents. Many smaller companies, such as those Caterpillar had envisioned as customers for its Russian-made construction equipment, were ruined.

"We asked ourselves some hard questions," said Stu Levenick, general director of Caterpillar Overseas in Moscow, "mainly about whether this was the right time to invest $50 million."

The economic collapse seemed to confirm the worst corporate fears about Russia: It is too unstable to operate here. Companies such as Pizza Hut and Hershey's pulled out, and many that had considered entering Russia shelved their plans.

Caterpillar could have easily followed the conventional wisdom. Yet a number of Western multinationals—not just Caterpillar but Nestlé, Lucent Technologies and others—coped with the economic crisis by settling deeper into Russia rather than pulling out.

They were not blind to the problems, so they developed a variety of strategies to cope. Most started by picking areas where the local government now supports business, regardless of broader upheaval in Russia. This is one such area. In St. Petersburg and the surrounding region, six American projects were expected to bring in more than $500 million of direct foreign investment in between May 1999 and the end of 2000.

Caterpillar pushed ahead with its plant, and production there was expected to begin on schedule in December 1999. Up the highway from Tosno, the Wm. Wrigley Jr. Company opened a new factory in the winter of 1999, and Gillette was building one next door. Philip Morris was constructing a $330 million plant, and in the spring of 1999 International Paper paid an estimated $65 million to acquire controlling interest in a local paper mill.

At the same time, Ford Motor was in talks with the government to invest more than $150 million in an auto plant in the region surrounding what was once the city of Leningrad.

Beyond this region, still known by its old Leningrad name, Bayerische Motorwerken announced a joint venture in the far western Kaliningrad region. Lucent Technologies began to produce fiber optics in the Voronezh region of central Russia. And Nestlé planned to invest $30 million in six existing factories throughout the country.

Many of these companies had bucked the prevailing corporate trend before, coming to Russia in the mid-1990s while competitors hesitated. That experience has made them less skittish than they might have been then about the turmoil that can damage emerging-market economies. Attracted by Russia's enormous potential to consume and produce their goods, these corporations have made a long-term commitment regardless of short-term disruptions.

"When will the crisis end?" Nigel Brackenbury, general director of Ford's operation in Moscow, asked. "It won't. It's the challenge for all of us in Russia to put together strategies to promote growth in the conditions we have. It's not time to wait around for external circumstances to change and help us."

Indeed, while Western executives were relieved that Russia reached agreement in May 1999 on a $4.5 billion loan from the International Monetary Fund to avoid default on its existing debts to the international agency, they were paying much more attention to the action closer to the ground.

"From New York or Washington, Russia looks hopeless," said Scott

Blacklin, president of the American Chamber of Commerce in Moscow. "But you can have a successful business here and not at all be tied to reforms."

Even before the collapse, few foreign investors had the nerves for Russia. The government treats most businesses, domestic and foreign, equally poorly, burdening them with onerous taxes, hostile and corrupt bureaucracies and ever-changing regulations. Direct foreign investment in Russia totaled a paltry $2 billion in 1998, according to the American Chamber of Commerce in Moscow.

But the chamber expected direct investment in 1999 to at least stay at that level. One reason is that some places in Russia are easier to work in than others, and the willingness of certain regional and local authorities to cooperate with investors has been critical to keeping Western money here. The economic crisis has not made regions historically wary of foreigners any friendlier, but it has made fence sitters like the city of St. Petersburg more flexible.

"Before, the city's attitude was something like 'Kiss our ring, and maybe we'll do a deal with you,'" said James T. Hitch, managing partner at the St. Petersburg office of Baker & McKenzie, the law firm. "Now, it's like: 'You've decided to stay in Russia after the crisis? You're dedicated to us? Well, how can we work together?'"

The city understands that it faces competition for scarce investment from its neighbor, the Leningrad region. In 1997, the regional government developed a set of laws and tax breaks to attract investors. The region attracted about $290 million in foreign investment that year and the next and was expected to get another $350 million in 1999. "No crisis influences us," said Sergei Naryshkin, head of the region's committee on external economic relations. "We won't step back from our investment politics or from our commitments."

That attitude has seeped to the local level. Tosno, at a passing glance, could be any small Russian town. Old wooden shacks that have begun to list toward the swampy earth line its outskirts. The main road that cuts through the center of town is still called Lenin Prospekt, and one mild Saturday residents were out raking leaves in the parks and squares as they had during the many springs spent under Communism. Unemployment is widespread among the thirty thousand people of Tosno, and people pack the suburban trains to St. Petersburg to seek work there.

The town's young mayor and his staff are eager to draw foreign investment. As part of the Caterpillar deal, the town reduced the local portion of the profit tax. It helped win federal permission to cut the trees at the site. It worked with the local utility company to get Caterpillar the electrical power it will need, and it offered the Americans a forty-nine-year lease on the site, since private ownership of commercial land is still not allowed in Russia.

"What's most important to investors is the good will of the authorities," said the deputy mayor, Galina Karpova. "We're willing to help them solve their problems."

Many multinationals realize that Russia, stable or not, is ultimately too big a market to be ignored. In Russia, there's still great unmet demand for everything from chewing gum and beer to trucks and bulldozers. And when the ruble weakened badly, imports—paid for in dollars and other foreign currency—were suddenly out of reach for most Russians, who get their skimpy wages in rubles. That made local production look better.

"All the companies that were importing stopped," Hitch said. "By contrast, all the companies that were already producing here or in the process of doing so kept moving forward."

For those already here, the crisis forced them to work more effectively. Wrigley, like most makers of consumer goods, suffered a drop in sales of 20 percent to 30 percent. But the company gained market share from competitors in this period, it says, because it encouraged its sales force to work harder to get its products on store shelves to make up for a cut in advertising expenditures.

Another strategy will be to focus on the export market, as Caterpillar plans to do, until demand in Russia rises again.

That's not to say companies with direct investment have not suffered. Take United Technologies' Otis elevator business. Among the oldest Western businesses in St. Petersburg, Otis invested $20 million in building an elevator factory. The company also provides services for municipalities that still own most housing in Russia.

Cities in northwest Russia ran up debts to the company of 40 million rubles, which before the crisis was worth about $7 million. After August 17, 1998, when the ruble was devalued, that sum was worth $2 million.

"We lost five million dollars in one day," said Vladimir Marov, director of the Otis St. Petersburg plant. "The crisis hit us very hard. We've suffered over and over."

A man with deep laugh lines and the taut build of an aging bantamweight, Marov walks through the corridors of Otis's offices on the way to the factory floor. On one side of the corridor, people are working. The other half is empty, the beige tile etched with black circles from the wheels of office chairs that have been recently packed away. Otis has laid off about 10 percent of its St. Petersburg staff. In the fall of 1998, Otis St. Petersburg did not sell a single elevator, and the factory was idle for a month. It closed maintenance offices in a few cities and was struggling to get St. Petersburg to pay 23 million rubles in debt accrued before the crisis.

"No one had any experience with such a sudden fall, but we survived the best we could," Marov said. "The question came up among our leadership in the U.S. and Germany about whether we should continue. And we decided we should, because the potential is so big and things will calm down at some point."

That tempting potential and the vision, however elusive, of a stable Russia continue to draw automakers, despite a 60 percent drop in sales of foreign cars since the summer of 1998. Russians have typically bought about one million cars a year, only 10 percent of them foreign made.

In early April 1999, BMW announced the opening of a 50-million-mark ($27 million) joint venture in Kaliningrad to assemble cars and sport utility vehicles. General Motors is holding talks with Russia's biggest car company, Avto Vaz, to start a $200 million joint venture that would initially manufacture thirty-five thousand cars.

Ford has settled on the village of Vsevolozhsk, twenty miles northwest of St. Petersburg, for its new factory. The company already has an assembly plant in Belarus where workers put the final touches on Escorts and Transit vans that arrive nearly built. The Belarus plant can turn out six thousand vehicles a year, though in the six months after the economic collapse, it produced nothing. The Vsevolozhsk plant would have far larger capacity, starting at about twenty-five thousand cars a year with the possibility of expanding to one hundred thousand vehicles.

In 1998, the company looked closely at the entire project. It decided that to have the high sales it wanted in Russia, it had to manufacture locally. "Russia has significant future growth potential," Brackenbury of Ford said. "The question is, will there ever be a right time to come into Russia?" As far as Ford is concerned, now is as good a time as any.

Neela Banerjee
May 1, 1999

CASE 5

The Native Executive

At the height of the Asian financial crisis in 1998, Scott Fedje, an art director for a Fortune 500 apparel manufacturer, returned to his company's headquarters in the northwestern United States from a five-year stint in Hong Kong. Even though he got a promotion and a pay increase as a reward for his overseas performance, Fedje resigned a few months later to take a job with a design-consulting firm in San Francisco.

"I felt lost," said Fedje, who asked that his former employer not be identified. "Most of us who returned went from a position of high responsibility and a dynamic environment to a cubicle, a project and a whole month to make a single decision." He missed old colleagues who had moved on, he said, and he longed for the kind of cultural stimulation he had found in Asia. So when he was offered work in the Bay Area, he grabbed it, and now he heads the retail design division of the firm, Landor Associates.

Call it the exodus of the returned expatriates. Every year, thousands of executives like Fedje arrive home from foreign postings and bolt to greener pastures, often at a cost to their employers of $1 million or more that was invested in training and overseas expenses. Dr. J. Stewart Black, managing director of the Center for Global Assignments, a consulting firm based in San Diego that works with executives going and coming from abroad, said that two-thirds of the returning executives and their family members he had interviewed described repatriation as a more wrenching experience than the overseas postings themselves. "It's a staggering statistic and problematic for employers," he said.

Just as alarming for corporations is the defection rate of returning managers. Twenty-five percent leave within a year, double the proportion of departures by those who never go abroad, Black said. And the returned managers who leave typically go to the competition.

Black cited an extreme case of a company that over a two-year period lost every manager it had sent on international assignments within twelve months of their return—twenty-five people in all. The company "might just as well have written a check for fifty million dollars and tossed it to the winds," he said.

The biggest shock for managers fresh from foreign postings appears to be the change in their status from a big frog in a small pond to a small frog in a big one. Many also discover that the skills they acquired overseas, and the acquaintances they cultivated, are of little use to them now.

"It has left me depressed," said an executive at a large transportation company who came back to the United States at the end of 1999 after spending four years in Southeast Asia. The executive, who insisted on anonymity, added that he now felt like "just another cog in a bureaucratic wheel."

Family members can also go through reverse culture shock, compounding the pressure on the breadwinner. When her husband was sent back to the United States after two years in Tokyo for a small semiconductor company, Sylvia Dickinson of Menlo Park, California, felt out of sorts and concerned about her daughter's adjustment to American schools.

"People did not want to hear about our life abroad after two seconds," she said. "It's difficult to simply shut out a life-transforming experience like that. You don't just pick up where you left off either."

Her husband, Tom, worked on ad hoc projects until he was recruited away by Cirrus Logic, a competitor that she said now capitalizes on his international background. She has capitalized on it, too, starting Dickinson Consulting, a firm that counsels outbound and returning executives and their families. "Having been there and back, I can offer an empathetic ear," Dickinson said.

So, what do companies do to hold on to their talent? Robert Greenleaf, executive director at TMC, a consulting firm in Princeton, New Jersey, that specializes in preparing executives for overseas posts, says rule number one is to write down, in clear terms, what they expect the departing executives to achieve abroad and what they expect them to do when they come back.

Black cited companies like Monsanto that start thinking about next assignments for expatriates three to six months before they return. At Monsanto, two senior officials with international experience assess the skills that the overseas executive has gained on the tour of duty and review the job openings that are available. At the same time, the returning executive writes a report, assessing his skills and describing his career goals. The three then meet to decide his future.

Paul Kocourek, a senior partner at Booz, Allen & Hamilton, knows about repatriation. He went through it three times, after stints with the Peace Corps in Thailand in the 1970s, Bain & Company in Tokyo in the 1980s and Booz, Allen in Australia in the late 1980s and most of the 1990s.

His familiarity with the process enabled him to draw up a short list of hints for making a successful reentry. The returning expatriate, he said, should try flying home a number of times during the final stages of the overseas stay to cement relationships with people in the home office, meet with clients and discuss a future role in the company. And the executive should ensure that clients and projects are properly handed over to the overseas successor.

"Maintaining one's network and having a mentor or sponsor back at headquarters to keep tabs on you helps," Kocourek said.

Reentry can be especially wrenching if the home office has more or less forgotten about you. That is what Deborah Burks, a Chicago executive, said happened to her. Burks was dispatched to Hong Kong in 1998 to build a regional presence for the digital-media division of a Fortune 500 chemical company based on the West Coast. But despite what she said were significant inroads that she had made, the company decided to halt its expansion effort there.

"There was neither a contingency nor any accountability within the division or company," Burks said.

In 1999, she returned to Chicago, where she had been posted before—except that now she ended up in an office with little to do. She had sold her Chicago home, believing she would be away for an extended period, and had to shop for a place to stay. Her company told her of jobs available in a small town in Ohio, but she decided not to pursue them. In the end, she found a job as a director for new business development at R. R. Donnelley & Sons. She is not bitter, she said, and in fact believes that her international experience taught her invaluable skills in coping with changes in the corporate world.

"I would still do it over again but be more mentally prepared for the risk," she said.

As for employers, the best thing they can do to keep returning stars is to keep channels of communication open even long after an overseas assignment has been completed.

"If an executive is feeling unease, he should be able to speak up and have a nonthreatening forum to do so in," said Dennis Kaminsky, who spent two tours of duty in Japan for the plastics division of the General Electric Company.

"Coming home is always a wonderful feeling," Kaminsky said. "It's having the environment to express this and any other feelings that can make a world of difference."

Jobert E. Abueva
May 17, 2000

5

GETTING HITCHED

The Next Generation of Mergers and Acquisitions

> I'll never retire because I love this job. For me, the whole profession is a sport.
>
> —John H. Slade, ninety-two-year-old
> honorary chairman of the executive committee,
> Bear, Stearns & Company, May 31, 2000

Name just about any major industry, and chances are it recently witnessed the announcement of a once-unthinkable merger. Oil? Exxon and Mobil, two of the companies sundered from John D. Rockefeller's Standard Oil by trust-busting Roosevelt. Media? America Online, the bumbling Internet company of the mid-1990s, and Time Warner, Henry Luce's giant that ended up being swallowed. Cars? DaimlerBenz, the luxury brand that was once part of the German war machine, and Chrysler, the darling of minivan-loving middle America.

The mania of deals has not been restricted to the companies with names we all know, either. Over the last decade, the number of mergers each year has more than quadrupled, according to Mergerstat. Every year now, there are about eight thousand corporate combinations in the United States, and the number continues to grow.

As a result, making sure that an acquisition succeeds has become one of the most important tasks for many managers today. "For many companies," says Jim E. Fishbein, a consultant, "mergers have moved from occasional event to a routine, frequent part of doing business."

The process starts with financial executives who decide whether the numbers justify a deal. It then spreads to the lawyers and lobbyists who often must win an acquisition's approval from regulatory agencies—not only in Washington but also increasingly in Brussels and other faraway regions where the firms do business. Finally, the task falls to the employees left to sort out whose cheese is supposed to sit where, to borrow a phrase from a popular recent book.

Consider this chapter a primer on mergers, from their origins to their rarely smooth execution. Case studies, rather than theories, provide the best lessons. You will get an insider's view of corporate America's version of the dating game, played frantically by Frontier, Global Crossing, Qwest and U S West. You will travel to Washington to learn why the political landscape shifted in favor of big business—and where it still remains rocky. And you will visit some of the affected workplaces to see how some companies have tried to meld themselves.

This search for a deft management touch is as difficult as it is important. For though there is sometimes a surprising amount of common ground, there is often some unanticipated dissonance. Even when two companies do largely the same thing, they can have vastly different styles. And even when two groups of "latte-drinking nice guys" come together, they can find that stock options plans are harder to combine than coffee stations.

<u>CASE 1</u>

Expanding the Clientele

Nearly a century ago, the House of Morgan and its founder, J. Pierpont Morgan, preserved the American financial system in the midst of a widespread panic.

But despite the best efforts of the bank that bears J. P. Morgan's name, in recent years it could not preserve itself.

Over the last twenty years J. P. Morgan has undergone a remarkable renovation, infusing what had become a sleepy bank devoted simply to lending money to big governments and corporations with the pioneering spirit of the House of Morgan. Morgan was the first modern American commercial bank to break out of the restrictions imposed on banking in the 1930s during the Depression, becoming a contender on Wall Street by underwriting stock offerings and advising on gigantic mergers.

But as much as the company strained to reclaim its former glory, it was not able to find a comfortable position in the modern financial world. So Morgan put itself on the block, talking with a number of banks around the world before reaching a deal in September 2000 to be acquired by the Chase Manhattan Bank for about $31 billion.

In the end, analysts said, Morgan's downfall may be that it tried too hard to remain what its founder had built—a behind-the-scenes adviser to the richest and most powerful, with a driven but insular culture. It shied away from the wave of banking mergers so prevalent in recent years. And Morgan found it had become an anachronism in a financial world dominated by mass rather than class.

"Nobody like them is succeeding," said Alden Toevs, an executive vice president of the First Manhattan Consulting Group. "The companies they are competing with are just much bigger in terms of capital and product lines."

Morgan is not alone. Shortly before its deal with Chase, two other midsize Wall Street firms, Donaldson, Lufkin & Jenrette and PaineWebber, also agreed to be bought, both by huge diversified Swiss banks.

Paradoxically, J. P. Morgan is giving up its independence only a year after its biggest regulatory burden—the Glass-Steagall Act—was lifted. Passed in 1933, the law separated commercial and investment banking and forced the Morgan Stanley brokerage firm to be split from J. P. Morgan.

Through the 1970s, the Morgan bank was content to lend money to big governments and corporations and to manage the assets of the heirs to the fortunes of the turn-of-the-century robber barons and other wealthy individuals. But as its big corporate borrowers were able to raise money directly by issuing stocks and bonds, the company realized its traditional business was wasting away.

Given the choice of changing its clients or changing its products, declared its former chairman, Lewis Preston, in the 1980s, J. P. Morgan should offer its existing clients the ability to trade securities and agree to underwrite their financial offerings. This set in motion a twenty-year game of cat and mouse with Congress and the banking regulators as Morgan found more and more regulatory loopholes that allowed it to act more and more like a brokerage firm. Indeed, when Congress finally repealed Glass-Steagall in 1999, Morgan had already become much more like its old partner, Morgan Stanley, than a traditional commercial bank.

But repeal freed Morgan's competitors to go after its business, even as it accelerated the mergers among its rivals. Morgan executives, in the bank's exhaustively deliberate style, studied and stewed over myriad possible combinations, but never were willing to dilute what they saw as the company's unique culture and heritage.

"This was the last bank on Wall Street that wanted to surrender its independence, and in retrospect this proved to be a real handicap," said Ron Chernow, the author of *The House of Morgan,* the definitive history of the

bank. "The other commercial banks weren't hampered by a sense of tradition and were able to grow at greater speed."

Ten years ago, Chernow noted, Morgan had the highest stock market
value of any bank in the country. Now its value is one-tenth of the biggest,
Citigroup.

The financial world is increasingly dominated by two kinds of institutions.
On one side are investment banking powerhouses—Goldman Sachs, Morgan
Stanley Dean Witter, Merrill Lynch, perhaps Credit Suisse and Deutsche
Bank—that manage the raising of capital, brokering of mergers and trading
of anything with a price. Competition in this business is so intense that even
successful second-tier players are choosing to sell to larger rivals.

The second sort of giant that has evolved out of the commercial banks are
financial conglomerates that sell all manner of investments, loans, deposits
and insurance. The archetype of this company is now Citigroup, which incor-
porates Morgan's longtime rival Citibank, along with the Salomon Brothers
and Smith Barney brokerage firms and the Travelers Insurance company. And
the corporate ancestor of the entire conglomerate is the antithesis of everything Morgan: the Commercial Credit Corporation, which began by lending
money to lower-income people before it was transformed into a global leader
by the driven deal making of its leader, Sanford I. Weill.

While Morgan has managed to crack the top ten in annual score cards of
underwriting and advisory deals, it has never been able to climb to the very
top where the bulk of the profits are earned.

Morgan in some ways was trapped by its earlier success doing business
with tycoons and Fortune 500 companies, according to Chernow, and
could not take advantage of the burgeoning markets managing the money
of main street America.

"They felt their competitive advantage was to trade on the romanticism
and illustrious tradition that no one could match," Chernow said. "But
when the entire world of Wall Street was going down market, they felt that
by lessening their standards they would water down their mystique."

Similarly, Morgan's focus on the very largest corporate customers
recently left it with little involvement in the most dynamic sector of the
economy, small technology companies.

In recent years, Morgan has tried to address these flaws with modest
efforts. It started an Internet business meant to serve the affluent rather
than the truly wealthy. And it tried to get involved in financing Internet
companies. But the results have been mixed. One of Morgan's most prominent Internet deals was the financing of Boo.com, an ambitious attempt to
create a global Web site selling women's sportswear. Morgan helped Boo

gain investments from some of the most wealthy families in Europe, but after running through $135 million, Boo was liquidated in May 2000.

Morgan is now likely to see itself become a part of Chase, an agglomeration of banks that had hardly been in its league. To be sure, some of the ancestors of the current Chase have their own storied histories. The Bank of Manhattan Company, after all, was founded in 1799 as a water company. And Chase in the 1970s, run by David Rockefeller, was a leading banker to the Arab world. But the institution now using the Chase name was formed when two underperforming New York banks—Chemical Bank and Manufacturers Hanover—merged in 1991 as a way to preserve capital drained by a decade of overindulgent lending. In 1995, what was then called Chemical bought Chase, which itself was struggling to meet profit goals. Chemical was clearly in control but took the more prestigious name.

"They have a history of making acquisitions and integrating them successfully; that is enviable in an industry that has not done this well," Toevs said. Still, Chase, with its extensive branches and wide-ranging clientele, relies on a corporate culture drawn more from the streets of New York than of the rarefied air breathed by those at Morgan.

"The Morgan folks are always wearing their elite status on their sleeves," Toevs said. "That's got to help the Chase franchise."

Saul Hansell
September 13, 2000

CASE 2

A Doubly Hostile Takeover

On a balmy Saturday in mid-June 1999, seventy of Joseph P. Nacchio's closest friends and family members gathered at his northern New Jersey home for boccie ball and a late supper to celebrate his son's high school graduation. Also attending were a few colleagues, including Jack Grubman, who had worked with Nacchio at AT&T years before.

Grubman, a top telecommunications analyst at Salomon Smith Barney, had helped advise Global Crossing on its recent mergers with U S West Inc., the smallest regional Bell company, and the Frontier Corporation, the nation's fifth-largest long-distance company, based in Rochester. Global, like many young telecommunications concerns these days, hopes to use fiber optic cables to transmit data over the Internet. U S West and Frontier would give it what it needed most: revenue and customers.

But the rumor on Wall Street the week before the party was that one of Global's rivals, Qwest Communications International, was on the verge of making unsolicited offers for the two companies. If true, it made for an awkward situation on Nacchio's backyard deck: Nacchio was Qwest's chief executive. "There's a lot of speculation out there about when you are going to come with an offer," Grubman said at the party, a swing band playing in the background.

Nacchio said he replied with a shrug, "We may, we may not."

Nacchio was in fact about to embark on the largest double hostile takeover in American history. As he crawled into bed that evening, he was almost giddy. "I think we both had a lot of trouble sleeping that night," said his wife, Anne Esker Nacchio, "not because we were worried, but because we were excited."

The next day, Qwest made offers to buy both U S West and Frontier for a total of $55 billion in stock and cash, in effect topping Global's stock offer of $47 billion. Soon, scores of bankers, lawyers and negotiators began shuttling between Denver, where both Qwest and U S West are based, and lawyers' offices in New York as often as commuters on a subway. The result was a July 1999 compromise, for U S West to merge with Qwest and for Global Crossing to acquire Frontier—a deal that most analysts agree gives each company the prize it needed most.

But what many participants had hoped might be worked out amicably in days, instead took weeks of almost Machiavellian maneuvering. Clandestine meetings were held in airport hangars and hotel rooms, far from prying eyes. Tempers flared as the battle at times seemed personal. And Denver's most celebrated billionaire was forced to step in and broker not one but two vital relationships. Without his effort a compromise might never have been reached.

Not everyone was savoring the victories, however, especially investors in Qwest and Global Crossing; on July 23, Qwest stock was 42 percent off its fifty-two-week high, and Global 35 percent.

"Despite being a sensible solution, this is not a happy one for everyone involved," said one person involved in the talks. "A lot of value was lost by investors in this whole escapade."

"A Lot of Adrenaline Flowing"

Nacchio was a little nervous as he drove to the offices of Kekst & Company, a New York public relations firm, on June 13, 1999, the morning after the graduation party, where he planned to announce the offers.

Qwest's bid was simple: The company was willing to pay $55 billion in stock and cash for both U S West and Frontier, about 22 percent more than Global Crossing's all-stock offer was worth based on the previous Friday's closing prices. The move was risky; not only was Qwest trying two hostile takeovers at once, but both targets had signed merger agreements with Global Crossing months before that would be tough and expensive to break.

Nacchio, who grew up in a scrappy Italian neighborhood on Staten Island, attacks competitors with a take-no-prisoners style. But even his friends say that sometimes his abrasive personality makes him an easy target for detractors. He was described in *The Economist* as having "all the swagger and verbal braggadocio of Joe Pesci's mobster in the film *Goodfellas*." Nacchio took offense to the stereotype, and wrote a letter to the magazine in response: "The overwhelming majority of Italian Americans are not mobsters," he said.

The day Qwest announced its bids, Nacchio recalled, "I had a lot of adrenaline flowing." Minutes before the news release went out, he called Joseph P. Clayton, chief executive of Frontier, to tell him of the bid. Philip F. Anschutz, the secretive billionaire who owns 39 percent of Qwest and is chairman, called Solomon D. Trujillo, chief executive of U S West. Nacchio thought a call from Anschutz, whom Trujillo knew, might "take the edge off," he later recalled.

Trujillo turned down several requests to be interviewed for this article.

The news of Qwest's offer, though unwelcome, came as no surprise to executives at Global Crossing. They had worried that Qwest and a partner might enter the bidding war. Global's top management conferred immediately with its advisers at Salomon, but there was little to do except wait and see how investors reacted. Robert Annunziata, the chief executive, was barred from commenting publicly about Frontier and U S West until Global filed documents with regulators. And, anyway, Global had a provision in its merger contracts that allowed it to review any competing bid.

Meanwhile, Qwest investors revolted. On the day after the announcement, the shares collapsed 24 percent, to $34.125, in record trading volume. That was troubling for Qwest, because the company was offering its own stock as currency. When the stock price dropped, so did the value of its dual offer, making it almost comparable to Global Crossing's. Nacchio and his advisers had clearly miscalculated the market response.

As one investment banker not involved in the deals said at the time, "This will be a Harvard Business School case study someday on how not to launch a hostile takeover."

Qwest's attempt to promote the deal during that week's road show was equally disastrous. Investors bought Qwest with the promise of owning a supercharged growth company. But if Nacchio bought U S West, Qwest's growth rate would be halved. "I think the whole strategy is absurd," said Robert Gensler of T. Rowe Price, the mutual fund company in Baltimore, one of many analysts to balk at the move.

By the time Nacchio got back to his Denver office on Thursday, June 17, 1999, he had six hundred e-mail messages waiting. No one, Nacchio said, seemed to understand Qwest's rationale, least of all the news media. "*Business Week* has a story coming out, and you are not going to like it," Nacchio recalled a board member telling him that day. Nacchio had been interviewed, he said, but instead of a news article, the magazine published an editorial criticizing his bids, calling him "a telecom bureaucrat dressed up in Internet clothes."

Nacchio did not mask his anger. In a conference call with advisers later that afternoon, he lashed out. "What is going on here?" he barked, according to one person on the call. "Why can't we get any good press?" Nacchio later told aides to try to set up meetings with top editors at major news outlets so he could explain his plan. Nacchio said he thinks some news accounts were planted by Global to try to undermine his offers. "It demonstrated they hadn't done their homework on me, and I wasn't going to back down," he said. He called the stories "hurtful." (Annunziata of Global Crossing said neither he nor any of his executives planted negative reports.)

But Nacchio's public relations campaign did little to sway the audience he needed most. That same day, Frontier reaffirmed its merger with Global Crossing, which is based in Bermuda; four days later, U S West did the same.

Their message was clear: Sweeten the offers or go away.

"A Ton of Bricks on Your Heads"

On June 22, 1999, nine days after Qwest made its offers, Nacchio was awakened by a telephone call from Anschutz, Qwest's largest shareholder, wishing him a happy fiftieth birthday. "How do you feel?" Nacchio said Anschutz asked him. "Tired," Nacchio replied, "but I'm not sure if it's age or if it is this deal."

Nacchio and his negotiating team, which included Craig Slater, who is one of Anschutz's trusted advisers, had begun a "Dear Sol" letter-writing campaign to pressure Trujillo of U S West to accept Qwest's offer. Instead, advisers say they annoyed him, and Trujillo demanded that they stop. Qwest was also planning to make revised offers that were more palatable, but exactly how was up in the air. Among other things, U S West wanted protection in case Qwest's volatile stock plummeted further.

Nacchio and Anschutz discussed several different options—more stock or a guarantee of cash, perhaps—and decided to keep Qwest's board members on standby in case a quick vote was needed on a revised bid. By day's end, it was: Frontier shareholders would be offered a guaranteed forty-eight dollars in stock and twenty dollars in cash, and U S West shareholders sixty-nine dollars in stock, for each share.

The total value of the offers—about $50 billion—was not as rich as the first, but seemed better than Global Crossing's. And both companies' stockholders would be protected from volatile price swings as well, something Qwest hadn't offered originally. Qwest planned to make its revised offer the next morning.

Nacchio, who had been working at home in his library, took a few hours off that night for a quiet barbecue with his wife and two sons. (Their birthday gifts to him that day included the *Godfather* trilogy on video and a promise to wash and wax his Porsche.) And he called Grubman of Salomon, in part to send a message to Global to back off.

Nacchio was still fuming about the *Business Week* editorial, and he said he told Grubman that "it was a bad tactic for Global to go after me personally." He also told Grubman that another bid was coming, saying, as Grubman recalled it and Nacchio confirmed, "I'm going to drop a ton of bricks on your heads."

The new bids posed a problem for Global Crossing. Its founder, Gary Winnick—a financier and a former colleague of Michael R. Milken—had turned a $15 million investment in an undersea cable into more than $5 billion of Global stock. For Global to succeed, it needed the cash and customers Frontier and U S West could provide. Winnick's biggest fear was losing Frontier, because he coveted its long-distance network.

He knew it would be inappropriate to approach Qwest directly about a compromise, so on the afternoon of June 26, 1999, according to people close to the talks, he stopped by the Malibu home of a trusted friend, Ken Moelis, a Donaldson, Lufkin & Jenrette executive in Los Angeles. The two walked on the beach, and Winnick asked Moelis: Could he help with Anschutz?

Moelis, who was not advising Qwest, called Lou Friedman, another Donaldson banker who was, and told him about the visit. Maybe a deal could work, Moelis thought. Qwest, the nation's fourth-largest long-distance company, was interested in U S West mainly for its local customers. And Frontier, while important, was less vital to its strategy.

It took executives and bankers two days to negotiate a meeting of about eight Qwest and Global executives and advisers at the O'Hare Hilton in Chicago on June 30, 1999. "Everyone was terrified," one person close to the talks said. "No one trusted each other. They didn't want leaks. The implication was it would show weakness."

When the two camps convened at 10 A.M. in room 3002, a Salomon banker laid out Global's concerns first: Winnick was prepared to give U S West permission to negotiate with Qwest as long as Qwest was willing to drop its bid for Frontier that day. No way, said Slater, Anschutz's adviser. "This isn't going to be unilateral disarmament," he said, according to people who were there. "It's trust, but we'll keep our nuclear weapons pointed at you." Slater said Qwest would drop its bid for Frontier only when a deal with U S West was struck.

For two hours, the two teams bickered. "Part of the negotiation with Global Crossing was helping Qwest get in to U S West to talk," said one person close to the talks. "U S West could have hidden behind legal issues if it wanted to." By noon, Slater and his team were so frustrated that they threatened to walk out of the negotiations and called their pilot to fetch them. But after three more exhausting hours, they were no closer to a compromise.

A flurry of calls were made over the next twenty-four hours to both Winnick and Anschutz. Those led to an informal understanding the next day that allowed U S West to negotiate with Qwest as long as Qwest agreed to drop its bid for Frontier when a deal with U S West was signed. Also, Global would receive half its original $850 million breakup fee. That afternoon, Winnick and Anschutz confirmed the informal understanding by telephone. Later that day, U S West said it would begin talks with Qwest. Frontier also said it would hold talks with Qwest.

Maneuvers, and a Deal

An agreement between Qwest and U S West might never have been reached without the stealthy maneuverings of Anschutz, the press-shy Denver billionaire who made his fortune in oil and railroad investments. Most recently, he had sold the Southern Pacific Railroad in 1996 for $5.4 billion, tripling his $1.8 billion investment.

Like Winnick, Anschutz is guarded and private, driven to finding opportunities where none are clear. But in this case, his motivation was self-evident: to further protect his 39 percent investment in Qwest, which since June 13, 1999, had lost one-quarter of its value. As the largest shareholder, he had the most to gain in welcoming Trujillo into the Qwest fold. "Guys like Anschutz and Winnick, they want to make money," said one person involved in the talks. "They don't want to be known as the guys who remade the telecommunications industry."

Because U S West had originally approached Global about a merger of equals, it was not technically for sale. So Trujillo and his board were demanding a merger with equal power. One concern was that Qwest had no experience running a local telephone business. And Trujillo wanted to make sure that his ideas and those of his management team would get an equal airing once the companies were combined. "U S West was concerned about Qwest slashing and burning its management team," a person close to the talks said.

In fact, mutual suspicion pervaded every aspect of the negotiations, to the point that seemingly trivial details like a demand by Trujillo to drop a sentence and move a paragraph in the news release would snag the deal's signing for hours. (He prevailed on the sentence, which said he would report to Nacchio; the paragraph, explaining each of the top executives' titles, ultimately stayed put.)

Anschutz began talking about management issues with Trujillo on Thursday, July 8, 1999. One solution discussed was to name Trujillo president of the local and wireless business and a vice chairman of the combined company. But that was a nonstarter; U S West feared that a vice chairmanship would be perceived as one step away from early retirement.

Talks between executives in New York stalled over the weekend, too. Slater was running in Central Park the following Saturday when he received a call on his cell phone from Allan R. Spies, U S West's chief financial officer, informing him that the day's planned negotiations might be postponed, said a person close to the talks. Slater and his team went to the offices of Davis Polk & Wardwell, the lawyers advising Qwest, to await Spies's call. The meeting never happened, and Qwest's advisers ended up watching the Women's World Cup soccer finals on a television in the law office library.

Four days after discussions began in earnest, negotiators struck paydirt. Slater and Spies, along with two other executives from Qwest and U S West, met at U S West's hangar at a small airport outside Denver on July 12. The four men mulled over a compromise that had surfaced earlier: naming Anschutz, Nacchio and Trujillo cochairmen.

Nacchio would still be chief executive. But to make that palatable, Trujillo would have the authority to present his own ideas to the board, even if Nacchio disagreed. Trujillo would be named president of the local and wireless business. And top jobs at the combined entity would be divided equally between executives from the two companies.

Anschutz didn't love the concept at first. "Phil thought the market would perceive him as an arbitrator," said one person close to the talks. "He was the referee, and he didn't want to be." But he soon warmed to the idea, as did Nacchio, who was traveling that day. Later that afternoon, Anschutz went to Trujillo's office, and the two men agreed that it was an arrangement they all could live with.

With management issues all but behind them, negotiators spent several long days and late nights—until the boards' meetings on Friday night—working out the details.

The drama of Qwest's battle for U S West overshadowed the story of Frontier. After preliminary discussions stalled, Rolla P. Huff, president and chief operating officer, said he called Nacchio on July 13—the same day Nacchio and Trujillo had dinner at the Brown Palace Hotel in downtown Denver to discuss their future—to gauge whether he was serious about buying Frontier. Nacchio said he was, but Huff said he suspected then, as he does now, that Nacchio was not as interested in Frontier as he was in U S West.

But Will It Work?

The Qwest and Global Crossing compromise was greeted with little fanfare on Wall Street. Analysts called it the logical outcome, as did the principals.

"At the end of the day, we thought U S West was good, but we had our limits on what it was worth," said Annunziata of Global Crossing.

Nacchio said, "It was OK to let Frontier go."

Communications companies, like Qwest and Global, are aware that if they do not transform themselves—placing one foot in the new digital universe of the Internet and the other in the traditional world of cable or copper wires—they risk likely death. In essence, that is at the core of the brawl for Frontier and U S West.

But betting on an unpredictable future takes its toll. "I'm just physically tired," Nacchio said, sounding weary on a telephone call from Boston, one of several cities he visited on a whirlwind road show to discuss the merger. "I've only seen my wife three times in the past three weeks."

Nacchio says he is confident that Qwest's merger with U S West will succeed. But it will be several years before he, or Qwest investors, know for sure. Still, "Qwest can never be the same," Nacchio said. "Once we started, we knew we could never go back to what we were before."

Laura M. Holson
July 25, 1999

CASE 3

Trusting Trusts

Teddy Roosevelt plotted the beginning of the end of John D. Rockefeller's oil empire at a secret meeting at the White House on a summer night in 1906. Surrounded by his attorney general and other key cabinet members, he mapped out the antitrust suit against Standard Oil that prompted Henry Clay Frick, the steel baron, to complain on behalf of his fellow oligarchs, "We bought the son of a bitch, and then he didn't stay bought."

It took five years for Roosevelt to win his case in the Supreme Court, breaking up Standard Oil into thirty-four companies. And for the better part of the next seventy years, Washington's economic agenda was dominated by the high-stakes politics of curbing the power of big enterprises: the regulatory zeal of the New Deal, the oil cartel cases of the 1950s and 1960s, the failed—and now foolish-looking—thirteen-year pursuit of IBM, the breakup of the Bell System.

But something has changed in Washington in the past decade or so, something that has taken the issue that Woodrow Wilson called "these vast aggregations of capital" off the country's political agenda, even as it lives on in courtroom arguments about the legality of Microsoft's strategies to dominate the electronic ether.

In late 1998, when two of the biggest remaining parts of the old Rockefeller empire, Exxon and Mobil, were recombined in the world's largest merger, Washington yawned. Richard A. Gephardt, the pro-union, proconsumer voice of the Democratic Party's left wing, spent the day complaining loudly—about the Clinton impeachment inquiry, and he has yet to say anything about the deal, according to his office. In fact, scarcely a politician of any stripe headed for the cameras to question whether the $75 billion deal was good for the country, for workers or for consumers.

The same silence greeted the deal that created Citigroup, which was the largest financial services company for a few minutes until Deutsche Bank bought the Bankers Trust Corporation in December 1998, and Cargill Inc.'s move to snap up Continental Grain, one of the few huge concerns that farmers could turn to if they didn't like the prices Cargill was offering for their harvest.

President Clinton, only steps away from the room where Roosevelt held forth ninety-two years earlier, was hardly pounding the podium. "My position on mergers," he said, "has always been that if they increase the competitiveness of the company and bring lower prices and higher-quality services to the consumers of our country, then they are good, and if they don't, they aren't."

Clinton's fence-sitting reflected the odd politics of an era of prosperity tinged with uncertainty. A few years ago downsizing was a brewing political issue; though layoffs continued, job growth had been so strong that that issue had been defused.

Less than a decade ago, when Japanese corporations snapped up Rockefeller Center and two Hollywood studios, many in Congress were in an uproar over the sale of American icons to foreigners. But, with the Dow bobbing at record levels and analysts declaring the triumph of American-style capitalism, neither the Deutsche Bank acquisition nor DaimlerBenz's purchase of the Chrysler Corporation in the spring of 1998 yielded a similar furor.

Many theories have been offered to explain this new passivity about the evils of Big Everything: the pace of technological change, or the realities of borderless competition in a year of global tumult, or the confusing business currents that at once celebrate the global reach of American-based multinationals and the entrepreneurial spirit of small businesses.

And perhaps it's just temporary—if prices start going up again at the pump, or if the American economy falters, there could be a renewed clamor to rein in corporations viewed as too big, too powerful or too heartless. But whatever the reason, noted Senator Paul Wellstone, the Minnesota Democrat who was among the few in Congress still exercised about the concentration of corporate power, "Once upon a time this was a burning issue, and now it's not even on the table."

The government's antitrust case against Microsoft seems at first blush to be the notable exception: it was hard to turn on the television in 1998 without hearing about the company's supposed scheme to dominate the Internet browser market, or its secret strategies to flatten competitors. (Imagine the muck Ida Tarbell could have raked with access to e-mail.)

But among politicians, the case was rarely mentioned. No one ran for office on a platform of Gates-bashing the way Roosevelt once called Rockefeller's crowd "the biggest criminals in the country." At a rare high-profile hearing in 1998 on the long-term effect of mergers, Alan Greenspan, the chairman of the Federal Reserve, argued that the government was inept at determining in advance those mergers that would create competitive problems and would be wiser to wait and see.

"I would feel very uncomfortable if we inhibited various different types of mergers or acquisitions on the basis of some presumed projection as to how markets would evolve, how technology would evolve," he said, "because history is strewn with people making projections that have turned out to be grossly inaccurate."

Greenspan's view was challenged at the hearing, chiefly by Joel I. Klein, the assistant attorney general in charge of antitrust, and Robert Pitofsky, the chairman of the Federal Trade Commission, which was set to review the Exxon-Mobil merger and presumably would force the company to divest some assets. Pitofsky noted that undoing the damage after employees of an acquired company have been fired, after its plants have been closed and after top management has moved on, "is enormously expensive."

But the fact remains that few lawmakers dare to venture deep into this territory, even though it sustained generations of their predecessors. "The biggest reason is the mix of money and politics," said Wellstone, who was intensely focused on the issue as he was considering a run for his party's presidential nomination. "For both parties, these are the heavy hitters, the monied interests who have a huge impact on the tenure of people in Congress. Not too many people want to challenge them."

Of course, that was also true in Roosevelt's day, even if Frick and other monopolists came to regret their support of the president. But Wellstone noted a second reason: the quiet arrival in Washington of "a set of shared assumptions about what is necessary these days for survival in a global economy."

The first is that while bigger is not always better, it may be the only way to extend one's reach abroad. "The ability to be a global player and to be competitive anywhere in the world has become more important as all the traditional walls of regulation, state ownership and time barriers have come down," said Daniel Yergin, chairman of Cambridge Energy Research Associates.

The second assumption is that technology moves faster than antitrust cases. When the government began its push against IBM in the late 1960s, the microprocessor had just been invented. By the time the case was abandoned, the microprocessor was revolutionizing the computer industry, and IBM was missing the boat. It caught up, but market dominance was no longer an issue.

And the breakup of the Bell System, while leading to lower long-distance rates and helping to promote technological advances, has also driven millions of consumers up the wall. For many, the only thing more annoying than trying to figure out how to get a phone fixed is answering dinnertime calls from solicitors trying to sign up customers for a new phone service nobody has ever heard of.

In the end, today's trust busters are no longer politicians but technocrats and regulators who, in the first few months after the merger announcement, would be reviewing neighborhood-by-neighborhood what to do about streets that have both a Mobil and an Exxon station. Almost no one was talking about blocking the merger itself, a merger that a decade ago Exxon would not have dared to think possible.

David E. Sanger
December 6, 1998

CASE 4

800-Pound Gorillas

A nice irony of Judge Thomas Penfield Jackson's June 7, 2000, decision is that he rejected the suggestion of smashing the world's most powerful software company into a bunch of "Baby Bills," and instead proposed to split Microsoft into two behemoths that would dominate their respective markets.

In fact, a major legacy of the Clinton administration will be that it encouraged one of the greatest periods of industrial concentration in American history, affecting old and new sectors ranging from oil and pharmaceuticals, to telecommunications, broadcasting and the Internet. Call it the Age of Oligopoly.

Corporate mergers have grown so frequent and so large, said Robert Pitofsky, the chairman of the Federal Trade Commission, that "there's not a week that goes by that we're not called upon to review a big merger that has significant implications for the marketplace."

The Seven Sister oil companies have shrunk to five (or even fewer if you consider the joint marketing and production agreements between them); the seven Baby Bells are now four; and American and foreign car producers, once great rivals, are now intertwined to the point where it is difficult to figure out who actually manufactures the Mercedes, Chrysler, Nissan or Volvo next to you at a traffic light.

As headlines that week made clear, no corner of the economy appeared untouched. Executives from the parent company of American Airlines were in talks about possible mergers with Delta or Northwest, prompted by United Airlines's decision to acquire USAir. The Federal Communications Commission approved AT&T's acquisition of MediaOne, troubling consumer advocates by clearing the way for the emergence of a company that will control about a third of the cable television market, large television programming units, and the biggest high-speed Internet service.

There may be a new round of packaged food mergers, set off after Unilever, the maker of Lipton Tea, Ragú tomato sauces and Breyers ice cream, offered $20 billion to buy Bestfoods, producer of Skippy peanut butter, Mueller's pastas and Thomas' English muffins.

While there are undoubted economic benefits to consolidation—cheaper goods, more uniform quality and better distribution—economics and antitrust theory cannot measure the fundamental changes in the character and quality of life that comes with size. For example, economic analysis won't tell how to deal with, say, the merger of banks and insurance companies and the potential privacy threats that result when one company holds both your medical and financial records.

The gospel that bigness is not necessarily badness has been preached on both sides of the political aisle for about twenty years. During the twelve years of the Reagan and Bush administrations, an era widely remembered for frenzied merger activity and devotion to a laissez-faire regulatory approach, there were 44,518 mergers and acquisitions in the United States, with a combined value of $2.17 trillion, according to Thomson Financial Securities Data. By contrast, the Clinton administration has witnessed 71,811 corporate deals valued at $6.66 trillion so far.

"We live in perhaps the most dynamic economy in at least a generation or more," Pitofsky said. "There are many firms trying to adjust to new economic circumstances and global competition, striving to find new efficiencies. That's all fine with us. It's the relatively few mergers that present problems."

Over all, however, the days of *Small Is Beautiful,* the title of E. F. Schumacher's 1960s paean to smallness of economic scale, now seem a quaint relic of an earlier age. "We can't go back to a Jeffersonian world or a literal Brandeis concern about human-sized institutions because we'd pay a terrible efficiency price in terms of technological innovation and global competitiveness," said Harvey J. Goldschmid, an antitrust expert at Columbia Law School. "The trick is to take account of the modern needs for efficiency but still use antitrust to give us workably competitive markets."

When is a marketplace sufficiently competitive in the minds of regulators?

"Antitrust authorities don't worry about consolidation per se, they only worry about it when it gets to the tipping point," said Robert Litan, a former antitrust official in the Justice Department and now director of economic studies at the Brookings Institution. That point, in many cases, is reached when a market is effectively controlled by just one or two players, he said.

There have been some notable instances when the Clinton administration blocked or restructured mergers that would have passed unscathed under the Republicans. Still, more than 95 percent of the cases reviewed have encountered no resistance from federal antitrust officials.

Thus far, only a handful of critics and lawmakers have raised concerns about the increasing size of corporations and concentration of markets, though some are questioning whether antitrust law is able to factor in the noneconomic costs of all the deal making.

When the FCC, for instance, approved AT&T's merger with MediaOne, only one of the commissioners expressed any significant concern about the declining number of media voices that will result from the deal.

Noting that the commission's approval means that five companies will control forty of the fifty-nine viable cable networks, the commissioner, Gloria Tristani, wrote, "It's time for the FCC to realize that we are not dealing with bottled water or sneakers, but with the dissemination of news and information—the lifeblood of our democratic way of life. In the last few years, the number of entities that control what people watch on television has dwindled to alarming levels. With this decision, the FCC has failed yet again to stem this crisis and ensure a robust marketplace of ideas."

Mark Crispin Miller, director of the Project on Media Ownership and a professor of media studies at New York University, said current antitrust tools fail to recognize what is actually lost by all the mergers.

"The danger of media concentration lies not in the risk of prices getting higher, which is what antitrust measures," Miller said. "The real danger is much subtler. You're talking about the disappearance of alternative views. You're talking about an exponential increase in conflicts of interest. You're talking about fewer interests having greater market power. You're talking about the rise of trivial programming. These are consequences that are extremely troubling, that worry most Americans, but that don't attract any kind of sustained political or judicial attention because they are not simply economically quantifiable."

At present, the march to oligopoly seems irreversible. Microsoft, if broken up into separate operating systems and applications companies, will hardly be high-tech start-ups in a garage. They will cover the world with their products. "Technology will not go backwards and the integration of markets will not go backwards and the growth of the global shareholder, putting more and more countries and companies under the microscope of investor scrutiny, will not go backwards," said Daniel Yergin, whose book, *The Commanding Heights,* is about the changing balance between governments and international markets.

But the same forces that have helped propel growth could slow it down, if not reverse it. Globalization has been financed largely by the world's investors, particularly institutions like pension and retirement funds, which relentlessly seek higher returns for their money. This has put enormous pressure on companies to find new markets and produce ever stronger quarterly earnings.

An economic downturn could cause investors to pull their money out of stocks, and lead governments to erect barriers to free trade. This would make it harder and less profitable for multinationals to sell their products around the globe.

Still, the world shouldn't hold its breath waiting for businesses to shrink. There is just too much commercial logic on the side of size. The real job ahead is for governments and individuals to learn how to benefit from and to some extent control the vast corporations the age has spawned.

Stephen Labaton
June 11, 2000

CASE 5

Bridge Building

When Gerald M. Levin, Time Warner's chairman and chief executive, urged the assembled press corps to look at the body language among the executives on stage one day in January 2000 as proof of how harmoniously his company would blend with America Online, the row of men in the spotlight fidgeted in uncomfortable silence.

Then Robert W. Pittman, president of America Online, leaned back and put his arms around his Time Warner neighbors. If the gesture did not necessarily provide assurance of a happy cultural mesh, it did draw laughter and managed to defuse an awkward moment.

Pittman, once a high-profile figure in New York's elite media scene who began his corporate career running The Movie Channel at a predecessor company to Time Warner, now carries around a Libretto notebook computer and conducts business through America Online's instant message feature. With a foot in both worlds—and an affinity for the limelight—he is expected to be a key figure in stitching together the old media with the new.

"Think of me as a forward scout," Pittman said later that week from Palm Springs, California, where he and Richard D. Parsons, who were to share the job of chief operating officer at the merged company, to be known as AOL Time Warner, were speaking to a group of investment bankers from Salomon Smith Barney. "The truth is these two companies are a lot alike. What we both think about is the consumer, what are people doing, and how do we serve them and create new value."

By most accounts, the two companies are more similar than they appear.

America Online has long fancied itself a mass-media company, and many of its top executives have been drawn from the ranks of traditional media companies. The people who run Time Warner's entertainment properties, particularly in Los Angeles, pride themselves on being quick to make deals. And the dress code has relaxed even at the company's more buttoned-down editorial offices in New York, where ten years ago men were virtually required to wear ties.

Apparently, Time Warner has casual dress five days a week, one America Online senior executive said yesterday with some relief.

Indeed, at AOL, the buzz held that the merger with Time Warner would be easier than had been that with Netscape Communications, the Silicon Valley software company America Online acquired in 1998. Many of Netscape's star programmers have since departed.

Time Warner executives in turn said they expected the merger with America Online to run far more smoothly than Time Inc.'s notoriously prolonged integration with Warner Communications after they merged in 1989 to form Time Warner.

"These are Dockers guys," said a senior executive at Time Warner from the Time Inc. side of the business. "Latte-drinking nice guys. These are not Hollywood killer types."

Still, the melding of an Internet company at which jobs change weekly and employees are compensated largely in stock options and a corporate hierarchy known for its devotion to tradition may encounter some difficulties. At America Online, where instant messages hyperlinked to the company's stock price flit across computer screens all day, there was off-the-record dismay as the company's stock fell after the announcement.

At Time Warner, there was a David-and-Goliath issue, the sense that an august old-media institution had been felled by a smaller, more agile competitor. "There is a recognition that new media is big, that this is a sea change, that this is momentous," said one executive, who insisted on anonymity. "And somehow this company with a fifth of our revenues and far less cash flow came along and took us over. We've seen it before. How did World-Com buy MCI? But it's a little different when it happens to you."

Time Inc. was once a company that embodied a certain Ivy League gentility. In the 1950s and 1960s, after the editors closed an issue of the magazine, a waiter brought a cart with wine and hard liquor for a celebratory toast. Now, some Time Warner executives believe that the merger with Warner Communications ten years ago and the ascension of Levin has brought about a certain anodyne quality, almost a neutral environment.

There is no drinking in the office. The headquarters building at Rockefeller Center in midtown Manhattan is a big, rather bland monolith. A nest of wires runs along the ceiling of the *Time* magazine offices, and in the right frame of mind can resemble the corporate environment portrayed in the 1985 movie *Brazil,* which satirized a postapocalypse corporate culture.

One Time Warner executive said that Levin purposefully affects a mien of utter calm. "He has had a charisma bypass," the executive said. Parsons, he added, is a consummate politician, evenhanded and almost benign in his ability to assuage demands and dented egos from all sides of the Time Warner corporate edifice.

By contrast, at AOL's headquarters next to Dulles Airport in the Washington suburbs of northern Virginia, the company's chairman and chief executive, Stephen M. Case, not long ago held regular beer parties on Fridays, and Pittman has weekly staff meetings that are often raucous. Built on a sprawling site that was once a British Aerospace hangar, America Online's headquarters consist of two glass creative centers referred to as CC1 and CC2. Whether an art director at *InStyle,* Time Warner's successful new celebrity lifestyle magazine, would consider the work done in them to be creative is unclear.

And while Pittman was careful to emphasize the similarities of the two companies, he may well try to import America Online's faster pace and more experimental method to the newly merged company.

"I once said something about how hard it is to get your mind around the pace," said Don Davis, the relatively new chief operating officer of AOL's interactive properties group. "Pittman goes, 'Aw, what's the matter? You'll get no sympathy in this room.' It's kind of like you're on the moon. It's a perspective that's hard to describe."

The relentless rate of change may be why some other efforts to combine new and old media have flopped. Most recently, the attempt by Barry Diller, who controls USA Networks, to merge his cable holdings with Lycos, an Internet search engine and information portal, failed when a major Lycos shareholder opposed the combination because it did not offer a premium.

Still, traditional media companies have landed in more trouble trying to delve into the Internet on their own. Time Warner is often held up as a text-book example of such failures. The company's experiment in interactive television in Orlando, Florida, for instance, cost thousands of dollars per household and never quite worked. And though Time Warner was ahead of its old-media colleagues in creating Pathfinder, an umbrella site on the World Wide Web for all of its properties, the venture lost millions of dollars and was scrapped in 1999.

"The history of Time Warner has been an internal clash of cultures, that's what's kept them from being able to put together a Web property that works," said Tom Wolzien, a media analyst at Sanford Bernstein & Company. "Internal politics destroyed it, they shredded themselves."

With access to AOL's twenty million subscribers, the unwillingness of Time Warner's many divisions to devote their resources to the Internet may change. Selling the idea to them, and uniting them behind it, is most likely to be largely left to Pittman.

Levin has made a point of welcoming Pittman back, saying that some of the best work Pittman had done at America Online was rooted in what he had learned as a builder of brands and consumer marketer at Warner. Pittman, several executives with long tenure at Time Warner said, is perceived as a known quantity. Friendly with many Time Warner managers, he and his wife, Veronique, dine regularly with Levin and his wife. Don Logan, the chief executive of Time Inc., said the two men see themselves as kindred spirits, bonded by their passion for marketing, and both are from the South.

"In a sense, it's like coming home," Pittman said.

But with the company's headquarters to be split between New York and Dulles, he had not decided yet just where he will live, Pittman said. He owns homes in Great Falls, Virginia; Manhattan; Jamaica and Telluride, Colorado. Pictured on the cover of *New York* magazine in 1990 as the "Couple of the Minute" with his first wife, Sandy, Pittman has since remarried and has two sons, one from his first marriage and one from his second. In 1999, he made *Forbes* magazine's list of the four hundred richest Americans.

The son of a United Methodist minister from southern Mississippi, Pittman has carved out a reputation as archmarketer. From his first job as a teenage radio disc jockey, he has had a knack for sensing what the consuming public wants, or at least how to package it and sell it.

At a Thanksgiving gathering on an uncle's farm in Holly Springs, Mississippi, when Pittman was in the second grade, the horse he was riding threw him off and kicked him in the face until it was so bloodied that nobody could tell what was still left underneath. A trip to the hospital determined that his right eye had been lost. Tom Pittman, who witnessed the accident, believes that the glass replacement sharpened his brother's determination to understand other people's motivations, the better to fit in himself.

"He never could play ball because he could never see where the ball was coming from," says Tom Pittman, who is the publisher of a newspaper in DeSoto, Mississippi. "But he became a pretty keen observer of human nature and what other people were interested in, how to determine that, how to fit in with that. He learned to do that very well. Even the sports guys liked him."

After building WNBC in New York into the leading television station in the country, Pittman landed at Warner Amex Satellite, where he helped to found MTV. When Viacom bought MTV—along with the other channels Pittman helped to create, VH1 and Nickelodeon—he briefly headed his own company, Quantum Media, at which he introduced Morton Downey Jr. to television. Returning to Time Warner in 1990 at the behest of Steve Ross, who was chairman, Pittman acquired the Six Flags theme parks and bolstered the parks' attendance and brand awareness. When a controlling share of Six Flags was bought by a new investor, Pittman was unable to reach an agreement on what his equity stake should be, and he departed to run the Century 21 real estate corporation.

He joined America Online just as the service was imploding. Having decided that it needed to switch to flat-rate pricing to keep its customers, AOL proceeded to sacrifice its lucrative per-hour connect fees and simultaneously enraged its customers by being totally unprepared to handle the ensuing spike in usage of its network.

Pittman is credited with stabilizing the company, expanding its customer service and, significantly, selling it as a credible stock to Wall Street investors. Some three years after his arrival at the company in October 1996, AOL stock had risen 3,100 percent.

"People say AOL exists because of Steve, but it works because of Bob," said Mark Stavish, America Online's chief of human resources.

Henry R. Silverman, chairman of the Cendant Corporation, Pittman's former boss at Century 21 and the godfather of his younger son, said Pittman's role at the world's largest media company would have less to do with the touchy-feely blending of corporate cultures and more to do with his traditional strength: selling.

"Bob's a marketing guy," Silverman said. "What Bob did best at AOL is he got the stock up and he gave the company a currency that enabled it to acquire Time Warner. I would assume that would be what he's expected to continue to do. He'll be asking what he's always asked: 'What can we sell, whom can we sell it to and at what price can we sell it.' "

Amy Harmon and Alex Kuczynski
January 12, 2000

CASE 6

The Real Work of Merging

David Hadfield still winces when he recalls the 1989 merger of Coopers & Lybrand and some international operations of Deloitte, Haskins & Sells. "We figured they're both accounting firms, they trade in the same markets, so of course their cultures would be the same," said Hadfield, who was a consultant with Deloitte at the time. "We couldn't have been more wrong."

Deloitte, he explained, was far more free-spirited than the control-minded Coopers. And it took three years of employee defections and financial bleeding—and finally a new management team—to get the firm past its culture clashes.

So in 1998, when Coopers and Price Waterhouse merged to form the $15.3 billion megafirm PricewaterhouseCoopers, they made sure to avoid the same nightmare. Ten months before the deal was completed, each firm assigned four executives to a merger integration team, which in turn named Hadfield as its global transition director.

"If no one has full-time responsibility for making a merger work," he explained, "you'll mess up what could have been a perfectly good deal."

There is nothing new about the idea that a merger or acquisition can give rise to cultural conflicts, to quarrels over pay systems, to information systems that don't communicate with each other and to various other problems. Indeed, researchers routinely say that anywhere from one-half to three-quarters of mergers never provide the low costs, added market share or other benefits that management promised shareholders—or that they take much longer than expected to do so.

But until recently, corporations acted as if the only way to better those odds was to look more closely at whether a potential partner's markets and products really meshed with their own, and then to negotiate harder if the deal still made sense.

Now, though, they are also training their magnifying glasses on all the possible glitches that could come after the deal is done—and seeking ways to prevent them.

"We've walked away from companies with autocratic leaders because their employees wouldn't fit in with our team culture," said Ammar Hanafi, director of business development for Cisco Systems, the maker of computer networking equipment. "We even walked away from one that had fancy artwork on its walls, because we doubted it would fit into our culture of frugality."

By April 1999, Cisco, based in San Jose, California, had acquired thirty-two companies since its founding in 1986. It has fifteen full-time people dedicated not only to making mergers work, but also to steering management away from marriages that might be undermined by issues of company culture.

As deal making continues its rampant transformation of corporate America, the concept of in-house merger managers keeps gaining converts.

Allied Signal, General Electric and Lucent Technologies all now have specialists dedicated to the integration of merged companies. In February 1999, AT&T—busy digesting Tele-Communications Inc. and setting up joint ventures with British Telecom and Time Warner—promoted Harold W. Burlingame, its executive vice president of human resources, to the new position of executive vice president of merger and joint venture integration.

"What's changed is that companies are paying as much formal attention to postdeal integration as they pay to the predeal part of mergers," said Bruce A. Pasternack, a senior vice president at Booz, Allen & Hamilton, the consulting firm.

Consultants say the list of such companies grows daily. "Lack of attention to cultures and systems has caused a tremendous number of deals to blow up, and that's shown companies that slapping functions together is not the same as integrating them," said Mark N. Clemente, president of Clemente Greenspan & Company, a management consulting firm.

Recent history has been rife with learning opportunities. Accounting irregularities take only part of the blame, for example, for the implosion of the Cendant Corporation, the $14 billion company created when HFS and CUC International joined forces in late 1997. Most business experts also implicate the mismatch in styles between the controlling and numbers-oriented Henry Silverman, HFS's chief, and the strategy-minded, people-oriented Walter Forbes, the head of CUC.

At AT&T, a good part of Burlingame's new job is to ensure that the company does not repeat with TCI the mistakes it made when it acquired the NCR Corporation in 1991 and McCaw Cellular in 1994.

In both of those cases, AT&T let efforts to coordinate sales pitches, product development and client contacts simmer on a back burner. AT&T

never made money on NCR, which it eventually spun off to shareholders. And while AT&T's cellular business eventually prospered after the acquisition of McCaw, Burlingame believes the company took far too long to absorb its purchase. "We lost a chance to blow the competition out of the water," he said.

There are many reasons that merger integration has emerged as a discipline, with its own dedicated personnel. Corporations have whittled away at headquarters staffs, and the support people who survived—and might be logical candidates for merger duties—rarely have much slack in their schedules. Moreover, top executives recognize that unless they hold individuals accountable for shepherding an acquired company, integration issues could fall to the sidelines.

The number of mergers and acquisitions is at a dizzying high. In 1998, the Securities Data/Thomson Financial Company, a research firm, counted more than twenty-three thousand deals worldwide, worth $2.5 trillion; in just the first quarter of 1999, $840 billion in deals reached fruition worldwide.

Lucent, the big telecommunications equipment maker, bought 18 companies in less than three years of existence. Tyco International, an industrial conglomerate, bought 110 companies in the first six years of L. Dennis Kozlowski's tenure as chief executive, which began in 1993.

"For many companies, mergers have moved from occasional event to a routine, frequent part of doing business," noted Jim E. Fishbein, a vice president of Rath & Strong, the consulting arm of the Aon Corporation.

The deal frenzy has driven prices for acquisitions sky-high, making shareholders unforgiving of deals that do not add to earnings immediately. So the ability to integrate a new company quickly—and wring out some costs in the process—has become a major factor in how a merged company's stock performs.

"Companies have to come full-steam out of the gate to justify the premiums on deals," said Ronald N. Ashkenas, managing partner of Robert H. Schaffer & Associates, a consulting firm in Stamford, Connecticut.

Hercules Inc. certainly knows that. In July 1998, when it announced its purchase of BetzDearborn, another company in the specialty chemicals business, for $2.4 billion in cash and $700 million in assumed debt, it promised investors that by the end of 2000, it would achieve $125 million in synergies—merger-speak for cost savings.

Well before the deal was completed that October, Hercules assigned executives from the two companies to integration teams. Vincent J. Corbo, president of Hercules, presided over the teams, sending each to a different unit to find potential cost cuts and devise schedules for achieving them. He also set up an "integration program office," with a full-time head responsible for seeing that the timetables were met.

Corbo says the merged company is ahead of schedule on reducing costs. But it is still suffering the types of culture clashes that led to the abrupt departure of William R. Cook, Betz's former chief executive, shortly after the companies merged.

"We knew that at Hercules decisions are made analytically, while Betz was managed more intuitively," Corbo said. "But it made sense to get the people in place and the cost synergies planned for before we tried to merge the cultures."

In fact, companies that make frequent acquisitions have found that, after a while, they can handle cost-cutting and personnel issues almost by rote. Their merger integration specialists are high on the learning curve when it comes to disposing of excess real estate, melding pension plans, coordinating accounting systems or handling other important but typical merger chores. Spared of having to reinvent the wheel in those areas, they have more time to study the cultural and market issues that make each merger unique.

"It's a lot speedier if the same people handle the myriad things that are similar in acquisitions and the business units concentrate on melding products, markets and cultures," said Patricia F. Russo, the executive vice president who oversees Lucent's merger integration group.

Gary P. Yeaw, who in 1998 became the first director of human resources for mergers and acquisitions at Allied Signal, the industrial conglomerate, agreed. "You want to customize every integration, but you don't want to start from scratch each time," he said.

Internet technology has made it easier to build banks of institutional memory and advice. A couple of years ago, General Electric pulled together separate teams from human resources, finance and more than a dozen other corporate functions and set them to interviewing GE people who had been involved in some of the hundreds of deals that the company has done in the last few years.

A result is an elaborate site on GE's internal computer network, sorted by subjects like culture or compensation, so that people responsible for those issues can quickly find anecdotes gleaned from past deals, names of GE contacts and even tips on how to choose the right leader for an integration team.

"The Web page's contents, printed out, would fill enough file folders to line an office wall," said Gary M. Reiner, chief information officer for GE. "The intranet is the first viable medium for sharing best practices."

For those who have been wounded by past mergers, remembering the worst practices is even more important.

In hindsight, Burlingame of AT&T concedes that the whole notion behind the NCR deal—that the communications and computing worlds were themselves merging—was flawed. But he believes AT&T exacerbated the problems by not coordinating goals with NCR early on.

"The two companies retained different visions," Burlingame recalled. "AT&T figured it could build on NCR's customer base to sell full-service networks, but NCR just wanted to use our brand name to sell their hardware."

Burlingame is already trying to ensure that cable employees from TCI and their telephone counterparts from AT&T travel the same road from the first day. High on his list are training programs aimed at keeping TCI employees, who have concentrated on serving local markets, from working at cross-purposes with AT&T employees, who are trying to expand national markets.

With Burlingame so new in his job, he might do well to pick up some tips from Hadfield at PricewaterhouseCoopers. Since July 1998, Hadfield has designed employee-retention programs, redeployed some partners to new posts, sent other partners for merger-related training, dispatched people to explain the merger to clients, streamlined purchasing and otherwise cut costs—and made sure that the firm's 150,000 employees are up-to-date on the integration process.

Hadfield credits the integration program for the company's success in retaining nearly all of the nine thousand partners who had been most important to the two firms before they merged.

Unlike PricewaterhouseCoopers, EPS Solutions Inc.—also born of a merger of accounting and consulting firms—has no legacy of failure to guard against. But its integration challenge is perhaps the most dire around.

The company, based in Costa Mesa, California, was formed on December 14, 1998, from the merger of thirty-six smaller firms. Overnight, thirty-five former entrepreneurs were playing second or third fiddle to one large organization. And 1,344 employees who had worked for tiny companies were working for a middle-sized one that now plans to go public.

Long before the December D-day, Christopher P. Massey, the prime mover behind the new company and now its chief executive, met with the other business heads to form integration teams that, as soon as the deal was final, would visit every office to answer questions. They charged one person with integrating all the computer systems. They hammered out a stock option and benefits plan.

When the deal was done, the executives were ready with a thirty-page booklet that detailed compensation plans and career opportunities. It addressed frankly the culture shocks that might be ahead but also devoted considerable ink to the benefits of combining client bases and cash flows.

"We wanted employees, from Day One, to be able to go home and prove to their spouses that there was a lot of security," Massey said. "And we needed to prove to ourselves that we really could turn all those different firms into a single company with a single culture."

And he had to prove it fast. EPS closed six additional acquisitions in March 1999.

Claudia H. Deutsch
April 11, 1999

6

THE TALENT SQUEEZE

Recruiting and Retaining Employees

[When I was at Kodak], the board of directors fired the CEO . . . and held a meeting of fifty managers. Roberto Goizueta, who was the chairman of Coca-Cola at the time, told a story at the meeting about his grandfather, who raised boxer dogs. He said if the dogs were more than 30 percent white, they were considered defective and had to be destroyed. He said that was the problem with Kodak management: It was too inbred, and we had to bring new people in. Those of us in the room who'd been trying to make changes were fuming. After you're accused of being a dog, when the phone rings and it's a headhunter, you listen. Next thing you know, I was CEO of a $240 million company.

> —Katherine M. Hudson, chief executive officer,
> Brady Corporation, August 23, 2000

In an Internet company, you need talent faster than you can hire it. You have to take whoever is in the company and move them at the speed of light in terms of their abilities. You have to compress ten years of learning and making mistakes into two. I call it radical mentoring.

> —Candice Carpenter, cofounder,
> iVillage, November 3, 1999

"At our company, diversity is more than just a slogan; it's a way of life." "We encourage work-life balance because happy employees are productive ones." "We invest in our people to maximize their potential." "We are all about hiring the best people."

Does any of this sound familiar? Of course it does. Over the last decade or so, seemingly every large corporation in the country has adopted nostrums like these. After laying off thousands of employees in the 1990s, companies found themselves with flatter organizational charts and a new need to motivate people, rather than simply issuing them orders. The tight labor market of recent years has also forced companies to devote more attention to hiring people and to keeping them. Many workers simply have more options than they once did. And keeping the best people can be even more critical in bad economic times.

For workers, then, the issue becomes figuring out which companies actually live up to their slogans. For the managers, the key question is whether a stated commitment to a happy workplace—even when accompanied by sincere intentions to back up that commitment—is enough to improve a company's efficiency.

The answer to that question, unfortunately, is an unequivocal no. Companies that proclaim lofty human-resource ideals and then fail to live up to them often find themselves in worse shape than those that simply keep quiet and operate in an old-school way. Why? The overly ambitious firms set their employees up for disappointment and set themselves up as possible examples of hypocrisy. In the end, they are left with frustrated workers, and the companies are almost sure to find that future change will be more difficult to accomplish.

Two of the case studies in this chapter offer a contrast between a stated desire to change and an actual commitment to it.

Years before he became Hewlett-Packard's chief executive, Lewis E. Platt had to confront the reality of balancing work and family because he was a widower and the sole adult in his house for a couple of years. As a result, he says, he gained a new understanding of the challenges many women must face and wanted to be sure they were promoted in adequate numbers. He vowed to change Hewlett-Packard.

Likewise, General Electric—many people's nominee for the best-managed company in America—says diversity has been one of its top priorities since the 1970s. Back then, the company even put on a skit for senior executives about a sexist boss who refused to promote his secretary. Lately, GE has intensified its efforts to promote minorities and women.

Two big companies, both with a commitment to diversifying their executive ranks, right? Well, maybe. One of those companies now has a woman as its chief executive and claims to have the same turnover rate for female and male executives. The other, it turns out, has about half the portion of female corporate officers as the average large American company, and not one of its large divisions is run by a woman.

In these stories—and in one about a recruiting cartel, another about the benefits of failure and others about the world of hiring, retaining and promoting people—you can discover the danger of worthy goals alone. In today's labor market, companies and managers have to figure out ways to live up to those goals, or to pick up the pieces when they don't.

Either way, their best employees are likely to stick with a company that keeps its word. Whether they'll need to change jobs to do so is another matter.

CASE 1

The Cracked Glass Ceiling

Hewlett-Packard's elevation of Carly Fiorina to the post of chief executive in July 1999 solidified the company's reputation as a bastion of egalitarianism in a male-dominated corporate world. With more than a quarter of Hewlett-Packard's managers women—including one who was a main rival of Fiorina for the top job—it seemed incontestable that the glass ceiling that stops the rise of female executives at so many other companies had been shattered.

But who hurled the rock?

The surprising answer: a middle-aged white guy who never thought much about women in the workplace—until he was thrust suddenly into the challenging role of single parent.

The struggle of Lewis E. Platt, now the company's chairman, to juggle the competing duties of father and breadwinner when he was a rising senior executive nearly two decades ago had a happy ending for Hewlett-Packard. And his success in turning company policy around from the traditional "man rules the roost" culture to a gender-blind ethos holds an important lesson for the rest of corporate America: a little direction at the top can go a long way.

It all began in 1981. Back then, Platt was a general manager, and Hewlett-Packard was what he describes as a "white male haven," populated by graduates of engineering schools in dark suits with starched white shirts. He was, he says, quite comfortable working in that male-dominated environment and leaving the child-rearing and housekeeping chores to his wife of sixteen years, Susan.

Then, his world fell apart: Susan died of cancer, and suddenly, he was the one who had to make dinner for his two daughters, Laura and Caryn, then nine and eleven, get them to school, make sure they did their homework in the evenings and even find the time to go grocery shopping.

"My mother had really been the one running the show on the home front," said Caryn, who now runs her own social services business. She has memories of standing with her father and her sister in a supermarket aisle wondering whether there were enough varieties of Hamburger Helper, one of the few dishes Platt could prepare, to dine on that week.

His sudden vulnerability, Platt says, shattered his old assumption that any difficulties women had in the workplace were of their own making. "Here I was a white male, doing really well at HP," Platt recalled in an interview at the company's headquarters in Palo Alto, California. "I was suddenly thrust into a different role." In the position of having double duty at home and at work, "I couldn't cope any better than they did," he said.

For six months after his wife's death, he said, his coworkers allowed him to grieve and concentrate on getting his personal life in order instead of putting his full energy into his career. "I was probably a pretty marginal performer," he admitted, but he came to understand the ebb and flow of careers. "One day I would be back and give the time and energy to be a senior manager," he said.

As the months rolled by, his life remained frantic, he says, a never-ending grind of traveling, working late in the office, getting up early to be with his children and turning to grandparents or nannies to care for them when he was not around. At one point, he debated leaving Hewlett-Packard; but as a lifelong employee, who had joined right out of business school in 1966 and worked his way up the ladder, he soldiered on.

When he married again in 1983, his second wife, Joan, took over the household responsibilities, freeing him to indulge his workaholic tendencies. But rather than retreating to his old way of thinking, he found he sympathized with the plight of the average working woman more than ever. Joan Platt had two daughters of her own, Amanda and Hillary, then nine and seven, and surrounded as he was as the sole male, he had little choice but to look at their side of things, noted his daughter, Caryn. "We would gang up on him pretty mercilessly," she recalled. All four daughters are now working.

Named a vice president in 1983, Platt continued his ascent at Hewlett-Packard, managing various parts of the company's computer business before becoming an executive vice president in 1987. During that time, more women were rising to the level of manager, but few were making it to the highest ranks.

By the time he became chief executive in 1992, he says, droves of those women managers were leaving. "The pipeline didn't look very good," he said. After an outside consultant conducted interviews with many of these women, he came to realize that despite his own open-mindedness on the subject, the company's policies were not flexible enough to accommodate their lives outside the workplace.

What concerned him in particular were the women in their late thirties who left the company to devote more time to their children, never to be seen again. "They were gone," Platt said. "We were no longer connected to them."

So he decided to take action. Working with other top executives, Platt developed what for Hewlett-Packard was a new workplace strategy. Over the next several years, the company began to encourage employees to adjust their workweeks, arrange flexible work schedules, work at home if necessary and even share jobs—all so that they could meet their personal responsibilities. They could even take sabbaticals—yearlong unpaid leaves from the company—no questions asked.

While many companies offer these options, few corporations actually encourage their use. Hewlett-Packard did. Platt made speeches, reminding managers that they needed to consider seriously any of their employees' requests to take advantage of this new flexibility, and he put his name on memos sent to managers across the world. "Work/life issues are a business priority," one statement said. "Attention to work/life issues strengthens HPs competitive edge and improves teamwork within HP."

Even high-level employees take advantage of the new flexibility. Janice Chaffin, an eighteen-year Hewlett-Packard employee and general manager in charge of providing large computer systems to companies, for example, shared that position, just one rank below division president at the company, for a year.

Chaffin says she has never come under any pressure to put in time in the office for the sake of appearance—her bosses' boss even encouraged her to make clear to her own manager, who was known for spending nearly every waking hour at the office, that she would not do the same. "It was never an issue," she said.

Nearly all employees determine their own hours to some extent, according to the company, and large numbers opt to work at home at least some of the time. About 12 percent have formal telecommuting arrangements, and employees are routinely asked about how receptive their managers are to their needs in balancing work with the rest of their lives.

Perhaps most important, Platt has been vocal on the issue, according to Jerry Cashman, the company's director of programs that encourage work/life balance and diversity. He also likes to remind male colleagues of some of the built-in disadvantages women operate under; he never tires of noting that while the vast majority of them are married to men who work, two-thirds of male managers have stay-at-home wives.

Platt says the new policy is not just the right thing to do—it is the smart thing. "Anything you can do to attract and retain the best talent is really critical," he said.

The results, in fact, have been dramatic. In the early 1990s, the turnover for women was twice that of men, according to the company; now, the gap has been eliminated and the rates are almost identical. Moreover, the company says it loses fewer than 5 percent of its employees each year, compared with an industry average that the consulting firm William M. Mercer puts at 17 percent.

Brenda Vathauer, a high-powered marketing manager, says the freedom to set her own agenda persuaded her to return to Hewlett-Packard after her maternity leave. But she found herself in an odd position: she did not want a part-time job, which she noted is too often considered a "subjob" at most companies, but she did not want to work the sixty hours of a typical full-time job, either.

The solution: she teamed up with another working mother to share a full-time management position in customer service. Each woman now puts in three ten-hour days a week, each receives three-quarters pay and benefits—and each gets to spend four days a week at home, counting weekends. "You can keep your career more on track," explained Karen Walker, her partner in the enterprise and a mother of three.

Men make use of the company's programs, too. Bill Hornung, also a customer-service manager, describes himself as "a telecommuter poster child" for other men because he works at home so can he care for his two children, five and nine, when his wife, a flight attendant, is in the air.

To be sure, Hewlett-Packard is not an equal-opportunity utopia. Platt readily admits that the company has had difficulty recruiting and promoting blacks. The company said it does not disclose the percentage of managers within certain ethnic groups.

Even so, to the outside world, the promotion of Fiorina to chief executive—she is only the third woman now heading a Fortune 500 company—was seen as a groundbreaking event. And though it was greeted as policy as usual inside the company, some Hewlett-Packard employees reveled in the symbolism. Just as the victory of the American women's soccer team provided important role models for young women, so did the selection of Fiorina, they say.

Bart Coddington, who works with analysts studying the computer industry for the company, says his three-year-old granddaughter, Sydney, "will grow up with all that.

"I'm just so excited for her," he said.

Now that the white, middle-aged guy responsible for ushering in this era of equality will step down as chairman at the end of 1999, what about the woman who replaced him as chief executive? When she was appointed, Fiorina made a widely reported, controversial assertion that there was no glass ceiling. She has since told colleagues that her remark may not apply throughout corporate America, and she has emphasized the need to look for talent wherever it can be found, regardless of sex, race or age.

As for Platt, he is leaving it up to the company's employees to make sure Hewlett-Packard does not revert to its old self. Specific programs are not important, he says. "It's the core values."

Reed Abelson
August 22, 1999

CASE 2

Diversity in a Meritocracy

In late 2000, John F. Welch, who had a remarkable twenty-year run of earnings growth and near cultlike devotion as chief executive of the General Electric Company, was making plans for a successor. And the three frontrunners fit a pattern. All were gung-ho results getters for the company—and all were white men.

GE promoted three other executives to stand ready to replace any frontrunner who bailed out if he was not anointed as Welch's successor. These three, too, fit the mold: stellar growth-and-earnings producers, and all white men.

Where are the women? The blacks? The Latinos? The Asians?

Together, these groups make up about 40 percent of GE's domestic workforce, but they are not easy to find in the top executive corps of GE, which is regarded in many management circles as America's most admired corporation. Just 6.4 percent of its corporate officers are women, compared with an average of 11.9 percent for all the Fortune 500 companies, according to a 1999 survey by Catalyst, a nonprofit research and advisory group that studies women in business.

Of the twenty businesses that provided 90 percent of GE's earnings in

1999, only one is headed by someone who is not white: GE Industrial Systems has an African-American president and chief executive, Lloyd G. Trotter, who is also a senior vice president of the parent corporation.

And the first woman to become chief executive of a GE business—Sandra L. Derickson, at GE Capital Auto Financial Services—left unceremoniously in 1999 after the fast-growing auto-leasing unit posted a sharp earnings decline and had to be restructured. A man replaced her.

GE has had diversity on its agenda for at least three decades, and its efforts to retain women and minorities have intensified in recent years.

"We have put a lot of programs in place to make sure that GE's global diversity is real and lasting, and we measure our progress," Welch said. Responding to questions by e-mail, he conceded that GE isn't "where we want to be yet," but pointed to current efforts to move more diverse talent through GE's managerial "pipeline."

Lest anyone think that Welch has gone touchy-feely in his final year at the helm, he stressed that diversity was a bottom-line necessity today.

"Diversity isn't just a nice corporate program," he said. "It's a business and a global reality. The 1990s have been largely about global growth and going after the brightest minds, wherever they may be in the world."

He added, "I believe the future has never been better for a truly diverse GE."

In the here and now, however, GE's all-male and nearly all-white leadership slate raises intriguing issues. After all, it is no longer unheard-of for large American companies to be led by women or minorities—American Express, Maytag and Hewlett-Packard are high-profile examples. Catalyst has measured steady annual increases in women corporate officers since it started counting in 1995, and Spencer Stuart, the executive search firm, reports a small but growing minority presence in American boardrooms.

Under Welch, GE has become a gold standard for management practices. Detractors may criticize its mass layoffs and chemical spills, but its managerial training and promotion practices inspire widespread praise and imitation. To many in corporate America, GE is a meritocracy par excellence—a place where managers are judged on their ability to meet tough financial goals, not on whether they speak with the right accent, attended the right schools or had the right father.

Why, then, the white, male leadership slate? Is there something about this acclaimed corporate culture that is inhospitable to women and minorities?

Dozens of interviews with current and former GE managers turned up much agreement that GE's efforts at promoting diversity had fallen short, at least until recently. But there was no unanimity about why. "It really is a paradox," said Karen Nelson, a former GE Medical Systems marketing manager who served as the diversity director of that business from 1991 to 1994.

Some pointed to the company's practice of grooming talent through frequent relocations, saying that it was tougher on women, and unappealing to minority managers, who would have to drag spouses and children to parochial towns. Others said GE's engineering history was the reason, arguing that today's statistics reflect the difficulties that all engineering businesses had in attracting women and minorities as trainees years ago.

Trotter, GE's most senior black executive, thinks those theories let management, including himself, off too easily. "If I had managed my business the way I had managed diversity, I think I'd have gotten fired," he said, noting that GE requires every business unit to be first or second in its market, or risk sale or closure. There is no such requirement for diversity.

The priorities have now changed, Trotter said, adding that new measures to recruit and retain more African-Americans, designed by GE's black managers themselves, were more likely to work. These initiatives, which have more recently been adapted by GE's women, Latinos and Asian-Americans, pose no challenge to GE's culture of meritocracy, but try to bolster participants' confidence, groom them for promotion and give them a better idea of how they fit into the corporate structure.

Still, others who are knowledgeable about GE's workings wonder whether diversity can be achieved within a system that prizes growth and earnings above all else.

Nelson, for one, said that she savored the adrenaline highs of working in GE's tough culture, but that she began to believe that this same culture was burning out the very women and minorities she was working so hard to recruit, to say nothing of herself.

"I would get four hours of sleep a night," recalled Nelson, who gave birth to her second child while serving as diversity officer for the United States, Canada and Latin America. "I was traveling so much I knew all the porters in the airport by their first names. I would stagger home at midnight and get back up at 4 A.M. We had staff meetings at 7:30 in the morning, and you had to be there."

GE tried to accommodate Nelson, granting a postpregnancy family leave, and letting a nanny bring the baby to the office for midday feedings. But Nelson knew that accommodations could hurt as well as help, suggesting special treatment in a system that values a lean and mean image.

Increasingly troubled by work/family conflicts, and uncertain that diversity could ever take root in such arid soil, Nelson resigned in 1994 and is now president of the Leaders Forum, a nonprofit group in Milwaukee that promotes African-American business interests.

"Frankly, I don't know how to begin to change the GE culture," she said. "All we were saying was, 'Let's level the playing field.' Now, do we really want to say, 'We have to change the game altogether?' "

The company's efforts to promote women and minorities began in the early 1970s, when civil rights victories were bearing fruit in many American workplaces. A women's advisory panel was convened at the company, affirmative action guidelines were issued, and Welch's predecessor, Reginald H. Jones, traveled to Washington to become chairman of the National Advisory Council on Minorities in Engineering.

In the early 1970s, the General Electric Foundation went so far as to commission a one-act play to raise management consciousness. In the play, a male executive refuses to promote a secretary, then has a nightmare in which he is endlessly patronized by women. He wakes up screaming, "I'm not a statistic!" and, as the curtain falls, promises to stop blocking women's careers.

The early initiatives put more women into jobs as welders and foremen, and even attracted some minority managers, like Trotter, who joined in 1970. But they did little to change demographics at the top.

After Welch became chief executive in 1981, some people saw reason for optimism. True, Welch had come out of GE's plastics business, a division known for its free-wheeling frat-house culture, and he began selling GE businesses, laying off tens of thousands of workers and instilling a harsh, Darwinian ethos through the company. But by eliminating whole layers of middle management that had been predominantly white and male, Welch raised hope in some circles that he was clearing the way for diverse up-and-comers.

In 1992, an article in *Working Woman* magazine contended that the "Welch management revolution" bore a striking resemblance to then-current feminist management theories: Welch was trying to flatten hierarchies, encourage teamwork and have managers pool information across rigid turf lines, the article said, just as feminist scholars were declaring women to be quicker to share information, cooperate and encourage teamwork on the job.

It was that atmosphere that convinced Anne Poirson, a computer scientist, to go to work for GE as a systems designer in the early Welch years.

"I researched different corporations around the country, and found out that GE was supposed to be one of the best for women," she recalled.

"There was equal pay, promotional opportunities." And Poirson also approved, in theory, of Welch's campaign to reshape and "de-layer" GE.

But in practice, Poirson found herself thrown in with a lot of frightened, white, male middle managers who believed that they were fighting for their survival—and that she was the enemy.

"A lot of managers told me they were intimidated by me," she said. "I was a young woman in charge of some big projects, and I had a lot of clout. I was bringing in computer systems that were upsetting the power structure of the whole company. At one point, my productivity was rated on how many jobs I eliminated."

Poirson said she soon found herself excluded from key meetings and denied the secretarial help that she wanted. One day, she said, her boss told her point-blank, "I'm making twice as much as you are, and someone is going to figure out that there should be two of you, and then they won't need me anymore."

The entrenched layers of middle managers were being thinned, all right, but Poirson stopped hoping that women would rise in that environment. The whole point of restructuring was to strip away bureaucracy and improve earnings, she said, but because there were fewer management positions to go around, those who survived faced multiple workloads.

Poirson resigned in 1986, after five years with the company, to go into business for herself. She now has her own software consulting firm and says she has more control over her career.

"Someone in my position is not going to stick around at GE and wait for equality to simmer through the corporation," she said. "Yes, it's a very good company, but in my particular case, I didn't think it was going to pay off for me."

Cheryl Watkins Snead, an engineer, told a similar story. One of the first black women to receive an engineering degree from the University of Massachusetts—Welch's alma mater—she said GE appeared eager to recruit female engineers. She joined the company in 1981 and moved quickly through a series of assignments in the United States, the Caribbean and Asia.

But eventually, Snead said, she found herself wondering: Did all the transfers really mean that she was moving up?

"Not just at GE, but in corporate America, there are only so many management slots," she said. "It gets to the point where your moves are lateral, not vertical."

Had more women been near the top of the corporate flow chart, Snead said, she might have felt more confident that her labors would pay off one day. But the two minority women on GE's board today—Andrea Jung, an Asian-American who is president and chief executive of Avon Products, and Ann M. Fudge, the African-American who is executive vice president of Kraft Foods—arrived in 1998 and 1999, after Snead had resigned and founded Banneker Industries, an outsourcing firm.

To be sure, no one at GE ever contended that a main goal of restructuring was to advance women and minorities.

"For us, the eighties were about getting our business model right, 'delayering' and creating a 'boundaryless culture,'" said Welch, using GE language for lopping off tiers of the corporate organization chart and encouraging employees to go directly to senior managers for information rather than inching up the chain of command.

But years later, it was clear that the focus on earnings and market share had left diversity an orphan. GE's leaders realized that they would have to address what they called the company's "social architecture" if they wanted to stop losing people like Poirson and Snead. They decided to apply "work out"—a group-analysis process used to solve business problems in the 1980s—to diversity. About sixty well-placed executives were called to the corporate headquarters in Fairfield, Connecticut, in early 1991.

Among them were fifteen African-Americans, who decided to sit down privately beforehand to sharpen their presentations. Trotter said he had a revelation as he walked in.

"I had been around the company for eighteen years, and I only knew three of the fifteen people in the room," he said. One of diversity's most powerful advocates at GE, he suddenly realized he could not possibly promote talented blacks if he did not know who they were. "It was a mirror test," he said. "I looked at myself and said, 'Am I using all of the necessary energy and the skill moving people up the ladder?' And the answer was, 'No.'"

Steven D. Thorne, then a GE human resources manager, said it was not just that GE's black executives were too busy working to seek out one another. In general, African-Americans at GE were reluctant to call attention to themselves, he said, because the company's culture promoted color-blindness. If you were supposed to rise or fall on the basis of performance, what good would it do to bring up race?

"It was a way of avoiding making waves," said Thorne, who became the corporation's top diversity officer in 1999. "You put yourself at risk if you set yourself out."

At that first meeting, however, those fifteen black managers began to think that if minority recruits at GE kept playing the corporate game by the colorblind rules, they would never even know who their teammates were, much less score. Certainly, they began to think, there was some way of bringing African-Americans together and promoting their interests without challenging the meritocracy itself and creating a backlash.

When they raised the idea with Welch, he asked them what they had in mind. They had no answer.

"We went back and said to each other, 'If he ever asks us that again, we don't want to be in that position,'" Thorne said.

For the next year, on their own time, black managers studied glass-ceiling issues and minority retention at other corporations, trying to learn what practices brought lasting gains, and which of those might work in GE's culture. They also polled other black managers at the company, asking what they thought might be useful. They moved cautiously, Thorne said, fearing that if they threw together an ill-conceived program that failed, they would not receive a second chance.

In the end, they settled on an in-house self-help network, called the African American Forum. Started in 1992, its mandate is narrow: to demystify GE's personnel policies, to provide a setting where GE blacks can meet one another and to develop a formal mentor program, in which GE's senior executives are required to participate. GE says it is keeping track of which mentors' trainees receive promotions and is rating the mentors accordingly.

Outside critics may find this disappointingly tame, but the GE planners chose to avoid any hint of advocacy, special status or quotas. They figured that a narrow focus on self-improvement, well within the confines of GE's existing culture, would draw more members—and that a large group with limited goals would accomplish more over time than a small group that tried too much.

David A. Thomas, a Harvard Business School professor of organizational behavior who has studied diversity initiatives in large companies, agreed with that thinking. Corporate minority networks that succeed, he said, tend to have goals that jibe with the company's philosophy and can point to the participation of top executives.

The July 2000 gathering of the African American Forum attracted eighteen hundred participants, including Welch and most of GE's other senior executives based in the United States. Participants say the meetings provide something simple but important: a place where they can meet top executives without the usual pressure of being outnumbered by whites.

"In my first year and a half, I knew every corporate officer," said A. Louis Parker, president of direct products for GE Financial Assurance, who came to GE in 1996 after stints at IBM, Automatic Data Processing and Morgan Stanley. "It was very different from where I had been before. I've heard about diversity at other places, but GE is the first place I've felt it."

As the African American Forum began receiving plaudits like that, other groups at GE took note. Managerial women started planning their own self-help network in 1997, researching possible structures for a year and deciding that they, too, would restrict their mandate to narrow, nonconfrontational goals.

There were no calls to celebrate women's "web thinking" or other supposed feminine advantages now being promoted in some theorist circles. In interviews, many GE women said they enjoyed the intense, no-holds-barred environment at GE and wanted their group, called the Women's Network, to help them better compete on those terms.

Nor did the network's founders put work-family issues on their agenda. Though much research shows that these issues affect corporate women more than men, the GE women said they believed that the problems required individual solutions and that they did not want to lobby for one-size-fits-all remedies.

Instead, the Women's Network has focused since 1998 on coaching women in public speaking, in making effective presentations and in exuding leadership qualities. It also links participants with senior-executive mentors. GE, meanwhile, has asked Catalyst to conduct follow-up interviews with high-level women who leave the company, to make sure that there were no hidden gender issues driving them away.

None of this will catapult any women or blacks—or the Asians and Latinos now organizing their own groups—past those white men at the front of the pack in time to claim Welch's job. But the many consultants who study GE and try to graft its practices onto other corporations are watching the latest efforts to see what they accomplish.

"I think that by some of the programs that Jack Welch is pushing, he's kind of admitting that we have to do some special things" to accelerate diversity, said Noel M. Tichy, a professor of organizational behavior at the University of Michigan who ran GE's management training center from 1985 to 1987 and now writes and consults extensively on its management practices. "That doesn't mean you don't have standards, and you're not going to be a meritocracy. I would put them as one of the companies

that's pretty seriously driving this agenda. I don't know why it took them
so long."

Mary Williams Walsh
September 3, 2000

CASE 3

Demand-Side Staffing

For more than three months, Kevin Meeker, owner of Philadelphia Fish and
Company, a restaurant and bar, put up with a cook whose obsession with
the stock market often took his mind away from the soup. The twenty-two-
year-old employee checked his Motorola shares every half hour on his
pager and periodically slipped out to the dining room to get the bartender
to turn on CNBC.

Not so long ago, Meeker said, he would have warned the cook to knock
it off and fired him if he did not comply. But not in the recent job market.
Instead, he turned a blind eye to the goofing off, and said he would probably still have the man on the payroll if he had not quit on Mother's Day
after being asked to work beyond his eight-hour shift.

"I think the attitude among workers right now is, 'I could always go and
get another job,'" Meeker said. "Now, that cook's working for another
restaurant around the corner."

Checking on stock prices is the least of it. Increasingly, employees are
testing the boundaries of the American work ethic as employers, hammered
by recruiting and training expenses and fearful that they will be unable to
fill job openings, make allowances for just about every form of misconduct.
Offenses like frequent tardiness or absenteeism, apathy and even insubordi-
nation that would have merited a pink slip in the mid-1990s are being
shrugged off as inconveniences.

The new management rule of thumb, it seems, is that a warm body is
better than no body.

Take Suzan Windnagel, director of human resources for a credit union in
San Jose, California. A woman who worked for her was frequently late,
gave customers incorrect information and just did not feel like learning new
computer skills.

If not for the tight labor market, Windnagel said, she would have dismissed the slacker within four months. Instead, she spent a year and a half

counseling her, lecturing her and desperately trying to train her. Nothing worked, and, finally, she had to let her go.

But she said she is neither surprised nor particularly upset about the sloppy work habits she sees around her these days. "Workers, not bosses, have the upper hand," said Windnagel, who has been a human resources manager for more than two decades. "Managers today know how hard it is to recruit people, so they put up with more. I don't blame workers at all."

Most people still put in an honest day's work, of course. It is just that the lazy, the rude and the nonproductive have an easier time of it.

Doug Peterson, vice president for human resources at the Shape Corporation, an automotive supplier in Grand Haven, Michigan, for example, said most of the company's one thousand workers are productive and disciplined. Yet Peterson acknowledged that he harbors underperformers.

"Have we held on to people where in years past, we would have fired them?" he said. "The answer is yes."

The reason for the leniency is that at any given time, the company has an average of forty unfilled jobs.

Because skilled trades are such tough positions to fill, Peterson said, he tolerated for nearly a year a hot-tempered staff electrician who often threatened coworkers. The company tried to counsel him and even signed him up for anger-management training, but finally dismissed him. "Five or six years ago, we would have not put up with that," Peterson said. "The person would have been gone immediately."

To combat worsening tardiness and absenteeism, he said, Shape has chosen the carrot over the stick. In 1999, it decided to give workers seventeen hours of personal time off a year on top of their vacation days—and to pay them ten dollars for each of those hours they do not use. "We're giving incentives for people to be at work," he said.

Adaptec Inc., a maker of software and computer components in Milpitas, California, illustrates the starkness of the change taking place in the workplace. In 1994, almost one-third of the people who left the company had been fired, according to Rick Olivieri, the director of compensation and benefits. In 2000, that proportion is down to 2 percent. "It's a real war for people out there right now," Olivieri said.

But leniency carries risks, warns DeAnne Rosenberg, author of *Hiring the Best Person for Every Job*. Most notably, accommodating shirkers can hurt office morale, she said.

Rosenberg cited the case of a home health-care administrator in Boston who yelled constantly at her coworkers, fobbed off work on colleagues and treated clients disrespectfully. Over eight months, ten coworkers complained to her supervisor, but he refused to reprimand her, much less fire her. "He kept saying: 'It's a hard labor market. At least the little she does, she does,'" Rosenberg said.

Ultimately, the coworkers took matters into their own hands. They came in on a weekend, packed up the administrator's belongings and moved her desk and chair to another floor, she said. When the administrator came to work on Monday, they pretended she was not there and talked about her as if she had gone to another company.

She quit that day.

Obnoxious behavior is one thing. Illegal behavior is another.

Mark Spring, a labor and employment lawyer in Sacramento, California, said that executives at one of his client companies, a national book and music chain, merely gave a written warning to a manager who had ordered two subordinates to move a marijuana plant from his office to his home during work hours, he said.

In another case, a bank slapped the wrist of an employee who had been caught downloading pornography from the Internet, revoking his Internet privileges for thirty days and sending him to a sensitivity-training course.

Both the book and music chain and the bank exposed themselves to potential litigation by their inaction, Spring said.

Referring to the bank employee, he said, "If this had happened in the early nineties, he would have been fired because of the recession and because at the time everyone was nervous over sexual harassment."

Barring blatant wrongdoing, though, many companies are pursuing the path of least resistance.

"If a slacker comes in to work at 10 A.M. instead of 8 A.M., maybe the company needs to rethink that worker's schedule," said Erisa Ojimba, compensation expert for Salary.com, a salary-resource Web site based in Wellesley, Massachusetts. "Maybe they're not their most productive before 10 A.M."

Eve Tahmincioglu
July 19, 2000

CASE 4

The Failure Skill-Set

At age thirty, Michael Barach quit a lucrative job as a vice president for marketing for a $100 million furniture company to take charge of a start-up called Cartoon Corner—a concept similar to the Disney Store, but with generic cartoons on the merchandise.

The company was forced to dissolve within three years, partly as a result of his miscalculations and partly as a result of bad timing. That left Barach, who had graduated at the top of his business class at Harvard, broke and dispirited, but also dying for a second chance. "I was unbelievably hungry," he recalled. "I felt that I was behind my peer group."

It was just this hunger that appealed to the venture capital firm Bessemer Venture Partners, which installed Barach as chief executive of Motherna-ture.com, an Internet site offering natural products, in 1998. A year later, he argued that his failure at Cartoon Corner made him a sharper chief executive at Mothernature.com. "I am much more humble and paranoid," he said. He is so convinced that at least one setback in a career is crucial to shaping business judgment that he looks to hire executives who have had similar disappointments. "All my senior managers had something happen along the way," he said.

Not long ago, only winners needed apply in corporate America. An executive who presided over a new product that flopped had little hope of being promoted or getting a better job elsewhere. An entrepreneur who crash-landed a start-up was unlikely to get cash from venture capitalists for his next brainstorm.

But a decade's worth of talk from business schools and corporate trainers about the glories of risk-taking, combined with a shortage of executive talent in the current economic boom, has given a dash of class to failure. An executive or an entrepreneur who has cratered once is suddenly a sexy hire.

"Failure is a badge," said Irv Grousbeck, an entrepreneurship professor at the Stanford Business School. These days, he says, managers who have made errors and suffered for them are wanted not just by Internet start-ups but increasingly by Fortune 500 companies eager to make themselves more competitive against small businesses that move fast and take chances. "It is not just that these people had guts enough to take risks," he said. It is also assumed that "they learned under the whip of urgency."

This is not to say that job candidates with stellar, unblemished records need worry about going on unemployment. Nor does it mean that any failure will add the right kind of luster to the résumé. A botched start-up will probably do; after all, it puts the candidate in the company of such successful entrepreneurs as John Chambers, the president of Cisco Systems Inc., and Alexander d'Arbeloff, the chairman of Teradyne Inc., each of whom has at least one disaster to his name. Also acceptable, but requiring a convincing explanation of what went wrong, are management blunders in corporations.

Moral lapses, however, are widely viewed as unredeemable. "Anything related to issues of integrity, trust and ethics are fatal flaws," said Rebecca Guerra, vice president for human resources at eBay, the online auction house.

Not all industry sectors find that failure has the same cachet. Nowhere is it more in vogue, of course, than Silicon Valley, where new technology companies like to brag that they are shattering the old corporate mold with their venturesome employment policies.

"Failure is as much a credential as success—even, perhaps, more so," said David Cowan, a venture capitalist in Menlo Park, California, who has installed chief executives with checkered track records at a half-dozen Internet start-ups. "If they are coming off a failed business, they have an innate understanding of the consequences of running out of cash, and they focus on long-term issues earlier on than other people."

Even conservative employers, like banks and accounting firms, are coming around to the notion that failure is tolerable in small doses. Gene Manheim, a partner with Herbert Mines Associates, a New York recruiting firm, said they might have no choice. "The pool of talent is already too small to thin it out again by eliminating those who have failed," he said.

Over the last decade, Arnold P. Cohen, a retail executive, played a leading role at three well-known clothing concerns—London Fog Industries, Today's Man Inc. and J. Peterman—as each descended into serious financial trouble or went bankrupt. Despite this fiasco of a management record, everyone who has worked with Cohen sings his praises in one area: merchandising. With executive talent in retailing scarce, American Malls International, a Washington, D.C., real estate developer, hired him as the merchandiser for its new malls in Japan.

The volatile job market is also fueling the trend. Job-hopping by managers has become more common in recent years as corporate America has downsized, and companies are hiring more people in their forties and fifties. By definition, these corporate longtimers have more bloopers in their backgrounds than newly minted M.B.A. graduates.

Deloitte & Touche, the big management-consulting firm, which used to focus on fresh-faced M.B.A. graduates, has started to reach for people in their thirties and beyond. "We need people with practice and experience and, hey, if you are out there competing in the world, life happens," said Jim Wall, who is in charge of hiring at Deloitte & Touche.

Wall predicted that the firm would be hiring even more people with compromised records. "We are going to see a lot of M.B.A. students who heretofore had mostly considered opportunities in investment banking and corporate strategy but now are taking the fly right out of business school on some start-up venture," he said. "Some are going to be successful, and some of them are not, and it is the latter group that isn't going to want to come back. Are they still valuable as talent? You bet."

Notice his choice of words. For all the new luster of failure, career counselors say, employers generally prefer euphemisms to describe it. "We are interested in people who have worked beyond their comfort zone," said Nancy Eberhardt, whose cheeky title is queen of culture for Carl M. Freeman Associates, a real estate developer in Potomac, Maryland. "The person we like to see is the person who took a risk to do something bigger than they were."

Leslie Kaufman
October 6, 1999

In November 2000, Mothernature.com announced that it would be dissolving. "What does not kill you makes you stronger," Michael Barach said in a December 2000 interview. "I feel like I was a pioneer. We achieved what we wanted to achieve. In the end, however, e-tailing just does not add up. We understood that, which is why we are liquidating, not just waiting to go splat."

CASE 5

Keeping Talent Through Cooperation

LearnLinc, a small educational software company, needs an experienced project manager. There is a woman at MapInfo, a larger software company nearby, who fits the bill.

Almost anywhere else, Degerhan Usluel, the chief executive of LearnLinc, would go a-wooing on his own. But this is Troy, New York, a place where "thou shalt not raid" has become a new commandment. Usluel called Michael D. Marvin, MapInfo's chairman, and struck a deal in which the woman would work for Usluel for two years, then return to MapInfo. "We're getting the person we need, and MapInfo gets a free retraining program for a valued employee," Usluel said.

Forget how hard it is for high-technology companies to hold on to talent in a climate of cutthroat recruiting. Here in New York's Capital Region, an area of about a million people that ranks low on most wish-I-lived-there lists, local software companies are not only staying off one another's turf, but are also nurturing one another's employees.

"If someone stays in town, you may get him back," explained John C. Haller, one of MapInfo's founders. "If he goes to California, he's gone forever."

Such thinking has fostered a merry-go-round of job hops. Haller, for example, was feeling restless after ten years with MapInfo; Marvin arranged for him to teach classes at the Rensselaer Polytechnic Institute (RPI) here and to consult with Poweradz.com, a smaller local start-up, until his juices were flowing again. Six months later, Haller returned to MapInfo as chief technology officer.

Three years later, in December 1999, Haller and Steve Lombardi, another MapInfo employee, were starting a new Internet company with MapInfo's money. "I had just gotten a great job offer in California, and they knew it would take an Internet project to keep me here," Lombardi said.

Holding on to employees is an uphill battle here. Despite the looming presence of RPI—and a growing base of about two hundred software companies with combined revenues of about $300 million in 1999—the Capital Region of Albany, Schenectady and Troy is noted mainly for bleak weather and state politics. "There's still this perception that California is the golden world, that the Northeast is this cold and rusty place," said Michael H. Wacholder, director of the Rensselaer Technology Park, home to most of the software companies.

That is why the companies collaborate instead of competing. They take turns playing host to monthly beer parties for younger employees. They exchange salary information, evaluate one another's business strategies and critique one another's presentations to venture capitalists.

And they gang up on anyone who breaks the unwritten rules. A few years ago, one local company began wooing employees from its neighbors. Usluel let it grab one LearnLinc programmer. "But I said, 'You take one more person from me, I'll spend whatever it takes to buy two from you,'" he recalled. A year later, the company approached someone at MapInfo. Marvin called the chairman, gently reminded him that he "wasn't playing by the rules" and implied that he would be frozen out of all local activities if he persisted with raids. The MapInfo employee stayed put, and other local software chiefs say the would-be raider has kept his distance since.

But tales of rivalry are far outnumbered by those of collaboration:

- Over the course of eleven years, Joseph M. Clement was the first human resources chief at Chart Inc., MapInfo, Comsoft and, lastly, IA Systems, which makes software for the banking industry. In each case, as soon as he grew restless, his bosses helped him land a new job within driving distance of the old one.

- Kathy Dinardo, Marvin's administrative assistant, had breakfast with Donna Bonaquisiti, who was seeking a job at MapInfo. Dinardo liked her but knew that LearnLinc needed an office manager, so she sent her there. Bonaquisiti got the job.

- In November 1999, Clement met someone at a job fair who did not seem right for IA Systems; at his suggestion, another local company, Aptis, took the man on. Conversely, Clement called a former colleague at MapInfo the following month for leads on sales staff. "She gave me the name of someone she thought was great, but figured would be a better fit for us," Clement said.

MapInfo's name keeps cropping up in these stories. As the oldest and biggest of the area's high-technology firms—in 1999, it expected revenues of close to $100 million for its statistical map-making products—it incubates much local talent. But most important, it is home to Marvin, who is so much the spiritual mentor of the informal Capital Region software circle that the other chiefs often call themselves the Marvinettes.

Marvin got hooked on the idea of a technology center here in 1986, when he was with RPI's Center for Industrial Innovation. Four recent graduates approached him about heading MapInfo, the software company they wanted to start. "These were twenty-one-year-old boys," he said. "They needed an adult, and I loved the challenge of proving a high-tech company could make it in Troy."

Marvin was MapInfo's first and third chief executive, and he remains its chairman. In between he ran LearnLinc, Usluel's brainchild, until Usluel felt ready to take over. Marvin was also a cofounder of the Exponential Business Development Company, a venture capital firm that provides seed money for local high-technology concerns.

He has single-handedly kept several in town. "Mike Marvin said he'd give us seed capital if we stayed here, and persuaded us that we could learn plenty from the other companies," said Karthik Bala, another RPI alumnus, who had planned to move his video game start-up, Vicarious Visions, to California after graduation in 1997.

MapInfo people helped Vicarious Visions build a compensation plan for its game developers, and other local chief executives are helping the company forge a strategy for syndicating games on the World Wide Web. Vicarious Visions expects $8 million in sales in 2000.

The Marvinettes switch mentor and student hats with remarkable ease. Mark J. Chudzicki, founder of Poweradz.com, which helps newspapers with their Web sites, said he received some great gratis tips from Bala on how to put newspaper content online. Chudzicki, in turn, recently helped LearnLinc tackle some sales forecasting problems. He is now conferring with other local executives to find a job for one of his people, who just doesn't fit the chemistry of the company, but who Chudzicki still thinks is an asset to the region.

"It's the critical-mass thing," he said. "You've got to keep good people in the area even if they don't fit your company."

Of course, that raises a question: What happens to all the gemütlichkeit if the region comes to be viewed as an established technology center?

Even Marvin has no illusions. "Once that happens," he said, "the raiding will probably occur."

Claudia H. Deutsch
December 19, 1999

CASE 6

The New Employee Loyalty

In the tightest labor market in decades, entrepreneurs are finding that keeping their best workers happy—and loyal—is one of their most compelling missions.

And in going beyond the usual thank-you notes and bonuses, creative cosseting counts. At Assigned Counsel Inc., a kind of temporary-employment service for lawyers, executives have arranged lawn care for an employee for bringing in a large account, and treated others and their spouses to dinner for working especially hard.

The firm, based in Wayne, Pennsylvania, will even set up home offices for the lawyers it places, "as long as they're responsive to the client," said Samuel A. Frederick, a principal at the agency.

Frederick and other executives at Assigned Counsel, which made *Inc.* magazine's 1998 list of the five hundred fastest-growing companies in America, met with their peers in Nashville for the magazine's annual gathering of the winners. While the group tackled more than a few heady topics during the three-day event, the most pressing issue for the entrepreneurs—whose companies, on average, are just eight years old—was simple: keeping good employees and hiring others like them.

In other words, it was ideas like the free lawn care that really got their attention, not the more predictable ones like private equity finance, taking a company public and other ways to advance their fortunes. "Everybody kind of has that aspect down," said William R. Botti, founder of Computer Networks, a systems integration company in Pleasanton, California; that, after all, is why they were invited to the gathering in the first place.

"The problems we have in finding, motivating and keeping quality people is an overall theme that everybody's talking about," Botti said.

Some of the more flamboyant gestures by small businesses to keep their employees have made headlines. For example, Arcnet, a Holmdel, New Jersey, company that designs and builds wireless communications systems, gave leased BMWs, with fully paid insurance, to all of its workers who had been on the job at least a year. That meant twenty-eight of its fifty-seven employees, ranging from administrative assistants to architects. Like other companies, Arcnet has found that rewards, large and small, prove much cheaper than new rounds of recruiting and training.

At an *Inc.* roundtable on employee retention, several people talked with frustration about how offering stock to employees made their companies run like committees—and made them feel that their influence had been diluted. Then Gary L. Quick, founder and chief executive of Quick Solutions, a computer consulting company in Columbus, Ohio, raised his hand. What he said made almost everyone in the room—including Botti and his wife and partner, Janet M. Botti—wonder why they hadn't thought of the same thing.

Quick explained that after an employee has been aboard for three years, the company pays to have the employee's house cleaned once a month. It is an investment that costs $60 to $120 a month, depending on the size of the house, but the payoff is much more valuable, Quick told his colleagues.

"We were all just sitting there going, 'Great idea,'" Botti said.

Quick was an executive recruiter for eighteen years before starting his own consulting business. If those years taught him anything, he said, it was that "the warm and fuzzy things really work with employees." Pasta baskets for new employees and cookies on birthdays—all sent to employees' homes—go farther than cash, he said.

"This goes to the home, this goes to the spouse, and the way I look at it, you get more bang for your buck," Quick said.

Giving employees a twelve-hundred-dollar-a-year vacation allowance, too, can inspire loyalty in a way that a cash bonus can't, he said. Originally, he said, he thought of offering an annual cruise to employees with at least three years at the company—there are about 60 of them among its 250 consultants.

"Then some of the people started asking when we announced it if they don't want to do the cruise, can we do something else?" he said.

The cruise idea evolved into a flat twelve-hundred-dollar vacation allowance. "The only restriction we make," he said, "is you have to use it in one shot."

An employee, Quick said, is more likely to remember "an elk-hunting trip in Alaska" than some money in his pocket.

"Everyone's after our employees, so we want to make it real difficult to lose them," he said. "We take turnover personally."

Liz Murray Garrigan
August 8, 1999

7

WHEN MANAGING

BECOMES LEADING

Getting the Most Out of Your Team

At a plant meeting recently, I told the staff I found a defect in a furnace at the end of a production line. One person wanted to know how I found the problem. I simply said, "I asked." The employees were afraid I would be mad, but I said no, now we can get to work and figure out how to fix things.

—Fred Poses, chief executive officer,
American Standard, September 6, 2000

You try to get people to come to the right conclusion themselves. I have some other operating principles: Ignore the chain of command. Cultivate people who will disagree with you. And beware of the management fad of the year, especially if it is known by three letters.

—Stephen P. Kaufman, chief executive officer,
Arrow Electronics, January 5, 2000

You may have played the orange game at some point, perhaps during the miserable life stage known as adolescence. It goes something like this: A group of twelve-year-olds gathers for a party, often in the basement of a house, away from parental eyes. If the children are not quite ready for Spin the Bottle, they will find a convenient citrus fruit, stand in a boy-girl-boy-girl line and pass the fruit from one neck to the next, without ever using their hands. As the twelve-year-olds shimmy next to each other to complete the orange transfer, they giggle out of excitement or embarrassment.

Now imagine your horror if some decades later, you walked into a conference room at your office and found yourself scheduled to play the game with, of all people, your coworkers. If you worked for a certain travel company in New York, you may not have to do any imagining. You may, in fact, have played the orange game recently, as this chapter will explain, and you may be wondering whether corporate motivational programs are actually more painful than adolescence.

The sad truth is that despite the wads of money that corporate America spends to boost morale or create "bonding" experiences among workers, many training programs have little useful impact. Even those that do not cause people to cringe are often inefficient. Many occur in a retreatlike setting, far away from the office and its politics, and resemble a packaged vacation tour more than anything else. They seem to have little to do with the day-to-day realities of the workplace. Consider the paintball war that an Indiana company held shortly before laying off some employees, and the fact that a company spokesman later said that the game enabled employees to cope with the layoffs more easily.

What, then, can a manager do to keep the troops happy and productive? Whatever it is, it does not have to happen around a conference table or a PowerPoint presentation. Some initiatives are directly responsive to specific needs; some are meant to foster a particular ambience. Some of the most successful may even seem odd or counterintuitive.

In the following pages, you will read about companies that have set aside rooms for hardworking employees to catch a quick snooze and refuel. You will hear about hotel executives who set up a day care center for their workforce, only to realize they overlooked a central fact of their workers' lives and had to start all over again. You will meet a sales coach who says, oddly, that most salespeople spend too much effort trying to persuade customers to buy things. And you will learn about an orchestra that has no conductor but does have a few things to teach corporate bureaucrats.

You will also have a chance to watch some of the nation's largest organizations, like the United States Postal Service and the Enron Corporation, try to institute change and nurture both the company and its employees. By the time you make it to the end of the chapter, you should be thinking of oranges as a source of vitamin C, not camaraderie.

CASE 1

Motivational Missteps

Nanette Solow remembers the day she stood in a row with ten coworkers, tucked an orange under her chin and transferred it to the space beneath a colleague's chin. The goal was to move the orange down the entire line in less than five minutes. But there was a deeper purpose: to build teamwork, enhance communication and promote problem-solving. And, oh yes: to have a hoot in the process.

"My team got so good we did it in four minutes and thirty seconds," said Solow, a travel-industry marketing executive in Manhattan. "It was child-like and fun and fairly inoffensive."

It worked, too—for about a day. But after the fun ended, employees returned to their desks, submerged themselves in daily chores and forgot about the great fruit exchange.

Why? Because they knew management played by a different set of rules than those the seminar organizers had preached, Solow said.

"People were still not getting raises, and they felt underappreciated," she said. "It didn't matter how fast we transferred oranges. It was demoralizing."

Solow's sentiments are being echoed by a lot of employees these days, especially in a climate in which more and more corporations—at least 70 percent, according to some estimates—are relying on external training programs to build leadership skills and companywide bonding.

According to the American Society for Training and Development in Alexandria, Virginia, companies spend about $55 billion a year on formal training of all kinds. Often, they use elaborate and eccentric methods to put their point across, like paintball wars, fighter-pilot simulations and a course at the BMW Performance Center in Spartanburg, South Carolina, that features driving a car while blindfolded.

Trouble is, many of these programs have no practical value.

"With corporate training, it's often: 'Let's spend the money and hope for the best,'" said Cary Cherniss, a psychology professor at Rutgers University and cochairman of the Consortium for Research on Emotional Intelligence in Organizations, a coalition of researchers and practitioners from business schools, government, consulting firms and corporations. Unfortunately, he added, "It takes a lot of time and effort to unlearn old ways of thinking and acting and develop new neural circuits; it's unlikely these programs have a lasting impact."

Promoters say training seminars can do some good by fostering team-work. "So many companies are looking at ways to bring in new energy, they want to know how to take it to the next level," said Anthony Bourke, vice president of Afterburner Seminars, a half-day program in which management teams experience training and combat techniques used by fighter pilots. Both Bourke and the company's founder, James Murphy, author of *Business Is Combat,* are Air National Guard pilots with a combined thirty years of sales-training experience.

"Here they're at an off-site meeting, and we set a tone that's different from anything they've ever done before," Bourke said.

But that may be precisely the problem. While many programs bolster self-esteem and promote good cheer—it can be fun, after all, to pelt the boss with paint—most take place away from the office and all the frustrations and power struggles that go with it. As a result, critics say, they tend to create an artificial, almost vacation-like atmosphere that has little relevance in the real corporate world.

Like all new recruits at Deloitte Consulting in Manhattan, for example, Lou DiLorenzo had to take a weeklong training program. While he had a good time, he says, he didn't really learn much. "What I found is that you went to these classes to learn how to do research, say, but there was no link to the office. It was just like being at college and taking a class," he recalled. He is now on a task force to overhaul the firm's training program.

Hard times can quickly expose the limitations of training programs. In 1998, the Vandor Corporation, a diversified manufacturer in Richmond, Indiana, with one hundred employees, sent employees and managers to an intense paintball war cum leadership-training program with Leading Concepts, a company in Louisville, Kentucky. Everyone raved about the experience, but when the company found itself in a sales-and-profit squeeze a few months later, it laid off several people.

"As employees witnessed team members being axed to their left and right, they ultimately lost trust and rapport with management, and they undermined their entire investment with us," said Dean Hohl, the president of Leading Concepts. (A Vandor spokesman, Bruce Richardson, disagreed. "It's true that lack of trust is a natural reaction to a downsizing," he said. But, he added, the paintball war probably helped employees cope with that ordeal.)

Providers of management-training seminars acknowledge that some programs lack substance, though they generally argue that theirs fit into the useful category.

"When programs work, they pay for themselves, most within the first five years or so," said Daniel Goleman, cochairman of the Consortium for Research on Emotional Intelligence in Organizations and author of *Working with Emotional Intelligence*. But, he added, "when programs fail, they waste time and money."

Roger Lewin and Birute Regine, cofounders of Harvest Associates, a business consulting firm in Cambridge, Massachusetts, believe that most training programs do not work because they perpetuate an us-versus-them mentality. Managers, they argue, are not really interested in establishing genuine team structures, nor are they interested in overhauling their power base. And since training programs are imposed from the outside in, many employees resent them.

"Organizations are dynamic, interconnected human systems, not machines," said Regine, who with Lewin is the author of *The Soul at Work*. "If you want an organization that's adaptable, robust and flexible, the nexus of change is relationships. People need a sense of community. When people feel they're part of something they're more willing to change."

So what is the answer? Regine urges managers to skip the love fests at lakeside resorts and sit down with employees for serious heart-to-heart talks about what makes them tick—what they care about, what their goals are and what their fears are. Then they should try to motivate them the old-fashioned way—with raises, promotions and other positive reinforcement.

"How are people interacting? Are managers providing opportunities for people to connect on all levels?" she asked. "It's incredible the impact that has on people. You need to gauge what is essentially human—people's desire to participate, contribute and be part of something greater than themselves."

Abby Ellin
March 29, 2000

CASE 2

Delegating Leadership

It seemed to be magic. Music burst forth from two dozen string and wind instruments in perfect synchronization, without a conductor to summon it.

An hour later, during a break, the business school students who had been watching the chamber orchestra rehearse had the same question: How did you all start playing at the same moment?

"Body gestures," Eriko Sato, the first violinist on the piece, Telemann's

Water Music, said as she shrugged her shoulders to demonstrate. The musicians watch one another closely, they explained, and as each new movement begins, they know where to look for their cue.

This is Orpheus, the orchestra with no conductor and the ultimate flat, nonhierarchical organization. Its members had come to the Zicklin School of Business at Baruch College, the only M.B.A.-granting public school in New York City, to explain how they won three Grammys in 1999 and have become an annual fixture at Carnegie Hall without ever having an onstage boss.

It was a compelling sight: artists who make about thirty thousand dollars a year teaching would-be executives who will probably bring home twice that in their first year out of school. But Orpheus has more in common with some of America's largest companies than the casual observer might think. The group has become a living, and entertaining, microcosm of a management theory that has been transforming corporate America throughout the 1990s.

Spurred first by the corporate downsizing that began the decade and then by the Internet explosion that is ending it, hundreds of American companies are trying to become "flatter" by removing management layers between top executives and people in the field. The movement began as an effort to cut costs, but it has picked up steam, even during the current economic expansion, as executives try to reshape their companies to react quickly to technological change.

"Speed is becoming the most important criterion for growth and survival," said C. K. Prahalad, a professor at the University of Michigan Business School who has advised Citicorp and Oracle. "That is taking decision-making and accountability to levels that are closest to the business."

A 1996 survey of large companies by the Center for Effective Organizations at the University of Southern California found that 78 percent had removed at least one layer of management in the previous decade, while 14 percent reported getting rid of at least three.

The proponents of flatter structures are some of the best-performing companies of the 1990s, like Wal-Mart and Cisco Systems. "The more nodes in a communications link, the more likely it is that bad information goes up to the top," said Steven Kerr, the vice president for leadership development at General Electric, which has tried to remove management layers. At their worst, Kerr added, bureaucratic organizations can resemble the childhood game of telephone, in which children line up and pass a whispered message from one to the next, only to have the end result barely resemble the original statement.

Orpheus—named for a mythological Greek character whose beautiful music tamed wild beasts—has never needed to eliminate layers because, onstage at least, it has never had any. Julian Fifer, a cellist, and a few friends founded the group in 1972 with the aim of replicating the give-and-take of small chamber music groups in the larger setting of a chamber orchestra.

For every piece, a core group of musicians meets to decide how to play it. The first violinist, known as the concertmaster, typically leads the rehearsals, distilling the core group's plan into one voice. During pauses, other musicians call out suggestions, or objections, and hold smaller debates within their section of the orchestra.

When disagreements arise, Orpheus members try to talk them out until they reach a consensus. Failing that, they take a vote.

It is not always smooth sailing. In 1998, Fifer, who had stopped playing with the group in 1990, stepped down as its executive director, a job in which he oversaw the group's schedule and business matters. His resignation came after he had clashed with group members who thought Orpheus was spending too much time on international tours.

Without a conductor to make final decisions, smaller matters can be tricky, too. At the Zicklin School rehearsal, the students noticed that some musicians had spoken much more often than others and wondered whether more outgoing people had too big a say in decisions. Many of the musicians smiled, to acknowledge that this was an issue, but said they tried to speak up frequently only when they were members of the core group.

As a whole, however, they are not shy about offering criticism. At Zicklin, for example, Nardo Poy, a violist, stood up at one point and said, "I know it's water music, but it sounds like it's a little at sea." At another break, Sato politely but firmly dismissed a criticism by waving her hand and saying, "We are working on this."

In a standard orchestra, where the conductor is king, such give-and-take is virtually unheard of. Much as a corporate vice president's word can be final in a highly structured company, musicians do not question a conductor during rehearsal. One result is a message that is clear but, Orpheus members said, stifles creativity.

Renee Jolles, a violinist who plays with the group frequently, said, "When you play with a conductor, it's easy to sit there and do what you're told." Orpheus members, by contrast, are willing to lend advice to other musicians, knowing that critiquing the performance is not the job solely of one person.

"Orpheus gives every individual the opportunity to lead," said Harvey

Seifter, the current executive director. "But it also creates an imperative that everyone pull together."

That seeming contradiction has helped the group land consulting gigs. In 1999, Kraft Foods invited Orpheus to its Illinois headquarters in an attempt to teach product managers to be more honest about their disagreements, Seifter said. And in 2000 and 2001, the orchestra is holding seminars for hospital administrators in the United States and for companies in Berlin and Paris. Eventually, Seifter said, 10 percent of the orchestra's income could come from such activities.

Companies, for their part, are hoping that shedding bureaucracy will help them replicate the connection that Orpheus members, who often devote hours to hashing out musical decisions, feel to the group. That connection can reduce employee turnover, which has become a crucial issue for businesses as the unemployment rate has fallen to its lowest level since 1970.

Sturman Industries, a mechanical-valve designer in Woodland Park, Colorado, might be considered the Orpheus of the corporate world. The 140-person company is split into twelve functional groups, each with a coordinator who oversees administrative functions and can make final decisions when a consensus is unreachable. Other than the coordinators and the company's president, Carol Sturman, nobody has a title.

"It's not the easy route," Sturman said, because people are used to working in a more structured environment and are sometimes confused about what to do. But it has paid off: Sales at Sturman, a privately held company, were expected to increase 60 percent in 1999. And since moving to Colorado from California, the company said it had lost only four employees in three years, a remarkable retention rate in the current labor market.

The move toward flatter organizations shows little sign of abating. Management textbooks, which once extolled "seven-by-seven" companies that had seven levels of management and assigned seven workers to most managers, now trumpet the elimination of hierarchy.

Business schools besides Zicklin are training their students to work in a less structured world, too. At the Wharton School at the University of Pennsylvania, for example, Professor Michael Useem has brought an improvisational acting group into his classroom and led a group of M.B.A.s on trekking trips in the Himalayas, all with an eye to better understanding how less structured groups interact.

"When you have a hierarchical structure, you can get away with having managers who get people to do things because of their position," said Mike

Jenner, who teaches leadership at the University of Chicago. The more relevant question now, he said, is "how can you manage the performance of others when you don't have the power over them?"

David Leonhardt
November 10, 1999

CASE 3

Employee Service

The management epiphany for David Reid came at a center for the disabled in Chattanooga, Tennessee.

Reid, an operations division manager for United Parcel Service Inc. in Salt Lake City, got to where he is by getting things done, and he has not always been sympathetic, he said, to requests from employees for time off to tend to family matters.

But in the spring of 2000, while participating in a UPS community service program for managers, he assisted disabled residents at a center called Orange Grove. There he worked with a woman who uses a wheelchair because of cerebral palsy. The entire focus of her life was to muster enough energy from the only motion she could make, a slight tilt of her head, to drive the chair. "It's easy to take things for granted until you see something like that," said Reid, a twenty-six-year UPS veteran who oversees about six hundred workers.

The experience was a moving reminder of the harshness that life holds for some people, he said, and it made him cringe at the memory of his own coldheartedness years earlier in dealing with a part-time employee. The man had called in asking for time off because his wife was having trouble managing with their disabled child. Reid told him to get to work or risk losing his job.

"I guess it's never too late to learn a lesson," he said.

It is the sort of lesson that United Parcel wants to teach all its upper managers. With 340,000 employees of every imaginable ethnic background, the lowest paid of whom start at about $8.50 an hour, the company invests some $500,000 a year to send managers through the four-week program.

The program puts them to work with nonprofit organizations in one of four locations: New York, Chicago, Chattanooga and McAllen, Texas. Their duties range from building houses with Habitat for Humanity and visiting rural areas of Appalachia to see the impact of poverty on children to mentoring young men, boxing food for the needy and assisting adults with physical disabilities.

Corporate volunteerism in America has been increasing since the early 1990s to the extent that companies even use it in their marketing. But advocacy groups say it is rare to find a program as intensive as that devised by United Parcel. Since the program was created in 1968 in the wake of the civil rights movement, more than twelve hundred UPS managers have taken the detour from their ordinary duties to get a taste of life at the low-income barricades. About fifty participated in 2000.

The program is a much-needed reality check, according to Don Wofford, a community relations manager in Atlanta who oversees it. "You can get locked into that 'I've got boxes to move and people to move those boxes' thing," he said, "but those people have to move themselves, and those people have to be treated fairly and with dignity to do it well."

United Parcel makes an effort to send participants to unfamiliar territory to add zest to the experience. Even so, not all of them relish it. "Some individuals have been assigned, and others have been sentenced," Wofford said.

Mark Colvard, a division manager in Toledo, Ohio, was one of the assigned. Colvard went to McAllen, about six miles north of the Mexican border, to work in a poor Hispanic community at such tasks as serving lunch at a hospice, doing chores at a home for the elderly and working with incarcerated youths.

"I really wanted to take an opportunity to try to help a culture that does not even have the basic entitlements such as food stamps and Medicaid," he said.

While there, he helped build an eighteen-by-twenty-foot addition that doubled the size of a house where a family of seven lived. Although he and his fellow UPS managers were drilled in basic Spanish, communicating on the building project at times boiled down to stretching a tape measure to the length and width desired or putting an "X" on a piece of plywood where a door should go.

"You really find out how good a listener you are when you don't understand what someone is saying," Colvard said. And that effort has made him a better manager, he says. "I wasn't as open as I am now," he said. "I take more time with people, probably to a fault because I end up with a ton of work left on my desk at 7 P.M."

Terry Baumberger, a union steward for two decades in the Toledo operation, has seen the change in Colvard. "The man moves so fast his shadow couldn't keep up," Baumberger said. But now, he added, Colvard seems more relaxed. "I think he takes time now and slows down a half a step," he said. "That's good in this job."

Colvard said the experience had also forced him to take a harder look at the struggles of people in his workplace. Before he went to McAllen, he said, he had turned down a temporary worker's request for a permanent job, calculating that his budget could not handle the extra expense. But a conversation with the employee at a vending machine and a review of the case resulted in a change of heart.

He justified his decision with a mental calculation about the potential savings in overtime, he said, but the real reason was that "it was the right thing to do."

Even so, he joked: "I'm closer to my business plan than I've ever been. If my experience in McAllen has anything to do with that, I need to go back next year."

Some employees find the encounters with the poor so searing that they do go back. Patti Hobbs, a communications manager working for the United Parcel airline division in Louisville, Kentucky, is organizing a reunion of the group she was in that did a stint in 1999 at the Henry Street Settlement, a social service agency on the Lower East Side of Manhattan.

One highlight, she said, will be a barbecue under the Major Deegan Expressway like the one they helped a nun set up there for homeless people. At that event, the executives laid out a feast of grilled chicken, hamburgers, potato salad, baked beans and even a birthday cake for a homeless woman named Sharon.

Afterward, Hobbs joined the nun for her nightly run to take food to the homeless. The nun climbed up a small hill past mounds of trash four feet tall and called out a man's name, she recalled. Suddenly, an arm reached from one of the piles and took the food.

The man was a former stockbroker, the nun told her, who had lost everything, including his family, to cocaine addiction. "I'll never forget that as long as I live," Hobbs said. "This is really an opportunity provided so you don't forget where you came from or what employees are going through."

Barbara Whitaker
July 26, 2000

CASE 4

Encouraging the Entrepreneurs Within

Two words sum up the management philosophy of the Enron Corporation, according to its president, Jeffrey K. Skilling: loose, and tight.

"We are loose on everything related to creativity," said Skilling, who came here in 1990 to help transform Enron from a regulated natural-gas pipeline company into the energy industry's most freewheeling cowboy.

"We like to have smart people try new things," said Skilling. While other energy companies collect engineers, Enron has hired hundreds of M.B.A.s in recent years from top universities—about 150 in 1999 alone—and even the occasional liberal-arts major just out of college. "We stick them in the organization and tell them to figure something out," he said.

So where does "tight" figure in? With intense controls, imposed whenever Enron signs a long-term contract to deliver a commodity, like gas—a $600 million computer system tracks the company's financial exposures— or when it comes time to evaluate those smart people's performance.

"Risk-taking, anytime, is managed centrally," Skilling explained.

In less than a decade, lassoing loose and tight into a single strategy, Enron has emerged from its unlikely perch in the utility industry as a model for the new American workplace—every bit as much as the Silicon Valley start-ups that usually come to mind when the subject is entrepreneurship or innovation.

In the process, the company has opened huge new profit centers: by building power plants and pipelines in Asia, Europe, Latin America and the United States; trading natural gas and electricity in wholesale markets at home and overseas; and applying its financial expertise to create hedging instruments for the energy industry and other commodity businesses.

Its stock, meanwhile, sharply outperformed the Standard & Poor's 500 in the 1990s—a time when its old peers in the gas business badly lagged behind the market.

New management approaches abound: Walls have fallen within its fifty-seven-story headquarters tower, the better to promote cross-pollinating conversations. Through internships and mentor programs, seasoned executives help even the lowest-ranking new employees find an interest—and then challenge them to start a new business for the company.

Skilling says he does not care how people dress when they come to work, or whether expense accounts are filed on time. Or even if, after an all-out effort, a venture fails—like Enron's heavily publicized push in 1997 to become the nation's leading retail marketer of electricity, as states like California opened the power business to competition. The executive who led that effort is now in charge of spending perhaps eight times as much to sell long-term power contracts to big companies.

"If you try new things," Skilling said, "some will work, some won't."

What is it like to work in such an environment? To hear Enron employees tell their stories, it's a tightrope walk—exhilarating, if sometimes scary.

Moving Up, Forty-six Floors

Two hours with David W. Cox is as exhausting as a full day with someone else. Nearly six feet tall, Cox is a blur of motion on a forty-fifth-story trading floor, where he oversees a staff of thirty as a vice president.

Their business is one that Cox invented: writing swaps contracts that allow big consumers like newspaper publishers to hedge against fluctuations in the price of paper.

Enron wrote $4 billion of the contracts in 1998. And Cox, who started the 1990s working in the basement as a five-dollar-an-hour graphics clerk, sounds amazed that he is ending the decade heading one of the company's fastest-growing new enterprises.

For Cox, the door to entrepreneurship was opened directly by Skilling. Then a newcomer himself to Enron, Skilling, a former consultant at McKinsey & Company, was building the company's wholesale trading of natural gas, and Cox was helping to prepare materials for his presentations.

Skilling, he said, was constantly challenging employees to find ways to take advantage of the turmoil that impending deregulation had unleashed in the gas industry. "He made us feel that there was nothing we could not do," Cox recalled.

After three years, he persuaded Skilling to find an outside concern to handle Enron's graphics needs—and then left to join, and eventually buy, the small company that absorbed the work. About twenty-five Enron employees went with him.

The business grew quickly. Cox was soon also supplying graphics for Conseco, the insurer, and Sprint, the long-distance telephone company, offering long-term contracts for the service at a fixed price that included the cost of paper.

In 1995, though, paper prices surged, doubling because of high demand and tight manufacturing capacity. Put on the spot, Cox tried to freeze his paper costs, but was rebuffed by every producer or broker.

Sensing an opening, he got in touch with big paper consumers. Historically, those buyers had simply ridden the up-and-down cycles of paper prices: When costs were low, publishers, for example, would build up big supplies, but that piled expensive inventory costs on their books. And when supplies shrank, they often had to absorb quick price increases.

Cox's idea was to package financial deals that would guarantee paper users predictable prices—if not the lowest prices—for the long term. Publishers would sign long-term contracts with a financial partner. If the price they paid to their suppliers was higher than the contracted price, the partner would make up the difference; if the price was lower, the publisher would pay the difference to its partner in the hedge. The deals would be very much like those Enron was making with users of natural gas and other commodities.

Eventually, he convinced the Times Mirror Company and Media News Group, both publishers of big-city newspapers, that the concept had merit. Next, he called his mentor, Skilling, who quickly embraced the idea as a logical extension of Enron's financial deal-making. He invited Cox to return to Enron to set up the business. The five-dollar-an-hour clerk would become a vice president with a six-figure salary.

Over time, paper users have warmed to the concept. The value of the contracts rose twentyfold last year, to $4 billion, representing about 1 percent of the global paper market. Cox expects the contracts' value to quadruple between 1999 and 2001.

Cox attributes his entrepreneurial instincts to being, literally, a survivor. As a nineteen-year-old crewman on an oil industry supply boat that broke up in twenty minutes during a storm east of New Bedford, Massachusetts, he learned a crucial lesson. "It was a life-defining moment," Cox said. "I realized that life was so precious"—and that most anything was within reach if he tried hard enough.

Looking for Change

Lynda R. Clemmons was not a classic hire for an energy company. She had been a history and French major at Southern Methodist University in Dallas and then spent an unhappy year after graduation concluding that investment banking was not to her liking.

But she had hedged her bets a bit in college, by minoring in business. And she wanted to work for a company in the middle of major change. So, she joined Enron—where, she said, her bosses seemed to have faith that she could beat her own path.

Based on her previous experience, she started out working as an analyst in mergers and acquisitions. But Clemmons found that she was more attracted to the breakneck world of natural gas and electricity trading on the thirty-first floor of Enron's headquarters.

After transferring to work with the traders, she grew fascinated with the market for emissions credits, in which power companies that pollute less than they are allowed sell pollution rights to dirtier utilities.

As her new job put her in contact with executives of coal-fired utilities, Clemmons learned that they had another need: a hedge against the vagaries in weather that confound energy producers. During heat waves, for example, utilities must either restart—at great cost—their mothballed generating units, or buy power in wholesale markets where prices have spiked.

"They had been fantasizing about some kind of product to protect them against the weather for many years," Clemmons explained, sipping hot tea at a Starbucks stand in the headquarters lobby. Enron had been pondering the problem, too, she said, but "no one had put the case together before."

So Clemmons did, setting up a one-woman enterprise within Enron Capital and Trade, the company's financial unit, to develop a contract that essentially would let utilities buy insurance against the weather.

Initially, she approached Enron's trading, legal and credit departments for help on specifics, and checked in once a day with a supervisor. "I didn't have somebody holding my hand saying 'OK, this is how it's done,'" she said.

As the venture blossomed, she was able to get people assigned from other company areas to work for her. "You create your own network," Clemmons explained. But with the added support came stricter controls, like having to complete a daily profit-and-loss statement. "It becomes very clear very quickly if you are losing a lot of money," she said.

The most difficult part of the project, she said, may have been overcoming the skepticism of older, male executives in the utility industry, many of whom already considered Enron a threat to their business because of deregulation. And even more of whom were taken aback by her youth when she showed up with her charts and graphs.

"But you're younger than my daughter. Why should I listen to you?" Clemmons recalled being asked more than once.

Nevertheless, her persistence and cool, matter-of-fact manner eventually won their confidence. With the first transactions lined up, Skilling took the new business to Enron's board for approval.

In two years, Clemmons and her staff, which numbers thirteen, have sold about $1 billion in weather hedges. Essentially, she has created a new industry; companies like Koch Industries, the Southern Company and Utilicorp United compete with Enron for utilities' business.

Clemmons, meanwhile, is in demand as a speaker to explain her new field. She recently was chairwoman of a conference on risk management that drew five hundred participants.

And she is just getting started. She figures that American companies with big exposure to weather-related risks have more than $1 trillion in yearly revenues; utility deregulation and the weather extremes driven by the El Niño phenomenon can only spur demand.

"We've only scratched the surface," Clemmons said.

Spreading the Word

The business that Thomas D. Gros is building for Enron remains untested. But his entire career seems to have been aimed at the opportunity.

He studied aerospace engineering, worked as an analyst for the Central Intelligence Agency, earned an M.B.A. and set up a natural-gas trading operation—competing against Enron—for British Petroleum. He also did a stint on Wall Street with Chemical Bank.

But Gros—wiry, precise and impatient—quit that job in 1996. "I could not impact directly the bottom line of the firm," he said.

So he took a job at Enron, in charge of marketing commodity-trading services to big industrial customers. And as he set up an office for the operation in midtown Manhattan, he stumbled upon his entrepreneurial opening.

To connect his team's computers to those at Enron's headquarters in Texas, he ordered an expensive T1 telecommunications line. But it provided far more capacity than the office needed.

The trader in Gros saw the potential for profit in the spare bandwidth. "I wanted to see if there was a way to sell it to get some value for it," he said.

He quickly realized that he was not alone; many other companies were locked into contracts that wasted telecommunications capacity. Enron itself had built excess capacity into its internal fiber optic network, and had acquired even more with its purchase of Portland General Electric, an Oregon utility, in 1997.

He floated the idea within the company, drawing the interest of traders and other employees. "When people here see an opportunity, they want to participate," he said. "We do not ask permission to spread the word. We just do it."

He was able to spend freely on travel to sell the concept; when he needed larger sums—fifty thousand dollars in start-up expenses, for example—his boss was able to authorize the outlay.

"There wasn't any budget per se," Gros said.

In 1998, the company approved his plan to start a bandwidth exchange and to trade for Enron's own account. His title is now vice president for global bandwidth trading.

After Gros puts his new marketplace in operation, there is still much to sort out, from the ground rules of trading to the technology that will support it. And there is competition: At least three companies are already operating bandwidth exchanges, though Gros says the others focus on voice communications while Enron will offer a spectrum of communications capacity.

For now, Gros is using Enron's excess capacity to keep his growing team connected. A video link, for example, ties staff members in Houston to colleagues in New York, maximizing what he calls informal collisions. "The really creative ideas," Gros said, "don't come on a schedule."

Agis Salpukas
June 27, 1999

David Cox left Enron Pulp and Paper in July 1999 to work on developing content distribution services for Enron Broadband Services, a new multi-billion-dollar business. As managing director, Cox helped forge a twenty-year agreement with Blockbuster to stream video-on-demand to consumers' homes.

Lynda Clemmons left Enron in the spring of 2000 to start Element Re, a unit of XL Capital Ltd. She is president and chief operating officer of Element Re, which provides weather risk management insurance, reinsurance, and financial products.

In June 2000, Thomas Gros moved from Enron Broadband Services to Enron NetWorks, the company's e-commerce business incubator, to work on the development of a back office outsourcing product. He is a vice president for e-commerce.

CASE 5

The Model of Conciliation

In the early 1990s, the United States Postal Service had an employee crisis on its hands. Not the workplace shootings that made headlines and added the phrase "going postal" to the American vocabulary of violence. Those incidents, while often deadly, were isolated.

What really threatened the agency's productivity and morale was an avalanche of complaints by angry, frustrated employees to the federal Equal

Employment Opportunity Commission. For years, charges of racial discrimination, sexual harassment and other management abuses poured into the watchdog agency from the Postal Service, and the volume of informal complaints had built up to an incredible thirty thousand filings a year, more than from any other single employer. Some of the complaints escalated into costly litigation, while others festered.

But in 1994 as part of a settlement of a class-action lawsuit, lawyers at the Postal Service, one of the nation's largest employers, started one of the most ambitious experiments in dispute resolution in American corporate history. They created a program called Redress to settle disputes using neutral outside mediators, and tested it in a few cities before rolling it out nationally in 1997.

The results were spectacular: In the first twenty-two months of full operation, from September 1998 through June 2000, 17,645 informal disputes were mediated under Redress and of those, 80 percent were resolved.

During the same period, formal complaints, which peaked at fourteen thousand by 1997, dropped 30 percent. The lawyers estimate that the program has saved the agency millions of dollars in legal costs and improved productivity, to say nothing of the gains in intangibles like job satisfaction.

Now, two of the Postal Service's lawyers, Cynthia J. Hallberlin, former chief counsel, and Mary S. Elcano, former general counsel, have left for private practice at the Brown & Wood law firm in Washington, and are taking a similar program, which they have named Wins, on a road show. They are convinced that if mediation worked wonders for the Postal Service, it could do so at any company or organization.

Already, the World Bank has signed on for a review of its mediation program, and others, including investment banks, dot-coms and recognized brand-name manufacturers, are interested, the lawyers say. What is selling them, they say, is Redress's record.

Corporate America certainly needs the help. High-profile racial discrimination and sexual-harassment class-action lawsuits filed in recent years against industry giants like Texaco and Coca-Cola are only the tip of the litigation iceberg. Employment discrimination cases nearly tripled between 1990 and 1998, to 23,735 filings in federal district courts, according to the Justice Department.

To be sure, companies are not sitting on their hands. A survey of Fortune 1000 companies in 1997 by the Cornell Institute on Conflict Resolution found that the majority were doing some form of what is known as alternative dispute resolution to avoid litigation.

But Elcano and Hallberlin say they possess one thing that no one else can offer: a huge database of statistics and exit surveys, which they say proves how valuable their form of mediation, called transformative mediation, was to postal workers.

In it, the parties involved control the process and the outcome.

"We have found that companies are very interested in transformative mediation," Hallberlin said, "because of its promise to not just solve the problem at hand, but to help the parties communicate more effectively in the future."

Before Redress was created, Postal Service employees embroiled in disputes with their bosses followed procedures that could drag on for years. Generally, they would begin by filing an informal EEOC complaint. They then had the choice of dropping the matter or going down the bureaucratic path of filing a formal grievance, starting an official investigation with all its affidavits and hearings. Ultimately, they might file a lawsuit.

The Redress program aimed to short-circuit that process by offering disgruntled workers mediation. If a person who filed an informal complaint agreed, a meeting would be set up; a mediator would hear both sides of the dispute and, in most instances, help propose a solution within a day.

Sometimes, all the worker wanted was for his boss to say he was sorry. "The power of an apology became very significant," Elcano said. "People would walk away from litigation with that because they felt it was an honest give-and-take."

For example, one supervisor called all of his mail carriers by a number, Hallberlin said. One carrier thought it was demeaning and filed a complaint. When confronted about it in mediation, the supervisor said he had had no idea that some people found the practice offensive and said he would stop it immediately. Case closed.

"You're never going to get rid of conflict," Hallberlin said. "You just want to handle it better."

Robert A. Baruch Bush, a law professor at Hofstra University who helped design a training program for the three thousand outside mediators in Redress, said the goal was to shift conversations between employees and their supervisors from destructive to constructive. "If that happens," he said, "it becomes a more open corporation, and then the parties themselves in most cases will be able to define what's bothering them and how to fix it." Resolution is a by-product, he added.

Redress is intended to make mediation available at any stage of the grievance process, not just at the beginning. In one class-action racial-discrimination lawsuit that had originated in an EEOC complaint, black postal workers in Florida accused a white postmaster of making racist remarks about their work habits. They sought his dismissal, Hallberlin said.

It never came to that or to a dollar settlement, she said, because both parties agreed to bring in an outside mediator. In the end, the postmaster apologized, wrote a check to the NAACP and joined the Postal Service's diversity committee. "In future dealings, he had a more harmonious post office," Hallberlin said.

Elaine Kirsch, an outside mediator working in New York, recalled a case involving a postal supervisor and an employee, both women, one white and one black, neither willing to back down. The dispute was over the employee's repeated lateness, Kirsch said, but really it was about a lack of communication. After yelling at each other for one and a half hours, she said, the two became quiet.

Kirsch said she took the opportunity to point out that the two had more in common than they had thought. Sometime after that, she said, the supervisor and employee returned to hammering out particular issues and rehashing events. Finally, one said words to this effect: "You never lied. You always say what you mean."

The ice was broken, Kirsch said, "and from then on it was easy as pie." It turned out that the employee was often late because she had trouble finding care for her asthmatic child. She agreed to call her supervisor when this happened and her supervisor agreed to be more understanding.

To keep tabs on Redress's progress, the Postal Service hired Lisa Bingham, director of the Conflict Resolution Center at Indiana University. "Quantifying has been one of the problems with the field of dispute resolution for some time," Bingham said.

Her exit-survey research showed that postal employees and their union representatives and supervisors were highly satisfied with the process and the mediators. And, to a lesser degree, the parties were satisfied with the outcome.

Mary P. Rowe, an adjunct professor at the Sloan School of Management at MIT, said Redress "was large, elaborate and better evaluated than virtually any other component or system like it."

And, said Rowe, a longtime ombudsperson at MIT, there was no reason that programs like Redress should not thrive in the private sector. "Conflict management programs should function in every milieu," she said.

Not everyone is a big fan of mediation, of course, least of all the plaintiffs' bar. "Damages are often the best way to make up for how someone has been harmed," said Pamela Coukos, a lawyer for Mehri, Malkin & Ross, the Washington firm that handled the class-action lawsuit against Coca-Cola.

"Money can be a measure of how much respect you are given by a company." At the very least, Coukos said, workers with grievances should have a choice between litigation or some type of nonjudicial dispute resolution.

And in fact, such dispute resolution is widespread. Of the 606 companies surveyed by Cornell, for example, 88 percent reported using mediation at least once in the preceding three years and 79 percent reported using arbitration, which like mediation employs outside neutral parties, but unlike mediation, reaches a binding solution.

Today, said David B. Lipsky, the Cornell professor who conducted the 1997 survey with Ronald L. Seeber, companies are moving from a piecemeal approach to unified programs.

In 1999, for example, the Prudential Insurance Company of America in Newark started its own program called Roads to Resolution. Oliver B. Quinn, the program director, said Prudential took the step to develop a system that offered mediation and arbitration in light of the litigation erupting elsewhere.

And as part of its settlement of a multimillion-dollar racial discrimination case, Texaco created an Ombuds program in February 1998. Later that year, the company folded it and other programs like mediation and arbitration into a problem-resolution system.

As a result, Carole A. Young, director of the Ombuds program, said a court-appointed task force had determined that litigation had been reduced by nearly half in the first year.

In the meantime, the good news continues for the Postal Service. Karen Intrater, one of the lawyers who came up with the idea of Redress, said the program had been so successful it was catching on among government agencies.

"It's not a magic pill, but you can see the difference," Intrater said. "I've never seen anything that has such a potential for change as this."

Mickey Meece
September 6, 2000

CASE 6

The Child Care Formula

In October 2000, Marriott International will fire its second salvo in the nation's work-family conflict, opening a $2.5 million, 120-place day care center in a refitted historic building in downtown Washington.

The company's first assault on employee child care problems—a twenty-four-hour day care center in Atlanta—promised much when it opened in 1997 but delivered disappointing results. Now Marriott, having analyzed what went wrong, is prepared to try again, offering not just a refined version of company-sponsored child care but also insights for the many Americans who have wondered why, in one of the world's richest countries, it is so hard for companies to offer decent, affordable places for employees to put their children.

Fewer than 10 percent of American businesses offer some form of child care assistance to employees, said Faith Wohl, president of the Child Care Action Campaign, and the assistance is usually limited to discounts and referral services. Nationwide, parents currently pay sixty cents of every dollar of child care, she added, while governments at all levels pay thirty-nine cents, and the private sector—both companies and tax-exempt philanthropies—pays just a penny.

Marriott, one of the few companies to experiment with child care on site, began monitoring the work-family travails of its staff early on. Almost 85 percent of its employees are wage earners who push room-service carts, haul luggage or answer phones deep into the night.

Years before the current labor shortage made child care a hot-button workplace issue, Marriott discovered that these hourly employees were so overwhelmed with family chores that supervisors were essentially spending 25 to 50 percent of their time on social work.

"They were doing everything from finding subsidized child care to driving people to doctors' appointments," said Donna Klein, Marriott's vice president for diversity and workplace effectiveness.

Marriott was not dying to be in the day care business, she added, but its managers knew that if they ignored staff problems, they could badly tarnish the chain's reputation for customer service.

In the beginning, Marriott sought a solution on the supply side: If working parents could not find day care, the thinking went, it must be because there were not enough places. So Marriott would build its own center, employees would put an end to jury-rigged dealings with aunties and grannies and women down the street, and productivity would surge.

In Atlanta, Marriott's two downtown hotels, the Marriott Marquis and the Marriott Suites Midtown, formed a nonprofit partnership with two other hotels in the neighborhood and floated bonds to finance construction of a day care center.

And not just any day care center. The Inn for Children, as the center was named, was to offer not only around-the-clock child care and early-learning programs, but a full range of social services as well: nutrition counseling, family-crisis referrals, dental screenings, a pediatric infirmary, credit counseling and even mammograms.

On opening day, Atlanta's mayor cut a chain of paper dolls, and the local news media pronounced an end to the lodging industry's child care crisis. And then, to everyone's dismay, the children did not come.

The cost was a big reason. To cover the interest on its construction bonds, the hotel partnership charged $110 to $135 for a fifty-hour week of child care, depending on the child's age. That may have been on a par with other licensed centers in Atlanta, but it was out of the question for the wage-earning families the hotels wanted to assist. "If you're making twenty-five thousand dollars a year, that's twenty-five percent of your income," Klein said.

The hotels had expected the workers to make use of scholarships and state financial assistance to reduce their costs to as little as twenty-five dollars a week. What they did not realize was that the wage earners' hectic lives left them little time to line up the aid.

Employees working day shifts could not go across town to submit applications during business hours. Some did not have cars. Recent immigrants lacked required documents and could not read forms printed in English. And some employees had an aversion to going near any government office.

Faced with running this gauntlet, most employees stuck with the woman down the street.

With slots going empty and debts to pay, the hotel partners opened the center to the children of nonemployees. Today, of the 250 mostly low-income children finger-painting and eating peanut butter sandwiches at the Inn for Children, only twenty-five are children of Marriott employees.

The lesson in all this? The day care problem is not one of supply, but affordability, Klein said. If a company charges fees high enough to cover the cost, many employees will not be able to afford the service.

So Marriott is using a different model for its Washington center. Instead of linking with peers from the private sector, it joined forces with the General Services Administration, which has operated day care centers since 1985, and the city of Washington. Instead of floating bonds, Marriott and the GSA split $1.3 million in capital costs fifty-fifty, and Washington granted $1 million to pay rent for seven years.

The partners also lined up grants and scholarships from foundations and local businesses, so low-income families would not have to maneuver the state-aid bureaucracy. Community groups and Washington law firms offered pro bono legal work and managerial assistance.

And this time, no one is saying the center will put an end to all employee child care woes.

"If we could get, maybe, thirty Marriott children out of a hundred and twenty places, we'd definitely look at it as a success," Klein said, noting that the chain has three hotels within a four-block radius of the center, with about eight hundred hourly workers. Government employees' children are expected to fill most of the other openings.

But if the project succeeds, she said, it will be duplicated in other cities where Marriott has hotels, the federal government has employees and municipal financing is available.

"Ten years ago, we thought, 'Oh, we can make a huge difference,'" Klein said. "But now, we realize that this is a systemic issue, which has to be solved, certainly, with business as a key player, but with public-policy involvement as well."

Mary Williams Walsh
September 13, 2000

CASE 7

Napping on the Job

Sterling McCullough doesn't mind getting caught napping at work. A half-dozen times in the last year, he has disappeared down a little-used hallway at Deloitte Consulting in Pittsburgh, stretched out in a leather chair and nodded off.

His bosses don't care. That is because Deloitte, where McCullough is a senior manager, has created a nap room for employees.

Falling asleep on the job may be a cardinal taboo of the workplace, but a smattering of companies around the country are defying common wisdom and actually encouraging the practice. They are discovering that it increases morale—and productivity.

"Our society is chronically sleep-deprived," said Dennis W. Holland, director of alertness management at the Union Pacific Corporation, the nation's biggest railroad, which adopted a pro-napping policy in 1998. "It's worse than it was in the past, and we have to address it."

Both Union Pacific and its main rival, the Burlington Northern Santa Fe Railway Corporation, allow conductors and engineers to take sleep breaks of up to forty-five minutes, as long as the train is stopped and another crew member is awake. Other employers, including a handful of Silicon Valley companies, have set up nap rooms, some of which offer reclining chairs, blankets, alarm clocks and even classical-music CDs to lull workers into slumber. British Airways permits pilots on transoceanic flights to catch a few winks so they will be fresher for landings. Even the U.S. Army, convinced by recent sleep research, has begun telling officers to permit, and take, naps when possible.

Employees generally welcome the idea, though many can't shake off a feeling of guilt when they initially indulge. McCullough remembers the first time that he ventured into the company's nap room, closed the door and uneasily lowered the ceiling-to-floor shades. "You're looking for a camera or a tape recorder," he said. "You're wondering, 'If I snore, will they catch me?' The first time, it's kind of scary."

As more managers bedded down, employees took the cue and joined them, said the human resources director, Sandy Francis. During the day, the room is now occupied more than it is vacant, she said.

"Sometimes, those twenty minutes give you energy to go on for a few more hours, rather than faking lucidity for the rest of the day," said Frank M. Ligons, a business analyst who says he used to try to beat fatigue by staring blankly at the work on his desk.

The nap-at-work movement remains nascent, to be sure, but it gives hope to anyone who has ever nodded off in front of the computer screen or sneaked off to the storage closet, bathroom stall or space under the desk—as the character George Costanza did in one *Seinfeld* episode, to limited success.

With Americans sleeping roughly 20 percent less than their great-grandparents did, it is no wonder that two out of five workers report that fatigue regularly interferes with their ability to function, according to the National Sleep Foundation in Washington. The problem is likely to worsen, too, thanks to the Internet explosion, all-night television, twenty-four-hour stock trading and other temptations of the information age.

Most of the new nap policies began bubbling up two or three years ago. Since then, some pioneers have struggled to convince workers that lying down on the job really is OK. When Burlington Northern authorized the practice two years ago, it said conductors and engineers could sleep only if they radioed in the plan to headquarters. "It was a complete failure," said Alan L. Lindsey, the railway's general director for safety and rules. "People would make fun of them" over the radio.

So the company dropped the restriction and gave all fifteen thousand employees who work on trains carte blanche to curl up when the train was stopped and a colleague was awake. By early 2000, Burlington Northern will allow eight thousand track workers to nap, too. "We know this has always been going on," Lindsey said. "Now, we're putting a structure to it."

Of course, the napping movement is not exactly sweeping the nation. No major white-collar employer has publicly adopted a pro-sleep policy. Wal-Mart, the country's largest employer, says its 815,000 workers are free to repair to company lounges for quick rests during their scheduled breaks, but not to doze on the job. In general, bosses worry about sanctioning any innovation with goof-off potential, especially when e-mail and computer games are already vying for employees' attention.

Still, advocates of workplace napping say it is the wave of the future. After all, it has a proud history in many lands as the siesta, and doctors say afternoon drowsiness is part of the body's natural rhythm, not just a response to a heavy lunch. "You hit that two-to-three-o'clock period, and you think, 'Nap! I need to lie down,'" said Kimberly Oliver, the marketing director at OP Contract Inc., an office-furniture dealer in San Francisco that set up a nap room when it expanded in 1998. Now, when she is hit by "sleep coma," as office workers call postlunch fatigue, Oliver heads to the nap room, plunks down on a chaise longue, puts on eyeshades and listens to a CD of Pachelbel's *Canon,* provided by the company.

The scientific argument for naps has won over branches of governments, too. The army sends sleep specialists to elite training grounds, to tell rising officers that troops should "nap early and nap often," said Colonel Gregory Belenky, a doctor at the Walter Reed Army Institute of Research, who often delivers the speech.

A cottage industry is even popping up to exploit the trend. *The Art of Napping at Work,* by a Boston University professor, William A. Anthony, and his wife, Camille, hit bookstores in the fall of 1999. Workplace napping "is not an easy sell," the book acknowledges. But, it adds, "Neither, for that matter, was fluoride in the drinking water or women wearing slacks to work."

The Company Store, a New Jersey–based seller of textiles, offers an "executive napping kit," complete with a pillow and an earlier book by the Anthonys for seventy-nine dollars. And Mark R. Rosekind, a sleep researcher at NASA, left his post two years ago to start Alertness Solutions Inc. For a fee, it advises companies on how to fight employee fatigue.

David Leonhardt
October 13, 1999

CASE 8

Selling Without the Sucker Punch

Michael Stock, a salesman at Jennifer Leather Furniture on lower Broadway in Manhattan, was trying to convince us that an armchair was worth every penny of the $1,799 on its price tag. He caressed the soft hide, described the exotic oils massaged into its grain and suggested that we recline on its plump cushions. Fiddling nervously with his gold tie, he ramped up his sales pitch every time we prepared to move on.

He had no idea what he was up against.

My companion was Jacques Werth, who, after forty years in the selling business, reckons that he has gone on calls with 312 top sales representatives in twenty-three different industries. No mere student of salesmanship, Werth is a self-styled theorist on the subject—and, needless to say, a consultant. With nothing particular in mind to buy, I asked him to come along to appraise the help as I browsed big-ticket items, things priced at one thousand dollars or more.

Clearly, Stock was not going to rank with the great ones in Werth's eyes. Werth lighted on a chair similar to the one that caught my fancy, but considerably cheaper. "There is four hundred and fifty dollars more leather in the other chair?" he asked.

"Yep, generally," Stock replied, looking suddenly young.

"Maybe it's more durable," I suggested.

"If you stretch fabric from each of the chairs over a drum and beat them, this one would definitely last longer," Stock said, gesturing to the more expensive item.

Werth raised an eyebrow, but Stock continued. "Pull the corners," he said. "You can really feel the difference in quality there."

I murmured our thanks as we headed out the door.

"Call if you have any questions," Stock yelled, undeterred.

Out on the sidewalk, Werth shook his head sorrowfully, as if he had just witnessed an accident that could have been avoided. But his criticisms are not what you might expect. He does not blame Stock for angling hard, but for trying at all.

"From the sight of us, he should have been able to tell there was maybe a five percent chance we'd buy," Werth explained. "With a few questions, he could have determined we weren't ready—and then spent his time doing something productive, like paperwork."

Reached later, Stock had a defense for his performance: he thought

Werth and I were spies from Jennifer Convertibles, the owner of the store, and rude ones at that. "Normally, I would have been even more up," he said. "I would have gone even more all out."

More, however, is less in Werth's universe. He has distilled a lifetime's worth of vending wisdom into a philosophy—and a book—*High Probability Selling*.

His thesis is simple: Sell to people who want what you have. Figure out who those people are by asking them. Ask as many questions as you need to see if they are good prospects. Be radically honest. Do not fudge in order to pique people's interest. If there is no obvious match, cut them loose—quickly.

It all sounds absurdly obvious, until you consider that the twelve million Americans involved in direct sales are usually told just the opposite—that, with enough skill and persistence, anyone can be persuaded to buy anything. P. T. Barnum, perhaps the most famous salesman of all, summarized this view of human nature: "There is a sucker born every minute."

Werth does not look the part of a rebel against time-honored wisdom. His deep-set blue eyes sink into dark circles; his thinning silver hair is brushed neatly to the side. His speech, which betrays his roots in working-class Queens, never rises above a conversational tone. Physically, he resembles a reduced-scale version of the barrel-chested actor Brian Dennehy, who, coincidentally, was starring in a fiftieth-anniversary Broadway revival of Arthur Miller's classic, *Death of a Salesman*.

But Werth is no Willy Loman. After leaving New York Community College (now New York Technical College) in Brooklyn at age nineteen, he took a job selling forklifts and worked himself up to the top spot in the company's sales force. Eventually, he made a career of taking over failing businesses. Over the years, he says, he has rescued ten firms, from an Italian sports-car dealership to a plant that manufactures machines used to make silicon chips.

The thread connecting these varied projects, he said, was reeducating and reinvigorating the sales forces with his no-pressure, to-the-point methodology. Now a millionaire, he works primarily as a consultant helping troubled companies—and as an evangelist, trying to convert others to his system.

At each step along the way, Werth has made time to follow whatever top salesmen and saleswomen he could find as they went about their work. Whether they knew it or not, he said, the bulk of these successful sellers used similar strategies. They sought out a great deal of information about buyers and built long-term, intimate relationships. As a result, they were able to know their customers' needs and fulfill them. Just as important, they could also discern who had no need for their products.

The best salesman Werth has ever seen, he said, is David Grob, whom he called the sales champion of the semiconductor equipment industry. Werth describes with reverence the day he followed Grob, who worked for him at the time, to Motorola for a first call on a new product manager.

Grob started by asking the new manager questions—where he had come from, what jobs he had held, to whom he would be reporting. When the product manager said that his own boss was about to be replaced, Grob told him that the replacement would be coming from Motorola's Philippine operation.

The product manager was surprised and impressed, and he asked Grob if he knew the man. "Of course," said Grob, who then described the client's boss-to-be in great detail. Later, Werth learned that Grob kept in-depth organizational charts of the company—indeed, that he came close to knowing as much about the power structure at Motorola as the people who worked there did.

Interviewed from his home in Phoenix, Grob, now an independent sales representative, confirmed Werth's interpretation of his work, saying it was important to know the internal chain of command in client companies, from "operator to vice president."

By contrast, Werth argued, most salesmen spend a lot of wasted time looking for an "in" at a company—that is, for anyone who will take an interest in the product. But such people, he said, are usually just looking for an education about what's offered and are seldom ready to buy from the sales representative making the pitch.

As a result, sales agents end up trying to be aggressive, wily and deceptive enough to force a sale on a party not yet ready to do business. Werth pointed to a help-wanted ad in a newspaper seeking "an elbow-throwing, hard-hitting applicant," saying it was typical of the mentality of most sellers' bosses. They think that sales are made when someone is trying hard, he said, rather than when someone is offering a desired product.

Certainly, self-help books and trainers emphasize secret tips and clever strategies for making sales. One popular book, *Guerrilla Selling: Unconventional Weapons and Tactics for Increasing Your Sales,* teaches ways to sneak into organizations—going in the back door carrying doughnuts, for example—to make contacts.

Another best-seller, *How to Master the Art of Selling* by Tom Hopkins, offers all sorts of tricks for finding sales prospects. The book suggests visiting new businesses and telling the proprietors you want to get acquainted so you can refer customers to them. Of course, you drop off your card and hope they will pass business back your way. Hopkins also favors linguistic devices—ending statements with phrases like "isn't it?" and "don't we?"— because they are incremental ways to get a prospect to say "yes" to a pitch.

Hopkins is unfamiliar with Werth's approach, but he expressed skepticism that focusing on a narrow field of high-probability customers could be a winning strategy. To become a successful real estate salesman, Hopkins said, "I couldn't wait on my butt until people came to me; I had to go out and knock on doors." He said his skill was his ability to "create a need for my product through good presentation."

Werth does not deny that persistence or even old-fashioned arm-twisting sometimes works. By his own precise calculus, 16 percent of the top sales agents he has evaluated were able to succeed by being "slick, glib, deceitful con artists."

But Werth thinks that such success comes at a terrible price: the people doing the selling are miserable. Think of the success-obsessed but self-loathing real estate hustlers in David Mamet's *Glengarry Glen Ross,* a play that Werth praised for its verisimilitude.

In the instructional seminars he runs, Werth is reminded constantly of how people in sales can be full of self-loathing and doubt. When he asks how they feel when they are making sales, typical responses are "like a supplicant" and "vulnerable." Asked how they feel when they fail to close deals, they say "resentful" or "like a failure."

Such findings of unhappiness have plenty of anecdotal corroboration. *The Force,* a 1994 book by David Dorsey, followed the top copier salesmen for Xerox and found that even those making six-figure incomes had become walking wounded from the stress of making quotas. One top producer took a chain saw to the family Christmas tree; another tossed a frozen turkey down a flight of stairs.

From the point of view of both the seller and the buyer, it would seem that Werth's techniques would make selling a more pleasant experience. In theory, Werth's salesman is just the guy you want to deal with—someone who offers only as much information as you want and only about products in which you are truly interested.

In practice, of course, this approach takes some adjusting to. During our shopping trip, Werth followed me into the luxury ABC Carpet and Home store on lower Broadway in Manhattan. We were immediately approached by Tevfik Askin, an almond-eyed clerk from Turkey. He started out amiably enough but very soon seemed to grow bored and uncommunicative.

The conversation went something like this:

Reporter: Do these carpets need to be special-cleaned?

Askin: Depends on the spill.

Reporter: Let's say orange juice; my son dribbles a lot of that.

Askin, shrugging: It depends on the carpet.

Reporter: OK. How about a wool carpet?

Askin: Depends which one; they are all different. Do you have one in mind? If not, you should try the rack.

Then Askin was gone.

Later, he would explain that while he is willing to work with everyone, "some people are like blanks, and you send them to the racks so that they get some idea where to start." After that, he said, he works with the customer—and has sometimes made sales even to people starting with almost no sense of what they wanted.

At the point of contact, however, I was unimpressed. I offered Werth my assessment: "Not very knowledgeable."

"No," he said, contradicting me because he had recognized a high-probability salesman at work. "He knows this stuff, but he knows we're not ready to buy. There is a lot of floor traffic here, and he would rather get a better prospect. He's good."

Leslie Kaufman
February 7, 1999

CASE 9

Company Culture

Not everyone seeking transcendent peace and spiritual growth can live a life of reflection in a cloistered monastery. In the real world, somebody has to fix flat tires.

And then they can meditate. That is how it works at the Tires Plus stores in the Midwest, where Tom Gegax, the cofounder, gives his workers time for meditation, shiatsu massage and nutrition classes.

"We're always looking for ways we can be more evolved," said Gegax one rainy morning in the summer of 1999, as the rhythmic chanting of Indian song on the disk player soothed the bumps in the road. "It takes psychological growth, spiritual growth, a striving for wellness."

It is Zen and the art of the tire business. While old-style tire shops might smirk at the touchy-feely style at Tires Plus, it seems to be working with the customers, or guests, as they are known here. With more than 150 stores in nine Midwestern states, and sales of $160 million in 1998, Tires Plus has become something of a cultural institution here in Minnesota, a state with a history of social progressivism.

Gegax, who uses the title "head coach," has a modest office—no bigger than anyone else's in Tires Plus's Minneapolis headquarters, which was designed with the principles of feng shui, the ancient Chinese philosophy of blending architecture and spiritualism.

"Keeping ego in check is the number one goal," said Gegax, tall and silver-haired, with a gentle manner and a soft voice that is barely above a whisper. "It's about servant leadership."

Gegax comes by humility from experience. He fell into deep depression in 1989 after what he describes as a "three-ring wake-up call." He was divorced from his wife of twenty years. His business was failing. And he discovered a cancerous lump in his throat while shaving.

"I couldn't get out of bed," he said. "And when I did make it into the office, I just went in and shut the door."

He went through extensive therapy, quit drinking and stopped eating meat. He said he began to coach himself about how to live.

Gegax, a hard-charging basketball player who now has a clean bill of health, has written a book about his journey, *Winning in the Game of Life: Self-Coaching Secrets for Success*.

In the book, edited with the help of the younger of his two sons, Gegax says people are fixed on a notion of success that can be hollow, no matter how big the paycheck.

"Our eyes are bleary from reading business success tomes and taking notes at 'achievement' seminars," he writes. "Still, we're left asking the same questions: What makes us tick? What makes us sick? What drives us? While the average American works more hours than ever, little of the effort actually helps us understand anything about ourselves. Crowded out by the often-manic push for success, simple reflective inquiry barely hits anyone's radar screens."

To Gegax, who grew up in small-town Indiana, the son of a man in the mausoleum business, simplicity is among the highest of virtues. There is nothing very complicated about his philosophy. Reduced to its essence, it is: Take good care of yourself, and show kindness to others.

"If you do good things, it will translate into being good for business," he said. "But don't do it for that. Do it for human reasons. Otherwise, people will sense it."

Each month, he spends two hours with every group of about forty newly hired workers. And he congratulates them for having the courage to select a field that may not seem glamorous to the rest of the world.

"How many of you at graduation looked up into the sky and pondered your future and said, 'Tires!'?" Gegax asks them.

After his own graduation from Indiana University in 1968, Gegax went to work for Shell Oil. At twenty-nine, he bought three old Shell garages and went into the tire business with a partner, Don Gullett. To show their connection, a string runs from Gullett's office, through the walls, to Gegax's office.

"We try to take one little corner of people's lives and make it a little better experience," he said.

Tire shops, he said, have never had a reputation as particularly cozy places. They are often dirty, he said, and the workers can be surly.

At Tires Plus, the workers—they are called "teammates"—wear white shirts and greet each customer with a handshake. Each store has a coffee table, a television set and a hookup for a computer laptop. There are toys and videos for children. And customers can walk onto the shop floor, provided they wear safety glasses, to watch the mechanics at work.

In a male-dominated business where a macho ethic has sometimes prevailed, Tires Plus preaches diversity. There are rules against insulting anyone over their race, gender or sexual preference, and workers—still mostly men—are required to challenge anyone they hear making a disparaging remark. "If you say nothing," Gegax said, "that is tacit approval."

For employees, the Tires Plus headquarters has a full-time "wellness coordinator," a fitness room, a quiet room for meditation, a table for shiatsu massage and bulletin boards with health information.

But no one is required to take good care of themselves. "We have people who drink, smoke and have a horrible diet," Gegax said, "and we love them, too."

Dirk Johnson
August 29, 1999

CASE 10

Play Clean

To say that D. Clark Ogle is miffed is a wild understatement. His company, Johnston Industries, a $300 million textile manufacturer based in Columbus, Georgia, says that it has been the victim of corporate espionage. Outside consultants hired by a competitor, he contends, posed as a prospective investor and a graduate student to gain access to Johnston's trade secrets.

And not just any competitor, but Milliken & Company, a sixteen-thousand-employee giant that won a Malcolm Baldrige National Quality Award in 1989. "Obviously, the things Milliken did hurt us," said Ogle, Johnston's chief executive. "They took away opportunities our people had found for niches we were exploiting somewhat on our own. Then, basically overnight, we had a competitor in there knowing our processes."

Johnston is suing Milliken over the matter. Milliken has stated that it will defend itself "vigorously" and that its long-standing policies forbid its employees or consultants from illegally obtaining proprietary information from competitors.

What irks Ogle most, though, is that Milliken takes pride in a corporate mantra often repeated by its chairman: "steal shamelessly."

According to Christopher E. Bogan, chief executive of Best Practices, a management consulting firm in Chapel Hill, North Carolina: "The concept of 'steal shamelessly' is really grounded on the concept of 'don't be afraid to borrow.' It's a dramatic statement that no individual, no company, no team, no industry can corner all good ideas. It doesn't for a minute suppose that you should steal proprietary information or trade secrets."

Perhaps, but Ogle contends that couching the concept in words like "steal" is just plain wrong. "When you take something that has negative connotations, just the subliminal message you send to your culture is different," he said.

Tom Peters is not totally surprised by Johnston's allegations. Peters and Nancy Austin wrote about Milliken in 1985 in *A Passion for Excellence*. "From my experience, the ethical standard there is very high," Peters said. "But they are also a very aggressive company. If you have an action-at-all-costs mentality, even if your ethical standards are high, sometimes people are pushed to do stuff they shouldn't have done."

Is it possible to promote the kind of omnivorous aggressiveness implied by the "steal shamelessly" slogan without also promoting behavior that crosses the line into unethical or even illegal territory?

The original, benign meaning of "steal shamelessly" may be lost on employees new to the business world. In the 1980s, when the slogan took hold, most corporate cultures had a strong bias against anything "not invented here," as the phrase went, and companies rarely acknowledged borrowing ideas from anyone, least of all rivals. Now, it is commonplace to grab others' good ideas, and even to share one's own.

"The good news is that people love to share stuff," Peters said. The bad news is that if even one employee takes the phrase too literally, the rallying cry can seem like a dirty-tricks license.

Bogan, a coauthor of *Benchmarking for Best Practices,* a 1994 book about the practice of measuring and comparing a company's methods and results against competitors', said, "It's very easy to misinterpret what benchmarking is and what good it can provide for organizations, because people will wrongly think it condones illicit behavior."

Preventing that misinterpretation is the challenge. It calls for making the keep-it-aboveboard message as loud and clear as the gung-ho, go-get-'em message.

Peters gave this advice: "State your case very clearly: 'Yes, we are aggressive. Yes, we are action-oriented. But if there's anything that ever shows up gray on your record, ethically speaking, you're either in serious trouble or you're out of here.' "

For a manager, it is a useful test to ask yourself whether you'd have to fire someone if actions under consideration were ever found out. Milliken, in its statement, said it did just that, dismissing its consultants when "claims were made about the propriety of the collection techniques being used." But after-the-fact sanctions can be taken to mean "Just don't get caught." The message that some holds are barred needs to reach employees beforehand, with as much vigor and boosterism as "steal shamelessly" had in its nascence. Perhaps the new slogan should be: "Play hard, but play clean."

Jeffrey L. Seglin
January 17, 1999

8

RUNNING THE SHOW

Handling Transitions at the Top

I had to fight my way in [to the family business]. My father said stuff like: "Who needs you. Don't talk to the customers. Who said you could order paper clips?" He was as tough and mean to me as he could be. I appreciate that training now; you have to be able to hold steady in the buffeting winds.

—Tama Starr, chief executive officer,
Artkraft Strauss, December 29, 1999

I surround myself with mentors. One of the lessons I learned is from David Ogilvy: Hire people bigger than yourself, and you'll end up with an organization of giants. It sounds obvious, but another lesson I learned in the last six years [since I started my company] is there's an awful lot I don't know.

—Mark Jacobstein, chief executive officer,
Small World, September 27, 2000

General Electric was supposed to be showing corporate America how to handle the transfer of power from one chief executive to the next. Its celebrated boss, John F. Welch Jr., had been running the company for nearly two decades by the time the year 2000 dawned, and Welch had repeatedly said that grooming a successor was one of his most important tasks as chairman. He also said that he would exit gracefully in early 2001.

However, in the autumn of 2000, just weeks before GE unveiled its new leader, Jeffrey R. Immelt, events interceded. Welch decided to buy Honeywell, and he said he would stay on until the deal closed—at least the end of 2001—to oversee the combination of two industrial behemoths. Depending on one's point of view, it was either a necessary step to ensure a smooth transition for his successor or the prototypical example of a CEO who cannot quite say good-bye.

Either way, though, it was another illustration of just how tricky the process often is. Take a look at the recent experience of some other Fortune 500 companies. The Coca-Cola Company spent years grooming M. Douglas Ivester as the heir apparent to the legendary Roberto C. Goizueta, only to watch Ivester's unceremonious departure twenty-eight months later. Other huge firms, like IBM and AT&T, have decided that not one of the hundreds of executives on their payroll had the skills to lead and have looked outside for a new chief executive.

Choosing a new person to run the show, and then managing the handover, is often a watershed event for companies. In this chapter, you will have a chance to watch organizations that have struggled through the process: a real estate company with a cozy board that did not want to admit the extent of its problems, a famous dance troupe whose founder failed to take steps to assure that its legacy would continue after her death, and a cattle ranch that did not easily react to changing times. You will also have an inside view of a patriarch with an imaginative method of avoiding competition among members of a younger generation. And you will see a mild-mannered chief executive deftly walk in the footsteps of a famous predecessor.

The uncomfortable truth is that overseeing a big company is probably more difficult than it has ever been. (Of course, the rewards are bigger too; chieftains now make more than $10 million a year, on average.) Investors have less patience than they once did, and technological change, global markets and foreign competitors can all turn a bad year into a good one in a matter of weeks. Even smaller companies and family businesses are more vulnerable to the vicissitudes of markets.

Immelt is known for his technological savvy, his skill at motivating subordinates and his quickness at implementing innovations at the medical-systems unit he ran. He will need to draw on all of those strengths to fill his boss's shoes at GE. There's one other skill he may have to master some day: choosing a successor and then bowing out gracefully.

CASE 1

All in the Family

There is no family feud over succession at S. C. Johnson, no pack of obstructionist cousins demanding larger dividend checks. The 113-year-old family business has not gone the way of Milwaukee's Schlitz Brewing Company, collapsing after the family owners lost control. No one has been inquiring about the rise and fall of the storied Johnson empire.

Instead, on a summer day in 1999, in a tiny, elegant sitting room at the Racine, Wisconsin, headquarters of the old Johnson Wax empire, three of the four Johnson children were seated knee to knee on a white sofa, listening to their father, Samuel Curtis Johnson, explain to a visitor his unusual plan to sustain one of the nation's largest family-owned businesses by splitting it asunder.

That plan—to carve the $5 billion enterprise into three unequal parts, giving each interested child a separate company to run—was more than thirty years in the making, Johnson said, and born out of earlier brushes with family disaster. Framing it has entailed patient planning and study, an eye toward history and careful stroking as the children were positioned for the future, each like a delicate chess piece.

"I read every article in a major publication about family enterprises," said Johnson, who is usually called Sam, as he described a succession plan that would fall into place in 1999 and 2000. "We think about what are the things that destroy family enterprises."

Like his siblings, Sam Johnson's first child—also named Samuel Curtis Johnson, but called Curt—heard horror stories about the collapse of other family enterprises as he was growing up. Rather than demand a birthright to ascend to his father's role, Curt Johnson has agreed to run a unit of the business that sells to industrial customers. His sister Helen Johnson-Leipold was named chief executive of the family's recreational products business in March 1999.

And in 2000, the giant consumer product unit—with a stable of familiar brands including Drano, Windex and Raid—was to be entrusted to their brother, Herbert Fisk Johnson, who is named for his grandfather and great-grandfather and is called Fisk. (Winnie Johnson-Marquart, their little sister, hasn't wanted to run a business. She has four children, lives in Virginia and works part-time for S. C. Johnson in public affairs.)

"Sure this is unusual," Sam Johnson said emphatically, speaking later in his office. But he is resolute that giving his children autonomy is the recipe for a successful transfer of power. "One thing I know about brothers working for brothers," he explained, "is that it always has the potential for disruption."

If families like the Schlitzes, or the Binghams of Kentucky, whose media company dissolved as father battled son and brother battled sister, afford case studies in what can go wrong in the passing of the generational baton, the Johnsons would like to believe that their story will be a case study in what can go right.

In a series of interviews here, the family, which rarely talks to the press, spoke passionately and eloquently about finding its own path to family succession.

To commune with their family roots, the Johnsons retraced the path of an airplane trip that Sam Johnson's father made to the Brazilian jungle in 1935. To work through hard problems of governance and finance, they turned to a network of family advisers and consultants. And always, the children felt the gentle prodding of their father, who lured a reluctant generation back into the fold so that the core enterprise might have a chance to remain in family hands for the next one hundred years.

Of course these Johnsons, the fifth generation, face all the questions that come with taking over a family business. Are they qualified beyond mere blood? Can they distinguish themselves—without feuding—in a competitive corporate environment? And will their decisions about succession prove to be in the company's best interest, or just the family's?

There is no tried-and-true formula to success in family businesses, but there is a sense among historians that the best model may be the Johnsons'—no model at all, really, just subtlety and nuance.

"Every family dynastic situation has to find its own solutions, and they have to be tailored to a family's particular quirks and personality," said Alex S. Jones, who wrote about the Binghams, longtime owners of the *Louisville Courier-Journal,* and, with his wife, Susan E. Tifft, about the Sulzberger family, which controls the New York Times Company.

Yet it's often the quirks—and more fundamental flaws, like pride, greed or sloth—that snuff out family business dynasties. Few even field a fifth generation of family managers.

"How unusual is it for a company to be in the fifth generation?" said Joseph Astrachan, a professor of family business at Kennesaw State University in Georgia. "There's a zero-point-two probability."

A Good Farm Team

Founded in 1886 by an earlier Samuel Curtis Johnson, Sam Johnson's great-grandfather, who sold parquet floors before venturing into floor wax, the company blossomed as Johnson Wax early in the twentieth century. Its ascendancy—and its unconventional spirit—came into public view in 1939, when the company hired Frank Lloyd Wright to design its headquarters in Racine, a building best known for its huge, open interior spaces and the golf-tee-like columns that held up the floors above. (Two years later, Wright designed Wingspread, the majestic Prairie-style Racine home where the current Sam Johnson grew up.)

S. C. Johnson also has a tradition as a benevolent enterprise. Before such donations were fashionable, the company gave 5 percent of its pretax profits to charities. A profit-sharing plan begun in 1917 gives 25 percent of the company's earnings to employees, who also have access to a 146-acre park and a vacation resort in northern Wisconsin.

Herbert Fisk Johnson, the second to lead the company, called the Johnson approach "enlightened selfishness." And to this day, S. C. Johnson is considered one of the nation's most conscientious corporate citizens, repeatedly designated by *Fortune* magazine as one of the "100 best companies to work for."

Its early products were waxes and enamels, but in 1954, Sam Johnson, then twenty-six and the head of product development, emerged from a company lab with the formula for Raid House and Garden Bug Killer, the first water-based insecticide that could be used safely on plants. Within a decade, it was one of the company's best-selling products.

Within a few years, the labs developed Pledge furniture polish, and then Edge, the first gel-based shaving cream. Publicly, the company declared that innovation was its hallmark; privately, the mantra was that each Johnson heir would make a major contribution.

"My grandfather set the tone in the 1920s, and my father came with international growth and technology," Sam Johnson said proudly. "Each generation brings something different."

Transitions, however, weren't always smooth. When Herbert Fisk Johnson Sr. died suddenly in 1928, he left no will. A struggle ensued for control of the Johnson empire, pitting brother against sister. Eventually, a sixty-forty split gave control to Herbert Fisk Johnson Jr.

"It took my father ten years before he was able to settle my grandfather's estate," Sam Johnson recalled. "Fortunately, it didn't wreck the family. My father said, 'I'm never going to let that happen to my son.'" In his will, he clearly designated Sam as his successor.

Sam Johnson wasn't going to let it happen again, either. After his father had a stroke in 1968, Mr. Johnson, by then the company's president and chairman, took a year off to reflect. When he returned, he outlined a plan to begin "downstreaming" his assets, setting up trusts for his children and grandchildren.

He diversified the company in the 1970s, buying makers of outdoor recreation equipment to form what would become Johnson Worldwide Associates, the publicly traded company that Helen Johnson-Leipold now heads, and starting the Johnson Bank, which is now one of the largest banks in Wisconsin.

These steps, he acknowledges now, were made as much out of fear as logic. "I thought the wax company might get smothered by Procter & Gamble," said Johnson, whose wealth is estimated at $3.6 billion by *Forbes* magazine. "I also thought these companies might make a good farm team for the children."

Schools for Scions

First, Johnson had to convince his children to join the team, which he always said was large enough for everyone. It wasn't easy. They all had distinct interests—and trepidations about their legacy.

Initially, Helen Johnson ventured off on her own. After earning a degree from Cornell University (all four children, and their parents, went to Cornell, where the business school is called the Johnson Graduate School of Management), she worked at an advertising firm, moonlighted as a bartender and then opened her own restaurant in Chicago.

"I wasn't ready for the company," she said. "There were very high expectations for the next generation. So I knew everybody would be watching. You also want to prove yourself to yourself."

Curt Johnson also took a detour. After Cornell, he got an M.B.A. at Northwestern and then dabbled in real estate and venture capital.

"I didn't have an interest in the family business right away," he said. "Initially, I was interested in small business."

Only Fisk Johnson trained specifically to work at S. C. Johnson. He studied chemistry and received an M.B.A. and then a Ph.D. in applied physics at Cornell before joining the company in 1987.

"I always knew I wanted to come back," he said. "I thought we had something unique here."

By 1990, Curt and Helen had come back, too, and their father orchestrated the children's training, taking care that one never had line authority over another, that each found a way to demonstrate his or her strengths.

"We never talked about who would be the ultimate successor," Johnson said. "They were all in the mode of trying to qualify."

Top executives helped in job placement. "They weren't assigned to a bed of roses," recalled Neal Nottleson, a former chief financial officer. "Fisk was in an extremely competitive environment, and Curt was general manager of Mexico in a difficult period." Helen had a tough assignment involving the marketing of a hair-care product, he added.

A family council was formed. Johnson, his wife, Imogene, and all four children met regularly to discuss the business and the family. There were also family advisers with expertise in estates and other matters.

Ultimately, Curt, Helen and Fisk each had a private audience with their father to declare a primary interest. Curt, the last to join the company, carved out a niche on the industrial side, becoming the first to set his sights on a top post. ("That started the domino effect," Johnson-Leipold said.) Less sexy than the consumer brands—selling floor-care products, food sanitation systems and polymers—the business had been overlooked as a growth vehicle, he believed.

Helen, the athletic tennis player and diver, got the recreational business, which had gone public in 1987. And Fisk, the scientist, got the big prize, leadership of the core consumer business.

The Johnsons say there was little jealousy or competition, little currying of their father's favor. Yes, they "fought like cats and dogs" as youngsters, Johnson-Leipold said, but as adults, they just fell into place, largely because of their father's attention to the details.

"We each found our spot," she said. "Curt was the wheeler-dealer entrepreneur, Fisk was the technician and I was the one interested in marketing."

Their cousins, the Louis family—thirty-eight living descendants of Herbert F. Johnson Jr.'s sister—had virtually no say in the succession, despite their nearly 40 percent interest in the old Johnson Wax empire.

Remembering the internecine battles of the 1920s and 1930s, the Johnsons long ago determined that the Louis family would have no role in running the business. According to Dr. Herbert Johnson Louis, that hasn't always gone over well.

"Some of my kids aren't too happy," said Louis, a surgeon who lives in Arizona. "But I would hope that if they became superb businessmen, the Johnsons would have to consider them. They'd be silly not to." None of the Louises now works in the business.

Louis's side of the family had early concerns about the current succession. "Anybody who's looking at a fifth-generation company has to be very suspect about who's taking over," Louis said. "But I have absolute confidence in Fisk." And Johnson, he added, has been a superb communicator: "He doesn't let turmoil boil over."

Onward Bound

Indeed, the Johnsons—for all the dysfunction one can imagine their circumstances spawning—seem a remarkably congenial bunch. They bank at

Johnson Bank and eat at Johnson-owned restaurants. They love the outdoors; they love shared adventures.

The most important came in 1998, when Johnson suggested that he and the boys reenact a trip his father made to Fortaleza, Brazil, in 1935. Johnson's father flew a Sikorsky S-38 amphibious aircraft fifteen thousand miles, from Milwaukee to the Brazilian rain forest and back, to study an area rich with carnauba palm trees, a key ingredient in Johnson wax, and to open a school there. In a copy of a book he published privately about the "journey of his life," Herbert Jr. wrote to his son: "Sammy, I hope you take this trip someday."

In 1996, Sam, Curt and Fisk Johnson went scuba diving in Indonesia, hoping to recover the original Sikorsky plane, which had sunk in the Manokwari Bay in 1938, after the Johnson family had sold it. They found nothing. So they had a replica built. The "Spirit of Carnauba" took off from Racine in October 1998, with a few squabbles along the way as father and sons jockeyed for the pilot's seat.

"Dad gave new meaning to the term 'backseat driver,'" Fisk Johnson said.

After stops to refuel and rest, they arrived nearly a month later in Fortaleza and were joined by the rest of the family. More than just an Outward Bound–style adventure, there was something almost mystical about this pilgrimage to what the Johnsons call the "Tree of Life," their way of connecting the carnauba to the company's mythology.

"This trip has provided us with an opportunity to talk about some of the issues and opportunities facing the family businesses," Curt Johnson wrote in an Internet posting to Johnson employees. "I feel connected to the visioning process my grandfather experienced when he made this trip."

Pursuit of Profit

With a succession plan in place, the Johnsons now face the prospect of leading what soon will be three companies into the future.

Curt Johnson's unit, Johnson Professional, now has its own building in Racine, a crisp, new, redbrick structure whose lobby pays homage to Johnson Wax and the Johnson family. He hopes to rev up sales, and after the company is spun off, the family may consider taking it public to finance its expansion.

Johnson-Leipold's business, Johnson Worldwide, has struggled as a public company, its stock lagging behind even the anemic Russell 2000 index of small-capitalization stocks over the last few years. Revenues amounted to just $356 million for the twelve months ending in June 1999.

Still, Johnson-Leipold is happy with her role in the family enterprise. "We all came with slightly different strengths," she said, adding, "You're not in it for yourself, and it doesn't matter which piece is bigger than the other."

In the consumer business, Fisk Johnson faces his own formidable set of challenges.

According to his father, revenues are growing about 8 percent annually. But the gains in the past few years have come from acquisitions. In 1998, S. C. Johnson, as the familiar part of the business is called, bought Dow Brands, whose products included Ziploc bags and Fantastik cleaner. Those operations must be integrated, and new sources of growth found.

"Most of their consumer goods businesses are slow-growth businesses," said John Nevin, a marketing professor at the University of Wisconsin, who has followed the company for decades. "And so they're going to have to do it through innovation or the acquisition of innovative businesses."

Wall Street analysts say the company also continues to face stiff competition. "They face a formidable competitor in Clorox, which understands how to build a brand," said William H. Steele, an analyst for Banc America Securities.

Still, Johnson ranks first or second in market share in nearly every major category where it competes. According to Information Resources Inc., a market research firm in Chicago, Raid and Windex hold 60 percent shares of the United States market for products in their categories; Drano has a 43 percent share among drain cleaners, and Edge is the top-selling shaving cream.

Johnson executives say they are seeking growth overseas and benefiting from huge sales of Glade scented candles, a relatively new product line. Though it cannot distribute stock options, the company says that its compensation plans are competitive with publicly held companies, and that it has no trouble attracting and retaining top talent.

Fisk Johnson says that he recognizes the pressure to create new and innovative products, as his father did, but that he won't rush out with something just to prove himself. "I don't plan on making any bold moves," he said—the kind of comment rarely heard from the chairman-to-be of a publicly held corporation.

The Children's Hour

Johnson, however, remains confident about both the company's prospects and his children's preparedness.

"So far, so good," he said with a smile, sitting in an office decorated with model planes and fishing gear. "They're all well qualified to do what they're doing, and now it's up to me to let them do it."

He even has a plan in place to resolve disputes, a board made up of the four children and three advisers they selected.

"If one of us goes berserk, there's a system to remove that person," Johnson-Leipold explained; the advisers will break any ties.

Johnson is distancing himself from day-to-day operations; his office is three miles from company headquarters. "I'm seventy-one years old, going on seventy-two, and seventy-two seems to be the magic age to vacate one's seats on boards and things like that," Johnson said reflectively.

One thing he cannot influence at all is whether his children will be able to keep the enterprise in Johnson family hands into the sixth generation, in which there are already eleven potential chief executives.

Conservation and environmental issues will get Johnson's attention, and he will oversee Johnson International, the 850-employee financial services company that sprang from the Johnson Bank. He even plans to open up his own banquet facility in downtown Racine, right next to Johnson-Leipold's restaurant.

"Everything is in place," Johnson said. "The management is in place. The product line-up is in place. There are no looming problems. I can step aside without any serious worries."

And in any event, "it's up to them," Johnson said of his children. "I can't operate from my grave."

David Barboza
August 22, 1999

In October 2000, Fisk Johnson was named chairman of S. C. Johnson. Sam Johnson remained chairman of Johnson International and became chairman emeritus of S. C. Johnson as part of the transition. Johnson Worldwide has changed its name to Johnson Outdoors Inc.

CASE 2

Board of Directors v. Artistic Director

Things looked bleak for the Martha Graham dance company in the spring of 2000 when it canceled its scheduled performances for the year, suspended operations of its school and acknowledged that it was virtually bankrupt.

Six weeks later they looked even bleaker.

The company board had changed the locks on the warehouse where it keeps its costumes and scenery out of fear that its former artistic director would take them. That artistic director, Ron Protas, whom Graham herself chose to carry on her work, was operating by cell phone from a location he refused to reveal and was working to prevent the company from performing any of Graham's dances.

Many of the troupe's seventeen members were discussing whether to organize a boycott of the modern dances they had worked so hard to master and perform, to choke off Protas's ability to license them to other companies.

And Protas was talking of establishing a new company to supplant the one that Martha Graham left him in charge of.

The undancerly wrestling match at times took on aspects of an opera bouffe, but for many in the dance world too much was at stake for any laughter.

Hanging in the balance, they said, is the legacy of America's great master of modern dance, which, without a school to teach her particular technique or a permanent company to display her oeuvre, could become the stuff of textbooks for dance history courses.

"It is an end of an era," said Chrystelle Bond, a dance historian at Goucher College in Maryland. "It's a very sad commentary when people destroy the art in the process of trying to save it. Dance is a living tradition, and once you kill the school, there's a danger that the repertory could be lost in just a few years." The school has five hundred students.

In her autobiography, published at the end of her long life, Graham left no doubt about whom she would place in control of her choreography, her company and her extraordinary legacy, which spanned most of the twentieth century.

It would be Protas, she wrote, the untiring acolyte who for nearly twenty-five years shadowed her on rehearsals and tours with a yellow legal pad and dark, oversize glasses, scribbling down her dance commentary and absorbing her technique. He was the devoted aide who nursed her back from serious illness and bouts of alcohol-induced isolation and depression, enabling her to create and produce more dances when the prospects for this seemed dim. It was this man, she wrote, to whom she "entrusted the future of the company."

Nearly ten years later, in July 2000, the Martha Graham Center of Contemporary Dance, encompassing the Graham dance company, school and junior troupe, is struggling to survive the internecine warfare. Protas, who was ousted as artistic director and as a board member, still owns the rights to Graham's works and controls the Martha Graham Trust, which licenses the Graham dances both to the center and to others.

All of this puts Protas at the center of the storm. His scornful critics say that his mercurial personality makes him the most reviled man in dance. That is a tough label for a person with the charm to joke that he doesn't dance a step except for the merengue he mastered decades ago at a Fred Astaire school.

"I'm not a saint, but they seem to blame everything but the Crucifixion on me," he observed dryly.

He is zealous and sometimes prickly in seeking to guard Graham's image and the more than 180 dances that established her as a revolutionary modern dancer and choreographer. Graham, who died at ninety-six in 1991, started what is now the nation's oldest dance company in 1926 and created stark dances and highly dramatic ones that used her movement vocabulary, the Graham technique.

Protas, a restless man with tight tousled curls and a voice that dips into a slow whisper to punctuate points, took over full control as artistic director of the company after Graham's death. That meant he made critical decisions about casting, selection of the season's ballets and appointment of the rehearsal directors who coach dancers. The company long had an international artistic reputation, but it also had a checkered financial history and a touring schedule that was declining in the last years of Graham's life.

The son of a New York businessman and a housewife with a passion for theater, Protas met Graham in the late '60s when he was a freelance photographer and was intermittently attending law school, which he never finished.

The relationship, he said, grew as he tended her while she was hospitalized in her seventies for diverticulitis. It was a dark period in her life when, she wrote, she stopped dancing and started brooding alone, drinking too much and eating too little.

Today even Protas's fiercest critics give him credit for helping to revive Graham's interest in her career. But Protas said he knew that company members mocked the relationship by calling him and Graham the Harold and Maude of dance.

"Her act of choosing me created jealousy and animosity because all the other dancers felt that they should have been chosen by her, and that is a big part of it," Protas said.

His opponents portray the dispute in other ways. "Ron thinks that because Martha was treated as an icon that he would get the same treatment as her heir," said Judith G. Schlosser, a Graham Center board member for more than twenty years. "It took us several years to figure out how to pass on the torch." She said that the board's goal was to make the company more businesslike to appeal to previously reluctant donors.

Encoded in the word "businesslike" is a sharp critique, by Schlosser and many others, of Protas's perceived way of doing business and dealing with dancers. He has alienated some potential contributors and theater presenters, who complain that in his zealousness to preserve the Graham legacy he became erratic and difficult and constantly sought to renegotiate matters that had already been decided.

"I cannot work with Ron Protas again," said Ken Fischer, president of the University Musical Society at the University of Michigan, which organized a Martha Graham festival in 1994. "I have another major project that I want to do with a Martha Graham dance in 2001. I've got the space reserved and the support identified. But I don't feel I can do it if I have to work with Ron. It's just too much dealing with him. He's always changing his mind."

Protas has also faced an undercurrent of derision because he does not dance himself. Critics say that resentment increased because of his brusque treatment of dancers, who were frequently reduced to tears by his critiques.

"How can he be coaching about movement if he has never done it?" said Camille Brown, who quit the company in 1994. "It's like talking about the ocean if you have never seen it."

Brown quit the company soon after filing a complaint with the American Guild of Musical Artists, the dancers' union, in connection with a rehearsal incident involving Protas. She did not pursue the complaint after the filing.

She said she was preparing for a role when Protas tied her hands loosely with rope because, he told her, the piece was about being bound and trapped. And, she said, he added that he would be back with duct tape.

"It was so humiliating," Brown said. "And there was no one in the building who would say, 'You can't do these things.'"

Protas said that this rehearsal method was used by Graham herself for the piece, "Errand into the Maze," as a way to connect with the experience of being restrained, which he said he told Brown.

Critics say as many as thirty dancers, administrators and support staff have left over the years because of Protas's management style. Protas maintains that turnover is natural in any arts organization and that it had been heightened by the company's financial turmoil. Those who have left include a former managing director, Todd Dellinger.

He left early in 2000 and broke into choking sobs recently when he recalled a "sick environment" in which "a bunch of addictive, high-strung personalities were living in a very dysfunctional office." At the top of the heap, he said, was Protas.

By all accounts, the strains between Protas and the board created warring camps and an atmosphere of deep suspicion, with differing accounts about who was responsible for the growing budgetary problems.

Protas maintained that in the previous two years he had disengaged himself from the administrative management of the company to concentrate on artistic matters. "They kept saying if you would just go away, everything will be fine," he said. "And I turn over management to them, and look what happens."

But Dellinger said that Protas had a hand in major transactions and decisions as small as selecting the company's postcards.

The feuding ranges beyond the deficit that brought the suspension of operations in May 2000, to issues as serious as Protas's maneuvers to replace the board's chairman and as small as his irritation with a consultant's penchant for open-toed sandals and napping on the office floor.

("He was a very good organizer and helped the board like never before," Francis Mason, the acting chairman, said of the consultant. But, he conceded, "Maybe he was sleeping under the desk.")

In the end, the board feared that donations would dry up if Protas continued in any management role. The Harkness Foundation for Dance had already withdrawn its support.

And so, in June 2000, with the school and company shut down, another crucial showdown was set over what is perhaps Protas's most powerful hold on the Graham legacy: his control over the licensing of her dances.

The board tried to negotiate a new agreement that would allow the company to perform the dances for ten years with minimal involvement from Protas in return for an annual fee about equal to his $100,000 salary as artistic director. But when his lawyer insisted that Protas keep some form of artistic control, the trustees countered with his removal from the board.

After that vote, four of Protas's supporters on the board resigned. "I don't know why they make Ron the bête noire, the scapegoat. I have no idea," said one of them, Princess Moune Souvanna Phouma of Laos. She added that at every meeting she attended it appeared the board was more intent on destroying Protas than on confronting its own financial shortcomings.

Some Graham dancers and teachers appealed to Protas to renegotiate despite the turmoil. When they got no response, they said, the dancers began to discuss the plan to boycott Graham's dances by other companies as long as they were licensed through Protas.

New battles may be brewing. No one was quite sure what would happen to the Joffrey Ballet's plans to rent costumes for a scheduled performance of Graham's "Appalachian Spring" in October 2000. Protas said the costumes were his to rent, but the Martha Graham Center pays for storage in a warehouse that it has outfitted with new locks. Protas does not have the keys.

In the meantime the company does not have enough money to move into its planned quarters in the vast basement of a new building rising on the former site of the company's school, which was sold to reduce debt.

The center began trying to organize classes at an alternative studio after plans for classes at the 92nd Street Y in Manhattan fell through for lack of money.

"You can't open a school without a dollar for teachers or the accompanist," said Pearl Lang, a former company dancer and noted choreographer. "It just makes me sick. If I work with one group, it seems as if I'm at war with the other."

From his office, Protas holds out the possibility that he might open a new school.

For those who have watched the warfare and sometimes been caught up in it, there is nothing less at stake than a language of dance.

Janet Eilber, whom the company hopes—money permitting—to name as Protas's successor, contends that the mess has to be fixed before the Graham technique becomes a memory. "Martha could be consigned to a history class in ten years unless there are new talent and new disciples," she said. "It will happen incredibly fast. In fact, it's already been happening."

Doreen Carvajal
July 6, 2000

CASE 3

An End to Family Control

Crossing a shady creek bed in South Texas nearly 150 years ago—in the middle of what many people called the Desert of the Dead—Captain Richard King had a vision.

Although he was a steamboat pilot with a thriving business on the Rio Grande, Captain King saw an opportunity to raise cattle on the parched, untamed land that surrounded him. He bought 15,500 acres, about twenty miles southwest of Corpus Christi, from a land grant known as Rincon de Santa Gertrudis. And he began carving out a ranching enterprise that would become an American legend.

His descendants built on his dream, creating one of the largest ranches in the country, with 825,000 acres in Texas and operations around the world.

Over the years, family members developed the Santa Gertrudis, the first new breed of cattle to be produced in the United States; advanced new methods of clearing brush; perfected the American quarter horse (not to mention breeding a line of Thoroughbreds that included Assault, a Triple Crown winner in the 1940s); and refined a system of land management and preservation.

But in recent years, as the cattle business has become less profitable and the family has grown larger and more costly to support, the vision seems to have blurred. Many think it faded altogether when the last King descendant to work the ranch, Stephen J. (Tio) Kleberg, was dismissed in April 1998 by the professional manager brought in three years earlier to lead the company.

In the year that followed, at least eight key employees quit or were dismissed. At a place where employees have been well tended for generations, managers say they felt uncertain about their future, with their work scrutinized and their decisions second-guessed.

"Maybe these changes have to happen," said Bill Baxter, a computer technology specialist at the ranch for seventeen years until he resigned in November 1998, dissatisfied after Kleberg's departure. "I just wonder if there's a good way to do that without destroying the legacy. It's sad to see the traditions die."

In fact, tradition has been under assault at King Ranch for years, maybe decades. Captain King's rule—the guiding principle of many of the white settlers of Texas—was that bigger was better. When he died, in 1885, the ranch had grown to more than six hundred thousand acres. It now consists of four units sprawled across five counties, one of them named for his Kleberg descendants. At one point, he imported the residents of an entire Mexican village to work his cattle; the children of these *kiñenos,* as they became known, were educated on the ranch, and generations were guaranteed jobs.

But traditional ranching activities have been a diminishing part of King Ranch's business, as Americans have reduced their consumption of beef and as more profitable uses have been found for the land, from oil drilling to quail hunting to tourism. And a portfolio of nonranch holdings has been developed to generate the dividends demanded by the eighty-four family shareholders.

Since Jack Hunt, who has an M.B.A. from Harvard and a background in agribusiness, took over as chief executive and president in May 1995, he has sold the ranch's lumber operations, a cotton warehouse in Galveston and a horse farm in Kentucky. He terminated some farming leases in

Arizona. The ranch is now looking to merge or sell King Ranch Energy, an oil and gas company.

In the meantime, King Ranch has bought a 5 percent stake in Agraquest, a Davis, California, company that makes natural pest controls for crops. In 1998, the company led a consortium, Consolidated Citrus, in the acquisition of Turner Foods, one of Florida's largest citrus growers.

The company, which is privately held, does not divulge financial information about its operations. But people close to it have said that in a good year, pretax profit from cattle can range from $1 million to $3 million. Hunting, they say, can bring in $3 million a year; sod, $16 million. A 1998 article in *Texas Monthly* magazine quoted "company insiders" as saying that overall revenues were $183 million in 1994, up from about $100 million in the late 1980s. The company has some 600 employees globally, about 160 of them working the Texas ranch land.

"I think we are very interested in continuing to grow and provide and meet the expectations of the shareholders," said Hunt, a reserved man who runs King Ranch from the company's office in Houston. "At the same time, we're absolutely committed to operate and maintain the South Texas property."

The family says that it, too, is committed to the ranch and that the best way to assure its future is by securing its viability.

In June 1999, Captain King's descendants were to gather in South Texas for their annual summer camp and shareholders meeting, a time when family members get reacquainted with the land and one another. They also consider the ranch's future—and with each passing year, that seems to become more of a challenge.

Calling in the Professionals

The ranch has struggled to support itself since 1977, when the shareholders laid claim to 75 percent of the royalties coming from gas and oil reserves on the ranch. That cash flow had given the ranching operations breathing room, and once it was gone, many operations were deemed unsustainable. The Thoroughbred racehorses were put up for sale, as were most of the overseas ranches. Only a fifty-thousand-acre ranch in Brazil remains, run by Kleberg's son Chris.

Corporate management at the ranch predated Jack Hunt. In 1988, seeing a need to diversify, the family hired Darwin E. Smith, the chairman and chief executive of Kimberly-Clark, the paper maker, as its first outside chief executive. He lasted only a year, and was replaced by an oil executive, Roger Jarvis. During their tenure, the ranch added a citrus grove and sod farm in Florida, an alfalfa hay farm in Arizona and a cluster of offshore oil and gas wells in the Gulf of Mexico.

While the family deferred, for the most part, to its professional managers, Tio Kleberg ran the ranching operations. A fifth-generation descendant of Captain King, with a bushy red mustache and a penchant for chewing cigars, he had grown up on the ranch. Descendants of the original *kiñenos* gave him his nickname, which means uncle in Spanish, because they saw him as cut from the same cloth as his uncle Robert J. Kleberg Jr., who led the ranch for more than fifty years, helping to save it in the 1930s when an estate tax bill posed a mortal threat.

Tio Kleberg went to work here full-time in 1971, when he was twenty-five, after serving in the army. "I was given a car and a set of ranch keys, and they said, 'Go to work,'" he recalled. "All I ever wanted to do was cowboy."

Already familiar with cattle, from his childhood on the ranch, he set out to master other aspects of the operations: brush-clearing, fence-building, the location of windmills. He learned every square inch of the land and participated in every roundup, happiest when he was out working the ranch rather than sitting in an office minding the books.

By 1977, Kleberg was head of ranching operations. But the ranch was already unprofitable, he said, and land management was becoming an increasingly important part of the business. He oversaw a shift from cattle to fostering wildlife development, for everything from hunting to bird watching, and expanded farming operations on parts of the ranch. Under his stewardship, the ranch brought in experts on cattle fertility and continued to build on the Santa Gertrudis, breeding them to be more productive.

People who know both Tio Kleberg and Jack Hunt, the Harvard-trained chief executive, are not surprised that they clashed. Both are said to be strong-willed, and each had a well-cultivated sense of how a ranch should be managed. Often, those visions conflicted.

In addition to his Ivy League credentials, Hunt came to Texas with more than twenty years of experience in agribusiness—fourteen of them at the 270,000-acre Tejon Ranch in southern California, long controlled by the Chandler family, owners of the *Los Angeles Times*.

Their final confrontation, Kleberg said, came after he was asked to examine whether the ranch's agricultural operations—sod, cane and citrus in Florida and cotton and sorghum in Texas—should be split from the ranching operations. After talking to the head of the Florida business, Kleberg concluded that the time wasn't right. The man had a young family, he explained, and a reorganization would require him to travel much more.

Soon, though, Kleberg said, he realized that his opinion wasn't being sought, that he was being told to split the operations. Shortly after report-ing his findings, Kleberg said, he was called to a meeting with Hunt and the chairman of the ranch board, Abraham Zeleznik, a psychoanalyst who is professor emeritus at Harvard. They asked him to resign.

Hunt plays down the resignation, noting that Kleberg joined the board of directors of the company at the time and still lives on the ranch. Keeping Kleberg involved "was an important element of the move," Hunt said.

Still, Kleberg's removal from the day-to-day operations unleashed some doubt about the stability of employment at King Ranch, a worry foreign to a company in which jobs have remained in families—both of Kings and *kiñenos*—for generations.

Among the eight people who have departed since Kleberg's resignation were several ranch managers and Hunt's own secretary, who had been with the company about nine years.

Hunt said that most of the people who left were pursuing better job opportunities. But the handful who were willing to discuss their departures described feeling under constant scrutiny, and they expressed frustration at what they saw as a lack of direction in King Ranch's operations.

Outsiders, too, felt the sting. "The best beating heart they had is gone," said Gus T. Canales, whose family was ranching here before Captain King put down roots in the area, speaking of Kleberg. "It's hard for those of us who have grown up with this lifestyle. We have more emotional ties, and maybe not so economically feasible feelings. But I think that the next gener-ation should give us a lot of credit for trying to change as fast as we can and still keep the affection for the land."

"Small, Gradual Changes"

Stripped of the romance of the West, what is happening at the King Ranch doesn't seem that different from a typical story of the corporate world: New management comes in and scrutinizes the operation for ways to make it more profitable.

In the case of King Ranch, that means asking questions like: What is the optimal mix of ranching and hunting? What is the best kind of feed grass? Should helicopters be brought in at $275 a day for rounding up cattle, or is the job best done the old-fashioned way, on horseback?

"It isn't like we're going to change the world," said Paul C. Genho, who was hired away from the Mormon Church's three-hundred-thousand-acre Deseret Ranch of Florida to head King Ranch's ranch and livestock oper-ations after Kleberg's resignation. "It's going to be small, gradual changes."

To illustrate the point, he stopped at a field where men were setting fence posts for a new weaning lot. The lot would be near grain bins, to eliminate the twelve-mile round trip previously required, saving as much as one hundred dollars a day.

Another change, Genho said, involved the ranch's developing a mineral supplement for cattle and producing it through outside contractors, for half as much as a commercially produced supplement had cost.

On a larger scale, Genho, who at Brigham Young University earned a doctorate in animal science with a specialty in cattle reproduction, continues to work on cross-breeding the Santa Gertrudis to develop cattle with higher weaning weights and greater growth potential. He also hires consultants to advise him on maintaining the most productive mix of bush and grazing land.

"Running a big ranch can't be intuitive," he said, glancing over acre after acre of scrub land.

A knowledgeable man with a good sense of humor, Genho takes a more hierarchical approach than his predecessor to running the ranch. Just a handful of managers report directly to him, compared with the dozen or so who reported to Kleberg. Those who have left the ranch since his arrival, he said, represent a mere 2 percent turnover rate.

For those who have stayed, he has introduced up-to-date incentive programs. For example, a cowboy, likely to be making around twenty thousand dollars a year, can make an additional 10 percent if he does three things: build three miles of fence, help cut production costs and get his high school equivalency diploma.

Also on Genho's agenda is getting back to some traditional ways of working cattle—putting in more time on horses and spending less money on the helicopters that have become popular in recent years for herding.

Asked about the observation by former employees that people were feeling nervous about their jobs, Genho said, "I can understand people's concern, but there's no intent to do anything but to treat those people right."

Doubts remain, however, about the ranch's future course. With the arrival of Genho, a Mormon and seventeen-year veteran of the church's Florida ranch, came rumors that the Utah church was positioning itself to buy King Ranch, too.

"That's totally ridiculous," Genho said.

Local cattlemen, too, say they see nothing to the rumor. But in the next breath, they'll tell you they never expected to see a day that a Kleberg wasn't running the ranch, either.

Hunting Down Some Profits

The pressures on King Ranch affect the entire Texas cattle industry. Cattlemen have stabilized American beef consumption after years of decline and have stepped up their search for export markets. But cattle ranching remains a low-margin business.

"The last several years, it's been extremely difficult in some years to make a profit, and in some years we don't make a profit," said Hilmar G. Moore, who serves on the King Ranch board of directors and is himself a fifth-generation rancher in Fort Bend County, just outside Houston. "You have to run a much leaner, meaner operation."

And it isn't just the cattle; ranchers also need to get more out of their land. Indeed, many ranchers view themselves more as land managers—on the prowl for profitable, sustainable uses of their acreage—than as cattlemen.

In Texas, for the most part, that has meant hunting.

King Ranch, historically rather secretive about its operations, came relatively late to the business of marketing its land as an attraction. But in the last decade, it has embraced the notion, leasing more than five hundred thousand acres to hunters at six dollars to twelve dollars an acre annually. In some cases, hunters lease the land directly. Outfitters also work in conjunction with the ranch to put together organized hunts.

"There are two kinds of hunters: those who have hunted on King Ranch and those who want to hunt on King Ranch," said Luther Young, an outfitter who has a contract to guide groups of quail hunters on the ranch.

Hunters, he said, are willing to pay as much as $850 a day for the privilege. For that fee, they must bring a gun, shells and an appetite; he provides lodging and gourmet meals at his bed-and-breakfast nearby, as well as transportation and dogs. The general stay is three days, he said.

Beyond the hunters, some fifty thousand people visit the ranch every year, most of them for scheduled tours of the property, others for birdwatching or wildlife tours. The company is exploring additional ways to use its natural resources.

"If you told me twenty-five years ago King Ranch would be hosting birdwatching and hosting tours, I'd say you've got to be kidding," said Steve Munday, vice president of the Southwest Texas Cattle Raisers Association. "But that's using their resources."

More Life to the Legacy?

Sitting in the bleachers of the rodeo arena at King Ranch, Jamene Toelkes reminisced as she watched Adan Alvarez put cattle in chutes for roping practice, his four-year-old daughter, Clarissa, in the saddle in front of him.

"When we moved here twenty years ago, we could have survived a holocaust right out here," said Toelkes, whose husband is the veterinarian at the ranch. There were four commissaries, one in each of the ranch's four units, to serve the needs of the hundreds of people who lived on the ranch.

Today, while some one hundred people still call the ranch home—and more than 130 children from the ranch and neighboring Kingsville attend a school on the property—many of the employees commute to work; the commissaries have all closed.

On her little finger next to her wedding band, Toelkes, whose family came to the ranch from Abilene, Texas, in 1978, wears a ring made from some of the diamonds her husband received, on tie tacks, for his twenty years of service. He gave each of his sons—Dell and Philip—a diamond-studded tie tack, as well.

Toelkes, who works in the ranch museum, said her husband told them: "When we made the commitment to go to South Texas, we all became a part of King Ranch history."

Can that heritage be preserved? "My children, neither ever wanted to be cowboys," she said. "Their tastes were too expensive." Dell is a land developer in Colorado City, Texas, and Philip is a partner in an engineering firm in Brentwood, California.

But watching Alvarez, a fifth-generation ranch resident, and his daughter, Toelkes nonetheless saw something that she hopes will never die. "This is what King Ranch is all about—the old teaching the young," she said as Clarissa guided her horse through the arena. "It's in her genes. It's horse heritage. Generations before her did this."

And the generations that come—what will they make of King Ranch? Toelkes paused, then came up with a knowing answer. "It will be," she said, "what the shareholders want it to be."

Barbara Whitaker
June 6, 1999

CASE 4

Following a Tough Act

It was Nickelodeon's twentieth-anniversary party at the Museum of Television and Radio in New York in June 1999, but Herb Scannell, the chief executive of the children's TV network, promised to be brief.

"I'm a Nick fan," he told revelers, using his network's nickname, "but

I'm also a Knicks fan," meaning he wanted to get home to watch the Knicks-Pacers game. Wrapping up his remarks five minutes later, he thanked Geraldine Laybourne, his celebrated predecessor. As he lauded her "inspiration and vision," his voice quivered and his eyes filled with tears.

It was vintage Scannell: deferential, almost self-effacing—the quintessential number two guy.

Except that he had been number one for three years, and built Nickelodeon, a division of Viacom Inc.'s MTV Networks, into a $1 billion multimedia powerhouse. When he took over from Laybourne, few thought he would do much more than stay the course she had set. Today, his detractors at the network, some of whom now work elsewhere, know better. So do Nickelodeon's rivals, who had hoped that Scannell would stumble.

Instead, he has taken Nickelodeon into animated feature films, highvolume licensing and merchandising, digital cable channels, an educational television partnership, Web sites and overseas expansion, all the while reaping more than half of all advertising dollars spent on children's television.

In the process, he has nearly doubled Nickelodeon's revenue and profits. And the doubters have learned an important lesson about Scannell: Beneath his boyish face and mild-mannered demeanor lurks the same hypercompetitive personality that drives those Knicks and Mets ballplayers he admires so much.

When he heard in the summer of 1997 that *Teletubbies,* the quirky British show for toddlers, was coming to the United States, he summoned his executive troops together to plan a counterattack. Never mind that the "Tubbies" were going to be shown on PBS, a noncommercial channel, and that nobody really knew how popular they would be; Scannell ordered everyone to find ways to pump up the promotion and marketing of *Blue's Clues,* Nickelodeon's year-old computer-animated educational show.

"He told us, 'Regardless of what they do, we have to be as aggressive as we can,'" Cyma Zarghami, Nickelodeon's executive vice president and general manager, said. Scannell even managed to get a balloon of Blue, the show's star dog, into the Macy's Thanksgiving Parade.

"He is extremely competitive," Sumner M. Redstone, Viacom's chairman, said. But, he added: "He's quietly competitive. You don't have to shout to compete."

On the other hand, if you are too quiet, people may not realize you're a fighter. That was Scannell's problem in 1996. He had toiled in the shadow of the charismatic Laybourne, a combination Pied Piper and business shark who in seventeen years had made Nickelodeon not only the most popular children's network in America but also the most popular cable network, period.

Associates remember how Laybourne sometimes unleashed a temper that matched her passion for her work. By contrast, Scannell came across as an amiable and thoughtful logistics specialist who rarely even raised his voice.

"Without question, my reaction and that of a lot of other industry people was, 'Can he fill her shoes?'" Jack Irving, executive vice president and media director for the advertising agency Saatchi & Saatchi New York, said. "People felt he was a behind-the-scenes kind of guy. People thought he would have a tough time."

So did his superiors. Scannell's background was in programming and marketing, and they wondered whether he had the financial expertise or strategic vision to lead Nickelodeon into the twenty-first century. Tom Freston, president of MTV Networks, actually moved into Laybourne's office for six weeks, acting as president and evaluating Scannell's every move.

One thing he found was that Nickelodeon's successful "zigzag" strategy, as it is called inside the network, came straight from Scannell's gut. "When others zig, we zag," Zarghami said.

For example, Scannell had the idea of making Saturday night a special night for children's variety programs, calling it "Snick," for "Saturday Night Nick." And, with Saturday morning hours the stronghold of the broadcast networks, he suggested using Sunday mornings to premiere Nickelodeon's cartoons. "He didn't just step in and inherit something," Laybourne pointed out. "He inherited his own hard work."

Scannell said many of his best ideas came to him at home, an apartment in lower Manhattan where he lives with his wife, Sarah, and their four-year-old daughter, Caroline.

And though a company car could be at his disposal, Scannell takes the subway to work. "Only three stops on the express train," he explained.

One of his first moves as head of Nickelodeon was to challenge the two powerhouses of children's animation, the Walt Disney Company and Time Warner Inc.'s Warner Brothers. He persuaded his bosses to invest $350 million to build an animation studio in Burbank, California, that now has five series and four feature films in production for Nickelodeon, and some direct-to-video films in development.

Indeed, Nickelodeon's first animated feature film, *The Rugrats Movie*—made in the fall of 1998 in partnership with Viacom's Paramount Pictures and Arlene Klasky and Gabor Csupo, creators of the popular *Rugrats* television show—became the first non-Disney animated film to gross more than $100 million.

Meanwhile, the licensing and merchandising division of Nickelodeon mushroomed in the three years since 1996 into a $100 million business, largely on the strength of characters from *Rugrats* and *Blue's Clues*.

Scannell also took advantage of the broadcast networks' shift toward filling the 8 P.M. time slot with sexy sitcoms and other adult fare. Since 1985, Nickelodeon from 8 P.M. on had been showing classic sitcoms like *The Brady Bunch* and *I Love Lucy* under the promotional banner "Nick at Nite." But in October 1996, Scannell moved children's shows into the 8-to-8:30 P.M. slot, and in 1998, he expanded them into the next half-hour. The moves worked: More children watch Nickelodeon between 8 and 9 P.M. than watch any other network, even though the broadcasters reach 99.4 million homes, compared with Nickelodeon's 75 million.

In 1998, Scannell again caught his rivals off guard. They had expected Nickelodeon to announce an educational channel. What they failed to foresee was that he would start it in partnership with the best-known name in educational television, the Children's Television Workshop, producers of *Sesame Street* and other highly praised public television shows. The result was a commercial-free educational channel called Noggin, which began in February 1999. "I felt putting us together was like one plus one equals three," Scannell said. "It would be building a new model that has its own strength, rather than have two independent guns going at each other and turning it into a shootout that would cost everyone a lot of money."

Noggin has already become one of the channels most sought after by cable operators. So has Nickelodeon GAS (short for Games and Sports), another spin-off.

Through all his maneuverings, Scannell has taken advantage of an almost total recall of television history that gives him a gut instinct on how audiences will react to new shows. He even uses TV lore to describe his parents. His father was a social worker in Harlem and later in Suffolk County, where he and his three older siblings grew up, and his mother was a Puerto Rico–born caseworker for Catholic Charities. "My mother and father were like Ricky and Lucy, only in reverse," he said, referring to Lucille Ball and her Cuban husband, Ricky Ricardo, on *I Love Lucy*.

When Scannell got the chief executive's job, according to Jeffrey D. Dunn, Nickelodeon's chief operating officer, he gave himself a crash course in his weakest area, finances, constantly pestering Dunn with questions while pushing his department heads to set higher goals. "This is where the competitive streak served him well," Dunn said. "For Herb, it wasn't just, 'How does this work?' but 'How are we going to win, how are we going to take it to the next level?' It was empowering."

Not everyone thought so, though. Between 1996, when he took over, and June 1999, eight high-level executives left, including the heads of marketing, licensing and the movie division, as well as Rich Cronin, who had been running the spin-off channel TV Land and left to head the Fox Family Channel.

One former executive, who insisted on anonymity, said Scannell had set unrealistically steep financial goals for some departments, trying to goad certain managers to become more competitive. This person said that if the network's advertising executive had not locked up advertisers to two- and three-year deals in 1997, the network might have seen a drop in ad revenue in 1999 as its Nielsen ratings dropped slightly.

But the network attributes that loss of market share to increased competition from the Cartoon Network and, to a lesser extent, the Disney Channel and the Fox Family Channel. Most advertising agencies agree.

Another executive, still on board but also speaking on the condition of anonymity, said some longtime department heads simply did not respond well to the higher challenges Scannell had set for them.

"He made people deliver," Zarghami, the network's general manager, said. "The ones who were delivering were the ones who stayed."

Scannell still has his critics within management ranks, though they understandably decline to speak for attribution. Some say that compared with Laybourne he is a micromanager, while others grouse that his drive to increase sales is putting at risk Laybourne's mantra, "Kids first."

For example, the week before the *Rugrats* movie was released in November 1998, Nickelodeon removed the show from its 7:30 P.M. time slot, and ran a promotional spot saying, "The Rugrats have gone to Hollywood, but they'll be back at their normal time next Monday."

Some parents complained that their children had been disappointed not to see the show. Others resented the gimmick, which, naturally, led many children to ask, "What's Hollywood?" and then, "Can I go see the movie?" But the move did help sell tickets, bolstering Nickelodeon's bottom line.

Viacom does not report Nickelodeon's results separately. But cable analysts at Paul Kagan Associates, a media consulting firm, project revenue of $865 million at Nickelodeon's domestic network in 1999, up from $570 million in 1996, and $431 million in cash flow, a measure of profit, compared with $291 million in 1996.

When ancillary businesses and Nickelodeon's international earnings are added (it has channels in Latin America, Britain, parts of Europe, Australia, Japan, Indonesia and South Africa), the division is expected to earn about $500 million on revenue of nearly $1 billion.

Fred Moran, who follows Viacom for ING Baring Furman Selz, said Nickelodeon was "probably the fastest-growing established, nonstart-up, media-related entity."

"Wall Street's focus with Viacom has been on whether Blockbuster would turn around, or on the performance of the studio, driven by *Titanic* and other successful movies," Moran added. "But the quiet, always predictable leading performer among Viacom's assets is without question Nickelodeon."

Lawrie Mifflin
June 17, 1999

In September 2000, Scannell was also named president of TNN, formerly The Nashville Network and renamed The National Network. He was charged with leading the team that will manage, rebrand, and reposition TNN as a general entertainment network.

CASE 5

A Too-Cozy Board

First the founder was in charge. But then came an accounting scandal, and he stepped aside—sort of. Replacing him were two other executives: his wife and the man who oversaw accounting. But then another accounting scandal became public, and they stepped aside, too—sort of.

Now who's running the company? A member of the board who has supposedly been overseeing the company's executives since the day it went public in 1994.

This is JDN Realty, an Atlanta-based real estate investment trust that was one of the industry's most respected firms in the 1990s. It is also one of the prime developers for Wal-Mart Stores. But in early 2000, JDN disclosed that it had been making under-the-table payments to two of its own executives for years, that it improperly billed its two largest clients, that it defaulted on its main bank loan and that it would have to restate all of its earnings since 1994. Law firms across the country have filed class-action lawsuits. JDN's stock dropped 43 percent from February to April 2000.

"The more you look into this, the stranger it gets," said Patrick S. McGurn, a vice president at Institutional Shareholder Services, which advises large investors on corporate governance issues. "There is so much wrong with this that it's almost the plot for a satire."

More seriously, management experts say, JDN's travails offer a case study of the problems that can befall a public company that continues to operate like a private one. At a time when companies are going public at a record rate, and many are flouting widely accepted management guidelines, the lessons are particularly relevant. At the core of JDN's troubles, corporate governance specialists say, is a board that is too closely aligned with management to be an effective advocate for shareholders. The directors are a small inbred group—mostly men who have business ties to JDN or personal ties to J. Donald Nichols, the founder, and his wife, Elizabeth. Most have been board members since the company went public in 1994. The board even lacks a nominating committee.

JDN executives, through a spokesman, and board members declined to comment. A lawyer investigating the company's problems on behalf of the board said the directors had aggressively responded to the company's problems. "The interests of the shareholders have been paramount in their minds," said John Latham, a partner at Alston & Bird in Atlanta.

To analysts and investors, however, JDN's problems—jeopardizing almost every relationship the company has and undercutting its financial statements since 1994—are deep enough that an independent board would have discovered them sooner. Even after they became public, the company reacted in ways that have ensured bad news will continue to dribble out, the critics say.

In February 2000, for example, Elizabeth Nichols was one of two JDN executives on a conference call to analysts in which the company emphasized that J. Donald Nichols, her husband, did not seem to have benefited personally from the off-the-books payments.

Then, on April 12, the company said it would not publish its 1999 earnings by the end of the week, violating a two-week extension it had previously received from the Securities and Exchange Commission.

The company also acknowledged the billing "discrepancies" in previous deals with its two largest customers, Wal-Mart and Lowe's, a home improvement retailer. The problems, which analysts said amounted to overstating costs, leave JDN open to legal claims from the two companies, it acknowledged.

After the market closed that day, J. Donald Nichols resigned as chairman, according to Latham. He had already stepped aside as chief executive in February.

Now JDN faces the difficult task of regaining the trust of clients, analysts and investors who say they still have little solid understanding of the company's problems.

"Those things cause you to lose a significant amount of confidence in management," said one investor who had sold JDN shares in the previous two months.

And Wal-Mart and Lowe's, the two companies JDN wrongly billed for the construction, leasing and sale of shopping malls, were conducting their own inquiries, spokesmen for the companies said.

"Anytime we have to pay something we shouldn't, we take that very seriously," said Les Copeland, the Wal-Mart spokesman. If anything, he added, "We're going to overreact to it and manage it very carefully."

Until recently, J. Donald Nichols seemed to have a golden touch. After five years playing minor league baseball in the Baltimore Orioles' system, he switched to the business world, joining J. C. Bradford & Company, a Nashville investment firm, according to a 1998 article in *Forbes* magazine about his art collection.

He then struck out on his own, getting his first break by helping Wal-Mart build a store near his boyhood home in Franklin, Tennessee. His real estate business expanded in the 1980s, thanks in part to Wal-Mart's rise as the nation's biggest retailer. JDN went public in March 1994, and its stock consistently outperformed other real estate investment trusts, giving shareholders a 79 percent return between January 1995 and January 2000. Real estate indexes returned about 50 percent during that same period.

JDN "had a superior growth rate and a predictable earnings stream," said Andrew Jones, a real estate analyst at Morgan Stanley Dean Witter. "People really understood how they made money."

The executives did it by establishing solid relationships with the country's strongest retailers like Wal-Mart and Home Depot. JDN won a reputation for finishing its projects on time and, seemingly, on budget. Retailers, Jones said, "will pay a little bit more for predictability." In the highly leveraged real estate business, a small amount of additional cash flow makes a big difference to profits.

All the while, JDN continued to operate with largely the same board it had on the day it went public. Until J. Donald Nichols resigned, it included him and Elizabeth Nichols, along with William B. Green, a bank and real estate executive who knew the Nicholses from Tennessee, where the couple continue to live; Craig Macnab, a Nashville financial executive who also once worked at J. C. Bradford, one of the underwriters of JDN's first stock sale; and Haywood D. Cochrane Jr., a Nashville health care executive who says he met J. Donald Nichols through mutual friends shortly before JDN's initial public offering.

Of the two directors who joined since 1994, one is William G. Byrnes, a retired Alex Brown executive whom J. Donald Nichols praised for the vital role he played in shepherding JDN's public offering. The other, Philip G. Satre, is the president of Harrah's Entertainment and also has a Tennessee connection. For years, he was based in Memphis as a hotel executive.

The best evidence of the coziness between the directors and executives, critics said, is the lack of a nominating committee on the board. Without one, the choice of directors often falls solely to the chief executive. "That in itself ends up leading to a lot of cronyism on boards," said Ann Yerger, the director of research at the Council of Institutional Investors. "You want to know there are at least one or two independent directors asking the hard questions."

Three-quarters of public companies in the United States have nominating committees, according to a recent study by Korn/Ferry International, a recruiting firm.

But executives of many public real estate investment trusts, known as REITs, often continue to run them more like the private firms they once were, governance specialists said. As REITs have stumbled in recent years, investors have turned more attention to their management structures. At the Council of Institutional Investors' annual meeting in the summer of 1999, its members held a specific discussion about the industry, Yerger said.

At JDN, management experts said, a more independent board may not have been able to prevent the off-the-books payments, but it probably would have responded more forcefully once the scandal broke.

On February 14, 2000, the company announced that two executives, Jeb L. Hughes and C. Sheldon Whittelsey, had received $4.9 million in payments that JDN's earnings statements did not reflect. Many of the payments, the company said, were approved by J. Donald Nichols. The payments, which analysts said could have come in the form of cash or real estate, ranged from 4 percent to 20 percent of JDN's annual earnings between 1994 and 1998.

Nichols may have made the payments, Jones at Morgan Stanley said, in an attempt to retain the executives at a time when private real estate firms were doing much better, and paying more, than public REITs.

The company offered no explanation, however. It did announce that Nichols was stepping aside as chief executive but that he would remain chairman, in charge of maintaining "tenant relationships."

Under the circumstances, the company should have immediately dismissed J. Donald Nichols, said McGurn, the shareholder adviser, rather than "talking about reassigning him to other duties in the corporation."

Latham, the board's lawyer, said the directors initially chose to weigh

J. Donald Nichols's mistakes against the importance of his ties to big clients. "It's a business decision the board had to make," he said.

Elizabeth Nichols and JDN's chief financial officer, William J. Kerley, then took over as co-chief executives, and the board began investigating the payments, as well as searching for a new chief executive. On April 12, 2000, Kerley resigned, Elizabeth Nichols returned to her job as company president, and the board named one of its members, Macnab—the former J. C. Bradford employee—to the top job.

Analysts and investors, meanwhile, are still trying to figure out when the next piece of news will come and what it will contain.

"I've heard so many different things, I don't really know what's true and what's not," said Jessica C. Tully, an analyst at Wachovia Securities in Atlanta, who had downgraded JDN's stock to "sell."

David Leonhardt
April 13, 2000

In July 2000, Elizabeth Nichols announced her resignation as both the company's president and a member of its board. In November 2000, the Securities and Exchange Commission opened a formal investigation into the undisclosed payments to Jeb L. Hughes and C. Sheldon Whittelsey.

CASE 6

The Empty Executive Suite

Faced with an unforgiving stock market and a harsh business environment, many companies are experiencing another stark reality: a lack of management depth. As more and more chief executives are being rushed out the door by disappointed investors and impatient boards, companies are finding that there is a shortage of obvious candidates to fill these spots, according to executive recruiters and management experts.

Boards will be forced to reach out more broadly for candidates than they have in the past, they say, which may mean that women will be able to move up in these organizations more quickly. The current shortage of managers may also cause companies to rethink how they are grooming future executives.

"Companies have been developing talent on a slower timetable than they should be," said Thomas J. Neff, the chairman of Spencer Stuart, an executive recruitment firm in New York. As companies waste no time in ousting executives who stumble, the escalating demand may mean that companies have difficulty finding replacements. "It's not like there is an unlimited supply of talent to run all these companies," Neff said.

Chief executives are clearly being held to much higher standards today, and the turnover at the top appears to be unprecedented. Lloyd D. Ward at the Maytag Corporation, Richard A. McGinn at Lucent Technologies and Michael C. Hawley at Gillette are among the chief executives at some of the country's best-known companies that have left after they failed to deliver the performance that investors wanted.

From August to October 2000, 350 chief executives in the United States left their jobs, according to Challenger, Gray & Christmas, a Chicago-based firm that helps newly unemployed executives find new positions.

Increasing the pressure on companies is the need to find better candidates than they have had to in recent years, when a buoyant stock market and a booming economy made the choice of a chief executive less critical. "Good times mask mediocre management," said Gerard R. Roche, the senior chairman for Heidrick & Struggles International, an executive recruiting company based in Chicago.

While some recruiters say there are plenty of future executives who will one day be considered as successful as Jack Welch, the head of General Electric, they acknowledge that companies are unlikely to find people who have already proved they are up to the job. "They have already done their job and are tired of it or are doing a good job where they are," explained Russell S. Reynolds Jr., an executive recruiter who is now the chairman of the Directorship Search Group in Greenwich, Connecticut.

Unless boards are willing to consider a less-obvious choice, someone who has never been a chief executive, for example, the market looks narrow, said Rakesh Khurana, who is an assistant professor at the Harvard Business School and who is writing a book on the chief executive labor market.

As a result of the downsizing that went on during the 1980s and 1990s, "there was a significant thinning of management ranks," he said. Companies have also been reluctant to invest in developing future executives because managers are now unlikely to spend their careers at any one company.

In general, the development of talent within companies has been "a much lower priority," agreed Arthur Resnikoff, a consulting psychologist with Hagberg Consulting Group, which is based in Foster City, California. "Companies are not willing to put their money to work in that way," he said.

There are exceptions, of course. General Electric is an oft-cited example of a company that takes great pains to develop future chief executives, even when Welch appeared to be in no hurry to leave. And IBM is likely to choose a successor to Louis V. Gerstner Jr., its chief executive, from among its top officers.

The high rate of turnover among chief executives will force many companies to look more widely for candidates, both inside and outside their organizations. A result may be greater opportunity for female and minority managers, who have traditionally had difficulty reaching the executive suite, according to Andrea Redmond, a recruiter for Russell Reynolds Associates. She is aware of three chief executive searches being conducted by her company that include candidates other than white men.

"There are a number of women with very substantial titles, ergo experience, and a certain degree of readiness," said Sheila Wellington, the president of Catalyst, a nonprofit research and advisory group in New York that studies women in business.

But while Catalyst's census among Fortune 500 companies released in November 2000 identified about sixteen hundred female corporate officers, only 28.6 percent of them had the kind of responsibility that made them likely candidates for the top job, she noted. About twice the percentage of male corporate officers have such responsibility for profits or a direct relationship with clients.

"As one looks more carefully, there is somewhat less reason for optimism," Wellington said.

And some management experts wonder whether companies have been looking for the right candidates for chief executive, given the rapid changes within corporate America. Boards have erred in trying to find the candidate that is most like their last success, said James O'Toole, a business professor at the University of Southern California and an adviser to Booz-Allen & Hamilton, the management consulting firm. Directors "are looking for the safest person, and someone they're comfortable with," he said.

Instead of looking for the next Jack Welch, O'Toole said, directors should try to find someone who can create an environment where there is an abundance of managers who can move up. At Enron, for example, Kenneth Lay, the chief executive, has made a concerted effort to recruit managers and give them substantial responsibility, he said. While some of those people will fail or leave for other jobs, it adds to the company's overall management strength. Lay "has simplified his role," O'Toole said.

Boards may be slow, however, to recognize the need to find a different kind of candidate, even as they move quickly to replace someone who is struggling. Many have taken the unusual step of filling the executive suite temporarily by bringing back the company's former chief executive even when that executive may bear some of the responsibility for the company's current woes.

"It's almost going in the wrong direction," said Michael Useem, a management professor at the Wharton School at the University of Pennsylvania, who said he also believed that today's chief executives must possess a different set of skills than their predecessors.

Boards "haven't quite identified the problem yet," he said.

Reed Abelson
November 16, 2000

9-1-1

When Things Go Wrong

When young people come to me complaining about their horrible bosses, I say, "Aren't you lucky," because the more examples of bad management you see, the more you'll learn. I learned more from my worst boss than I did from my best boss. I was taking notes on how I would not manage.

—Geraldine Laybourne, chairman,
Oxygen Media Inc., October 6, 1999

In retrospect, it all seems so clear.

Iridium was a big, exciting new technology bet. But the global satellite phone venture charged too high a price and underestimated the ability of cellular phones to work in foreign countries. Technologically, Iridium may have been appealing, but a few lessons from Marketing 101 could probably have foretold its downfall.

Fruit of the Loom, meanwhile, was running on little other than the hucksterism of its chief executive. While he soothed investors and Wall Street analysts with his slick words, he was dumping his own shares in the company, using company loans for personal purchases and storing his Czech fighter plane in a Fruit of the Loom hangar.

And executives at Boeing, one of the world's most complex companies, were obviously pigheaded when they blithely figured they could more than double their output in less than two years. Anybody who truly understood the airplane business could tell that the combination of cutting costs, lowering prices, gaining market share and ramping up production was too much to accomplish in a short span.

It would be easy to read these and other tales of mismanagement in this chapter and play the Monday morning quarterback. You almost want to snicker at the hubris or shake your head at the greed or bumbling that characterized some of the best-known flameouts of recent years. And feel free: The flameouts were pretty spectacular.

But then take a moment to think about the many talented managers at these companies who had many good ideas and fully expected that they could execute their plans. Or the thousands of investors who kept the faith for far too long and now have shallower pockets as a result. Or some of us know-it-alls in journalism who wrote glowing accounts of these companies even as they laid the seeds of their downfall.

The fact is, it's often tough to recognize the signs of decline, particularly in a big, established company or any institution that has been around for a long time. That is especially true if the decline is slow and uneven. So a key lesson to take away from the stories in this chapter is to look for signs of trouble in even the calmest waters at a company. Perhaps you'll spot some parallels between your employer or your favorite stock and the case studies here. Perhaps your firm, like Value America, is run by entrepreneurs who are convinced that they can manage a large organization as well as they launched a small one. Maybe your organization has a grand expansion scheme that, at first blush, appears as if it just cannot fail—much as Boeing's plan to gain market share must have seemed to its executives.

Keep in mind the adage that those who have not learned from history are doomed to repeat it. Just ask longtime employees of AT&T. As they watched the Microsoft antitrust trial, they could not help but think of another giant company that was too big and too successful to be hurt by a bunch of regulatory meddlers.

CASE 1

Impossible Goals

Listening to Philip M. Condit and Harry C. Stonecipher talk about the difficulties facing the Boeing Company, the global aerospace powerhouse and national icon they jointly run, oddly brings to mind the feminist battle cry of the 1980s: They just don't get it.

After an awful year of monumental production foul-ups, $4 billion in unexpected accounting charges and lots of talk about illusive recovery plans, the news from Boeing only seems to get worse. In December 1998, the company stunned investors and its 232,000 employees with the announcement that it would cut as many as forty-eight thousand jobs by 2001—and still make only a negligible profit.

The news from the nation's single largest exporter rippled across the country like the storms that pour rain on Seattle, Boeing's then hometown, and then head east. President Clinton weighed in with his concerns about the company's health. And on Wall Street, shareholders—who had been led by Boeing to believe the worst was over—began selling in anger, even disgust. Boeing stock took a beating.

"This is one of the great American industrial franchises of the twentieth century," said John Hayes, an analyst at Independence Investment Associates, an institutional money manager that sold its stake of several million Boeing shares in 1997. "For the business to be in this kind of disarray is unfathomable. These guys have been doing this a long time. They should know how to build planes at a profit."

Yet in their first interview since announcing the latest cuts, Condit, the chairman and chief executive, and Stonecipher, the president and chief operating officer, spoke that December as if Boeing had no choice but to make the decisions that have laid it low—to sell hundreds of airplanes at cut-rate prices in 1995 and 1996 and then to nearly triple production rates, from eighteen airplanes a month to the current record rate of fifty-one.

"No one could have run this place successfully for the last year," said Stonecipher, the former chief executive of McDonnell Douglas, who joined Boeing after it acquired McDonnell in 1997 for $16 billion, creating a national monopoly in large passenger jets and the world's biggest military contractor and aerospace company, with more than $56 billion in revenues expected in 1998.

"The systems were overloaded to the point where it doesn't matter who was in charge," he said. "You could have worked it a lot of different ways; the result would have been the same."

Condit's credibility seemed especially weak, because he had to revise so many of his public positions over the course of 1998. Yet while contrite, he still had trouble, even in hindsight, viewing the company's actions as a colossal blunder. "I think we were very close to making it," he said of the ill-fated ramp-up in production. "So it isn't, gosh, you can look back and say, 'It was clear you wouldn't have.'"

Boeing's thirteen-member board was set to meet that month in the wood-paneled boardroom where Condit and Stonecipher were talking. And for the first time in anyone's memory, as the *Seattle Times* pointed out in an editorial, the ouster of a Boeing chief executive was being openly discussed by employees and on Wall Street.

"If I was on the board, I would be taking a hard look at whether to keep him," said Bill Whitlow, an analyst at Safeco Asset Management in Seattle and manager of a fund that holds 67,500 Boeing shares.

Seven of the outside board members declined to comment; three did not respond to telephone messages and one other board member could not be reached. While Condit acknowledged that he was in the hot seat, he said that he was working harder than ever and that he didn't think a change at the top made sense.

"I think we are better together than either one of us would be alone," he said, referring to Stonecipher, adding later, "I could not imagine a better partner."

Still, if Condit's days are numbered, Stonecipher may be positioned to cap his long career as Boeing's next chairman. That idea rankles many employees of the old Boeing—"heritage Boeing," in the company's post-merger parlance—because after years of bruising competition they, not McDonnell Douglas, had prevailed in the marketplace.

"I have heard internal comments that, 'Hey, we won, but now they are running the show,'" Whitlow said.

Boeing loyalists especially resent what they see as the heavy hand of Stonecipher, a blunt talker who became popular on Wall Street first by turning around the Sundstrand Corporation, a maker of aerospace components, and then by sharply improving McDonnell's financial performance before selling that company to Boeing.

As Boeing's problems worsened during 1998, Stonecipher's power appeared to have grown. He, rather than Condit, was seen as the man behind the departures of a number of Boeing executives with whom Stonecipher is said to have clashed, including the longtime chief financial officer and the head of the commercial airplane division.

Stonecipher, who had a large stake in McDonnell Douglas, was one of Boeing's largest shareholders; so was John F. McDonnell, the son of one of McDonnell's founders, who like Stonecipher was on the Boeing board. Condit, like other board members who came from the old Boeing, owned relatively little stock.

Investors and analysts credit Stonecipher with sharpening Boeing's focus on shareholder value. Boeing's decisions to increase greatly its communication with Wall Street, disclose earnings targets, announce large job cuts and buy back up to 15 percent of its stock all echo Stonecipher's previous stints at Sundstrand and McDonnell. (The company's new candor, of course, contributed to its problems, as promises and predictions have failed to materialize. But Condit said he still thought that Boeing should keep lines of communication open with investors.)

Stonecipher was also seen on Wall Street as a strong executive who holds his charges accountable, while Condit was widely viewed as a talented engineer who is out of his element running the country's eleventh-largest industrial company.

In the interview in December 1998, Condit and Stonecipher dismissed talk about differences between them as idle gossip. Condit said that they leaned on each other and often swapped roles, but that Stonecipher's job was to focus more on day-to-day operations while he concentrated on longer-term strategy.

Few people privy to the inner workings of Boeing's executive suite would comment on relations between the men. Current and former Boeing executives are reluctant to criticize them.

The two men could not be more different. Stonecipher is tough-talking, quick-tempered and unsentimental. He was raised modestly in the coal-mining regions of eastern Tennessee and worked his way up through General Electric for twenty-seven years, rising to become head of its jet engine business before spending seven years at Sundstrand and three at McDonnell Douglas. He has been married to his Tennessee sweetheart for more than forty years.

Condit grew up comfortably as an only child in San Francisco, where his father was a chemist for Standard Oil. He joined Boeing in 1965 after getting a master's degree in aeronautical engineering from Princeton and was quickly identified as a golden boy destined for greater things within the company. In addition to doing engineering work on a variety of airplanes, Condit had stints in sales and marketing. He was named president of Boeing in 1992, rising to chief executive in 1996 and to chairman in 1997. He has been divorced three times.

While Stonecipher is feared, Condit, who is known for his people skills, is genuinely liked. "I'm a little more aggressive than Phil," Stonecipher once told a group of potential investors in New York. "I'm more likely to shoot you and then ask you your name. Phil is likely to ask you your name and then shoot you."

Condit's crowning moment was in the early 1990s, when he led the team that designed the 777, Boeing's newest and most modern jetliner. In the course of that project, he promoted an uncharacteristic degree of teamwork that he has since tried to spread to the entire company.

A self-described lifelong learner, Condit received his Ph.D. in 1997 from the Science University of Tokyo. He is also not afraid to help Boeing executives—not the most introspective group—get in touch with their feelings. A few years ago, he hired David J. Whyte, a poet and motivational speaker, to run workshops with top managers. In one meeting at Condit's home, the executives were asked to write down negative stories about Boeing and toss them into a bonfire so that only positive, inspirational stories would remain.

By December 1998, executives were probably tossing Boeing's last five quarterly earnings reports into the blaze.

The company's difficulties building commercial jets have prevented it from capitalizing on one of the biggest sales booms ever. Though Boeing has only one competitor left—Airbus Industrie, the European consortium—and is building more jets than ever, it said it would make hardly any money in 1999 and 2000 from selling them. Analysts say that by the time Boeing fixes its problems, demand will have dried up.

In acquiring McDonnell Douglas, Condit wanted his rival's large military operations. Along with the space business of Rockwell International, which Boeing bought for $3.2 billion in 1996, they were supposed to help Boeing balance the ups and downs of the notoriously cyclical passenger airplane market. But even with all those new businesses, Boeing expects to earn only $1 billion this year, a meager 1.8 percent return on sales.

In hindsight, it seems obvious that Boeing's commercial airplane business was headed for trouble, given what the company was trying to do. Two years earlier, when demand for new planes began to pick up after a drought in the mid-1990s, Boeing made a bold bid to gain market share by offering steep discounts. Executives believed that plans to overhaul Boeing's production systems—which date to World War II and are still largely paper-based—would allow the company to lower the unit cost of each jet by 25 percent, so that it would make a profit even at the low prices.

As orders poured in, Boeing was forced to increase production to forty planes a month, from eighteen, in a year and a half. Rather than help, the efforts to consolidate four hundred separate computer systems, track millions of parts and digitize thousands of drawings added to the rising confusion. Parts shortages developed, and work fell behind schedule as thousands of new workers—hired to replace older, skilled laborers who took early retirement during the previous down cycle—could not handle the load.

At the same time, Boeing was trying to introduce several new models, each of which required certification by regulators in Washington and Europe, adding to the delays. In addition, many of its new orders were from new customers, which meant tens of thousands of hours of engineering work to customize the planes to their specifications.

By early October 1997, Boeing's assembly lines around Seattle had seized up. The company said it would halt production of its 747 and 737 jets for a month to catch its breath. Along with costly changes on the new 737, that resulted in a stunning $2.6 billion in accounting charges.

Investors were angry; Boeing had been insisting for months that reports of production difficulties were exaggerated. Over the next year, as the airplane division struggled to recover, a pattern developed. Executives led by Condit would try to put the best face on the situation. But just when it seemed things were turning around, the company would drop another bombshell.

A low point came in July 1998, when Boeing released its second-quarter earnings and, for the first time, offered earnings guidance to Wall Street analysts. While most analysts were estimating that Boeing would earn $1.64 a share in 1998 and $3.24 a share in 1999—down from as high as $5.00 before the production difficulties arose—Condit said the company expected to make $1.01 a share in 1998 and $2.02 a share in 1999.

Boeing's share price plunged, and analysts were irate. The next day, when Condit met in Boston with institutional investors and analysts, one analyst all but called him a liar. At a similar session in New York, another analyst implied that Condit was deliberately trying to drive down the price of the stock to buy it on the cheap.

Shaken, Condit returned to Seattle and told colleagues he never wanted to be put in such a position again.

But his credibility has continued to deteriorate. In the spring of 1998, Condit strongly defended Ronald B. Woodard, the head of the commercial airplane division, when many people were calling for his head. Five months later, he ousted Woodard, who had been in line to become Boeing's president. Insiders now say that Condit's mistake was not firing Woodard sooner.

Boyd E. Givan, Boeing's chief financial officer for thirty-two years, was also forced to resign after reportedly clashing with Stonecipher. "I thought they shot the messenger," said Dean Thornton, a retired Boeing executive. Givan was replaced by Deborah C. Hopkins, former chief financial officer for General Motors Europe, who started work in December 1998.

Condit said that if he finds fault with himself, it is in underestimating the challenge of transforming Boeing from a company of the cold war era, which valued engineering performance above all, to one that also values financial performance.

Now, he said, "we have unhooked ourselves from market share intentionally and said what we are about is running a profitable company."

Condit and Stonecipher said that the bad news in December 1998 was unavoidable, because the economic downturn in Asia would force the company to cut back its production in 2000 far more than it had thought.

The explanation is puzzling: For more than a year, the company's assessment had been much less pessimistic than those of outsiders; then, when some experts began to say that conditions in Asia were improving, Boeing was saying the situation was worse than ever.

"I think most of the world is really in denial about what's going on in Asia," Stonecipher said.

What really alarmed investors about Boeing's 1998 disclosures was the company's acknowledgment that margins on its commercial airplanes would be even lower in 2000 than in 1999. Boeing attributed the deterioration to expectations that it would sell more of its new models, which command lower margins than older planes. But the announcement raised analysts' concerns that it would take Boeing longer than anticipated to make its assembly lines more efficient.

Already, Alan Mulally, the new head of the commercial airplane division, has delayed the production modernization program; instead, the company will try to deliver planes on time and avoid penalties. "We are probably the least efficient we have ever been making airplanes," Mulally said in a December 1998 interview. Thousands of extra workers are on the payroll simply to get planes out the door, he said.

With the layoff warning, many of those people are fearing for their jobs, even as Boeing depends on them to help it out of a jam. "It's a helluva Christmas present to give Boeing employees," said Bill Johnson, president of the machinists union local that represents thirty-nine thousand Boeing workers.

The union, which struck against Boeing for sixty-nine days in 1995, was gearing up for negotiations in August 1999, and it believed it had Boeing over a barrel. The company wanted to introduce a new workweek to cut overtime and institute copayments on health insurance. The union would have none of it.

"We are not going to be mean," Johnson said. "We are just going to make sure we get the things we want. They cannot afford a strike in September. I see them somewhat on the defensive already."

Can Condit ride out the storm? On paper, the odds look to be in his favor. Only four of the thirteen board members, including Stonecipher, came from McDonnell Douglas. Eight are Boeing holdovers, presumably with loyalties to Condit, including such pillars of the Northwest as George Weyerhaeuser, the paper magnate, and Charles M. Pigott, the former chairman of a truck maker, Paccar Inc.

Even with Stonecipher in the executive suite, there is no clear succession plan. He would be popular with investors, but faces mandatory retirement in 2001. The only other obvious candidate within Boeing is Mulally, who has his hands full turning around the jet business and is not yet considered seasoned enough to be chief executive.

Bringing a new leader into Boeing from outside would be a dramatic step for the proud company. But it could hasten changes that Condit and his predecessors have talked about implementing for the last decade, with little apparent progress.

"Boards really aren't very compassionate," Stonecipher said. "The moment the board decides that somebody else can get this thing done for them, we will be out of here the next day."

Is Boeing at that point today? Stonecipher did not hesitate to answer. "No," he replied.

Laurence Zuckerman
December 13, 1998

CASE 2

Betting Too Early

There are two tenets of unshakable faith in all management bibles of the new economy. One is that being the "first mover" into a market is a huge advantage. Get there first, as Amazon did, and all the self-reinforcing "network effects" of the modern economy work to your benefit. It may not guarantee permanent leadership, but it makes life awfully difficult for the second, third and fourth movers.

The second, related tenet is that the future belongs to the big risk takers. Fear of failure is for losers. The American entrepreneurial edge is that business failure carries none of the stigma it bears in other nations. Failure here is a useful learning experience, increasing the chances of success next time.

What, then, to make of Iridium?

The global satellite phone system, which cost $5 billion to build, had been languishing in bankruptcy. And on March 17, 2000, Iridium asked the bankruptcy court for permission to shut down completely, liquidate its ground assets and spend up to $50 million over the following nine months to "deorbit" its sixty-six satellites, sending them hurtling into the Earth's atmosphere to burn up.

Dreamed up in the mid-1980s by engineers at Motorola, its creator and largest investor, Iridium was certainly a first mover and a bold risk-taking project. Yet it is nobody's idea of a noble failure; words like fiasco are more often heard. What are the lessons in the Iridium experience?

First, the project was fundamentally different from the kinds of business ventures that turn heads today in the Internet economy. Iridium really was a bold bet on the future, while most Internet ventures are not. The "network effects" work so predictably on the Internet because the network is in place. Iridium, by contrast, had to build a network of ground stations and launch its satellites into orbit.

Further, as a technology, the Internet is totally mainstream. Most Internet start-ups are built on a blend of incremental innovations in software and the pursuit of some market niche. If one venture fails, it is easy to move on to the next, refining the software a bit and going after a different market. This is not visionary risk-taking or innovation.

Big corporations are embracing Internet technology for the same reason—because it is an important tool for overhauling the way they do business, not because it requires much real risk-taking.

Iridium was at the other end of the spectrum, a giant long-range gamble on an unproven technology. For Paul Saffo, director of the Institute for the Future, it calls to mind a cowboy adage: Never mistake a clear view for a short distance.

In the postmortems written on Iridium since its filing for bankruptcy protection in August 1999, Motorola's hapless management of the project has come in for great criticism. Saffo agrees that management matters, but he said its role in big, pioneering, technology efforts tended to be overstated. Mostly, he said, Motorola bet too early on the wrong technology: "They zigged and the world zagged."

Iridium's litany of troubles are well known. Everything proved more costly than anticipated, from launching the satellites to making the handsets, which cost three thousand dollars apiece when the system went live in November 1998. The cost later fell by half, but too late to do much good. The equipment was clunky, with handsets the size of bricks and antennas like billy clubs. The hoped-for millions of customers never signed up. In March 2000, Iridium had fifty-five-thousand subscribers and debts of about $4.4 billion.

While Iridium sputtered, ground-based wireless phone service grew at astounding rates in Europe, Asia and the United States. Business travelers, the main market for Iridium's global service, soon found that they could simply use their cell phones in major cities around the world.

Michael Kleeman, a former consultant at the Boston Consulting Group who is a founder of a telecommunications start-up, said Iridium was blindsided by the rapid growth of ground-based competition. For its part, Iridium was dependent on its local partners around the world, twenty-eight traditional telephone companies and government-owned post, telephone and telegraph monopolies, known as PTTs.

"Iridium can be seen as the last gasp of the government telecommunications cartels, the last of the big telecommunications consortia tightly tied to the PTTs," Kleeman said. "And Iridium had the old mentality—'Build it and we'll force people to use it'—as opposed to, "Is there a market for this anyway?'"

It is also instructive to ask, what is the wrong lesson to learn from Iridium's failure? "The lesson you don't want to learn is that satellite telephony is a bad idea," said Peter Schwartz, chairman of the Global Business Network, a consulting firm. "Iridium was a radical new system that leapt into commercial use too soon."

Steve Lohr
March 19, 2000

The plan to let the satellites hurtle toward Earth was stopped in December 2000, when the Pentagon agreed to spend $72 million over two years for satellite service. That was the key step in persuading a court in New York to permit a successor company, Iridium Satellite LLC, to buy the assets of the bankrupt service for $25 million.

Iridium Satellite has a vastly scaled-down business plan. Besides providing service to twenty thousand military and government workers who already have Iridium handsets, the new company intends to offer the service to a small group of potential industrial customers like oil and gas companies who do exploration work in remote regions. Iridium Satellite's costs will be much reduced since it will not have the bankrupt company's debt load. Boeing agreed to operate the satellite system under contract.

CASE 3

The Mortal Brand

In 1997, Fruit of the Loom was trading at forty-four dollars a share, and nobody was questioning William F. Farley.

Sure, there had been smirks years before, when the hunky chief executive donned underwear to star in a television commercial, and raised eyebrows about a man who once touted himself as White House material. But investors cared more about a company that ranked number fourteen in the Fairchild 100 survey of the world's most recognizable fashion brands. And analysts cheered a new marketing slogan, "Everybody Loves Fruit."

In March 2000, with Fruit of the Loom wallowing in Chapter 11 bankruptcy protection and the company's shares down to around $1.30, nobody loves Fruit. And all fingers are pointing at Farley.

A growing band of critics say there were signs everywhere that Farley, a veteran of the hugely leveraged takeovers of the 1980s, had been steering the company toward disaster for years.

They point, now, to a 1998 class-action lawsuit that charged Farley and other executives with insider trading, to $103 million in personal loans guaranteed for Farley by the company, to bloated pay packages and rich deals with Farley's private company, to simple mismanagement of underwear sewing plants.

Yet much of this had been disclosed in Fruit of the Loom's regulatory filings, and none of it stopped bankers from lending Farley tens of millions of dollars to solidify his control of the company. Or Wall Street analysts from enthusiastically recommending the stock to investors. Or respected investment banks from underwriting hundreds of millions of dollars in bonds, even as the company was coming unglued.

After years of inaction, and some would say complicity, the board of directors finally ousted Farley on August 30, 1999. Four months later, the company filed for bankruptcy protection. By then, investors were out billions. Fruit of the Loom reported it lost $576 million in 1999.

The financial world's failure to call a halt to the high jinks appears to be one more example of Wall Street's capacity to be blinded by charm—and by stories it wants to believe.

"I look back and say I should have never done it," said Donald Yacktman of Yacktman Asset Management, a big shareholder. "It was a big brand name, and it's hard to believe a company with this kind of market share could get killed like this."

But it did. Today, the fate of Fruit of the Loom is being played out in two locales—a Delaware bankruptcy court, and at the company's operational headquarters in Bowling Green, Kentucky, where a former executive has been called out of retirement to pick up the pieces.

Fruit of the Loom, a brand name first used by a Warwick, Rhode Island, textile mill in 1856, has asked the bankruptcy court for permission to begin liquidating Farley's assets. The company wants to use the proceeds to pay down a $65 million personal loan it guaranteed for Farley in 1999, and became liable for when he stopped making payments himself.

In his first interview since he was removed as chief executive, Farley defended his tenure and insisted his conduct was beyond reproach.

"Not a day goes by when I don't think about it," he said wistfully, "the questions of what could have been done, could we have escaped this ugly situation?"

But people are forgetting, he said, that he was the visionary who acquired Fruit of the Loom in a leveraged buyout in 1985 and built its sales to $2 billion. Blaming directors and managers for foiling his plans, he is threatening legal action, too, saying the company owes him about $100 million in severance and pension benefits.

Only one outside director of the company responded to telephone calls about the board's oversight of Fruit of the Loom, and of Farley. "It's a besmirch on my long history of integrity and honesty," said Henry A. Johnson, a director since 1988 and the retired chief executive of Spiegel Inc., the catalog retailer. "But I'll have to live with it."

"Dale Carnegie Personified"

Before the fall, Bill Farley was living the high life.

In 1985, *Forbes* magazine listed him as one of the richest Americans. He had a ski house near Aspen, Colorado, a home in Kennebunkport, Maine, and a lavish apartment on Lake Shore Drive in Chicago, where he played host to President Clinton at a 1998 Democratic fund-raiser. He dated the 1989 Miss America (he was one of the judges who picked her) before meeting Shelley McArthur, a Chicago model and singer who is now his fourth wife.

Farley grew up in Pawtucket, Rhode Island, the football-playing son of a postal worker, and said once, "I want to create companies in my own image." He pursued that vision at Fruit of the Loom. Obsessed with fitness, he installed athletic facilities at company plants. Cigarette machines were banned, and meetings often began with Farley leading his managers in aerobics.

He was charming and energetic, a deal maker—"Dale Carnegie personified," said one former colleague. But much of his wealth was tied to the stock of Fruit of the Loom. And things began to unravel there in 1997, when the company, which also owns the BVD brand, was facing stiff competition from apparel makers like Hanes, a division of the Sara Lee Corporation.

At the time, Farley's top executives were busy selling Wall Street on a massive revamping effort that would reduce costs by moving sewing operations offshore. To demonstrate management's confidence in the company's long-term prospects, Fruit repurchased $173 million worth of its own stock.

Wall Street analysts rallied behind Fruit of the Loom, helping bolster the shares to nearly an all-time high in the spring of 1997.

Just then, however, top executives began unloading huge blocks of their own holdings, some 1.4 million shares worth $46 million. And Farley did the bulk of the insider selling. He cashed in $39 million, most of it in April, May and June.

The timing was prescient. In early July 1997, Farley and other executives told analysts that something had gone terribly wrong and that profits would not meet expectations. Second-quarter profits tumbled, and by year's end there were losses of nearly $400 million.

The ensuing stock sell-off prompted the class-action suit by shareholders. Their lawyers argued that in early 1997, the top executives misled investors by painting a deceivingly rosy picture of the company's prospects, even as they dumped their own shares.

The suit, filed in federal court in Kentucky, also asserted that executives won those shares as bonuses by fraudulently bolstering the company's performance in 1996, flooding retailers with inventory and booking sales before customers paid. That gimmick artificially inflated earnings late in the year, the suit said, allowing top executives to qualify for stock options.

The company is fighting the suit. Farley said, "The case is absolutely without merit."

Fruit of the Loom made a modest recovery in early 1998; jobs were slashed and the company announced that it would create a parent company in the Cayman Islands to greatly reduce its tax costs. Soon, though, the chief financial officer and the chief operating officer resigned, and over the next year, there were constant foul-ups as the shift to offshore production careened out of control.

Ethan Schwartz, an analyst at Credit Research and Trading LLC, a securities firm in Greenwich, Connecticut, said that in the middle of 1999 he called some of Fruit of the Loom's suppliers to ask about its operations.

"About three hundred to five hundred spinning machines were inefficient," he said. "I talked to knitters who said they talked to Fruit and were given contradictory information about what to make and what color to use."

Already heavily leveraged, with more than $1 billion in long-term debt, the company's bloated expenses caused cash-flow problems. By the middle of 1999, its debt rating had plummeted into junk bond territory, and the stock price sank below five dollars a share.

Several executives blamed Farley for the missteps; the deal maker, they said, was not much of a manager. In an interview, Farley conceded that the restructuring was botched, but said his executives and board should have gone along with his plan to move production offshore three years earlier.

And these were certainly tough times in the basic apparel business. Low-cost producers like Gildan Activewear, a Canadian company that went public in 1998, were gaining market share, while others, like the Starter Corporation, were driven out of business.

By the summer of 1999, even Farley's handpicked board was fed up. At a meeting in Chicago, the board fired Farley, though he still controlled about 30 percent of the company's voting stock. Dennis S. Bookshester, a long-time board member, was named acting chief executive.

In an interview, John J. Ray, the company's general counsel, said there was no mystery in the decision.

"I think the operating results speak for themselves," he said. "They were abysmal."

High Pay and Huge Loans

It was only logical to blame Farley: he ran Fruit of the Loom like an emperor, according to interviews with more than a dozen former company executives. Besides selecting the board, he used company money to buy art for corporate offices and his home, gave Fruit's money to his favorite charities, even controlled a portion of the pension fund investments, picking the stocks himself.

He was among the nation's highest paid chief executives, according to Graef Crystal, the compensation expert, who has called Farley a "perennial compensation abuser." Farley earned over $40 million from 1996 to 1998, even though Fruit of the Loom lost $103 million during those years.

Any criticism of his pay, Farley said, was purely subjective.

"People are free to think whatever they want to think about its adequacy," he said. "I think my compensation was fair and obviously the board did."

Beginning in 1994, the company guaranteed three personal loans totaling $103 million for Farley. He acknowledged using some of the money for personal purchases and investments. Some of it, former executives said, went to expand his Chicago apartment.

A $26 million loan in 1998 allowed Farley to buy back securities owned by Leon D. Black, formerly one of his bankers at Drexel Burnham Lambert and now a partner at the Apollo Management investment firm in New York.

That debt was convertible into shares of Farley Inc., Farley's private holding company, which went into bankruptcy protection in 1991 with Fruit of the Loom voting stock in its portfolio.

Fearing that Black might gain control of Farley Inc., and thus the Fruit of the Loom shares, and block the Cayman Islands move, Farley said the board asked him to take out the loan to reacquire Black's shares.

Ray, the company's general counsel, disputed that account.

The $65 million loan that the board guaranteed in 1999 was intended in part to refinance the two earlier loans, according to the company.

Farley is unapologetic about the loans, which he said are standard perks in corporate America. "Go look it up," he said. "It's not unusual for a corporation to loan a senior executive money."

Management experts disagree. "This is most unusual," said Donald Sullivan, a retired compensation expert who worked for many years for the Towers Perrin management consulting firm in New York. "Private companies making loans is another matter, but public companies—not very often."

Farley's private companies also billed more than $100 million to Fruit of the Loom for management and investment banking fees between 1985 and 1996, according to company filings.

The arrangement, which began when Fruit of the Loom was a private company, was canceled in 1996, after complaints from institutional investors and several board members, according to former executives. Farley called the issue "ancient history," saying the fees were charged "at cost."

Investors remained skeptical. In September 1999, the Council of Institutional Investors, which represents large pension funds, criticized Fruit of the Loom's corporate governance practices. Among other things, the group objected to the Cayman Islands move, because it resulted in big tax bills for investors but shielded preferred shares that Farley owned from taxes.

"Not exactly a shareholder democracy in action," said Peg O'Hara, a spokeswoman at the council in Washington.

Alarms That All Ignored

Looking back, the fall of Fruit of the Loom seems almost preordained. But few heard the alarm bells.

Though the company's finances began deteriorating in 1997, Wall Street analysts never turned against the company. There were few "sell" signals, no reports that questioned management or the company's long-term prospects. In fact, when Fruit's stock collapsed in the early part of 1999, some analysts viewed it as a buying opportunity.

"Every day on Bloomberg it said, 'Here's Fruit of the Loom at six times earnings,' and people said: 'Six times earnings? How do I get some of that?' And soon, there were no earnings," said Matthew Hershberg, an analyst at Standard & Poor's.

Some analysts say they saw the problems but were persuaded that better times were ahead. "It was always possible to come up with a scenario where the numbers made sense," said John Pickler, an analyst at Prudential Securities. Farley was, after all, a master salesman. "I've seen Bill turn around a group of investors who were skeptical going into a meeting," Pickler said.

Meanwhile, corporate bankers were propping up the company. In 1997, Bank of America led a syndicate that financed the company with a $660 million revolving loan. Fruit of the Loom drew that loan down to nearly zero during 1999. And five months before the Chapter 11 filing, in March 1999, Bank of America and Credit Suisse First Boston led the sale of a $250 million public debt offering.

"I was amazed they were able to do that $250 million placement, because if you read the financials, the cash flow was already deteriorating," said Debra Downie, an analyst at Miller Tabak Roberts Securities, a bond dealer in New York.

Several bankers said privately that due-diligence efforts failed to turn up troubling signs that would have stopped the deals. The banks, they said, did not mislead investors in the bond offering, which was clearly described as "high yield." Bank of America and Credit Suisse First Boston declined comment.

Shortly after the bonds were sold, Fruit of the Loom announced a $9 million loss for the first quarter of 1999, and the price of the bonds collapsed on the open market. In March 2000 they were trading for pennies on the dollar.

Why didn't bankers speak up? Hershberg at Standard & Poor's laughed. "The fact is, Fruit of the Loom was a golden goose of the banking business," he said. "How many bankers are going to say: 'I forecast a long-term bankruptcy'?"

Artwork and a MIG Fighter

In March 2000, the company, operating on $650 million in new emergency financing from Bank of America, was trying to rid itself of less productive units. It had liquidated its Pro Player sports apparel division; the Pro Player name was expected to come down from the Miami Dolphins' football stadium. Pink slips went out to 280 employees at its Frankfort, Kentucky, plant, which was being closed.

Besides tangling with Farley over his loan guarantees and severance, the company was also pursuing other claims against him, including the possibility that he used company resources for a Czech MIG fighter plane he owned and stored at a Fruit of the Loom hangar in Bowling Green, according to lawyers familiar with the case.

Fruit of the Loom hired Christie's to appraise some of the art that Farley bought for the company, including four pieces by Frank Stella and a Roy Lichtenstein print.

Investors were hoping a white knight would ride in to rescue the Fruit of the Loom brand. Aris Industries, which owns the Members Only trademark, was exploring a deal that could give it control of Fruit of the Loom, according to executives close to the discussions. *Women's Wear Daily* reported that Wal-Mart may have been interested, too.

John B. Holland, who came out of retirement to assume his old post as chief operating officer, said things were looking up at Fruit of the Loom. "We're trying to manage the areas where there can be real cost improvements," he said. Demand is solid, he said, but profit projections are hard.

Meanwhile, Farley was spending many of his days in half-deserted offices high above Chicago, on the fiftieth floor of the Sears Tower.

On one afternoon in March 2000, a side of his old suite was filled with boxes ready to be shipped to Fruit of the Loom, which was once officially headquartered in these rooms. On the other side of the suite was Farley Inc., his old holding company, which had few holdings but large pension liabilities.

He had trimmed back his personal holdings. His yacht, "L'Acquisition," was sold a few years earlier. More recently, he had sold Hammersmith Farms, the fifty-acre Rhode Island estate where Jacqueline Bouvier grew up.

He wasn't facing personal bankruptcy, Farley said, but called his situation "ugly as sin." His huge holdings in Fruit of the Loom, which he borrowed against over and over, were nearly worthless.

Yet on that day, he was tanned and dapper, wearing a Versace suit. The optimism had not worn thin: he was still committed to Fruit of the Loom, where he remained a director, to his wife and their five-year-old son, Liam. And he was resilient. "What I do every day is I get up and I say, 'Suck it up,'" he said.

In a reflective moment, he conceded that the whole leverage game was wrong, that it was too complicated. Stock is a much more straightforward currency, he said. Investments in biotechnology, telecommunications, media and Internet companies were already in his plans.

"You can start your own e-commerce company and sell it at infinity," he exulted, pacing a conference room next to his office. "I'm saying the deals I'm going to do now are going to be all equity, no debt. Or virtually no debt."

That's a promise, he said.

David Barboza
March 19, 2000

CASE 4

Historic Lessons

Comparisons can be overdrawn between the ordered breakup of Microsoft and the dismemberment almost twenty years ago of AT&T. But veterans of the Bell System's split see at least one clear parallel: the sense of denial within AT&T was as strong then as it appears to be at Microsoft in 2000.

Harold W. Burlingame, an AT&T employee since 1962 and executive vice president of AT&T Wireless, was part of the phone company's breakup team in the early 1980s. Burke Stinson, who joined AT&T in 1969 and is a manager in its public relations department, was in a lower-level public relations job at the time.

Both men recall widespread disbelief that a breakup was inevitable—and fear and anger when it happened as planned under an agreement with the government.

"Instead of preparing for the future, people waited for a hue and cry from Main Street to force Washington to change its mind," Stinson recalled. "What Washington understood, and AT&T in its hubris didn't, was that the American public likes underdogs and competition and will vote to bring down any company it sees as too big for its britches."

AT&T's management took the obligatory calming steps. It protected pension plans and ensured that each newly independent company—a long-distance carrier and seven local phone companies—would start out with a strong set of assets and a viable balance sheet.

But management could not effectively dispute the obvious: some careers would be enhanced by the breakup, but many would be truncated.

AT&T had routinely rotated up-and-comers from the local phone companies through staff jobs at headquarters, with an eye toward grooming them for future management anywhere in the company. The breakup prevented the easy flow of people back and forth, forcing managers to choose their futures early on.

Many of the company's fast-tracked middle managers, including Burlingame, decided to stay at headquarters. "I felt the new AT&T would be an international business that would grow," he said.

For many, that belief escalated into condescension for those who joined the so-called Baby Bells.

"People who stayed at headquarters called the others 'Bell heads,' a pejorative term for people whose thinking was more traditional than adventuresome," Stinson said. "Their sense of what AT&T itself would become was steeped more in marketing promise than reality."

Instead, AT&T's unsuccessful attempts to move into computers and complex communications systems sent the company into a tailspin, prompting huge job cuts. And as competitors piled into its former monopoly markets, the criteria for success at the company were upended, leaving once-promising managers out on the street.

Like Microsoft facing the post-PC era, the new AT&T found itself in an environment unlike the one in which it had drawn the government's ire.

"We would probably have had to change anyway," Burlingame said, "but the breakup really accelerated the process."

Claudia H. Deutsch
June 11, 2000

CASE 5

An Oversized Umbrella

How's this for a strategy? Spot some societal or business problem, and set your scientists to inventing a solution. Buy a company with marketing expertise in the field, and merge it with the nascent technology. Give the scientists-turned-entrepreneurs options on the combined company's stock and sell, or "spin out," a chunk to the public, but hold on to as much as 80 percent yourself. Then use the proceeds to do it again and again.

That strategy has been behind both the meteoric rise and the humiliating fall of the Thermo Electron Corporation, the Waltham, Massachusetts, conglomerate that over a sixteen-year period spawned twenty-three fledgling businesses, in areas as disparate as measurement devices and hair removal. For most of that time, Thermo Electron, which started as a diversified technology company, grew briskly and its profits and share price seemed headed ever upward. But then earnings tumbled and the stock tanked, undone by problems at some of the offspring and by a corporate management stretched too thin.

Thermo Electron's stock, which entered 1998 hovering above forty dollars, had slipped below thirteen dollars by the middle of the year. It inched up after that, but by early June 1999 had still not reached twenty dollars.

Did the fault lie in iffy execution or in a fundamentally flawed strategy? Or, to ask the question in another way, should anyone else consider giving the concept a try?

Definitely not, said Jack L. Kelly, a conglomerate analyst at Goldman Sachs. "Too many public subsidiaries are confusing for investors, less flexible to manage and unworkable for anyone," he said.

Definitely yes, countered Rita McGrath, an associate professor at the Columbia Business School. "Having lots of public spin-offs lets you apply assets and knowledge to many marketplaces and applies public-market disciplines to inventors," she said.

Maybe, others chimed in.

"It works only if the parent company's management isn't psychologically overinvested in the spin-out," said Steven N. Kaplan, a professor of finance at the University of Chicago's Graduate School of Business, who said the best way to deter management from pouring more cash into floundering subsidiaries is to retain only a minority share.

Companies should limit themselves to an industry that they know well and that investors favor, added Robert S. Sullivan, dean of the University of North Carolina's Kenan-Flagler Business School. "The strategy is only dangerous if the parent has majority equity in too many unrelated companies," he said.

Of course, the idea of hatching new businesses out of corporate behemoths is not unique to Thermo Electron. Numerous companies have departments that nurture promising technologies. But those companies generally fold the resulting ventures into their core businesses, set them up as wholly owned subsidiaries or bring in partners. Taking the new ventures public is the exception.

"An IPO is our least likely exit strategy," said Thomas M. Uhlman, president of the New Ventures Group of Lucent Technologies.

The Xerox Corporation, which has taken two small ventures public, is in no hurry to kick others out of the corporate nest. "It's easy to say, 'This product is great; let's spin it out,'" said Brian E. Stern, senior vice president of Xerox Technology Enterprises. "Well, success takes a strategy and a huge amount of marketing money."

Thermo Electron learned that the hard way. Although many of the subsidiaries remain successful, a bomb-detection spin-out, for example, languished because it had few sales except after terrorist attacks. And Thermolase, a chain of laser hair-removal salons, was losing money, in part because its process turned out to have only a temporary effect.

"We got carried away with our own success," said George Hatsopoulos, Thermo Electron's chairman, who voluntarily ceded the title of chief executive in mid-1999 to Richard Syron, the former head of the American Stock Exchange. "We spun out businesses that weren't solid and did not meet our criteria for growth potential and management depth."

The Thermo Electron model has advantages. Stock options in their own companies can attract and motivate entrepreneurial people, while the continued involvement of a well-known parent can reassure investors. The parent can provide legal help and other support at low cost. It can give heads of subsidiaries stock options in one another's companies and in the parent as an inducement to share ideas and customers. And, by retaining 80 percent stakes in its subsidiaries, it can consolidate results, avoiding some taxes.

But for each plus there is a minus. Control by the parent company complicates any business that the spin-out may try to do with its parent's or siblings' competitors. Stocks of newly public companies often drop when the new company hits any snag, sending the stock options underwater. And there is a temptation to try to bolster the share price by rushing a product to market too soon.

"If some analyst writes a bullish report, the stock can soar beyond the company's reality, and plummet just as quickly when reality sets in," said Howard H. Stevenson, a professor of business administration at the Harvard Business School.

The reporting burden can be daunting, too. Having twenty-three public subsidiaries means producing twenty-three annual reports, filing ninety-two quarterly earnings statements a year, and enduring countless interactions with analysts and other investors.

Part of Thermo Electron's method is to put the Thermo prefix on the names of all its subsidiaries, a tactic that lends the new companies instant credibility but increases the odds that problems at any one of them will tar the whole group. "One subsidiary reports a bad quarter, and investors get the sense that things aren't right in Thermo-land," said Kelly, the analyst. "The company's almost too transparent for its own good."

Hatsopoulos said, "Putting the Thermo name on everything has been a double-edged sword."

Armed with hindsight, what would Thermo Electron do next?

First, slim down. It planned to sell some units entirely and buy others back in—some to shut down, some to reabsorb. Eventually, it hoped to whittle down to eleven subsidiaries.

"To let a part of the company, no matter how small, into the public eye, you must be sure of what you're doing, and that means putting an upper limit on the number of spin-outs," Hatsopoulos said.

Syron, the new chief, concurred. "This isn't a mutual fund with limited liabilities," he said. "This is a company with subsidiaries," he added, and "management must be able to oversee all of them."

From now on, the two men agreed, Thermo Electron will spin out only companies that have the potential to grow huge and will probably buy them back when they are mature enough to need professional management more than entrepreneurial flair. And it will fold them into its own businesses in instrumentation, medical devices and other areas that have been Thermo Electron's strengths.

"Sure, we made mistakes," Hatsopoulos said. "But this is still a business model that will be used widely in the twenty-first century."

Claudia H. Deutsch
June 6, 1999

CASE 6

Ethereal Value

Nagging question lingers as one new Internet company after another bursts into public view, offering glittering Web sites, charismatic founders, innovative business models, surging sales and soaring stocks. What, exactly, is going on behind the screen?

The answer, at least in the case of Value America, the once high-flying Internet department store based in Charlottesville, Virginia, is not pretty. It is also most likely not unique to the company, though a war among board members that broke out in late 1999 focused considerable public attention on the company. Craig Winn, a cofounder and the chairman, and his handpicked chief executive, Tom Morgan, departed. And the new chief, Glenda Dorchak, put forward a turnaround plan that repudiated much of what Winn did.

Amid the discord, each faction was in remarkable agreement about many elements of the Value America saga. They agreed the company had been mismanaged. They accepted that entrepreneurial founders of companies are often not the best executives to run them as they grow. And they said that things have gone so far off track for Value America that it would probably be better off if it were bought, at least in part, by a larger company.

As to what the management errors were and who made them, however, there is no shortage of debate.

Such recriminations—about tactics, people and plans—are likely to reverberate as the wings melt off many an Internet Icarus. Some companies are realizing that the rising tide of e-commerce did not lift their boats. And some investors are beginning to see the downside of backing companies that put growth over discipline.

Value America's board ultimately came to accept the view of Dorchak, who had been president, that the company had expanded too fast, selling a sprawling jumble of goods from barbecue grills to breakfast cereal, when most of its business was in computers and office products.

William D. Savoy, a board member, said Value America stumbled, as much as anything, because it lost the confidence of Wall Street. "They got themselves in a box by creating different expectations than what the company's core competencies were," said Savoy, who represents the interests of the Microsoft cofounder Paul G. Allen, a Value America backer.

Winn defended the broad selection and grand pronouncements to investors. And he contended that Morgan and Dorchak mishandled the company's marketing and botched a computer upgrade. "There will be no slow-growing e-tailing companies," Winn said. "I believe that entrepreneurs should eventually phase themselves out, and I handed an aggressive and well-managed company over to Tom in March 1999. In retrospect, the company needed the entrepreneurial spirit and leadership for another year."

Dorchak declined to be interviewed. Morgan said Winn did not criticize his leadership while he was chief executive.

Outside analysts and competitors raise a more fundamental question about the business model developed by Winn, who established Value America as the most virtual of companies. It holds no inventory, simply passing the telephone and Internet orders it received to manufacturers, which sent goods directly to the buyers. But in many cases, manufacturers were so lackadaisical about shipping that customers suffered unusual delays.

The scene at Value America in January 2000 could not be more different than on April 8, 1999, the day after its initial public offering. That day, the stock hit fifty-five dollars a share, giving the company a market valuation of $3.2 billion and making Winn, who owned 35 percent of the company, a paper billionaire for twenty-four hours. The shares slid steadily, closing at five dollars on January 7, 2000, for a market value of $224 million.

With the luxury of hindsight, investors might have seen some warning signs. The company's initial prospectus disclosed that its auditors found significant gaps in its inventory tracking system, although the issue was cleared up before the offering. And Dynasty Classics, the lighting company that Winn founded and ran from 1986 to 1993, wound up in Chapter 11.

None of this kept investors from flocking to the offering. And who could blame them, in a market where everybody is making it up as they go along?

Winn's energetic persuasion attracted a star-studded list of investors, including Allen; the FDX Corporation, parent of Federal Express; and Frederick W. Smith, its chairman. Winn also persuaded some of the world's biggest manufacturers, including IBM and General Electric, to sell their products through Value America.

After the offering, revenues grew even faster than projected. But so did expenses, and Value America's underwriter, Robertson Stephens, downgraded the company several times, out of fear that it was not getting the leverage it should from its huge expenditures on newspaper and television advertising.

Winn reacted to the falling stock price alternately by telling investors that they were applying flawed analysis and by making ever bolder promises about the company's future plans. That was a particular frustration to the company's management and board because Morgan, who became chief executive in March 1999, was supposed to be the one dealing with Wall Street.

By November of that year, Morgan, angry that Winn was meddling in management affairs, handed in his resignation. Winn convinced him to stay, but they continued to spar. Two weeks later, Morgan resigned again; this time, Winn accepted.

Those moves started a monthlong battle for the soul of the company. The board appointed Dorchak as chief and Wolfgang R. Schmitt, former chief of Rubbermaid, as chairman. They contended that the company should pare its product line and focus on serving business and government customers rather than consumers. Winn, then still a board member, disagreed.

Ultimately the board decided to back Dorchak's plan to switch gears and dismiss nearly half the company's six hundred employees. Winn and his cofounder, Rex Scatena, who owned 15 percent of the company, left the board.

The company was running through its cash, $100 million at the beginning of 2000, at a rate of $10 million a month. Smith of FDX has been put at the helm of a committee charged with considering a sale of all or part of the company.

Board members say Value America's technology would be of great value to a traditional retail company looking to catch up with the Internet leaders. But with Value America's founders gone and its strategies repudiated, buyers would have to think long and hard about what was left behind the screen.

Saul Hansell
January 9, 2000

In August 2000, Value America filed for Chapter 11 bankruptcy protection and closed its Web site.

CASE 7

The Contrite CEO

It seems that you cannot turn on the television or open a newspaper these days without some sober-eyed chief executive offering a personal act of corporate contrition.

In television advertisements, Jacques A. Nasser, chief of the Ford Motor Company, explained that he was doing his best to replace the Firestone tires said by regulators to have led to eighty-eight deaths in the United States. Masatoshi Ono of Bridgestone/Firestone did the same in full-page newspaper ads. And James E. Goodwin, chairman of United Airlines, owned by UAL, bought commercial time to offer an apology for the company's recurrent flight delays.

Media analysts said they expected to see these chief executives step in front of the camera. Such appearances are now part of a chief executive's job, the analysts said. And they predict that other leaders whose companies get into trouble will have to do likewise.

Events of the last few years—including President Clinton's taking to the airwaves with a personal mea culpa—have primed audiences for this strategy, said Robert J. Thompson, founder of the Center for the Study of Popular Television at Syracuse University.

"Madison Avenue has finally realized that deep in the American heart is this powerful respect for honesty," he said, "and if you confess to something, you can get away with murder, sometimes literally.

"It used to be you never wanted them to see you squirm. All of a sudden, corporate America has recognized the apology as the quickest way to make bad things go away."

Putting a leader's face on a crisis response is almost a necessity now, whether for potentially fatal product flaws or annoyances like flight delays, said Sue Parenio, an associate professor of advertising at Boston University. Americans are so fed up with poor treatment from large corporate bureaucracies, she said, that they will accept reassurance only from the top official.

"When you call up and raise Cain about a product or service experience you had, the customer service reps say, 'yeah, yeah' and it's not cutting it," Parenio said. "Consumers have a lot more choices. If one company disappoints them, they are going to go somewhere else. They might live with you through a crisis, but only if they get to hear it from a top guy."

Or, as Robert J. Kopp, an associate professor who teaches marketing and advertising at Babson College, said, "People, in their gut, like to be able to personalize a company."

But does it work even when the personality is a plain-vanilla one? Ono's advertisements, which began appearing in newspapers on August 23, 2000, were an unadorned list of Firestone actions that left Kopp unimpressed.

"When the advertisement says that Firestone initiated a 'voluntary safety recall,' anybody who's been following this will get a chuckle about that," Kopp said. "It was voluntary, with a gun to your head."

Ono, who speaks little English, did not appear in Firestone's television advertisements, which instead featured John Lampe, executive vice president for the company's United States unit.

United Airlines had a more natural spokesman in Goodwin. On the heels of a print advertisement, United started running a TV commercial on August 24, 2000. It showed Goodwin walking through an empty airplane, presumably not one that passengers are waiting impatiently to board. It portrays him as a plain-talking, regular guy, the kind who could join a company as an accountant in 1967 and work his way up. It was shot in two hours. "There was no wardrobe, no styling, no makeup," said Julie Thompson, a spokeswoman for Fallon Worldwide of Minneapolis, which designed the ad and has handled United's other ad campaigns.

But the straightforward approach failed to persuade Susan Fournier, an associate professor at Harvard Business School who specializes in marketing and branding. She had been stuck in Chicago waiting for a United flight and had spent more than an hour in a line to get information. When she became aware of the ads, she was all the more critical. "The left side of my brain is saying, 'Yeah, right,'" she said.

Fournier said United could take a lesson from James E. Burke, former chief of Johnson & Johnson, who saved the reputation of Tylenol during the drug-tampering scare of 1982. Burke not only appeared on numerous TV interviews, but also gave public updates on all the company's actions, from removing products from shelves to introducing tamper-resistant packaging. "It had a lot of oomph behind it," she said. "There is the acknowledgment, and then there is the reparation and recovery."

Kopp agreed. "I would recommend the CEOs view these campaigns with some continuity and come back to us with a follow-up" with some concrete actions, he said. "Otherwise, people will think they are just putting their finger in the dam before it bursts."

United has no particular plans to put Goodwin back on the screen. Ford was similarly unsure of Nasser's future appearances. Carolyn Brown, a Ford spokeswoman, said that Nasser had received good reviews for his two television advertisements. Some 58 percent of focus group members said that after watching the first ad they had a positive view of Ford's handling of the recall; the percentage rose to 72 for the second commercial.

Reaching directly to consumers through paid advertising was an obvious choice, said Matthew Triaca, a United spokesman. "It was a great way to reach a large number of customers, direct and unfiltered," he said.

Not that these executives are always willingly their company's spokesmen. Nasser initially declined to testify at federal hearings on the tire recall, saying that others at Ford were better qualified to discuss specifics. Accused of being insufficiently open, he reversed himself during a news conference.

But he and other chief executives usually leave the news conferences to others. Thompson, the television scholar, called it part of the strategy. "The

general makes the grand rhetorical statement, and you send the foot sol-
diers out to deal with the arrows slung by journalists," he said.

Still, companies are ultimately accountable for the truth in their advertisements. Americans find it hard to reject a white flag, Thompson asserted,
but they are more cynical than ever. And while it's easy enough to put a
human face on a company, Thompson mused, people will ask, "In the end,
can a corporation really feel remorse?"

Julie Flaherty
September 3, 2000

*Masatoshi Ono resigned as chief executive of Bridgestone/Firestone in
October 2000 and was succeeded by John Lampe.*

·10·

VISITING OLYMPUS

The Corporate Legends

The best advice I ever got was from John Sculley. He would have ten great ideas a week: one would be absolute genius, one would be absolute garbage and the other eight would be somewhere in between. The problem was, he said, it wasn't easy to tell which were which. That's why I always ask for thoughtful, intelligent opinions on my ideas.

—Carl Yankowski, chief executive officer,
Reebok International, November 24, 1999

Perhaps this chapter should be entitled, "Dinosaurs." There just don't seem to be many executives who get the chance to be legends anymore.

In recent years, one corporate icon after another has made a change at the top, and the reality behind the transition has usually been unpleasant. The list includes Coca-Cola, Gillette, Lucent, Mattel, Procter & Gamble and Xerox—all global, multibillion-dollar corporations. Sometimes the executives' departures have been voluntary. More often, they have been only allegedly voluntary, or even admittedly forced.

All this is a recent development. Despite frequent talk during the 1990s about how difficult chief executives' jobs had become, CEO turnover at big firms remained constant. Average tenure even increased slightly during the late 1990s. But then the calendar turned, and the pink slips started coming. In 2000, despite a generally strong economy, about one in ten of the two hundred biggest companies in the country made a change at the top, according to Pearl Meyer & Partners, an executive pay consulting firm in New York. Given the importance that investors now place on immediate results, many analysts expect turnover to remain high in the coming years.

To put it another way, figuring out what makes an executive successful has never been more important. In this chapter, you will have a chance to spend some time with some of the best-known managers of the last three decades as well as with Peter Drucker, the best-known management thinker of the twentieth century, and the ubiquitous Bill Gates. When you are done, you may want to throw up your hands and ask, "Are there *any* similarities among these people?" That's a fair question. One was a stoic man known for his trademark fedora. Another is given to screaming at subordinates and once dressed up as Moses for a corporate party. A third is the embodiment of corniness, a fan of Cherry Coke, minor-league baseball and the very same Midwestern house he has lived in since 1958. Yet a fourth spread lies—real whoppers, too—to thousands of people in order to promote his business.

Look more closely, however, and you will see some crucial parallels. All, even those with the most overblown egos, had outsized talents and outsized commitment to their work. Every one of them mastered the humdrum details of how to run an organization. Every one made sure to stay connected to the everyday realities of his business. None of them let their fame or wealth get in the way of that.

Take our would-be Moses. He may not be the world's nicest man, but he is famous for remembering the names of people he has met only once, for example, and he encourages managers to accept criticism from their subordinates.

There is a useful analogy from the world of sports. The most successful athlete of the last years of the twentieth century was Michael Jordan, the Chicago Bulls star. Yes, he found time to make advertisements and a movie. And, yes, he thought his image was crucial. But he was also known as the last player to leave the gym after practice, the one who stayed for hours perfecting the simple art of getting a ball to go through a hoop.

In the corporate world, such nitty-gritty can easily be lost in the hubbub of a time when many chief executives flirt with celebrity. Investors must be soothed. Employees must be motivated. Outside board meetings and weekend golf tournaments must be attended. But with uncertainty greater than it ever has been—with rivals emerging from other industries and other countries, technology bringing change on a monthly basis and weeks of market volatility—there remains no substitute for revenue reports and department meetings and a mastery of detail. Behind their varying styles, that is the legacy of our legends.

The Capitalist Hero

If there's one thing that the thousands of pilgrims who made their way to Omaha, Nebraska, in May 1999 would be loath to say about Warren E. Buffett, it's that he's shameless.

But it's true. No other American chief executive may be so plain-spoken or so masterful an investor. Nor does any other American chief executive do so many hokey things. In the course of the annual, three-day gathering of investors in his company, Berkshire Hathaway—a get-together that he has called the capitalists' Woodstock—Buffett could be seen all over town. He donned an old-time baseball uniform to throw out the first pitch at a minor league game, to Hall of Famer Ernie Banks. (Buffett's number: $\frac{1}{16}$ in homage to Wall Street and its stock fractions.) He also signed autographs outside Gorat's, his favorite steakhouse. He played bridge, "the official game of Berkshire Hathaway," at a local mall—against a former world champion.

And during Berkshire's six-hour annual meeting here in Berkshire Hathaway's hometown, a session generally regarded as one of the best financial seminars conducted anywhere each year, Buffett ritualistically swigged Cherry Cokes and nibbled at See's candies and Dairy Queen ice-cream bars—all products of Berkshire holdings, all demonstrations of his penchant for concrete investments in things you can use every day.

Hucksterism? Of course. Buffett, a kind of Will Rogers character with John D. Rockefeller's bank account, has mastered the art. But Berkshire Hathaway shareholders don't care. Like teenagers at a marathon rock concert—or, perhaps, religious devotees at a revival meeting—some fifteen thousand of them came here to soak up his every word and gesture.

They waited in long lines wherever he went, simply to get their hero's signature on old photographs, annual reports he had written, ticket stubs, baseball caps, dollar bills or books. They shopped at Borsheim's jewelry store and the Nebraska Furniture Mart, Omaha businesses he bought for Berkshire because he thought their owners were brilliant merchants; they drove by the modest house that Buffett bought for thirty-two thousand dollars in 1958 and still calls home.

One visitor said he'd rather be in Omaha than at the Super Bowl. Another shareholder, Laurence Day of St. Louis, said he told his wife he preferred Omaha to Paris in the spring. And Richard Dejonckheere, a sports trainer from Belgium, remarked: "Like every good Moslem goes to

Mecca, I come here. Every shareholder or capitalist should go one time to Omaha."

It is like this here every spring around the first Monday in May—even in years, including this one, when Berkshire Hathaway stock is lagging behind the broader market and the investing world has been agog over technology companies instead of Buffett's favored consumer brands. After more than thirty years of whipping the Standard & Poor's 500-stock index, his followers happily make allowances for Buffett's minor miscues.

"I'm not worried," said Frank Booker, an investor who came from St. Simons Island, Georgia. "We've been through this before. And I don't know anyone else I'd rather have as the captain of my capital."

Partly, maybe mostly, such affection is fueled by the love of money. The faithful know that Buffett's investing catechism has generated astonishing returns. They can cite the figures by heart: a ten-thousand-dollar investment in Berkshire in 1965 would be worth about $65 million today.

But more is at work here. The pilgrims flock to Omaha because the huckster seems so sincere. With his focus on the long term and his antipathy for the trendy, Buffett may be out of step with Wall Street and much of corporate America, they say. But he represents something they find wholesome, true and uniquely American. By all accounts he lives simply, well below his means and with few of the trappings of wealth. And in a marketplace crowded with whispering insiders, accountants' obfuscations and boosters happy to promote stocks at almost any price, he speaks directly to his shareholders, in language they can understand and with the kind of wit and wisdom they can appreciate.

In short, shareholders say they come each year because Buffett and Berkshire embody not just value investing but values. Study hard, he says. Search out sound advice. Know your limitations. And ask the right questions.

"It's a philosophy of investing and a philosophy of life," said Jeffrey Crohn, who came here from Mount Kisco, New York, for the Berkshire meeting with his wife, Kathleen, and left with a new bedroom set, television cabinet and patio furniture from the Nebraska Furniture Mart.

The Crohns, who say they have seven shares of Berkshire's class B stock—the version that now sells for about twenty-five hundred dollars a share, versus the seventy-seven thousand dollars price tag that keeps the original class A shares beyond the reach of most investors—are now passing on those lessons to their children. "Buffett takes a very common-sense approach to life," Crohn said. "You achieve what you achieve through hard work and sound management."

Getting with the Program

There are moments during the Berkshire weekend when the Warren worship seems to get out of hand.

When Buffett stopped at Borsheim's, which was opened on Sunday just for shareholders, the store was mobbed, with shoppers spilling into the common area of the Regency Mall. Eager to record the moment, one woman yelled, "Honey, hurry up and take the picture!" as Buffett passed through. Later that evening, when he downed his trademark T-bone steak with a double order of hash browns at a shareholders' dinner at Gorat's, two hundred others, lemminglike, ordered the identical meal, the manager said.

Even the news media grew idolatrous. During a two-hour news conference in which Buffett and Berkshire's vice chairman, Charles T. Munger, waxed poetic about investing, one reporter interrupted to say: "Mr. Buffett, I want to go to a warm and fuzzy place. I'm very taken with the fact that your shareholders are very taken with you." As the session ended, the gathered reporters broke, uncharacteristically, into applause.

Not long after, Marc Norton of the *Louisville Courier-Journal*, who had posed a serious question during the news conference, nabbed Buffett in the parking lot and asked him to pose for a picture.

"Here, I'll whisper a stock tip in your ear," Buffett said, and he jokingly pretended to do so just as the picture was snapped. "What did he say?" another reporter begged to know as Buffett disappeared.

Buffett has taken note of the frenzied rise of his profile. "There's no question the celebrity aspect has gotten played up," he told the reporters. "But Berkshire shareholders know what they own."

Besides the little companies he hawks so unabashedly, in 1999 they owned a huge insurance business, made up largely of Geico, which sells auto and other insurance directly to consumers, and General Re, a reinsurer that Buffett bought in 1998. And they share in Berkshire's storied portfolio of stocks: by investing in companies with rich consumer franchises like Coca-Cola, Gillette, Walt Disney, *Washington Post* and American Express, Buffett has made Berkshire—a small company of which he gained control in 1965—into a company worth $116 billion.

"This is a unique person in the history of capitalism," said Stevin R. Hoover, a money manager from Boston who has been a Berkshire shareholder since 1982 and was on his tenth trip to Omaha. "He's made most of us a lot of money."

Buffett's style of value investing, however, is largely out of fashion these days. And that has made Omaha—and the figurative Omaha that exists wherever Berkshire shareholders reside—a peculiar outpost in a financial world enamored of momentum trading, the latest hot new offering and Internet stocks valued at multiples of their losses, not their earnings.

But Buffett remains the world's second-richest man—after only his friend William H. Gates, the cofounder of Microsoft—and is the architect of countless Berkshire fortunes. In fact, many people travel to Omaha simply to thank him for setting them on the road to riches—riches that they also tend not to flaunt.

"We're millionaires, but who would know?" said Ernest Arvesen, a retired banker from Atlanta. "Not our neighbors."

Not, that is, unless they looked in the closets and medicine cabinets of Buffett's devotees.

Day, the St. Louis investor, had his epiphany in 1982, when he was sitting on a beach in northern Michigan with a pile of Berkshire Hathaway annual reports. "I read them and I was totally absorbed," he recalled. "I said, My God, this is it." Now Mr. Day arranges his everyday life around Buffett's favorite stocks, living by the theory that the investor's sidekick, Munger, likes to call "eating your own cooking."

"I buy every one of Berkshire's products," Day said. "Gillette razors. Coke. And now I have Geico insurance." He recently was married—and naturally, his wedding ring was bought at Borsheim's.

The Oracle Speaks

Most shareholders, however, say they come to Omaha not to buy Berkshire goods but to listen to Buffett's lengthy question-and-answer session at the annual meeting—the formal raison d'être for the weekend hoopla.

For the 1999 gathering, they lined up as early as 4:30 A.M. outside the Aksarben (that's Nebraska, spelled backwards) Auditorium, which seats fourteen thousand. And when the doors opened two and a half hours later, Buffett was there to greet those who rushed through the turnstiles.

The billionaire then hopped into his Lincoln Town Car and drove out through the parking lot, waving to a long line of shareholders waiting to enter the arena.

When everyone was in place, Buffett and Munger entered the packed auditorium to a standing ovation, in what shareholders describe as a kind of parting of the waters as the two made their way toward the stage.

The two men quickly ran through the official business of the company. And then—when most annual meetings would abruptly be adjourned— they opened the floor to questions, which they answered patiently, often with a good deal of wit, until 3:30 P.M.

(Actually, Buffett answered most of the questions, with occasional philosophical musings from the generally silent, seemingly lifeless Munger,
whom Buffett introduced this way: "If you haven't figured it out, this
hyperkinetic bundle of energy on my left is Charlie Munger.")

The shareholders asked about everything—Buffett's investment philosophy, of course, and what the company would look like after his death. (He
has already named successors, he said—without naming names—and
"they'd be ready to take over tomorrow.")

They asked the personal, too. Was he interested in a career in music?
(No, though he sang "Tomorrow" at a benefit performance of the musical
Annie.)

What books would he recommend? *Personal History,* the autobiography
of Katharine Graham, the former publisher of the *Washington Post,* and
Common Sense on Mutual Funds by John C. Bogle, senior chairman and
founder of the Vanguard Group.

Shareholders also posed pointed queries about specific investing decisions, including why Buffett chose to sell a large number of shares in
McDonald's in 1998—shares that later skyrocketed.

"It was a mistake," he said, repeating what he told shareholders in the
annual report: "Overall, you would have been better off last year if I had
regularly snuck off to the movies during market hours."

And they asked about the prospects for core Berkshire holdings like Coca-
Cola, Gillette and Disney, whose chief executive, Michael D. Eisner, took a
break one day from the ugly trial over his feud with a former company executive to visit the Main Street USA of Buffett's 1999 annual meeting.

All those stocks had badly trailed the market in recent months, but Buffett gave no hint of souring on any of them. About Coca-Cola, in which
Berkshire had an 8 percent stake at the end of 1998, he said, "Through the
next twenty years, preference for Coke will do nothing but grow."

He steered away from stock recommendations or predications, however,
though shareholders repeatedly encouraged a leak. Despite his occasional
big bet on macroeconomic trends—he bought 111 million ounces of silver
in 1997, for example, expecting the price to soar with growing demand—he
declined to forecast interest rates or discuss the big economic picture. Buffett may sometimes seem like a hayseed, but he is not about to show other
market players his hand.

Again and again, Buffett said that he doesn't pay attention to the everyday swings in the market: "We don't worry about the performance of the
stock; we worry about the performance of the company."

True to his habit of talking down Berkshire's prospects, he acknowledged difficulty in finding good values in a highly valued market, and the near impossibility of keeping a $100 billion company's value growing at 20 percent or more a year, as his investors have come to expect.

Some shareholders, nervously challenging their guru, asked why he didn't embrace the technology stocks that so many other investors look to for growth. Buffett said that while the technology revolution has changed the economic landscape, he doesn't know how to evaluate the long-term prospects of such stocks—and that the values assigned many of them by the market indicate that other investors don't, either.

Taking bites from a Dairy Queen ice-cream bar, Buffett said he simply buys what he knows, then offered a judgment he has no doubt debated over many bridge games with his friend Gates. "The Dilly Bar," he said with a smile, "is more certain to be around in ten years than any single software application."

David Barboza
May 9, 1999

CASE 2

The Hit Maker

For a quarter-century that ended with his last blockbuster, the musical *42nd Street,* in 1980, David Merrick, the producer whose gift for creating Broadway hits was matched only by his genius for attracting publicity and making enemies, was the dominant showman in the Broadway theater. When *Time* magazine put him on its cover in 1966, it estimated that 20 percent of Broadway's workforce was in his employment. In a typical season during the 1960s he produced a half-dozen or more plays and musicals, on occasion as many as four in a single month. His parallel record of productivity and profitability has been unmatched by any single impresario before or since in the history of New York's commercial theater.

His headlines were nearly as numerous as his hits. Merrick, who died on April 25, 2000, at the age of eighty-eight, was famous for baiting critics, his own stars and his fellow producers, all to promote his wares. Frequently likened to legendary predecessors like P. T. Barnum and David Belasco, he preferred to glory in his image as "the abominable showman."

A study in darkness—with his tailored suits, sleek black hair, mustache, sardonic wit and low, insinuating voice—he went out of his way to resemble a villain out of Victorian melodrama. When Al Hirschfeld drew a particularly unflattering caricature of him as a Grinchlike Santa Claus, Merrick reproduced it on his annual Christmas card.

Among Merrick's successes were some of the most popular musicals of his era, including *Gypsy, Hello, Dolly!* and *Promises, Promises,* as well as *42nd Street,* his longest-running show and one of the longest-running productions in Broadway history. He introduced Woody Allen to Broadway as a playwright (*Don't Drink the Water*) and actor (*Play It Again, Sam*) and produced the 1962 musical (*I Can Get It for You Wholesale*) that catapulted a nineteen-year-old supporting player, Barbra Streisand, toward stardom.

His productions also gave signature roles to Ethel Merman (Mama Rose in *Gypsy*) and Carol Channing (Dolly Levi in *Hello, Dolly!*), and he worked with nearly every major songwriter of the Broadway musical's last heyday: Jule Styne, Harold Arlen, Stephen Sondheim, Jerry Herman, Harold Rome, Bob Merrill and the teams of John Kander and Fred Ebb and Harvey Schmidt and Tom Jones.

But Merrick didn't produce only high-gloss entertainment. He also presented Laurence Olivier's most celebrated postwar performance (as Archie Rice in *The Entertainer*), the breakthrough dramas of John Osborne (*Look Back in Anger*), Brian Friel (*Philadelphia, Here I Come!*) and Tom Stoppard (*Rosencrantz and Guildenstern Are Dead*) and two epochal Royal Shakespeare Company productions directed by Peter Brook (*Marat/Sade* and *A Midsummer Night's Dream*).

When few commercial producers would touch the declining Tennessee Williams in the 1960s and 1970s, Merrick took on his doomed projects, including a revival of *The Milk Train Doesn't Stop Here Anymore,* which had failed under another management only a season earlier. (It failed again.)

Dickensian Years of His Youth

The producer's secretive private life was as complex and contradictory as his theatrical credits. "I was born on November 4, 1954, the night my first big show, *Fanny,* opened on Broadway," Merrick once said.

In truth he was born in St. Louis on November 27, 1911, as David Margulois, the youngest child of a hand-to-mouth salesman, Samuel, and his wife, Celia. His parents were divorced when he was seven—"It was like living on the set of *Virginia Woolf,*" he once recalled—and the young David bounced among relatives through a grim but stagestruck adolescence he called Dickensian but never revealed in detail.

Years later he said that he refused to take flights whose routes passed over St. Louis, lest he be forced to land in the despised city of his youth.

A good student, he won a scholarship to Washington University in St. Louis, where he said he won second prize in a playwriting contest that Tennessee Williams, another underclassman, also entered. The young Margulois then went to St. Louis University, where he studied law, a trade that would prove handy in his notoriously tough theatrical contract negotiations. In law school he haunted a student playhouse, winning the role of Tubal in *The Merchant of Venice*.

Upon graduation he did become a lawyer, but, more crucially, he married a woman he had met in school, Leonore Beck, whose modest inheritance allowed the young couple to flee St. Louis for New York in 1939. A year later he walked into the office of Herman Shumlin, a prominent Broadway producer, and offered to invest five thousand dollars in a forthcoming comedy, *The Male Animal*. The play was a hit, and David Merrick, taking a new name inspired by the great eighteenth-century English actor David Garrick, was born. Excused from war service because of ulcers, he later went to work for Shumlin.

Of his early, minor producing efforts, the most revealing was a comedy called *Clutterbuck* in 1949. Though the show received indifferent notices, Merrick kept it alive for six months with discount tickets and a publicity stunt: each night during the cocktail hour of 5 to 6 P.M. he called hotel bars and restaurants all over town to page a fictive "Mr. Clutterbuck."

"Have You Seen Fanny?"

But it was *Fanny* five years later that elevated him to Times Square stardom. Convinced that Marcel Pagnol's cinematic trilogy set on the Marseilles waterfront could make a musical, Merrick flew to France three times to persuade Pagnol to give him the rights. After a bitterly unconsummated effort to enlist Richard Rodgers and Oscar Hammerstein II to write the score—a campaign that would lead to a lifelong feud with Rodgers—he settled on Harold Rome. The Broadway titans Joshua Logan and Ezio Pinza served as director and star.

Fanny did not get glowing reviews, and Merrick himself was said to be disappointed in it. But he sold the show relentlessly, plastering men's-room mirrors in midtown with suggestive stickers reading "Have You Seen *Fanny*?," running radio and television spots long before they were commonplace and taking the first full-page newspaper ads ever for a Broadway show. He also hired a sculptor to create a life-size nude statue of the show's belly dancer, Nejla Ates, installed it in Poet's Corner in Central

Park late at night, then alerted policemen and reporters so they could discover it at daybreak.

Publicity bred theatergoers, and *Fanny* made back its investment in a remarkably fast seventeen weeks, then ran nearly another two years. Thanks to a shrewd rental deal Merrick had extracted from the Shuberts for the Majestic Theater, *Fanny* was on a weekly basis the most profitable show in Broadway history up to that time.

Four back-to-back hits followed, including Thornton Wilder's *Matchmaker,* directed by Tyrone Guthrie, and Peter Ustinov's *Romanoff and Juliet.* The Merrick pattern of hoopla was set. When *Look Back in Anger* showed signs of faltering only four months after its 1957 opening, its box-office fortunes were transformed when a distraught woman in the audience jumped onstage at the Lyceum Theater and slapped Kenneth Haigh, who played the misogynist antihero Jimmy Porter, on behalf of wronged women everywhere. The story raged in the newspapers for three weeks before Merrick confessed he had hired the woman for $250. But by then *Anger* was on its way to running another fifteen months on Broadway and the road.

Many more public relations masterstrokes were yet to come, most famously and successfully the replacement of the entire cast of *Hello, Dolly!* with an all-black company headed by Pearl Bailey and Cab Calloway when its audiences began to wane in 1967.

When Merrick judged the prospects dim for a lesser musical, *Subways Are for Sleeping,* in 1961, he turned to the phone book to find men with the same names as the daily newspaper critics, who then numbered seven—a stunt he had long plotted but could never execute until the retirement of the *Times* critic with a one-of-a-kind name, Brooks Atkinson. Merrick took the critical impostors, among them a mailman and a shoe salesman, to a preview and dinner, then got them to endorse the show with such encomiums as "the best musical of the century." The full-page ad he drew up trumpeting these "raves" was rejected by the *Times,* but it ran in one edition of the *Herald Tribune* before editors killed it. That was enough to garner international headlines and keep *Subways* on the boards for a nearly profitable season.

Somewhat less benign was Merrick's manipulation at the opening of *42nd Street* in 1980. Gower Champion, the musical's director and choreographer, had died early the day of the opening, at age fifty-nine, of a rare blood cancer. But Merrick kept the news secret so he could announce it from the stage at the curtain call, to the screams and tears of a devastated cast and first-night audience. Again the show's notoriety and success were assured, but an ugly aftertaste lingered.

"Because I Am Mean—What Else?"

Though Champion had guided many Merrick hits, including *Hello, Dolly!*, the two strong-willed men, while desperately needing each other professionally, had always had a tempestuous personal relationship. Merrick referred to the director as "the Presbyterian Hitler," and during the troubled tryout of the musical *Sugar* in the 1970s, the producer's wife, Etan, had gone so far as to remove her knitting needles from a hotel suite for fear the men might assault each other. Now that Champion was gone, Merrick minimized the director's billing posthumously on *42nd Street* and fought to minimize royalties to his estate (and to the show's other authors) as well.

This nasty side of Merrick had always been apparent. When Anna Maria Alberghetti missed performances in the hit *Carnival!* in 1961, the producer announced he would challenge his star's claims of ill health by administering a lie detector test to her in the hospital. When out of town with a production in trouble, he would humiliate the creative personnel with tirades belittling their work, pit collaborators against one another, threaten to close a show and then bring in other writers behind the authors' backs.

Such was his detestation of Richard Rodgers that even after the composer's death, he took revenge on his elderly widow by seating her in the upper balcony at *42nd Street*. Once asked why he was reputed to be so mean, Merrick replied, "Because I am mean—what else?"

He was especially hostile toward actors, whom he likened to "unruly children," and the press. In the 1960s he sought to put Walter Kerr on the defensive by accusing him of being overly influenced by nudges he received from his wife, Jean, on opening nights. (When I was drama critic of the *New York Times* some twenty-five years later, he recycled the same stunt with me and my soon-to-be wife, Alex Witchel, to generate publicity for a poorly received revival of *Oh, Kay!*) When Stanley Kauffmann was drama critic for the *Times* in 1966, Merrick prevented him from reviewing a preview of Brian Friel's *Philadelphia, Here I Come!* by canceling the performance and announcing that "a rat" was loose in the theater's generator. The story made page one—publicity well worth the price of the tickets the producer had to refund.

His taunting of Howard Taubman, the critic preceding Kauffmann at the *Times,* was particularly notorious. What began as a funny tirade on Johnny Carson's *Tonight* show—Merrick accused the critic of removing "Wet Paint" signs on benches in Central Park—escalated when the producer descended into Nazi analogies. After Taubman threatened to sue, Merrick issued a rare apology.

The producer's known humanitarian gestures were few, but, as a consistent foe of racism, he forced the backstage unions to integrate their crews on *Jamaica*, a 1957 musical with Lena Horne and a largely black cast, by threatening to jettison the production if they did not. He also had a keen respect for his audiences. After the out-of-town ministrations of both Abe Burrows and Edward Albee failed to save a 1966 musical version of Truman Capote's *Breakfast at Tiffany's*, Merrick closed it during New York previews despite advance sales of $1 million (a mammoth amount for that time) that would have kept it alive for months. He refused to subject theatergoers to what he pronounced "an excruciatingly boring evening."

Of his fellow producers, he was contemptuous. "There's a horse's ass for every light on Broadway," he told the writer William Goldman in 1968. He refused to belong to the producers' league and at various times likened himself to a "lone wolf" and to an "alley cat that's not quite trustful, that's always watching for someone to leap on him." Merrick didn't mind if people hated him as he battled his way to the top.

Even so, he was not without his fans in the theater. Woody Allen, Arthur Laurents and Jerry Herman, among others, have praised his professionalism through the years. "He's the only man I know who's made a vice of honesty," said the playwright N. Richard Nash. But Merrick had no close friends among Broadway's elite, who he felt never accepted him. At the theater-district hangout Sardi's, he always insisted on sitting at a table in the back, with the tourists, rather than with other theatrical royalty up front.

Among his toughest industry critics, Merrick was chastised for not only his misanthropy and financial ruthlessness but also for being an importer and packager rather than a truly creative producer who initiated shows from scratch. But if many of his successes were indeed from London, his biggest hits, like *Dolly* and *42nd Street*, were his own inspirations, and often his imports benefited from improvements born of his obsessive attention to every detail of production and promotion. Though Merrick was also faulted for producing his riskiest dramas through the tax dodge of a foundation, his eye for fresh theater was such that even some of those experiments, like Brook's *Marat/Sade*, turned out to be box-office sensations.

A Lone Wolf from a Bygone Era

By the time of *42nd Street*, which brought Merrick back to New York after a brief and fruitless Hollywood sojourn producing movies like *Rough*

Cut and and *The Great Gatsby* during the 1970s, his Broadway had disappeared. He and the few other surviving lone wolves among Broadway producers—most notably Alexander H. Cohen—were relics from a bygone time. Almost all Broadway shows were now imports of productions previously seen in London, regional theaters or Off Broadway. In place of a single tyrannical producer who ruled by gut instinct and took sole responsibility for financing, mounting and promoting a production, there were committees of producers, often investors and theater owners.

These new producers were "bereft of ideas, vitality and imagination," Merrick said. "They're just businessmen who happen to be in the theater." By the 1980s the leading theatrical showmen aspiring to Merrick's stature were Joseph Papp and Cameron Mackintosh, a vocal Merrick admirer. But Papp worked primarily in the noncommercial confines of Off Broadway while Mackintosh initiated his shows in London's West End and rarely produced more than one a season, if that.

In 1983 Merrick had a stroke, which curtailed his freedom of speech and movement as well as his professional activities. He had long since given up his famous office, decorated in the bloody color known in the trade as "David Merrick Red," high above the St. James Theater down the block from Shubert Alley.

What Made Merrick Run?

The last of his nearly ninety shows, a 1996 stage version of the 1945 Rodgers and Hammerstein movie *State Fair,* was actually produced by others, but Merrick took it over by making a large and impetuous investment during its pre–New York tour. It flopped on Broadway, though not before the frail showman made a brief ruckus by suing the Tony Awards for ruling part of its score ineligible for Tony consideration.

Though Merrick's final promotional stunts on Broadway were an embarrassingly faint and farcical replay of his old tricks, they in no way diminished the judgment made by the producer Herman Shumlin, who gave the young David Margulois his start in 1940. Shumlin had observed before his death in 1979 that David Merrick's career was "a milestone in our modern theater, where the exploitation of plays has become a lost art."

But that lasting professional verdict still left unanswered the question of motive, which had obsessed Broadway for decades: What made Merrick run? For all the money he earned, and for all his efforts to keep every last dollar of it, there is no evidence that he enjoyed his fortune. He lived furtively, often in unpretentious midtown apartments, and was not a party giver or goer. He frequently spoke of being depressed.

One friend recalled a rare occasion in the early 1970s when Merrick briefly let down his guard and explained why his enormous success had failed to lighten his spirit. "I'll tell you what it's like to be number one," the producer said. "I compare it to climbing Mount Everest. It's very difficult. Lives are lost along the way. You struggle and struggle and finally you get up there. And guess what there is once you get up there? Snow and ice."

Frank Rich
April 27, 2000

CASE 3

The Motivator

He became famous for his appearance—the sideline stoicism, the courtly attire, self-restraint in the midst of a brutal sport and, of course, his hat.

But to his players, to his colleagues in the National Football League and to the state of Texas, Tom Landry, the longtime Dallas Cowboys coach, represented much more. He was a father figure, a football innovator, even the gentlemanly and noble symbol who helped buoy Texans at a time when a state's identity seemed all too wrapped in the stigma of the assassination of President John F. Kennedy.

Landry, who died on February 12, 2000, at the age of seventy-five, was the coach of what came to be known as America's Team. And if he appeared more professor or bank president than football coach, then that set a standard, too.

"He conducted himself with such dignity and poise, it set the example for how you should live your life," Charlie Waters, a Cowboys safety for eleven seasons, said of his former coach.

"People didn't understand the weight of his influence. Because he wasn't a yeller and screamer, people thought he didn't motivate or make people better with his approach and his presence," he said.

"But he had, for example, a look he gave his players, and we all hated it when he gave us that look," Waters said. "It was haunting, because the look said: 'Why are you letting yourself down? Why are you letting me down?' Tell me that didn't motivate. None of us wanted to disappoint Coach Landry."

The diverse, lengthy Hall of Fame career of Landry inspired many—contemporaries and competitors alike.

"People search for heroes in this world," Gil Brandt, a longtime Cowboys executive, said. "And years ago, some of those people turned on their television every Sunday and saw a guy who wasn't dissolving into fits of anger, who wasn't using bad language, who was mannerly and well dressed.

"And yet, he was still driven and competitive and won championships. Is that not a worthy hero?"

Wellington Mara, the New York Giants' co-owner, knew Landry as a former Giants assistant coach and later as the head coach of a chief rival. For twenty-nine years, when the Cowboys came to the New York area to play the Giants, the two would have dinner on the eve of the game.

"I guess his reputation is someone who's aloof," Mara said. "But there was a lot of fire burning inside him. You might know part of him by looking at him, but you didn't know it all."

Landry's impassive demeanor in public was indeed a trademark, but it concealed, for example, a dynamic football mind. He single-handedly revived the shotgun formation in the modern era of football. He devised the four-three defense—pro football's model defense—in the 1950s. He was the first to computerize the strategy and game planning of an NFL team in the 1960s, and his flex defense was revolutionary in the 1970s.

An engineering major at the University of Texas, Landry could draw up a football play so precise and interconnected that it looked like the plans for a high-rise building. And it would stand the test of time, too.

Respect for Landry in the NFL ran deep. After several years as the Giants' defensive coordinator, he became the first coach of the Cowboys in 1960, a hapless expansion franchise that won just four games in its first two seasons. But by 1966, Dallas was in the NFL championship game. Landry's Cowboys didn't have another losing season until 1986.

"Twenty consecutive winning seasons," George Young, the Giants' former general manager and now the league's deputy vice president, said. "That gets you plenty of respect."

Young often tells the story of his preparations for Super Bowl V, in which Landry's Cowboys played the Baltimore Colts, for whom Young was the offensive line coach.

The Colts prepared for the Cowboys defense they had seen on film all season, but Young kept asking, "What if they change it up on us?

"I was told: 'They won't do that. This has been Landry's defense for years and he's not going to change it now, not when he's playing the biggest game of the year.'

"Well, wouldn't you know, that's exactly what he did to us."

His former players, and his colleagues, acknowledged that much of Landry's reputation was well earned.

He was extremely private and not known for grandiose gestures or self-promotion. Some who knew him for fifty years never knew he was a bomber pilot in World War II who narrowly avoided death in a harrowing crash landing in the French countryside.

He liked to read and spent countless hours across four decades traveling the country in the off-season to appear at functions that raised money for the Fellowship of Christian Athletes.

Landry's reputation for keeping his players at a distance was legendary and well deserved.

"I think he forced himself to do that because he knew he'd have to be honest with players he had to release," Waters said. "And he couldn't be emotional about it."

Still, when the former Cowboys fullback Walt Garrison was once asked if he had ever seen Landry smile, Garrison answered, "No, I only played nine years."

Landry coached five Hall of Fame players in Dallas—Roger Staubach, Randy White, Bob Lilly, Mel Renfro and Tony Dorsett—and an equal number as an assistant with the Giants. He also helped develop two of the most prominent coaches of the 1980s and 1990s, Dan Reeves and Mike Ditka, both of whom played for Landry and then worked as assistants under him.

"He shaped my philosophy on everything," Reeves said. "I followed his philosophy on football and how he handled himself on and off the field. He was a tremendous influence on me."

Landry won two Super Bowls, in 1972 and 1978, and his teams appeared in five. While he was criticized for turning his players into robots, he coached a number of charismatic, iconoclastic players, including Don Meredith, Duane Thomas, Thomas (Hollywood) Henderson, Pete Gent and Lance Rentzel.

Moreover, he coached a different kind of team, one that relied on organization and ingenuity, a forward-thinking team that often seemed in contrast to the dusty, blood-and-guts tradition of earlier eras in the league. Symbolically, Landry's team played mostly on artificial turf and usually in the sun and often, for television purposes, late on Sunday afternoons, which cultivated its popularity.

Along the way, to some at least, Landry's teams put a new face on the city of Dallas in the mid-1960s.

"Part of Coach Landry's legacy," Waters said, "is what he did for our city and state. For a lot of people in America back then, all they knew about Dallas was that President Kennedy had been assassinated there. They associated the place with that great loss.

"The stigma was real and it was a burden we all inherited, including Coach Landry, who was raised in Mission, Texas," Waters said. "But Coach Landry helped us turn the corner on that with the way he handled himself—in bad times and good times. He was the conductor for all that changed."

He was the man on the sideline in the hat, an image so abiding that when he was inducted into the Cowboys Ring of Honor at Texas Stadium, a small outline of a fedora was placed next to his name.

"The image of the Cowboys started with Tom," Staubach said. "The Cowboys will always be more than just another team because of him."

And Landry's friends and admirers, Staubach included, insist that on occasion at least, the stoic coach did smile.

"Tom wanted to show Roger Staubach how to run a quarterback bootleg once," Brandt said. "And he got behind the center and ran the play, except that Tom had an old knee injury and he limped badly as he ran around that corner with the football.

"So Tom says, 'OK, do it like that.' And Roger took the ball from center and ran it just like Tom did, hobbling and limping all the way around the corner. Tom just burst out laughing and so did everyone else. Guys were falling down, they were laughing so hard."

Bill Pennington
February 14, 2000

CASE 4

The Software King

Bill Gates is stepping down—or up, or sideways, or something—from his position as CEO of Microsoft. Nobody seems to think that this will make much difference either to the way Microsoft is run or to the desire of the Justice Department to break up the world's most valuable company and humble its founder. But maybe the announcement provides a good occasion to reflect on the achievements of this elder statesman (forty-four years old!) of the new economy.

You might say that Gates is to business strategy what Heinz Guderian, the father of the blitzkrieg, was to military strategy. Germany didn't invent the tank or the bomber; but the German command understood, in a way that the British or the French did not, how these inventions changed the nature of war, and very nearly ended up conquering the world. Microsoft didn't invent either the personal computer or the point-and-click interface; but Gates understood, in a way that other contenders for empire did not, how these inventions changed the nature of business competition, and some think that he has come equally close to global conquest.

You could say that each of the two other companies one might have expected to dominate the new economy was the victim of a flawed philosophical premise. IBM's fallacy was that of crude materialism: accustomed to providing software free with its mainframes, the computer giant believed that market power rested in the hands of manufacturers, and did not realize its mistake until far too late. Apple, by contrast, suffered from naive idealism: Its managers believed that having the better idea, the better product, was in itself enough to ensure victory in the marketplace.

Only Gates seems to have realized the importance, in this new competitive realm, of "network externalities," which is economese for the incentive most of us have to use the same software—or video format, or typewriter keyboard—that everyone else uses. It's not a new concept, and around the time Gates was starting to build his empire economists were working out a theory of how companies should conduct themselves when network externalities are crucial. (Perhaps the leader among these theorists was Berkeley's Carl Shapiro; not coincidentally, Shapiro took a leave in the mid-1990s to become a top official at the Justice Department's antitrust division.) The essence of that theory is that you have to lose money to make money: Your product must initially be sold cheaply, even given away, until enough people are using it that the rest feel that they have no alternative.

This seems obvious now, but in the 1980s Apple thought that simply because the Macintosh was insanely great it could be sold at a premium price from day one. It was Gates who understood the power of ubiquity, and used that knowledge to build an unassailable market position. "Windows Ninety-five is Macintosh Eighty-nine," declared the losers bitterly when the struggle was all over. They were right, but that in itself tells you how much better Gates played the game.

Did Microsoft overplay its hand? Judge Thomas Penfield Jackson thinks so, and though many independent economists think that his "findings of fact" were rather one-sided—Nicholas Economides of New York University, whose Web site on network externalities is much admired among aficionados, describes the judge's report as "unusually harsh"—there is a reasonable chance that in the end Microsoft will be broken up into an applications company and one or two operating systems companies. But that will not be the end of the story, because Microsoft is unique only in the scale of its success. Monopoly is inherent in the logic of network externalities:

The normal life cycle of new industries will be one in which an initial field of competitors is brutally winnowed until only one major player remains. Indeed, investors are counting on this process: Since everyone now knows that you have to lose money to make money, and acts on that knowledge, only the eventual prospect of big monopoly profits can justify the prices now being paid for money-losing tech stocks. When does the legitimate attempt to capitalize on victory in a competitive race become an illegal abuse of market power? So far, nobody has laid down the ground rules.

So don't cry for Bill Gates, America. The truth is, he isn't leaving us—and even when he does, there will still be plenty of other Bills to pay.

Paul Krugman
January 16, 2000

CASE 5

The Father of Modern Management

Peter F. Drucker, revered as the father of modern management, has a new message for corporate executives: Find another line of work.

"The unique twentieth-century creation, the corporation, is not going to survive in the twenty-first century," he said, almost nonchalantly, in a 1999 interview.

Big companies, he said, don't seem to be able to thrive for more than thirty years, not even those like General Motors and Sears, Roebuck that have received advice from management gurus like himself. But another reason is seemingly contradictory: management skills have advanced so far that business has lost some of its challenge.

"In business, you are becoming bored, because we know so much," he said. "When I came in, nobody knew the routine and that made it exciting."

Few people in business today can remember when Drucker appeared as a management visionary in the 1940s. Drucker turned ninety in November 1999, and that prompted celebrations and reflections on his life and work.

Four hundred people, many from nonprofit organizations he has advised, held a birthday party at the Getty Center in Los Angeles. Drucker, a native of Austria, received that country's Cross of Honor for Science and Art. And at least two books had appeared in the last few years assessing his life and work.

Drucker wears hearing aids in both ears and walks with the help of a cane. But his mind seems as fertile and his pen as fluid as ever. He teaches a course for midcareer executives at the Claremont Graduate School, east of Los Angeles, where he has been based since 1971. He spouts facts, figures and historical tidbits from memory. The author of thirty-one books, he had recently written major articles for magazines like *The Atlantic Monthly* and *The Economist*.

"Writing is a compulsive neurosis," he said.

Drucker made his mark by viewing management as a subject in its own right, rather than as a collection of specific skills like finance and accounting. "He was the first person to formulate management as a professional discipline," said D. Quinn Mills, a professor at Harvard Business School.

Drucker recognized early on that a key to corporate success was to motivate employees. He also stressed marketing and innovation over finance.

His books, a mix of pungent generalizations and historical trivia, have been criticized as lacking academic rigor. Some business leaders consider his ideas dated. But his fans have included John F. Welch Jr. of General Electric and Andrew S. Grove of Intel. He also has a huge following among industrialists who rebuilt Japan after World War II.

"We owe him very, very much," said Masatoshi Ito, the founder of Ito-Yokado—a large Japanese retailer that controls the 7-Eleven chain—who came to the birthday party at the Getty Center and helped organize one in Tokyo.

Drucker does not like to be typecast as a management guru. He has written nearly as many books about economics, society and politics as about management. He has even penned two novels. He is an expert on Japanese art and once taught a course in it. Early in his career, he worked as a banker and a journalist.

Born and raised in Vienna, Drucker received his doctorate in international law from Frankfurt University before he was twenty-two and then remained in Germany. In 1933, after one of his essays was banned and burned by the Nazi government, Drucker moved to London and then, in 1937, to the United States.

In 1944, after publishing a book about business and society, he received an invitation from General Motors to study its inner workings. That led to his first management book, *The Concept of the Corporation,* in 1946.

He does his consulting and writing at home, in the modest house in Claremont where he has lived for twenty-nine years. He reads voraciously, both fiction and history, and does much of his writing on legal pads or a typewriter rather than on a computer, which he says makes him write too fast. Doris Drucker, his wife of sixty-two years, is a writer and physicist who has designed and manufactured a device to aid in speech therapy. The couple have four children and six grandchildren.

As for his view on the demise of corporations, Drucker says people will still work for a living but will not cast their lives with a single company. What Drucker calls the knowledge workers of today will save their best efforts for nonprofit social service organizations, where they can make a bigger difference.

"The twentieth century was the century of business," he said. "The next century is going to be the century of the social sector."

Drucker, spending an increasing portion of his time with such service groups, is the honorary chairman of the New York–based Peter F. Drucker Foundation for Nonprofit Management, founded by leaders of other non-profit organizations that he advised.

Although he is fascinated by the Internet, Drucker says his choice for the growth industry of the next thirty years is not e-commerce. "It's going to be fish farming," he said, explaining that on the oceans, "we are still hunters and gatherers."

Claremont, which named its business school after Drucker, is now estab-lishing his archives under the direction of Nan Stone, a former editor of *Harvard Business Review*. The archives will be largely available online, so Drucker's insights will be available to corporate managers well into the next century, even if the corporations themselves don't survive.

Andrew Pollack
November 14, 1999

CASE 6

The Deal Maker

Sanford I. Weill had just completed his latest coup—the one that vaulted him into the clear, free of any rivals or pretenders to the crown—and he was taking the stage at Carnegie Hall, where a single microphone descended from the floodlights. It was the annual shareholders' meeting of Citigroup, which had just earned more than any company had ever earned in a single quarter, and it was Weill's show. He had built the company, ledger by ledger, through a series of deals as remarkable as any in Wall Street history. And finally, it was all his. Even the stage and the velvet-cushioned seats, which, as a trustee and chairman of Carnegie Hall, Weill had restored, were, in a manner of speaking, his.

Weill carefully adjusted the mike, like a soloist testing the keys before a performance. Then, he cut to the subject on everyone's mind: John Reed, the thirty-five-year veteran who personified Citibank for so many years and whom Weill had ousted as cochairman. He praised Reed "as a great partner and a great friend"—words that were belied by his next comment, that Reed was returning from Brazil and was not in attendance. "He didn't know if he'd get a seat," a man in the audience cackled.

But the hall was filled with friendly faces, and Weill recited a list of Citigroup's assets as though they were his personal jewels. Reveling in the moment, he told the crowd that, like the nervous young broker he used to be, he still scans the business news before going to sleep: "That sort of tells me how many twists and turns I'm going to have in the night, and then I get up in the morning and see what happened and I'm excited to go to work." It was easy to forget all about John Reed, and about Jamie Dimon, the longtime protégé whom Weill fired, and all the other ex-partners and former allies who had been jettisoned along the way. Weill was on top, all by himself.

How was it that this superficially ordinary man, only moderately articulate and often lacking in grace, had created the most impressive money machine in modern times? Unlike Jack Welch, Weill will not leave behind any lodestar for future managers; unlike Warren Buffett, he has no special genius in finance. Yet it is Weill, the consummate pragmatist, who has put together the first global financial firm of the twenty-first century, linking securities, banking and insurance, and no one who knows him would call it an accident. The number of right calls that Weill has made in his long career is simply astonishing.

Part of his secret is his obsession for detail, which translates into a sort of intuitive genius. He is relentless when it comes to exploiting small opportunities and fearless about seizing big ones. The people closest to him describe him as a self-absorbed man who rises early and paces the floors, a born worrier who explodes at the slightest problem. This edginess is a factor in his success. "Sandy is insecure fundamentally," says Jack Nusbaum, the attorney who handled many of Weill's early acquisitions. "It drives him to be a perfectionist—to be a master of every piece in the puzzle."

Moreover, Weill has so co-opted his employees that his passion has spawned a kind of generalized corporate neurosis. He grills subordinates relentlessly; he solicits their ideas, badgers them, consumes them with demands. He takes it personally when employees leave and has obliterated any distinction between his private and professional lives. He and Joan, his wife and closest confidante for forty-five years, socialize extensively with people who owe their success (and their options) to Sandy. At New Year's, they invite Citigroup couples to their vacation home in upstate New York, which is adorned with framed magazine covers of Weill's triumphs. He never misses an awards trip, those polyester galas for high-achieving salespeople, where he schmoozes with starstruck employees. And he regularly shows up at the bar mitzvahs and weddings of employees' children. "He flew back from Hong Kong to attend my father's funeral in Trenton," recalls Joseph Plumeri, who recently retired from Citigroup. "This is a compassionate guy."

The terms of Weill's compassion are carefully circumscribed, though. A fiend for attention, Weill courts standing ovations almost everywhere he goes: board dinners, corporate meetings, charity events. His annual "surprise" parties have become a ritual joke—"God forbid there is no surprise one year," says a Weill friend. Charles Prince, Citigroup's general counsel, orchestrates these events, each of which involves a cornball theme (Weill dressing up as Moses or as a knight in shining armor) and, inevitably, rounds of toasts in which Weill is effusively praised.

People mostly tolerate Weill's ego because he seems so genuine, so utterly unposed. He still gets excited at the memory of his first ride in a corporate jet, still gets a thrill from celebrity. Mike Weinberg, a friend whom Weill met at Atlantic Beach in the 1950s and now an employee, recalls the two of them walking into Club 55, a topless restaurant in St. Tropez filled with sun-drenched jet-setters. "Sandy's looking around to see who's famous," Weinberg noted. "He was the most famous guy there."

The story of how he rose from humble broker to Wall Street conqueror would be unbelievable had he not rehearsed every aspect of it so many times. In some sense, every deal was a prelude to Citigroup; every personal battle with real and imagined threats to his authority was a forerunner to his confrontation with Reed. And today, though personally worth more than $1 billion, he seems obsessed with the goal of securing his legacy and putting his personal demons to rest.

In the spring of 2000 I was invited to visit Weill and his wife at their country home in Saranac Lake, New York. Hopping a Citigroup Gulfstream jet with Leah C. Johnson, Citigroup's press director, and Jerome Jousse, the company's executive chef, I landed at a tiny strip in the Adirondacks. A ruddy-faced Weill, dressed in jeans and a bright sweater tucked over an ample stomach, arrived in a red Toyota Land Cruiser, and soon he was driving us past tattered bungalows and modest lakefront cottages. I asked Weill how he had chosen such a remote spot, and he responded that in 1990, he had been distracted by work and his marriage had hit a rough spot. Joan suggested the Adirondacks as a place to spend time alone. "It was the best thing we ever did," Weill told me.

An unmarked drive led to a sprawling house flanked by a vegetable garden and a collection of green-and-white guest cottages. A lake was visible through a grove of pines. Apologizing for the mosquitoes, the Weills took me on a quick tour of their winterized boat dock, his fitness room and her two-lane indoor pool.

Weill, who grew up in Bensonhurst and Miami Beach, is often depicted as an up-from-nothing overachiever, though his sister, Helen Saffer, told me that the family was well off and that her brother was a typical child. Their father, a Polish-born dress manufacturer, drove a Cadillac, and Weill attended Peekskill Military Academy, where he excelled at tennis. Weill was an indifferent student at Cornell, and right before graduation he left school to try to persuade his father, who was living with a girlfriend, to return. His parents' divorce was a bitter blow. "It's because of that experience—family is very important to him," Joan observed. "Loyalty is important to him."

Sandy added that he has consciously tried not to imitate his father, a Runyonesque dandy who married three times. In fact, he has woven his marital vows into the corporate culture wherever he has worked. To an unusual degree, Weill expects spouses to attend retreats and to ask questions during strategy sessions. Before making a big hire or clinching a deal, both Weills routinely meet both the executive and the spouse on the other side. A lissome woman with rust-colored hair and peach-toned skin, Joan was dressed in faded jeans and a blue sweater. She described her role as playing devil's advocate. "My husband comes first," she noted, "but I try to get Sandy to look at both sides." What she doesn't say is that she also stoked Sandy's ambition. "She's the one who wanted him to do something," says their daughter, Jessica Bibliowicz. "She pushed him."

Joan Mosher's parents didn't much like the idea of Weill joining the family, thinking his prospects dim. He started as a runner on Wall Street and soon was promoted to broker. Joan, then a young mom, struggled with the bills, paying the milkman one month, the diaper man the next. "Sandy says I invented the concept of float," Joan said.

In 1960, the twenty-seven-year-old Weill and Arthur Carter, who lived across the hall from the Weills in East Rockaway, on Long Island, opened their own firm, along with a friend of Carter's, a frustrated songwriter named Roger Berlind, and a fourth man, Peter Potoma. Weill borrowed thirty thousand dollars from his mother for his share of the partnership.

Carter, Berlind, Potoma & Weill was a scrappy firm. Operating out of a two-room office on Wall Street, the partners aspired to be not just brokers but also investment bankers. In a business still largely divided along ethnic lines, the firm became known as "the Jewish DLJ"—an aggressive boutique that did quality research. It was a quirky place, everyone a bit of a character. One early recruit was Arthur Levitt Jr., the son of a longtime New York State comptroller. Another was Marshall Cogan, a flamboyant salesman with a degree from Harvard Business School.

Weill was the quiet partner. He would sit in the back, chomping on a cigar, watching the tape. According to Frank Biondi, who worked there in the 1960s and later was president of Viacom: "Sandy could tell a convincing story. He developed clients who trusted him." Eventually those clients would include Sonny Werblin, an owner of the New York Jets, Joe Namath, Wilt Chamberlain and Howard Cosell.

As time went on, Weill tired of being merely a broker for hire. He felt the stirrings of corporate ambition and grew eager to build a firm. A turning point came in 1967, when the firm brokered the acquisition of Reliance Insurance by Saul Steinberg. Though the partners pocketed a $750,000 fee, Weill was dissatisfied. "The next day Steinberg had a business," Weill recounted, "and we had to start all over again."

The following year, Weill got his first lesson in corporate politics. Carter tried to take over the firm, but Levitt organized a countercoup and forced Carter out. No sooner had the crisis passed than the firm, now Cogan, Berlind, Weill & Levitt—aka "Corned Beef with Lettuce"—faced another. As a small firm, it always cleared trades through the larger Burnham brokerage firm, but in 1969, Burnham could no longer handle the volume. Weill hired Frank Zarb, later a Nixon administration official, to set up a clearing operation in house. Much of Wall Street's business was still done by hand, and firms were getting buried in paperwork. It got so bad that, for a while, the stock exchange had to shut down on Wednesdays. Thanks to Zarb's back office, Weill's firm had the equivalent of a factory with excess capacity. Thus, in 1970, when Hayden Stone, a much larger, old-line brokerage firm, was about to go bankrupt, Weill's firm could gobble it up.

The acquisition was a pivotal moment. Using almost no cash, Weill bought a good brand at a depressed price and pawned off a third of its branches, adding considerable revenue with few additional costs. He also adopted Hayden's tonier name. This would be the template for all his later deals.

Hayden Stone's failure exposed a major weakness of Wall Street: The firms that raised capital for the country were themselves undercapitalized.

When Merrill Lynch went public in 1971, Weill and his partners followed suit—another turning point. By 1973, Wall Street was in a depression, and many firms were failing. Weill's stock plunged from 12½ to 1. But because of the IPO, the firm had capital and could weather the storm. Cogan, the biggest revenue producer, wanted to take the firm private again. He had a trader's mentality, whereas Weill was interested in building the firm and recognized the value of permanent capital. Once again there was a standoff.

"I was the swing vote," recalled Levitt, who later became chairman of the Securities and Exchange Commission. "I thought Sandy would be a better leader than Marshall." It was not intellect, per se, but a trait that, at the climax of Weill's career, would be visible to Citigroup's board as well. Nobody would work harder or focus on the business more incisively than Sandy. As Levitt said, "He would not accept defeat." Cogan was out; Weill was CEO.

One by one the other partners, who sensed that Weill was consolidating his hold on the firm, left. They still argue over who was responsible for Corned Beef's success (Carter, today, owns and publishes the *New York Observer*, and Berlind is a top Broadway producer), and they remain miffed over an anniversary party in 1985 at which their contributions weren't even acknowledged. "It's fair to say my feelings for Sandy are complex," Levitt acknowledged.

In the 1970s, Weill, often working closely with a young protégé named Peter Cohen, bought firm after firm, including H. Hentz & Co., Shearson Hamill and Loeb Rhoades. The formula was the same: buy distressed, prune costs, keep the best of the new and dump the businesses that didn't fit. "We had this machine," Weill said fondly. It was not unheard-of for a merger to be done over a weekend or a holiday at the Weills' weekend home in Greenwich, Connecticut.

Thanks to his nonstop worrying, Weill developed a reputation in the business world as risk-averse. This wasn't quite accurate; he took business risks in virtually every deal. What he eschewed were financial risks. He has never had a taste for debt, and his companies always run a prudent balance sheet. This is the way he runs his life, too. A Depression baby, Weill still keeps the bulk of his non-Citigroup assets in treasury bills, and even after he began to make a lot of money, he was notoriously cheap, said to sit forever in a restaurant until his companion reached for the check.

Though his stature was rising, Weill still lacked the qualities of a natural leader. He was fidgety and chewed his nails; he would sweat profusely before making a speech. Though famed as a cost cutter, he had little stomach for actually firing people himself. He could also be oddly shy. At a

Christmas party for the Hayden Stone employees, Mary McDermott, a company spokeswoman, saw him standing outside, clutching a drink. Weill explained, "I don't know anybody." McDermott said: "Well, come inside. You've acquired their company."

Perhaps to cover for insecurity, he was often a bully. "You'd be faced with a barrage of screaming; it was demeaning behavior," said Peter Cohen, who finally quit in frustration. Weill, though, wouldn't let his protégé go in peace. At the farewell party, Weill stormed into the room and berated Cohen for selling company stock, to Weill an act of disloyalty. Incredibly, Cohen soon returned to the firm. Despite Weill's insensitivity, his energy was hard to resist.

And he wasn't too stubborn to rethink an issue following an outburst. When Jeffrey B. Lane, a manager, suggested that Shearson, as the firm was then known, go into the money fund business, Weill screamed that he was an "idiot," forcing Lane to defend his view. The next day, Weill changed his mind. "He's screaming but he's listening," said Lane, who runs Neuberger Berman.

Like few CEOs, Weill scrutinized the most humdrum aspects of the business. When he toured the printing plant, he remembered the foreman's name. Like a young Sam Walton tending his inventory, Weill grasped that success would ride on the details. Yet he also thought in global terms. One day in the mid-1970s, Weill told Phil Waterman, one of his cadre of manager-friends, "I want to complete the twenty-four-hour cycle." Waterman had no idea what he meant. Soon after, Waterman was sent to Hong Kong to set up a branch.

In the early 1980s, the big financial news was the bankruptcy of the Hunt brothers, who had tried to corner the silver market. Sensing the riskiness of their giant position, Weill had presciently dropped them as clients before the bubble burst. Many brokerage firms suffered collateral damage, notably Bache, which sold out to Prudential Insurance the following year. Weill, who was in Hong Kong when the Bache deal was announced, "got that funny look," according to Waterman, who was with him. Weill figured that a wave of consolidation was in the offing, and that unaffiliated brokerage firms like his would be easy prey. He hurried to his hotel suite, placed a call to Peter Cohen and told him they should explore a merger with American Express.

Amex would end up buying Shearson, but after the deal closed, Weill casually let it slip, as he was stepping from a cab in front of his East Side apartment, that Cohen would not have a seat on the board. Stunned, Cohen went directly to the Amex CEO, James D. Robinson 3d, and successfully pleaded his case, which Weill regarded as another act of disloyalty. To this day, Weill remains full of vitriol for Cohen, as though he were the one betrayed.

The early 1980s were difficult for Weill. When he moved to Amex, as Robinson's number two, he gave up day-to-day control of Shearson, against the advice of Joan and just about everyone else. Even his father called from Miami and said, "Don't do it; it's your power base." But Weill was hooked on a grander dream—integrating Amex and Shearson by cross-selling products, like using Amex's charge card as a sales list for Shearson brokers. Even as early as 1982, Weill had a vision of financial services coming together under one umbrella. But Robinson was leery of diluting the brand appeal of his famous green card, and the effort fizzled. As a misfit in Amex's waspish boardroom, Weill felt increasingly uneasy.

Weill did, however, manage to make one of the most important deals of his career at Amex—securing the services of a Harvard Business School grad named Jamie Dimon. Dimon's father was a broker who met Sandy at an awards banquet, and the two families had become close. "It's the women that started the whole thing," said Joan. Impressed by Sandy's unprepossessing ways and his understanding of the nuts and bolts, Dimon wrote his college thesis on Sandy's acquisition of Shearson.

At Amex, Weill and Dimon went to work on the company's troubled Fireman's insurance subsidiary, developing an intense working style they would perfect over the years. Swooping into field offices, they encouraged employees to critique the performances of their bosses. Eventually, with his path at Amex blocked, Weill decided he wanted Fireman's for his own, and offered to take if off Amex's hands, provided the company indemnified him from future losses. The board, intimidated by Weill's reputation as a negotiator, demurred, leaving Weill with no choice but to resign. Incredibly, the young Dimon, who could have stayed at Amex or had his pick of new jobs, elected to follow his mentor into unemployment.

Aside from work, Weill's greatest passion is food. At Saranac, Jousse whipped up a dinner of short ribs in ginger soy, and a lemon tart with raspberry sauce. Then Weill cleared the table, and we moved to the den to watch Pedro Martinez outpitch Roger Clemens. It's not quite right to say Weill never relaxes. But even in casual settings, there's an agitation and a need for self-validation that never shuts off. Settling into an armchair, Weill kept running track of the strikeout totals, often beating the announcers to the call and looking my way to see that I had noticed. Between innings, he switched to the Bloomberg business channel to check on markets in Asia. Weill tracks his share price as keenly as a heart-attack survivor monitors his blood pressure, and he was beaming that markets were up in Japan, where Citigroup recently purchased a sizable stake in Nikko Securities.

The next day, regrouping in his cavernous living room, where stuffed elk heads line the walls, he picked up the thread of the story he'd been telling me, starting when he and Dimon were looking for work.

Taking an office in the Seagram Building, they sifted through potential deals and waited for the phone to ring. In 1986, a call came from an employee at Commercial Credit Corporation, a Baltimore-based loan company. The struggling firm, which lent money to working families from a network of four hundred grubby field offices, was everything that image-conscious Amex was not. In other words, perfect for Weill. He persuaded Commercial Credit's parent to install him as CEO and take the company public. Investors didn't know beans about the company; they bought the stock because it was Sandy, and that turned out to be a wise bet. A single share, which made its debut in 1986 at $20.50, has multiplied over the years into twelve shares of Citigroup stock, worth about $650. Weill invested $6 million and grabbed a horde of options.

To run the company, Weill at first commuted to Baltimore and worked his staff around the clock. "You were away from your family, your social life—it became personal," says Robert Lipp, a former Chemical Bank executive and part of a nucleus of executives who today run Citigroup. "There was never any formal long-range plan—that's what we did when we sat down at lunch." A critical part of the team was Dimon, a hothead known to roll his eyes whenever something struck him as foolish. He was also unusually open with his boss. Weill and Dimon's screaming matches were legion, but their arguments drew them closer and sharpened their business instincts. Together they focused on immediate, tangible problems; Weill, in particular, always zeroed in on the bottom line for next quarter, not some far-off future.

In 1988, Weill bought Primerica Corporation, owner of Smith Barney, a storied brokerage firm that—not unlike Hayden Stone—had fallen on hard times. Aside from Smith Barney, Primerica had an army of salespeople that peddled term life insurance and mutual funds. This gave Weill a chance to revisit the goal of cross-selling that had eluded him at American Express. Weill figured that with the right pipeline, he could widen his product base, just as a bookseller might branch into music. This is the old grail on Wall Street. Remember when Sears was going to peddle Dean Witter securities ("stocks and socks") in its department stores? Almost no one had made it work, but Weill wouldn't let go of the idea. He dispatched Marge Magner, a Brooklyn policeman's daughter (and today head of Citigroup's consumer bank) to Alabama with a simple message: Teach the Primerica financial agents how to sell consumer loans from Commercial Credit. As the business grew, Weill and company noticed an interesting detail: People who were offered a loan were less likely to default than people who went into a credit office and asked for one. The business developed by the new sales channel actually performed better.

In the early 1990s, Weill struck again, acquiring Travelers, which had been devastated by woeful investments in real estate. At about that time, he had a meeting with Hillary Clinton, who was promoting her ballyhooed health care reform. She scared the wits out of him, so much so that Weill shrewdly dumped Travelers' health care business, which he saw becoming a magnet for bureaucratic meddling. Meanwhile, he pushed the rest of the organization to sell Travelers insurance products.

Weill made these mergers work by emphasizing teamwork. Over and over, he would repeat, "The enemy is the guy down the street, not the one in the next office." Another favorite refrain was, "Return internal calls before external ones." Weill rewarded managers with stock, but he pointedly forbade them to sell. "The flag was nailed to the mast; if the ship went down, you went down," said Prince. In time, two-thirds of Travelers annuities would be sold by its sister companies, as would half of Commercial Credit's real estate loans. It's hard to think of any other corporation in America that has woven so many companies into a single fabric.

But Weill wasn't finished. In 1993, American Express's basic charge card business was struggling. Weill had never given up the dream of reacquiring Shearson. Now, sensing that its owner was weak, he pounced. The move was pure Sandy, and it put him back in the big leagues of Wall Street. But the question of who would run the Smith Barney division was problematic. To fill all the new senior positions, Weill repeatedly shuffled key allies in and out. He is a loyalist in the larger sense: loyal to the company. His ethos for teamwork has always been balanced by a pitiless instinct for profits and growth.

By the mid-1990s, Travelers, now the parent's name, was cruising. Weill seemed to be everywhere, presiding at awards trips, rallying agents in a Texas football stadium, hollering at bankers to get offerings to market. When a timer that controlled the lights at headquarters malfunctioned, Mike Weinberg, Weill's old chum, got an angry call—Weill had flown by at 1 A.M. and spotted the lights ablaze. Weill ran his empire like the family store, even hiring both his kids, Jessica and Marc. His trademark was prowling the halls, "managing by gossip," in the words of one associate. He wouldn't even allow his secretary to screen his calls, lest he miss a bit of news.

And then, the family began to sour.

In 1996, Weill started to pressure Dimon to put Jessica in charge of the asset management business. It was a big job for which Dimon felt she wasn't quite ready. Meanwhile, Jessica was increasingly aware that her growing prominence in the company was making life there awkward for her. She even felt forced to pull back from Sandy. "His life is about his business," she noted. "I couldn't be open with him because I had to go through channels."

In 1997, she announced that she was quitting. "I told him we were going to be father and daughter again," she says. "I didn't leave because of Jamie. It wasn't working."

Jessica, a charmingly effervescent woman, is a principal in a private venture that, interestingly enough, is acquiring small financial service firms. I had barely walked in the door when, without a hint of self-consciousness, she started talking about her own deals. She seems to have no regrets.

Weill didn't get over it quite so easily. He was furious with Dimon. But the two continued on, immersed in building Travelers. Amazingly, Weill charmed J.P. Morgan—which, when Weill entered the business, had been virtually closed to Jews—into agreeing to merge. But as negotiations proceeded, Douglas A. Warner III, Morgan's chairman, insisted that, after a transition period, Weill would have to retire. A petulant Weill told a Wall Street colleague that Morgan "would never sell to a Jew." The deal was dead, but a new prospect materialized instantly: Deryck Maughan, CEO of Salomon, called virtually the same day.

Salomon was a fractious and perennially troubled firm, but it had a global presence—which Weill needed to vault Smith Barney into Wall Street's upper echelon. Moreover, Weill had taken Maughan onto the board of Carnegie Hall, and the two got along. Weill's managers were dubious, pointing out that $9 billion was a steep price for a firm that largely depended on its skittish bond traders. But Weill was adamant about the need for an overseas footing. In September, the acquisition was announced, and Weill and Dimon met several senior Salomon traders at the Four Seasons. It should have been a joyous occasion, but as they sat down to drinks, Weill and Dimon started to argue over a seemingly trivial detail. Within moments, they were screaming at each other.

Fights between them were nothing new, but their quarrels had taken on a brittle edge. Dimon, who was now in charge of Smith Barney, was chafing under his mentor's rule. Reportedly, Dimon even tried to exclude him from the unit's executive committee meetings. Weill seethed, especially when the press started paying attention to Dimon. Then, when Heidi Miller, the young chief financial officer, was added to the corporate planning group, Dimon gave the welcoming speech. "Sandy got really upset," said a senior executive. "He felt that Jamie had scooped him." They had always been like a married couple, squabbling then making up. Now they made up less and less.

"It was still the company I was running," Weill told me. "I didn't like being cut out of the knowledge flow." In the midst of the Jessica business, they had tried talking it out with their wives, but that didn't help. "I tried to understand him," Sandy added. "I'm not a psychiatrist."

Jessica observes that her father's relationships work until the other party changes. "Dad doesn't evolve," she said.

When Travelers acquired Salomon, Weill, who wanted to ensure a smooth transition, told Dimon that he would have to share CEO duties for the new Salomon Smith Barney with Maughan, a former British civil servant. Dimon was stung. Then, Weill pressured Dimon to transfer Salomon's jewel, its bond arbitrage group, to his son, Marc, repeating in a small way the minuet with Jessica. Dimon and Maughan both advised against it, noting that the bond group was potential dynamite. Weill backed off. Marc, who until recently ran the company's investment portfolio, is a shy, angular man who has no taste for corporate power plays. He spent much of an hour-long interview rubbing his hands, playing with a telephone cord and tapping a foot. He recalled that his father wouldn't let him win at tennis, and that he yelled at Marc "probably more than at most people here." (Marc was on a leave of absence from the company.)

The Salomon acquisition arguably was Sandy's worst. Salomon, he realized, wasn't strong enough to be a truly global player. So Weill started to think about Citicorp, a target he and Dimon had eyed for years. U.S. law forbade a merger of insurance and banking, but Weill thought Congress would get around to changing the law. Announcing a deal might even force their hand. "Sandy's got guts," Dimon noted admiringly.

As it happened, John Reed had been searching for a way to galvanize Citicorp, and was convinced that the change had to come from outside. Then fifty-nine, he was thinking of retiring soon, and imagined that the older Weill would retire with him. Weill wanted the deal so bad he persuaded himself that the two would be a perfect match.

In April 1999, when the blockbuster merger was announced, Dimon was surprised to discover that he'd been excluded from the board, a replay of

Weill's insulting treatment of Peter Cohen sixteen years before. Though Dimon was named president, it was a hollow title, forcing him to share responsibilities not only with Maughan again, but also with Citicorp's Victor Menezes. Dimon could barely contain his anger; meanwhile, Maughan was getting along splendidly with Weill, always careful to lace his speeches with accolades for the boss.

Trying to implement two mergers at once—and dealing with the meltdown in world credit markets following Russia's loan default, which cost Salomon $1 billion—Dimon and Weill were frequently at odds. Dimon began to act out. He nagged Weill and sharply criticized some of his ideas. "I stuck my finger in Sandy's eye," he admitted. Avoiding his office at the shimmering Citigroup Center headquarters, Dimon stayed mostly at Salomon Smith Barney downtown, where he concentrated on fixing the investment bank. It was odd behavior for a corporate president and presumptive heir.

Reed, who viewed Dimon as the intellectual soul mate Weill could never be, tried to bond with him. He gave Dimon books to read and invited him on a business trip to South America. But Dimon feared that their budding friendship would anger Weill and pulled back.

At a black-tie dinner and dance, at the Greenbrier, a resort in the West Virginia mountains, it all came to a head. The party was the climax of an extended weekend conference for Citigroup executives and spouses, an occasion to celebrate the merger. But the Travelers and Citicorp cultures had not been gelling, and the mood at the conference had been tense. Toward midnight, Steve Black, a Dimon friend who had never gotten along with Maughan, offered to dance with Maughan's wife as a sort of peace overture. Maughan failed to return the gesture, leaving Black's wife standing alone. Dimon, who had kept to himself most of the evening, took it upon himself to confront Maughan. When Maughan turned away, Dimon grabbed him by the shoulders, spun him around, popping a button from his lapel, and thundered, "Don't you ever turn your back on me while I'm talking!"

Citigroup officially investigated the incident. Recollections varied, then Weill talked to Reed and got his agreement on what had to be done. Dimon remained in the dark. "I never saw it coming," Dimon told me, sounding like an abandoned spouse. "I thought one day we'd have a drink and work it out."

On November 1, 1999, a Sunday, Weill and Reed summoned Dimon to the office. "We've made some decisions," Weill began. "Deryck is going to work on deals. Mike Carpenter is going to run corporate with Victor. And third, we want you to resign."

Dimon said, "OK."

Suddenly overcome, Weill tried to embrace him. Dimon said, "No hugs, please."

When I brought up the subject of Dimon, Weill became pensive. In halting tones, he admitted the breakup was exceedingly difficult, and added that he hoped Dimon "would do great in the future." Dimon's new assignment—as chairman of Chicago-based Bank One—is not dissimilar from the many that Weill and Dimon took on together. It's a turnaround situation, a company with plenty of problems and untapped potential. If Dimon remains a sensitive subject for Weill, it is in part because he knows that Dimon is out to prove that he can succeed without his mentor. Recently, when a Citigroup colleague offhandedly referred to Dimon, Weill exploded: "Have you been talking to him?"

Dimon's departure, though, made Weill's life at Citigroup much less complicated. He was now free to focus on Reed, a man as introverted as Weill is extroverted. Ill at ease personally, Reed preferred to stay in his office and deal with his staff via memos. At monthly retreats, Weill would use the lunch hour to turn on the charm; Reed would go for a solitary stroll. A trim MIT grad, he loved to figure out the right corporate process and let somebody else handle it. He was enchanted with the idea of management as distinct from the thing itself.

Reed had even toyed with the notion of moving the corporate staff to some airy remove like Cambridge or Palo Alto, where they could ruminate away from the line managers who ran the businesses. In Weill's view, the line managers are the business, and he couldn't abide Reed's abstractions: "I have a hard time visualizing what something is like without having seen it," he said.

Contrary to glowing press reports, Weill and Reed started having trouble right away. Reed wanted to limit the dinners before board meetings to directors. Weill wanted to invite managers—and their spouses, too. Their differences were stamped on their companies. Travelers was lean and informal; Citicorp top-heavy and hierarchical. Strangely, its most powerful department was human resources, which had set up an elaborate "talent inventory" to monitor personnel. Like apparatchiks vetting appointments with the Communist Party, managers at Citi often had to wait months for HR to approve transfers. Former Travelers managers now had to wait as well. The head of HR, Lawrence Phillips, was a remote bureaucrat who often worked away from the main office. Weill was desperate to get rid of Phillips and to cut HR down to size.

Then there was the Internet. Reed had organized a separate division, e-Citi, to move the bank online. He figured his managers would be too set in their ways to adapt, so he created a new bureaucracy from scratch. The problem was, it didn't develop products—not very quickly, anyway. True to Reed's form, e-Citi operated more as a think tank than as a profit center, and with fifteen hundred employees it was blowing $300 million a year.

The losses and the delays infuriated Weill. In his view, only operating managers—who are accountable for profits and losses—could effect a synthesis, grafting new products (like an online "credit card") into up-and-running business units. More than any other area, e-Citi came to epitomize the two CEOs' differences.

The tension between the CEOs steadily worsened. Reed told associates that firing Dimon was a mistake. Then, about six months after the merger, the corporate bank, still divided between Citi and Travelers people, staged a two-day retreat at the El Conquistador in San Juan. Confusingly, Weill gave an upbeat assessment and Reed scorched the bankers for earning no better than a "C." But what raised eyebrows even more was their timing: Weill arrived early and left after lunch on the second day, just as Reed was arriving.

In the summer of 1999 the CEOs agreed to divide responsibilities: Weill would run the operating units and Reed would handle HR and his pet, e-Citi. Weill already had his own people running most of the businesses. And he was romancing two other important players: Robert Rubin, the former treasury secretary, who was hired in October as a third member of the office of the chairman (and, in effect, a peacemaker), and the former Citicorp's Menezes.

Before long, the merger of equals became a takeover. Weill's cost cutters hacked away at Reed's bureaucracy, eliminating $2 billion in Citigroup costs. Reed seemed not to recognize that he was in a fight. "He doesn't think in those simplistic terms," one of his lieutenants says. In a speech accepting the executive of the year award from the Academy of Management, a scholarly group, late in 1999, Reed likened the problems of the bank's two cultures to what he had learned from the literature on splintered families. Almost naively, Reed added that some of the press and certain executives "would rather not have it be a merger at all, but a power struggle."

That's certainly how Weill saw it. According to aides, it had become nigh impossible to get his attention unless it was on a subject, like e-Citi, on which he could score points against Reed. In February 2000, the management committee met at Boulders, a resort in Arizona. On the second day, they went around the room; each manager complained that having two bosses wasn't working. "We can follow any compass," Menezes said, "but we have to know where north, south, east and west are."

After the retreat, Miller, the CFO and one of the highest-ranking female financial executives in the country, defected to Priceline.com. Weill, reckoning that Miller had been frustrated by having to answer to two CEOs, exploded. (Miller, who also had frustrations with Weill, declined to comment.) Reed and Weill agreed on one thing—they couldn't fix the problem. They called a special meeting of the board for late February to decide who should be left standing.

Reed, Rubin and Weill each made a pitch and left the room. Reed, still dreaming of an outside savior, suggested they bring in someone new. Rubin said another newcomer was the last thing they needed. Making clear that he was not a candidate, he threw his support to Weill. Only Weill said clearly that he wanted the job.

Not all the directors were so eager to crown him. "A little humility might help," one told me, "a little self-knowledge." But ultimately, what other choice was there? "It wasn't easy," Ann Jordan, a board member, says of the seven-hour meeting. "It was done with great thoughtfulness. But if you look at Sandy's history—I mean, to take Commercial Credit where he did is an amazing history for a businessman."

Reed got a farewell party; Weill was in Brazil. He did not even phone in a tribute.

With the power all his, Weill is making progress welding the two companies together. Citibank cardholders are now buying five thousand policies from Travelers a month, and Salomon Smith Barney is doing twice as much business as before with clients of Citibank. Overseas, Weill is moving even faster.

After a recent trip to Hawaii, he went to Hong Kong and met in secret with the heads of Taiwan's leading insurance-banking-and-securities family. As it happened, Taiwan's markets were depressed, thanks to saber rattling with the mainland. His hosts staged a sumptuous banquet watered with a vintage Lynch-Bages. Weill returned with a 15 percent stake in Fubon Group, which is poised to expand into Southeast Asia. This, Weill believes, will be a ticket to China.

More broadly, he has a notion that, one day, Chilean teachers and Polish miners will each be buying, say, annuities from Travelers and term insurance from Primerica. The basic premise is that foreigners will gradually buy more American-style financial products, just as they have cell phones and hamburgers. "The consumer internationally is the big opportunity," Weill told me.

Partly because Weill has been so busy doing deals, his organization often seems on the verge of chaos. Managers complain of confusion in the upper ranks and openly question whether he's suited to run an empire of 190,000 employees. The days of "managing by gossip" are over, a fact that Weill seems reluctant to acknowledge. "The way he makes decisions drives you crazy," said one bedraggled executive. "Sandy is constantly stirring the pot."

Insiders say the company misses Dimon. Weill's senior managers—Rubin, Maughan and a group of longtime "friends of Sandy"—tend to be diplomatic with him. They take issue with Weill, but not as bluntly as Dimon did. "Sandy is on overload—he has too many decisions to make, and people are afraid to tell him the truth, which is what he always thrived on," a Salomon Smith Barney banker remarked. Not surprisingly, Citigroup has been stung by repeated defections, which Diane Glossman, a securities analyst who has tracked Weill's career, called "a serious issue for Sandy."

The board has told him to groom a successor within two years, but the betting inside Citigroup is that he will be around longer. "Sandy's agenda is to work for at least three years," said one executive. "He's talking about staying until he's seventy."

Weill wants to go out with another conquest, perhaps on the Internet, the updated version of a coast-to-coast broker network. He has rerouted e-Citi's budget and staff, and he is furiously pushing managers to develop a coherent approach to the online world. In July 2000, Weill, just back from Japan, was abuzz over the newest commercial applications for wireless. Soon after, he announced a potentially major deal with America Online to make payments and transfer funds. Citigroup also has plans to enable all its customers to access and service every account with a single click. Ultimately, Weill wants every television viewer to be greeted with a menu from Citigroup. "When you go to a hotel, you see that single screen," Weill told me, the most excited I had seen him. "I'd love to see, when you turn on the TV at home, the first thing you see is Citigroup."

On my last afternoon in Saranac, the Weills and I sat down to lunch. The way Weill was talking, it was clear that he'd been doing a lot of thinking about his place in history. He told me he has been looking for a biographer, and then he grew irritated that I hadn't brought up the subject of his philanthropic work. "I probably do as much as any CEO," he declared, glancing at Joan for affirmation. He might be right. In the early 1980s, while driving through Harlem with Joan, he remarked at the inconsistency between the high rate of unemployed youth and his company's inability to find skilled labor. Before long, he'd set up a program to teach finance in a Brooklyn high school. The program—it has Weill's pragmatic touch—mushroomed into the National Academy Foundation, which prepares students for careers in finance, travel and technology, in four hundred schools nationwide. Weill devotes serious time to it.

And in 1998, the Weills made an eye-popping gift to Cornell's medical school—said by Cornell to be worth $100 million. The school, like the Carnegie recital hall, has been renamed in the Weills' honor. For these and sundry other causes, Weill has been a fund-raiser nonpareil, a role that suits him. He loves to talk about his commitment to "giving back," much of it to New York City and to young people, as if reaching out to the Brooklyn kid that is still Sandy, striving for his first bit of achievement and acclaim. And though the curtain is drawing on his career, there is no evidence that he is ready to relinquish center stage. "The other night the doctors at the hospital had a dinner for me," he beamed. "It's so nice to walk into a room and have everyone applaud." Joan, as if on cue, came to his rescue. "Dear, you get that at home every night."

Roger Lowenstein
August 27, 2000

AFTERWORD

The nineteenth century didn't have the Internet or a European Union or management seminars where you stand in a circle holding hands. But it did have credit-rating agencies assessing the value of a company and its chief. They offered much more interesting fare than today's "financial-information providers," at times skewering risky borrowers as scamps or drunks. Like today's financial analysts, though, they often made bad calls. Pity, for instance, the anonymous author of an 1863 entry that concluded that a merchant named J.D. Rockefeller "is not much of a businessman." *Plus ça change* . . .

Wheeling and Dealing, Old School

With his large hands clad in delicate white gloves, Travis B. Blackman gingerly opened the sheepskin-bound book and blew gently on the onion-skin-thin pages to separate them. He treated the aged volume with the reverence normally reserved for a first-edition Dickens or Hemingway.

But all this fuss over a credit report? Or rather, over 2,580 volumes of handwritten credit reports that date back to 1841 and run through 1891? As unromantic as it sounds, for people who study the wheelings and dealings of days gone by, the R. G. Dun & Company Collection at Harvard University is the Holy Grail of business history.

For within the books' light blue pages, written in curvaceous script, are titillating details about whether a particular businessman drank too much or attended church, if he got his money from his rich wife or his business was a front for a brothel.

Ne'er-do-wells are boldly named, like one storekeeper in Halifax County, North Carolina, who in June 1873 was referred to as a "purchaser of stolen goods, a great scamp." Long before the existence of the Securities and Exchange Commission or the annual stockholder meeting, it was the credit report that told the real dirt on a business.

"These volumes represent the creation of a national business network," said Blackman, who oversees the use of the archives for what is now the Dun & Bradstreet Corporation, which donated them to the university in 1962. "Every nook-and-cranny village on the frontier, somebody was there sending a report to the company."

And these days, more people are noticing. The number of people poring over the collection almost doubled from about nine hundred in 1995 to approximately seventeen hundred in 1998. Blackman, who must sign off on all the books and theses that quote the Dun collection, said that a few years ago, he might have reviewed one or two manuscripts a month. Now he sees five or six.

Laura Linard, director of historical collections at the library, said use has increased significantly because more scholars appreciate the worth of business records. It is the most used of all the library's historical records, to the point that Linard is a little frightened for its safety. "The collection is very, very fragile," she said. "It's in incredibly poor condition, because these books were used during their lifetime, consistently, constantly."

To scholars, the credit assessments are invaluable for piecing together American business history, in part because they avoid corporate spin and show the view of a third party—in this case, the agents, or "correspondents," across the nation who reported back to R. G. Dun's home office on the creditworthiness of local carpenters, grocers and lightning-rod makers.

Robert C. Kenzer, a history professor at the University of Richmond, recently trawled the books for information on Civil War widows who took over their husbands' businesses. "They were broad in their perspective," Kenzer said of the Dun reporters. "They rate the elite and they rate the common people. Right next to the Rockefellers you find someone you've never heard of."

A June 1870 entry on one J.B. Alford, who sold groceries and liquors, read: "This man is said to be in thriving circumstances. He has some Real & personal estate & I think it is safe to trust him." Alas, the December 1876 entry read, "Failed abt 3 mos ago & went into Bankruptcy."

Sociologists and historians like Kenzer use the archives to study the growth of a particular industry, like pottery, or a specific topic, like Jewish-owned businesses before the turn of the century. Over the last twenty years, Kenzer has made many trips to Boston, researching subjects like black-owned businesses in the South. Once, he spent six weeks copying every page of one ledger. "It's pretty exhausting work," he said. "Fortunately, they had good handwriting."

It sounds like the kind of summer reading only a number-cruncher could love, and Harvard business students seem to agree. For although the archive is housed in the Baker Library at the School of Business Administration, it is used infrequently by Harvard's M.B.A candidates, most of whom are more concerned with strategic mapping and venture capital than the cost of antebellum dry goods. Only scholars with very good reasons—and white gloves—are allowed to handle the fragile books. The library no longer allows genealogical research.

Still, there are lessons from the past that young executives could take with them into the business world. For starters, there is the danger of first impressions. One entry from June 1863 reports that a produce merchant named J.D. Rockefeller "is not much of a businessman, but had some capital, it is said, advanced by his father, who is reputed well off." He turned out to be a good credit risk; that was the year he set up a refinery that blossomed into Standard Oil.

Then there is the power of courtesy, as demonstrated in some hand-written requests for payment. Who wouldn't cave at this gentle entreaty: "If you will kindly favor us with a check at your convenience, you will much oblige"?

The Dun correspondents were often inspiring in their objectivity, for although they reported on the race or religion of a business owner, as was common at the time, those facts did not necessarily affect their rating of someone's business acumen. Women, it seems, could sometimes get credit when men could not, because, as one researcher found, they were seen as "cautious" and "economical."

Drinking was another matter. "If you were intemperate, they were not going to extend you credit," Kenzer said. Ponder the fate of G.H., an Ontario innkeeper, listed as "fond of drinking and gambling. Considered bad stock unsafe for credit."

Millennium watchers could have taken comfort in the business disasters of the past. Kenzer, who is starting research on the Chicago fire of 1871, said: "The problem wasn't just the people who were burned out. You don't know who you owe money to, or who owes money to you."

"It might be similar to a Y2K issue," he said. "How do you recover when you lose a lot of information?" Chicago, after all, bounced back fairly quickly.

One can get a snapshot of the early career of businessmen like Frank Winfield Woolworth, who borrowed three hundred dollars from former employers to open "The Great Five Cent Store" in Utica, New York, in 1879. Or of the catalogue tycoon Richard Warren Sears, a telegraph operator from Minnesota who started a business in mail-order watches and in 1887 took up with a young watchmaker named Roebuck.

Surprisingly, Lewis Tappan, the founder of what would become Dun & Bradstreet, did not like the idea of credit. Tappan was a Calvinist whose motto was "Owe no man anything but to love one another." But after a depression in the early 1800s left businesses in tatters, the practical Tappan saw that lenders needed to know whom they could trust to pay debts. Twice a year, correspondents would send their reports to Tappan's office in New York, then called the Mercantile Agency. The subscribers or their personal clerks could come to the office to hear credit reports on their business associates, read in discreet whispers.

Robert Graham Dun took over the agency in 1859, and it would be known as R. G. Dun & Company until it merged with its main competitor, the Bradstreet Company, in 1933. Throughout that time, credit reporting grew along with American business. When the railroad expanded business horizons, correspondents traveled west to report on saloonkeepers and cattle ranchers. One correspondent wrote of his work: "One method was to go on the railroad as far as possible, then to visit the towns on horseback. I traveled many miles on the hot plains of Texas by saddle, buckboard or mail hack."

Among the correspondents, usually lawyers who received fees for collecting debts, were four future presidents: Ulysses S. Grant, William B. McKinley, Grover Cleveland and Abraham Lincoln. After Lincoln's assassination, an agency clerk marked up an entry on the president, drawing a weeping willow tree and a grave marker and writing in the words: "This office has had the honor of having Old Abe as a correspondent."

Grant's commentaries could be especially colorful: he reported that a particular young lawyer he evaluated had nothing but an office chair, a barrel with a board for a desk, and a fine young wife. Still, he argued that ability and ambition were as important as capital, and recommended credit.

Executives of the last century were sometimes branded by the company they kept. In 1869, a correspondent wrote that Hannah Griffith, a milliner in Springfield, Illinois, was "about to marry a fellow [of] no account." An entry two years later noted, with some relief, that that plan had fallen through.

Modern credit write-ups, of course, are far less prying, not even denoting whether a business executive is a Mr. or a Ms. The streamlining came about through a natural technological evolution. With the introduction of things like typewriters, telephones and fax machines to do the reporting and computers to do the analyzing, it was easier to have some sort of consistency in the reports, and easier to compare businesses within particular industries.

More important, Dun's clients started demanding more facts and less gossip. "Social mores change," Blackman said. "All of a sudden our customers stopped asking whether a person drank to excess and started asking things like 'How is World War II affecting this manufacturer?'"

Indeed, today's reports are strictly factual, with their tabulations based on bills, suits, liens and government filings, information gleaned from enormous databases. For all its pride in its almost 160-year history, Dun & Bradstreet might like to forget the references to a Jewish business owner as "another of the tribe" or the abbreviation "col'd" after the name of every black business. But it does allow today's researchers to track the role of different races and religions in the American economy.

Should twentieth-century businesses fear that future generations will entertain themselves with their credit histories? Blackman said no: New information on a company supplants the old, and when a business closes, its file is left all but blank.

"There will not be anything like this ever again, as far as a snapshot of American business history," he said.

Julie Flaherty
August 21, 1999

Acknowledgments

We gratefully acknowledge the extraordinary talent of the reporters and editors of the *New York Times,* who supplied us with an embarrassment of riches from which to choose the articles that appear in this book. We also thank the people who are quoted and profiled in these articles for letting all those nosy journalists peer into their business world and, often, their personal lives. We are indebted to Mitchel Levitas, director of book development at the *New York Times,* and Robin Dennis, associate editor at Times Books, for their smart advice, timely interventions and patience with us during the project. And we thank our families, friend and coworkers, most of whom are still speaking to us.

Index

ABC online, 78, 79, 81–82
African American Forum, 164–65
Alberghetti, Anna Maria, 286
Alford, J. B., 315
Allen, Paul G., 269, 270
Allen, Woody, 283, 287
Allied Signal, 147, 149
Alvarez, Adan, 232, 233
Amazon.com, 62, 84, 113, 254
American Express, 159, 279, 302–5
American Malls International, 170
America Online (AOL), 71, 78–80, 84,
   312
  Bertelsmann and, 58, 59, 61–64
  Time Warner merger, 51, 60, 67, 81, 93,
   123, 141–46
Amos, Wally, 52–56
Anderson, Steven, 9
Andsold, 62, 64
Annunziata, Robert, 129–30, 134
Anschutz, Philip F., 129–34
Anthony, Camille, 202
Anthony, William A., 202
antitrust, 85, 135–41, 293–94
Armstrong, C. Michael, 67
Arvesen, Ernest, 280
Ashkenas, Ronald N., 148
Asian financial crisis, 119, 253
Askin, Tevfik, 206–7
Assigned Counsel Inc., 174–76
Astrachan, Joseph, 215
Ates, Nejla, 284
Atkinson, Brooks, 285
AT&T (Bell system), 2, 66, 67, 71, 72

break-up of, 135, 137, 247, 264–65
  MediaOne merger, 138, 140
  merger integration and, 147–48,
   150
Austin, Nancy, 210
Avignone, Lou, 55

Baby Bells, 73, 110, 138, 265
Bailey, Pearl, 285
Bain & Company, 22, 23, 24, 121
Baker, Robert, 16
Bala, Karthik, 173, 174
Bankers Trust, Deutsche Bank merger,
  135–36
Bank One, 89, 309
Banks, Ernie, 277
Barach, Michael, 168–69, 171
Barclay, Jack, 6
Baumberger, Terry, 186–87
Baxter, Bill, 227
Baxter, Charles, 113
Beck, Leonore, 284
Becker, Dietrich, 110
Belenky, Col. Gregory, 202
Bentley Motor Cars, 3–6
Berkshire Hathaway, xiv, 277–82
Berlind, Roger, 299, 300, 301
Bertelsmann, AOL and, 57–65
BET Holdings, 41–43
BetzDearborn-Hercules deal, 148–49
Bibliowica, Jessica, 299
Bilkovich, Bill, 8, 9, 10
Bingham, Lisa, 196
Biondi, Frank, 300

Black, Dr. J. Stewart, 120
Black, Leon D., 260, 261
Black, Steve, 308
Blacklin, Scott, 117
Blackman, Travis B., 314–15, 318
blacks
    entrepreneurs, 41–43, 52–56
    discrimination lawsuits and, 195–96
    employees, 157–60, 162–65, 285
Bloomberg, Michael R., 27–37, 262
BMW, 199
    Rolls-Royce and, 3–6
board of directors
    artistic director vs., 221–27
    CEO choices by, 242–45
    management mistakes and, 247–54,
      257–58, 268–71
    too cozy, 238–42
Boeing, 66, 246–57
Bogan, Christopher E., 210, 211
Bogle, John C., 281
Bonaquisiti, Donna, 173
Bond, Chrystelle, 222
Boo.com, 112, 126–27
Booker, Frank, 278
Bookshester, Dennis S., 260
Botti, Janet M., 175
Botti, William R., 175
boundary of firm, 95–98
Bourke, Anthony, 180
Brackenbury, Nigel, 100, 116, 119
Bradach, Jeffrey L., 23–24
Bradford, J. C., 240
Brandt, Gil, 289, 292
Bridge Group, 22–25
Bridge Information systems, 35–36
Bridgestone/Firestone, 271, 274
Broadcom Corporation, 45–50
Brodwin, David, 60
Brook, Peter, 283, 287
Brown, Camille, 224
Brown, Carolyn, 273
Browner, Carol M., 7
Buffett, Warren, xii, xiv, 277–82, 297
Burke, James E., 273
Burks, Deborah, 121–22
Burlingame, Harold W., 147, 150, 264,
    265
Burlington Northern Santa Fe Railway,
    200–202
Burrows, Abe, 287
Bush, George (father), 64, 139

Bush, Robert A. Baruch, 195
Byrnes, William G., 240–41

cable television, 40–43, 50–52, 233–38
    concentration and, 139–40
    satellite vs., 66–67, 69–71
Cameron, Ian, 5
Canales, Gus T., 230
Carpenter, Candice, 152
Carpenter, Mike, 308
Carsey, Marcy, 51, 52
Carter, Arthur, 299–301
Carttar, Paul L., 24
Case, Stephen M., 59, 143
Cashman, Jerry, 156–57
Caterpillar, 89, 115–19
CBS, 60, 78–82
Cebuhar, Chuck, 70
Chaffin, Janice, 156
chains, independents vs., 19–21
Chajet, Clive, 56
Chambers, John, 169
Champion, Gower, 285–86
Channing, Carol, 283
Chase Manhattan–Morgan merger, 124–27
Chernin, Peter, 81
Cherniss, Cary, 179
Chernow, Ron, 125–26
chief executive officers (CEOs)
    contrite, for poor products, 271–74
    corporate legends, 275–313
    flamboyant, board led to disaster by,
      257–64
    succession, in family business, 213–21
    teaching hospitals and, 14
    transition to new, 213, 233–38
    turnover, xiv, 242–45, 275–76
    women as, 157
    see also specific executives
child care, 197–200
China, 69, 114, 311
Chrysler, xiv, 101
    DaimlerBenz merger, 123, 136
Chudzicki, Mark J., 174
Cieutat, Susan, 17
Cisco Systems, 75, 84, 147, 169, 182
Citigroup, 126, 135, 296–313
Clark, Kim B., 87–89, 91
Clayton, Joseph P., 129
Clement, Joseph M., 172, 173
Clemente, Mark N., 147
Clemmons, Lynda R., 190–93

Cleveland, Grover, 317
Clinton, Bill, 135, 138–40, 248, 258, 272
Clinton, Hillary, 305
Clyatt, Bob, 26
Coase, Ronald, 95–98
Coca-Cola, 194, 196, 275, 279–81
Cochrane, Haywood D., Jr., 240
Coddington, Bart, 158
Coddington, Sydney, 158
Cogan, Marshall, 300–301
Cohen, Alexander H., 288
Cohen, Arnold P., 170
Cohen, Peter, 301–3, 308
Colvard, Mark, 186–87
Commercial Credit, 126, 304–5
Condit, Philip M., 247–54
Conn, Charles, 95–97
Cook, William R., 149
Copeland, Les, 240
Corbo, Vincent J., 148–49
Cornell University, 197, 217, 313
corporate culture, 30, 32, 34, 47, 65
    diversity and, 160, 161
    cross-border merger and, 104–6
    aggressiveness and ethics and, 209–11
    old-new economy merger and, 93–94,
      142–46
    postdeal intergration and, 146–51
    returning overseas executives and,
      119–22
cost cutting
    cross-border merger and, 104–5, 107
    teaching hospitals and, 12–19
Coukos, Pamela, 196, 197
Cowan, David, 92, 170
Cox, David W., 189–90, 193
Credit Suisse, 126, 262
Crohn, Jeffrey, 278
Crohn, Kathleen, 278
Cronin, Rich, 237
Crooke, Robert, 35
Crystal, Graef, 260
Csupo, Gabor, 235
customer service, 112–14

DaimlerChrysler, xiv, 6, 103, 111, 123,
  136
Dallas Cowboys, 289–92
Daniels, Dean, 80
d'Arbeloff, Alexander, 169
Darwall, Christina, 91
Davis, Don, 143

Davis, Robert J., 26
Day, Laurence, 277, 280
Deangelo, Joseph J., 76
Dejonckheere, Richard, 277–78
Delain, Michael P., 74
Dell Computers, 84, 114
Dellinger, Todd, 224–25
Deloitte, Haskins & Sells, Coopers &
    Lybrand merger, 146
Derickson, Sandra L., 159
Deutsche Bank, 108, 126
    Bankers Trust merger, 135, 136
Dickinson, Daniel, 110
Dickinson, Sylvia, 121
Dickinson, Tom, 121
digital television, 66, 67, 71
Diller, Barry, 143
DiLorenzo, Lou, 180
diminishing returns, 83–85
Dimon, Jamie, 297, 303–4, 306–10, 312
Dinardo, Kathy, 173
DirecTV, 66–73
dispute resolution, 194–97
Ditka, Mike, 291
diversity, 153, 158–66, 209
Donald, Odie, 73
Dorchak, Glenda, 269, 270–71
Dorling, Christopher, 44
Dorling Kindersley, 43–45
Dornemann, Michael, 64, 65
Dorsett, Tony, 291
Dorsey, David, 206
Dow Chemical, 6–12
Downey, Morton, Jr., 145
Downie, Debra, 262
Drucker, Doris, 296
Drucker, Peter, 276, 294–96
Dumstorf, Joe, 76
Dun & Bradstreet archives, 315–18
Dunn, Jeffrey D., 236

Eagan, Tom, 72
Easthope, Tracey, 8, 11
Ebb, Fred, 283
Eberhardt, Nancy, 171
EchoStar Communications, 69, 70, 72
e-Citi, 310, 312
e-commerce, 98, 193
    Six Sigma and, 74–78
    overseas markets and, 112–15
    see also Internet; old economy, vs. new
      economy; Web

Economides, Nicholas, 293
economies of scale, 84, 85
Ehrman, John, 9, 10
Eilber, Janet, 226
Eisner, Michael D., 78–79, 82, 281
Elcano, Mary S., 194–95
EMI Group, Bertelsmann and, 60–61, 65
employee(s), xiv
  behavior problems, 167–68
  bonus system, 31–32
  delegating leadership to, 181–85
  dispute resolution and, 193–97
  diversity and, 158–66
  entrepreneurship and, 188–193
  ethics vs. aggressiveness and, 210–11
  failure as credential of, 168–71
  meditation for, 207–9
  motivational training for, 177–81
  recruiting and retaining, 152–54
  rewards for, 174–76
  sales training for, 203–7
  service programs for, 185–87
  sharing, by regional companies, 171–74
  sleep breaks for, 200–202
  underperforming, 166–68
  work/family issues and, 154–58,
    197–200
Enron Corporation, 178, 188–93, 244
entrepreneurship, 26–28, 39–56
  defined, 87
  encouraging, within company, 188–93
  Harvard Business School and, 86–92
  scientists and, 265–68
environmental groups, alliance with,
  6–12
Equal Employment Opportunity
  Commission (EEOC), 193–97
Ergen, Charles, 70
Ernst, David, 96–97
ESPN.com, 79, 81
Esrey, William, 2
Esser, Klaus, 107–12
executives
  diversity and, 158–66
  failure as asset for, 168–71
  need for change by, 294–96
  overseas, 105–6
  returning from overseas, xii, 119–22
  search for top, 242–45
  service with nonprofits as training for,
    185–87
  women as, 153–59, 244

  see also chief executive officers;
    entrepreneurship; leadership
Exxon-Mobil merger, 123, 135, 137, 138

family business, succession in, 213–21
family issues, 153, 160–61
  day care, 197–200
  flextime, 154–58
  overseas executives and, 120–21
Famous Amos, 53–56
Fanny (musical), 283–85
Farley, William, 256–64
Federal Communications Commission
  (FCC), 138, 140
Federal Trade Commission, 137
Fedje, Scott, 119–20
Feerer, Jeffrey, 7, 9, 10
Ferrari, Dr. Bernard, 15
Fields, Mark, 107
Fifer, Julian, 183
Fiorina, Carly, 154, 157–58
Firestone tire scandal, 271, 272
Fischer, Ken, 224
Fishbein, Jim E., 123, 148
flatter management structures, 14, 182–85
Fok, Canning, 110
Forbes, Walter, 147
Ford, 96, 116
  Firestone tire scandal, 271, 273
  Mazda merger, xii, 99–107
Ford, William C., Jr., 104
42nd Street (musical), 282–83, 285–87
Fournier, Susan, 273
Fox, 81, 237
Francis, Sandy, 201
Frederick, Samuel, 174
Freston, Tom, 235
Frick, Henry Clay, 135, 137
Friedman, Lou, 131
Friel, Brian, 283, 286
Frontier, Qwest takeover of, xiv, 124,
  127–34
Fruit of the Loom, 246, 256–64
Fudge, Ann M., 163

Galloway, Donald E., 77
Garrison, Sekiko Sekai, 32, 33
Garrison, Walt, 291
Gassner, Rudi, 64
Gates, Bill, xii, 57, 136, 276, 280, 282,
  292–94
Gegax, Tom, 207–9

Gehry, Frank, 39
Geico, 279, 280
General Electric, xiv, 58, 80, 89, 182, 270
   Appliances, Web site for, 73–78
   CEO of, 212–13, 243–44
   diversity and, 153, 158–66
   Medical Systems, 74
   merger integration and, 147, 149
General Motors, 66, 68, 73, 119
General Services Administration (GSA),
   199
Genho, Paul C., 230–31
Gensler, Robert, 130
Gent, Chris, 107–12
Gephardt, Richard A., 135
Gerstner, Louis V., Jr., 244
Ghosn, Carlos, 103, 106
Gillette, 116, 243, 275, 279–81
Givan, Boyd E., 252
Glass-Steagall Act, repeal of, 125
Global Crossing, xiv, 124, 127–34
globalization
   communications and, 110, 254–56
   cross-border mergers and, 100–12
   e-commerce and, 112–15
   international executives and, 106
   management and, 99–100, 115–19
   mergers and concentration and, 137,
     141
   neighborhood business and, 1–2
   technology and, xv
   returning executives and, 119–22
Glossman, Diane, 312
Go.com, 79–83
Goizueta, Roberto, 152
Gold, Dr. Warren, 18
Goldberger, Paul, 39
Goldman, Dr. Lee, 18
Goldman, William, 287
Goldman Sachs, 103, 108, 110, 126, 266
Goldschmid, Harvey J., 139
Goleman, Daniel, 181
Goodwin, James E., 271–73
Graham, Katharine, 281
Graham, Martha, 222–23
Green, William B., 240
Greenleaf, Robert, 121
Greenspan, Alan, 136–37
Greer, Linda E., 8–9
Grieve, Bruce, 53, 56
Griffith, Hannah, 317
Grob, David, 205

Gros, Thomas D., 192–93
Grousbeck, Irv, 169
Grove, Andrew S., 45, 295
Grubman, Jack, 127, 131
Guderian, Heinz, 292
Guerra, Rebecca, 170
Gullett, Don, 209
Guthrie, Tyrone, 285

Hadfield, David, 146, 150
Haigh, Kenneth, 285
Hall, Philip, 4
Hallbelin, Cynthia J., 194–96
Haller, John C., 172
Hamel, Gary, 27
Hammerstein, Oscar, II, 284, 288
Hanafi, Ammar, 147
Hanawa, Yoshikazu, 101, 103
Hartenstein, Eddy W., 67–68, 70–72
Harvard Business School, xii, 85–92
Hatamian, Mehdi, 47
Hatsopoulos, George, 267, 268
Hawley, Michael C., 243
Hayes, John, 248
Hebert, Diane K., 6, 7, 8, 9
Hello, Dolly! (musical), 283, 285–87
Hercules Inc. BetzDearborn deal,
   148–49
Herman, Jerry, 283, 287
Hershberg, Matthew, 262
Hewlett-Packard, 153–59
Hexter, Gary K., 103
Heymann, Nicholas P., 75
Hirshfeld, Al, 283
Hitch, James T., 117
Hobbs, Patti, 187
Hohl, Dean, 180
Holland, Dennis W., 200
Holland, John B., 263
Holley, Howard, 99
Home Depot, 73, 74, 77, 240
Honeywell, 74
   GE merger, 212–13
Hoover, Stevin R., 279
Hopkins, Deborah C., 252
Hopkins, Tom, 205–6
Horne, Lena, 287
Hornung, Bill, 157
hospitals, teaching, 12–19
hostile takeovers, 107–12, 127–34
Hudson, Katherine M., 152
Huff, Rolla P., 134

Hughes, Jeb L., 241, 242
Hughes Electronics, 66–73
Hunt, Anne, 8
Hunt, Jack, 227–30
Hunt brothers, 302
Hunter, David, 12–19

IA Systems, 172, 173
IBM, 86, 244, 270, 293
  antitrust and, 135, 137
IDC, 112, 114
Immelt, Jeffrey R., 212, 213
Infoseek, 80
International Monetary Fund, 116
Internet, 2, 27, 29, 36, 71, 78–98, 139
  boundary of firm and, 95–98
  cable vs. satellite access to, 69, 71–73
  "clicks and bricks" alliances and, 93–94
  large vs. small companies and, 83–85
  merger integration and, 149
  old economy companies and, 57–65,
    141–46
  order-and-delivery and, 73–78
  overseas markets and, 112–15
  portals, 79–83, 114
  start-ups, managers at, 170
  takeover battle and, 108, 127–34
  virtual marketing and, 268–71
  see also e-commerce; Web; *and specific*
    companies
Intrater, Karen, 197
Iridium, 246, 254–56
Irving, Jack, 235
iSky Inc., 72–73
Ito, Masatoshi, 295
Iwon.com, 80, 82

Jackson, Thomas Penfield, 138, 293
Jacobstein, Mark, 212
Japan, 100–107, 136, 295
Jarvis, Roger, 228–29
JDN Realty, 238–42
Jefferds, David, 97
Jenner, Mike, 184–85
Johnson, Bill, 253
Johnson, Henry A., 258
Johnson, Herbert Fisk "Fisk," 214,
  216–21
Johnson, Leah C., 298
Johnson, Samuel Curtis, 214–21
Johnson, Samuel Curtis, Jr. "Curt," 214,
  217–19

Johnson-Leipold, Helen, 214, 216–21
Johnson-Marquart, Winnie, 214
Jolles, Renee, 183
Jones, Alex S., 215
Jones, Andrew, 240–41
Jones, Reginald H., 161
Jones, Tom, 283
Jong, James, 34–35
Jordan, Ann, 311
Jordan, Michael, 276
Joss, Robert, 90–92
Jousse, Jerome, 298, 303
J. P. Morgan, 108, 306
  Chase merger, 124–27
Jung, Andrea, 163
Justice Department, 139, 292

Kado, Kei, 104
Kalbfell, Karl-Heinz, 3, 4, 5
Kaminsky, Dennis, 122
Kander, John, 283
Kanter, Rosabeth, 87
Kaplan, Steven N., 266
Karofsky, Paul, 53
Karpova, Galina, 118
Kauffmann, Stanley, 286
Kaufman, Stephen P., 177
Kearby, Gerald, 57
Keebler Company, 53, 55–56
Kelley, Dr. William N., 13, 18
Kelly, Jack L., 266, 268
Kennedy, John F., 289, 291
Kenzer, Robert C., 315–16
Kerley, William J., 242
Kerr, Jean, 286
Kerr, Steven, 182
Kerr, Walter, 286
Khurana, Rakesh, 243
Kindersley, Peter, 43–45
King, Capt. Richard, 226
King Ranch, 226–33
Kinzius, Kurt, 110
Kirsch, Elaine, 196
Klasky, Arlene, 235
Kleberg, Chris, 228
Kleberg, Robert J., Jr., 229
Kleberg, Stephen J. (Tio), 227–31
Kleeman, Michael, 256
Klein, Donna, 198–200
Klein, Joel I., 137
Kocourek, Paul, 121
Kopp, Robert J., 272–73

Kozlowski, L. Dennis, 148
Kreisky, Peter A., 62
Krugman, Paul, 294
Kurata, Kaoru, 103
Kwoka, John, 84

Labaton, Stephen, 141
Lalande, Kevin M., 90
Lampe, John, 272, 274
Lane, Jeffrey B., 302
Lang, Pearl, 226
large company
    alliances and, 98
    entrepreneurial management and, 86, 87
    mergers, with small company, 94–95
    new economy and, 83–85
Latham, John, 239, 241–42
Latinos, 158, 160
Laurents, Arthur, 287
Lay, Kenneth, 244
Laybourne, Geraldine, 27, 50–52, 234–35,
    237, 246
Laybourne, Kit, 51
leadership, 27–37
    delegating, 181–85
    external training programs for, 179–81
    servant, 208
LearnLinc, 171–74
LeClair, Steve, 74
LeFrak, Samuel J., 37–40
Levenick, Stu, 115
Levin, Gerald M., 141, 143–44
Levine, Arthur, 1
Levitt, Arthur, Jr., 300–301
Lewin, Larry, 15
Lewin, Roger, 181
Light, Jay, 86, 90
Ligons, Frank M., 201
Lilly, Bob, 291
Linard, Laura, 315
Lincoln, Abraham, 317
Lindsey, Alan L., 201, 202
Lipp, Robert, 304
Lipsky, David B., 197
Litan, Robert, 139
Logan, Don, 144
Logan, Joshua, 284
Lombardi, Steve, 172
Louis, Dr. Herbert Johnson, 218
Lowe's, 239, 240
Lucas, George, 44
Luce, Henry, 123

Lucent Technologies, 46, 116, 243, 266,
    275
    merger management, 147–49
Lycos, 62, 114, 143

McArthur, Shelley, 258
McCaw, Craig, 72
McClanan, Martin, 115
McCullough, Sterling, 200–202
McDermott, Mary, 302
McDonald's, 20, 281
McDonnell, John F., 249
McDonnell Douglas, 248–49
Macesich, Michael G., 94
McGinn, Richard A., 243
McGrath, Rita, 266
McGurn, Patrick S., 238, 241
McKinley, William B., 317
Mackintosh, Cameron, 288
Macnab, Craig, 240, 242
Magner, Marge, 304–5
Malone, John, 72
Mamet, David, 206
management. *see* board of directors; chief
    executive officers; employees;
    entrepreneurship; executives; flatter
    management; leadership
management mistakes, 246–74
    CEO's contrition and, 271–74
    disaster caused by flamboyant CEO,
        256–64
    impossible goals and, 247–54
    monopoly practices and, 264–65
    scientists-turned-entrepreneurs and,
        265–68
    "steal shamelessly" concept and,
        210–11
    unproven technology and, 254–56
    virtual marketing and, 268–71
management succession problems, 212–45
    board of directors vs. artistic director,
        221–26
    end of family control and, 226–33
    in family business, 213–21
    Nickelodeon and, 233–38
    too-cozy board and, 238–42
    turnover, and lack of depth, 242–45
Mandabach, Caryn, 52
Manheim, Gene, 170
Mannesmann, 64
    Vodafone takeover of, xii, 107–12
MapInfo, 171–74

Mara, Wellington, 290
Marov, Vladimir, 118–19
Marriott, 197–200
Marshall, Paul, 88–89
Martha Graham dance company, 221–26
Martin, Jerry, 10
Marvin, Michael D., 171–73
Mason, Francis, 225
Massey, Christopher P., 150–51
Mattel, 44, 275
Maughan, Deryck, 306–9, 312
Maytag, 159, 243
Mazda, Ford merger, xii, 99–107
Mead, Scott, 110
media companies
  mergers, 57–65, 85, 109, 123, 140–46
  traditional, and Internet, 78–83
MediaOne, 67, 138, 140
Medicare, 12, 15, 18
Meeker, Kevin, 166
Menezes, Victor, 308, 310–11
Mercer, William M., 157
mergers & acquisitions, 123–51
  alliances vs., 97
  antitrust and, 135–41
  "clicks and bricks," 57–65, 93–95,
    141–46
  cross-border, 99–112
  financial industry, 124–27, 301–13
  hostile takeovers and, 127–34
  integration after, 146–51
  number of, 148
Merrick, David, 282–89
Merrill, Bob, 283
Merrill Lynch, 2, 34, 108, 110, 126, 301
Messier, Jean-Marie, 108–10
methodfive, Pricewaterhouse merger,
  92–95
Microsoft, 44, 57, 63, 78, 80, 84
  antitrust suit, 135–36, 138, 140, 247,
    264–65
  Gates as legend and, 292–94
Middelhoff, Thomas, 57–65
Middlehurst, James, 43–45
Midkiff, Dave A., 10
Midland project, 6–12
Milken, Michael R., 131
Miller, Heidi, 307, 311
Miller, James E., 103, 105–7
Miller, Mark Crispin, 140
Miller, Terry, 8
Milliken & Company, 210, 211

Mills, D. Quinn, 295
minorities, 153, 159, 161, 163–66
Mobil-Exxon deal, 123, 135, 137, 138
Moelis, Ken, 131
Mohn, Reinhard, 61
Mongan, Edwin, 7–8
monopolies, 85, 293–94. *see also* antitrust
Moore, Hilmar G., 232
Moore, Thomas E., 73
Moran, Fred, 238
Morgan, J. Pierpont, 124
Morgan, Tom, 269–70
Morgan Stanley Dean Witter, 108, 110,
  125–26
Morrison, David J., 58
Mothernature.com, 169, 171
Motorola, 74, 205, 255
MTV, 78, 145, 235
Muehleman, Frank, 114
Mulally, Alan, 253, 254
Munday, Steve, 232
Munger, Charles T., 279–81
Murdoch, Rupert, 72
Murphy, James, 180

Nacchio, Anne Esker, 128
Nacchio, Joseph P., 127–31, 133–34
Namath, Joe, 300
Napster, 58, 65
Naryshkin, Sergei, 117
Nash, N. Richard, 287
Nasser, Jacques A., 106, 271, 273
NBC, Web sites and, 58, 76, 78–82
NCR, AT&G merger, 147–48, 150
Neff, Thomas J., 242–43
Nelson, Karen, 160–61
Netscape, AOL merger, 88, 142
"network effects," 254–55
"network society," 83, 85, 96
Nevin, John, 220
new economy. *see* old economy, vs. new
  economy
New England Medical Center (Boston),
  15–16
Newport complex, 37–40
News Corporation, 72, 81
niche markets, 84, 85
Nicholas, Henry T., III, 45–50
Nicholas, Stacey, 48
Nichols, Elizabeth, 239–40, 242
Nichols, J. Donald, 239–42
Nickelodeon, 51–52, 145, 233–38

Nissan, Renault and, 100–105, 107
Noggin educational channel, 236
nonprofits, 21–25, 296
Norton, Marc, 279
Noski, Charles H., 71
Nottleson, Neal, 217
Nusbaum, Jack, 297

Ogilvy, David, 212
Ogle, D. Clark, 209–11
O'Hara, Peg, 261
old economy, vs. new economy, 57–59
   boundary of firm and, 95–98
   Harvard Business School and, 85–92
   mergers and, 92–95, 142–46
   multimedia companies and, 59–65
   old-economy company, transforms to
     new, 66–73
   old-economy principles and, 83–85
   Six Sigma and Web site, 73–78
oligopoly, 138–41
Oliver, Kimberly, 202
Olivier, Laurence, 283
Olivieri, Rick, 167
Ono, Masatoshi, 271–72, 274
Orpheus chamber orchestra, 182–85
Osborne, John, 283
Osha, Joseph, 46–48
Otis Elevator, 118–19
O'Toole, James, 244
Ouimba, Erisa, 168
Oxygen Media, 50–52

Pagnol, Marcel, 284
PanAmSat, 69
Papp, Joseph, 288
Parenio, Sue, 272
Parker, A. Louis, 165
Parr, Barry, 112–15
Parsons, Richard D., 141–43
Pasternack, Bruce A., 147
Peters, Tom, 210, 211
Peterson, Doug, 167
Phibbs, Bob, 19–21
Phillips, Lawrence, 309
Piche, Michel, 10
Pickler, John, 262
Pigott, Charles M., 253
Pinza, Ezio, 284
Pitofsky, Robert, 137, 139
Pittman, Robert W., 141, 143–45
Pittman, Tom, 145

Pittman, Veronique, 144
Platt, Caryn, 154–55
Platt, Joan, 155
Platt, Lewis E., 153–58
Plumeri, Joseph, 298
Poirson, Ann, 161–63
Polly's Gourmet Coffee, 1, 19–21
Porter, Michael E., 86
Poses, Fred, 177
Potoma, Peter, 299–300
Poweradz.com, 172, 174
Poy, Nardo, 183
Prahalad, C. K., 182
Preston, Lewis, 125
Pricewaterhouse Coopers, 146, 150
   Methodfive merger, 92–95
Primerica, 304–5, 311
Prince, Charles, 298
Protas, Ron, 222–26
Prudential Insurance, 197, 302
PTTs, 256

Quick, Gary L., 175
Quinn, Oliver B., 197
Qwest Communications, U S West and
   Frontier takeover, xiv, 124, 127–34

racial discrimination, 194–97, 287. *see
   also* diversity
Rather, Dan, 81
Ray, John J., 260–61
Reagan, Ronald, 54, 139
real estate investment trusts (REITs), 241
Redmond, Andrea, 244
Redress, 194–97
Redstone, Sumner M., 234
Reed, John, 297–98, 308–11
Reeves, Dan, 291
Regine, Birute, 181
Reid, David, 185
Reiner, Gary M., 77, 149
Renault, Nissan and, 100–103, 106–7
Renfro, Mel, 291
Renssalaer Polytechnic Institute (RPI), 172
Resnikoff, Arthur, 243
Ressi, Adeo, 93–95
Reuters Group, 29, 35, 36
Reynolds, Fred, 81–83
Reynolds, Russell S., Jr., 243
Richardson, Bruce, 180
Riggio, Leonard, 62
Robinson, James D., 3d, 302–3

Roche, Gerard R., 1, 243
Rockefeller, David, 127
Rockefeller, John D., 123, 135–36, 314, 316
Rodgers, Richard, 284, 286, 288
Rogers, Tom, 79
Rolls-Royce, BMW vs. Volkswagen and, 3–6
Rome, Harold, 283, 284
Roosevelt, Franklin D., 123
Roosevelt, Theodore, 135–37
Rosekind, Mark R., 202
Rosenberg, DeAnne, 167–68
Ross, Steve, 145
Rowe, Mary P., 196
Roy, Colin, 110
Rubin, Robert, 310–12
Rubinfeld, Arthur, 21
Rugrats Movie, 235, 237
Ruskin, Seth, 28
Russia, 100, 115–19, 308
Russo, Patricia F., 149

Saffer, Helen, 299
Saffo, Paul, 255
Sahlman, William, 88, 92
Salomon Brothers, 30, 126, 132, 142, 306–7
Salomon Smith Barney, 307–8, 311
Samueli, Henry, 46, 47, 49
satellite communications, 109
    Internet service, 72
    telephony and, 254–56
    television and, 67, 69–70, 72
Sato, Eriko, 181–82, 183
Satre, Philip G., 241
Savoy, William D., 269
Scannell, Herb, 233–38
Scatena, Rex, 271
Schlosser, Judith G., 223, 224
Schmidt, Carsten, 64
Schmidt, Harvey, 283
Schmitt, Eric, 112–13
Schmitt, Wolfgang R., 270
Schrempp, Jurgen, 111
Schultz, Howard, 20
Schumacher, E. F., 139
Schumpeter, Joseph, 1, 2
Schwartz, Ethan, 259
Schwartz, Peter, 256
Schweitzer, Louis, 101–2, 106–7
S. C. Johnson, 213–21

Sculley, John, 275
Sears, Roebuck, 70, 317
Securities and Exchange Commission, 94, 239, 242 , 301
Seeber, Ronald L., 197
Seifter, Harvey, 183–84
self-employment, 26–27
self-help networks, 164–66
semiconductor business, 46–50, 205
sexual harrassment, 32, 168, 194
Shapiro, Carl, 293
Shaw, Russ, 114
Shearson, Amex merger, 302–3
Shechtman, Ronald, 33
Shedd (John G.) Aquarium, 21
Sheldrake, Michael, 1, 2, 19–21
Shumlin, Herman, 284, 288
Silverman, Henry R., 145, 147
Sinclair, Mary, 8
Sistron, Yves, 20
Six Sigma quality control, xii, 58, 73–78
Skilling, Jeffrey K., 188–90
Skloot, Edward, 24
Slade, John H., 123
Slater, Craig, 130, 132–33
Slywotzky, Adrian J., 58, 87
small companies, 86–87, 97–98
Smith, Darwin E., 228
Smith, Frederick W., 270–71
Smith, John F., Jr., 68
Smith, Michael T., 66–69, 72
Smith, Vince, 10
Smith, W. H., 44
Smith Barney, 126, 304–6
Snap.com, 58, 80
Snead, Cheryl Watkins, 162, 163
software companies, 84, 172–74, 292–94
Solow, Nanette, 179
Souvanna Phouma, Princess Moune, 225
Spaceway, 71–73
Spieler, Geri, 75
Spies, Allan R., 133
spin-offs, public, 266–68
Spring, Mark, 168
standardization, 84, 85
Standard Oil, 123, 135, 316
Stanford University
    Business School, 90–92
    UC San Francisco Medical Center and, xiv, 14–19
Starbucks, xii, 1–2, 19–21
Starr, Tama, 212

Staubach, Roger, 291, 292
Stavish, Mark, 145
"steal shamelessly" concept, 210–11
Steele, William H., 220
Steinberg, Saul, 300
Stephens, Robertson, 270
Stern, Brian E., 267
Stevenson, Howard H., 267
Stinson, Burke, 264
Stock, Michael, 203–4
Stone, Nan, 296
Stonecipher, Harry C., 247–54
Stoppard, Tom, 283
Streisand, Barbra, 283
Sturman, Carol, 184
Styne, Jule, 283
Sullivan, Donald, 261
Sullivan, Robert S., 266
Sulzberger family, 215
Sumitomo bank, 102–3, 105
Summers, Lawrence H., 83
Suzuki, Yoichi, 104
Syron, Richard, 267, 268

Tappan, Lewis, 317
Tatsumi, Sotoo, 103, 105
Taubman, Howard, 286–87
TCI, AT&T merger, 147
teamwork, xii, 177–81. *see also* leadership
technology
    antitrust and, 136–37
    e-commerce and, 112
    economies of scale and, 84–85
    Harvard Business School and, 89
    organizational change and, xv–xvi
    unproven, betting too early on,
        255–56
telecommunications, 114, 254–56
    mergers, 107–12, 127–34, 138–39
Telecommunications Inc., 67, 147
telecommuting, 156, 157
Telefónica de España, Lycos merger, 114
telephones, 83, 264–65
    cable companies and, 71
    Internet access and, 72
    wireless, 107–12, 246, 254–56
Telerate Plus, 35–36
television networks, Web sites and, 78–83.
    see also cable television; digital
    television; satellite television
Terra Networks, 114
Texaco, 194, 197

Thermo Electron Corporation, 265–68
Thomas, David A., 164
Thompson, Julie, 273–74
Thompson, Robert J., 272
Thorne, Steven D., 163, 164
Thornton, Dean, 252
Tichy, Noel M., 165–66
Ticketmaster Online, 96–98
Tierney, Thomas J., 23–25
Tifft, Susan E., 215
Tilbian, Lorna, 44
Time Warner, 62, 66, 71, 147
    AOL merger, 51, 59, 81, 123, 141–46
    EMI deal, 60, 61
Tires Plus, 207–9
Toelkes, Jamene, 232, 233
Toevs, Alden, 125, 127
transaction costs, 96, 97
Travelers Insurance, 126, 305–6
    Citicorp merger, 308–313
Triaca, Matthew, 273
Tristani, Gloria, 140
Trotter, Lloyd G., 159–61, 163
Trujillo, Solomon D., 129–30, 133–34
Trump, Donald J., 38
Tully, Jessica C., 242

Uhlman, Thomas M., 266
Unilever, Bestfoods merger, 139
Union Pacific Corporation, 200–201
United Airlines, 271–74
    US Air merger, 41–42, 138
U.S. Congress, 125, 136, 137
U.S. Postal Service, 178, 193–97
U.S. Supreme Court, 135
United Parcel (UPS), 185–87
University Health System Consortium, 15,
    16
University of California-Stanford Health
    Care, 14–19
University of Chicago Business School, 90
University of Illinois at Chicago Medical
    Center, 14, 18–19
University of Pennsylvania
    Health System, 13, 14, 16, 18, 19
    Wharton School, 90, 184
US Airways, 41–42, 138
Useem, Michael, 184, 245
Usluel, Degerhan, 171–73
Ustinov, Peter, 285
U S West, Qwest takeover of, xiv, 124,
    127–34

Value America, 247, 268–71
Van Abeelen, Piet C., 75
Vanderbeck, Sunny, 57
Van Etten, Peter, 17
Vathauer, Brenda, 157
Viacom, 43, 145, 234–35, 237–38
  online business and, 78–79, 81–82
Vivendi, 107–10
Vodafone, 107–12
Volkswagen AG, Rolls-Royce and, 3–6
Volvo, 101, 106

Wacholder, Michael H., 172
Walker, Karen, 157
Wall, Jim, 170–71
Wallace, Henry D. G., 102, 105–6
Wal-Mart, 182, 202, 238–40, 263
Walt Disney, 44, 235, 279, 281
  Go Network, 78–83
Ward, Lloyd D., 243
Warner, Douglas A., III, 306
Waterman, Phil, 302
Waters, Charlie, 289, 291, 292
Web sites
  old media companies and, 78–83
  overseas markets and, 112–15
  Six Sigma studies and, 73–78
Weill, Jessica, 305–7
Weill, Joan Mosher, 298–99, 303, 312–13
Weill, Marc, 305, 307
Weill, Sanford I., xii, 126, 296–313
Weinberg, Mike, 298, 305
Welch, John F. Jr. "Jack," xii, xiv, 74,
    158–59, 161, 163–65, 212–13,
    243–44, 295, 297
Wellington, Sheila, 244
Wellstone, Paul, 136–37
Werblin, Sonny, 300
Werner, Tom, 52
Werth, Jacques, 203–7
Weyerhaeuser, George, 253
Wharton School, 90, 184
White, Randy, 291
Whitlow, Bill, 249
Whittelsey, C. Sheldon, 241, 242

Whyte, David J., 251
Wilbraham, Angela, 29
Williams, Tennessee, 283, 284
Wilson, Woodrow, 135
Windnagel, Suzan, 166–67
Winfrey, Oprah, 52
Winkler, Matthew, 33, 34
Winn, Craig, 268–71
Winnick, Gary, 131–32
Witchel, Alex, 286
Wofford, Don, 186
Wohl, Faith, 198
Wolfe, Steven, 41
Wolzien, Tom, 79, 144
women
  executives, 50–52, 153–63, 165, 244
  sexual harrassment and, 32, 168, 194
  work/family conflicts and, 156–58,
    160–61, 165, 197–200
Woodard, Ronald B., 252
Woolworth, Frank Winfield, 316–17
Wossner, Mark, 63, 65
Wright, Frank Lloyd, 215–16
Wrigley Jr. Company, 116, 118
Wymbs, Keith J., 94–95

Xerox, 266–67, 275

Yacktman, Donald, 257
Yahoo.com, 36, 78–81, 97, 114
Yankowski, Carl, 275
Yeaw, Gary P., 149
Yerger, Ann, 241
Yergin, Daniel, 137, 140
Yoakum, Alaina, 93, 94
Young, Carole A., 197
Young, George, 290
Young, Luther, 232
Yudkovitz, Marty, 82

Zarb, Frank, 300
Zarghami, Cyma, 234, 235, 237
Zeleznik, Abraham, 230
Zicklin School of Business, 182, 183
Zimmerman, Andrew B., 93, 94

About the Editors

Brent Bowers serves as management editor of the Business Day section of the *New York Times*. Deidre Leipziger is the *New York Times*'s Business Day story editor.

Harold J. Leavitt is Kilpatrick Professor Emeritus at the Stanford Graduate School of Business, where he directed the Executive Program and taught management and organizational behavior for many years. His most recent book, *Hot Groups,* coauthored with Jean Lipman-Blumen, was named the best business book of 1999 by the Association of American Publishers.